SYMBOL AND INTUITION
COMPARATIVE STUDIES IN
KANTIAN AND ROMANTIC-PERIOD AESTHETICS

LEGENDA

LEGENDA, founded in 1995 by the European Humanities Research Centre of the University of Oxford, is now a joint imprint of the Modern Humanities Research Association and Maney Publishing. Titles range from medieval texts to contemporary cinema and form a widely comparative view of the modern humanities, including works on Arabic, Catalan, English, French, German, Greek, Italian, Portuguese, Russian, Spanish, and Yiddish literature. An Editorial Board of distinguished academic specialists works in collaboration with leading scholarly bodies such as the Society for French Studies and the British Comparative Literature Association.

MHRA

The Modern Humanities Research Association (MHRA) encourages and promotes advanced study and research in the field of the modern humanities, especially modern European languages and literature, including English, and also cinema. It also aims to break down the barriers between scholars working in different disciplines and to maintain the unity of humanistic scholarship in the face of increasing specialization. The Association fulfils this purpose primarily through the publication of journals, bibliographies, monographs and other aids to research.

Maney Publishing is one of the few remaining independent British academic publishers. Founded in 1900 the company has offices both in the UK, in Leeds and London, and in North America, in Philadelphia. Since 1945 Maney Publishing has worked closely with learned societies, their editors, authors, and members, in publishing academic books and journals to the highest traditional standards of materials and production.

Symbol and Intuition

*Comparative Studies in
Kantian and Romantic-Period Aesthetics*

Edited by Helmut Hühn and James Vigus

LEGENDA

Modern Humanities Research Association and Maney Publishing
2013

Published by the
Modern Humanities Research Association and Maney Publishing
1 Carlton House Terrace
London SW1Y 5AF
United Kingdom

LEGENDA is an imprint of the
Modern Humanities Research Association and Maney Publishing

Maney Publishing is the trading name of W. S. Maney & Son Ltd,
whose registered office is at Suite 1C, Joseph's Well, Hanover Walk, Leeds LS3 1AB

ISBN 9-781-907625-04-6

First published 2013

Printed in the UK by Charlesworth Press

Cover: 875 Design

Copy-Editor: Richard Correll

CONTENTS

PREFACE

This volume is related to the comprehensive investigations of the literary forms of philosophy around 1800 conducted within the research project 'Heuristics between Science and Poetry'. The latter project formed a component of the Special Research Center 482 at Friedrich Schiller University, Jena, entitled 'The Weimar-Jena Phenomenon: Culture around 1800'. In a cross-disciplinary collaboration combining approaches from the humanities, cultural studies and natural sciences, the Special Research Center 482 explored the uniquely productive and intensive communication and interaction that took place in and between Weimar and Jena around 1800. The over-arching aim of the research was to examine the interrelation of Enlightenment, Classicism, Idealism and Romanticism.

For financial and infrastructural support we gratefully acknowledge the Special Research Centre and its spokesperson Prof. Olaf Breidbach. We thank the Deutsche Forschungsgemeinschaft (German Research Council) for the provision of essential funding.

Special thanks to Dr Temilo van Zantwijk und Prof. Gottfried Gabriel for their collaboration and lively discussion.

Thanks also go to LMUexcellent for funding James Vigus's postdoctoral research fellowship at Ludwig Maximilian University, Munich, from 2009–12, where much of his work for this volume was completed.

The specific idea for this book arose in the course of a graduate seminar on symbol-concepts from Kant to Hegel taught by Helmut Hühn at the philosophy department of Friedrich Schiller University, Jena, in 2008. James Vigus was at that time a DAAD (German Academic Exchange Service) postdoctoral research fellow in Jena, whose research on Samuel Taylor Coleridge and Henry Crabb Robinson as mediators of German thought intersected with the work undertaken in Dr Hühn's seminar. As we discussed the *desideratum* to investigate a key selection from the extraordinary range of theories of symbol and intuition around 1800 — an ambitious project intended to build on recent advances in scholarship on Kantian thought, Weimar Classicism, Jena Romanticism and German Idealism, to explore affinities and contrasts between Anglo-American and German writers, and to trace certain traditions of thinking about the symbol into modern approaches in which continental and analytic aesthetics intersect — it became clear that the most appropriate method would be to commission a series of essays from scholars with diverse backgrounds and perspectives. We thank all the contributors to this project: without them this book would not have been possible.

Thanks go to Kathleen Singles for translating Chapter 3, to Katrin Grünepütt for translating Chapter 4, and to Aaron Epstein and Christian Kästner for translating Chapter 11, all from the German.

PREFACE

With regard to the production of this book, we are grateful to Graham Nelson for his very patient guidance throughout the whole process, to Richard Correll for editing the copy, and to Sue Dugen for compiling the index.

Non-English quotations are given both in the original language and in translation: such translations are by the author of the respective chapter unless otherwise stated.

NOTES ON THE CONTRIBUTORS

Jeffrey Einboden is an Associate Professor in the English Department at Northern Illinois University. His *Nineteenth Century U.S. Literature in Middle Eastern Languages* is forthcoming from Edinburgh University Press. He has also co-authored a translation with John Slater, *The Tangled Braid: Ninety-Nine Poems by Hafiz of Shiraz* (Fons Vitae, 2009).

Gottfried Gabriel is Professor Emeritus at Friedrich Schiller University, Jena. His works in the areas of epistemology, logic, aesthetics and philosophy of language include *Definitionen und Interessen. Über die praktischen Grundlagen der Definitionslehre* (Frommann-Holzboog, 1972), *Fiktion und Wahrheit. Eine semantische Theorie der Literatur* (Frommann-Holzboog, 1975), *Zwischen Logik und Literatur. Erkenntnisformen von Dichtung, Philosophie und Wissenschaft* (Metzler, 1991), *Grundprobleme der Erkenntnistheorie. Von Descartes zu Wittgenstein* (Schöningh, 1993; 3rd edn 2008), *Logik und Rhetorik der Erkenntnis. Zum Verhältnis von wissenschaftlicher und ästhetischer Weltauffassung* (Schöningh, 1997), *Ästhetik und Rhetorik des Geldes* (Frommann-Holzboog, 2002) and *Einführung in die Logik* (IKS, 2005; 3rd edn 2007). He is editor of the *Historisches Wörterbuch der Philosophie*, vols 11–13 (Schwabe, 2001–07).

Nicholas Halmi is University Lecturer in English Literature of the Romantic Period at the University of Oxford and Margaret Candfield Fellow of University College, Oxford. He is the author of *The Genealogy of the Romantic Symbol* (2007), editor of the forthcoming Norton Critical Edition of *Wordsworth's Poetry and Prose*, and co-editor of Coleridge's *Opus Maximum* (2002), the Norton Critical Edition of *Coleridge's Poetry and Prose* (2003), and the collection *Inventions of the Imagination: Romanticism and Beyond* (2011). His retrospective view of the *Genealogy* appears as 'Telling Stories about Romantic Theory', *European Romantic Review*, 23 (2012), 305–11.

Jutta Heinz is Senior Lecturer in the German Department at Friedrich Schiller University, Jena. In addition to her monographs *Wissen vom Menschen und Erzählen vom Einzelfall. Untersuchungen zum anthropologischen Roman der Spätaufklärung* (de Gruyter, 1996) and *Narrative Kulturkonzepte: Wielands 'Aristipp' und Goethes 'Wilhelm Meisters Wanderjahre'* (Winter, 2006), she has co-edited the *Wieland-Handbuch* (Metzler, 2008), the *Wezel-Jahrbuch* (Wehrhahn, 2002–08) and, with Jochen Golz, *'Es ward als ein Wochenblatt zum Scherze angefangen'. Das Journal von Tiefurt* (Wallstein, 2011). She is currently working on editions of works of Christoph Martin Wieland and Clemens Brentano.

Helmut Hühn is Lecturer in Philosophy at Friedrich Schiller University, Jena. He is director of the Research Unit European Romanticism and director of Schiller's

Gardenhouse, Jena. His book *Mnemosyne. Zeit und Erinnerung in Hölderlins Denken* (Metzler, 1997) won the Ernst-Reuter Award of Free University Berlin. He is editor of *Goethes 'Wahlverwandtschaften'. Werk und Forschung* (Walter de Gruyter, 2010), co-editor of the *Historisches Wörterbuch der Philosophie*, vols 1–13 (Schwabe, 1971–2007) and of *Benjamins Wahlverwandtschaften. Zur Kritik einer programmatischen Interpretation* (Suhrkamp, forthcoming 2013).

Jane Kneller is Professor of Philosophy at Colorado State University. Her major publications include *Kant and the Power of Imagination* (Cambridge University Press, 2007), *Novalis: Fichte Studies* (Cambridge University Press, 2003) and numerous essays and articles on Kantian aesthetics, on the philosophy of early German romanticism, and on the theoretical connections between the two.

Stephan Meier-Oeser is Lecturer in Philosophy at Freie Universität Berlin. Author of *Die Spur des Zeichens* (Walter de Gruyter, 1997), he is editor-in-chief of Leibniz's philosophical writings and letters (Series II and VI of the *Akademie-Ausgabe*) at the Leibniz-Forschungsstelle Münster. He is currently working on the history of sign conceptions from the late seventeenth to early twentieth century, and on the long-term history of views about the cognitive function of propositional and/or iconic representations.

Cecilia Muratori is Postdoctoral Research Fellow (LMUexcellent) at the Seminar für Geistesgeschichte und Philosophie der Renaissance, Ludwig Maximilian University, Munich. In addition to her monograph on Hegel's interpretation of the mystical philosophy of Jakob Böhme, *'Il primo filosofo tedesco': il misticismo di Jakob Böhme nell'interpretazione hegeliana* (ETS, 2012), she has translated the first seven chapters of Böhme's *Aurora* into Italian, with introduction and commentary (*Aurora Nascente*: Mimesis, 2007). She is currently researching theories of the animal soul in Renaissance philosophy and has published articles and reviews on the difference between animals and human beings from the Renaissance to the early nineteenth century, focusing in particular on ethical aspects. With the essay 'Descartes' Error and the Barbarity of Western Philosophy: Schopenhauer in Dialogue with Coetzee's Elizabeth Costello', she won the 2008 essay competition of the Schopenhauer Gesellschaft.

Jan Urbich is Research Assistant in the German Department at Friedrich Schiller University, Jena. His publications in the areas of philosophy and literature, aesthetics, Early German Romanticism and Critical theory include *Darstellung bei Walter Benjamin. Die 'Erkenntniskritische Vorrede' [epistemological preface] im Kontext ästhetischer Darstellungstheorien der Moderne* (de Gruyter, 2011) and *Literarische Ästhetik* (UTB Böhlau, 2011); he is co-editor of *Der Begriff der Literatur: Transdisziplinäre Perspektiven* (de Gruyter, 2010) and, with Helmut Hühn, *Benjamins Wahlverwandtschaften. Zur Kritik einer programmatischen Interpretation* (Suhrkamp, forthcoming 2013).

James Vigus is Lecturer in English at Queen Mary, University of London, specializing in the literature and philosophy of the Romantic period. Having completed his PhD at the University of Cambridge, he has worked as a postdoctoral research fellow at Friedrich-Schiller-University, Jena, and Ludwig-Maximilian-

University, Munich. Author of *Platonic Coleridge* (Legenda, 2009), editor of *Henry Crabb Robinson: Essays on Kant, Schelling, and German Aesthetics* (MHRA, 2010) and *Informal Romanticism* (Wissenschaftlicher Verlag Trier, 2012) and co-editor, with Jane Wright, of the collection *Coleridge's Afterlives* (Palgrave Macmillan, 2008), he is currently working on a long-term collaborative edition of the *Diary* and *Reminiscences* of Crabb Robinson.

Temilo van Zantwijk is Assistant Professor of Philosophy at Friedrich-Schiller-University, Jena, specialising in the history of philosophy and in particular German Idealism. He is author of the monographs *Pan-Personalismus. Schellings transzendentale Hermeneutik der menschlichen Freiheit* (Frommann-Holzboog, 2000) and *Heuristik und Wahrscheinlichkeit in der logischen Methodenlehre* (Mentis, 2009). His articles in this field include 'Intellektuelle Anschauung und literarische Form', in *Phantasie und Intuition in Philosophie und Wissenschaften*, ed. by Gudrun Kühne-Bertram and Hans-Ulrich Lessing (Königshausen & Neumann, 2011), pp. 63–91.

INTRODUCTION

Helmut Hühn and James Vigus

This volume brings together original contributions by a range of scholars of philosophy and literature to examine a concept that gained an extraordinary prominence in the wake of Immanuel Kant's *Critique of the Power of Judgment*: that of the 'symbol'. A symbol in everyday usage is a sign, perceptible to the senses, that evokes something other than itself. According to a straightforward definition offered by the semiotician and novelist Umberto Eco with respect to literary works:

> The symbolic occurs [...] when the author delivers an utterance or a sequence of utterances completely literally, until you notice at some point that this insistence on some aspect or detail is really exaggerated. [...] In view of this waste of narrative energy, this violation of the rules of economy, the reader wonders what the author is actually talking about. [You notice that] it's about something else.[1]

A symbol, however, is not always, or necessarily, conceived as being only 'about something else'. During the ferment in German philosophy around 1800, models were developed according to which the symbol also acquired a major self-referential dimension. This enabled the symbol to promise great explanatory power in cognitive theory. The autonomy, or refusal of external referentiality, of a symbolic work of art was (paradoxically) what held out the hope that readers and spectators might discern cognitive content in art — might learn, that is, about the powers of the cognizing subject itself. The newly charged concept of symbol was thus from an early stage connected to the (variously formulated) notion of 'intuition'.

A principal purpose of this collection is to present in a widely accessible form new research on the debates on the concept of the symbol from the late eighteenth to the nineteenth century. At the same time, we aim to show the value for Anglophone readers of investigating what may all too easily appear esoteric terrain laden with formidable terminology and even ideological motivation. Despite the linguistic hurdle, 'German' aesthetics are now gaining fresh currency. As Andrew Bowie has recently commented: 'the most influential recent moves in Anglo-American philosophy have involved a rejection of the empiricist assumptions on which analytical philosophy relies, in favour of a reassessment of the concerns of Kant and German Idealism, concerns which are inherently bound up with aesthetics'.[2] The present volume offers *comparative* studies because the early twenty-first century is not the first time at which anglophone thinkers have taken an intense interest in post-Kantian and idealist aesthetics: there was also a major contemporary reception, informed (we wish to suggest) not so much by the 'borrowing' or even 'plagiarism' that commentators have often emphasized, as by the fact that these writers confronted a similar set of problems to that of their German peers.

Before reviewing the individual contributions, we shall offer, first, a concise introduction to the concepts of 'intuition' and 'symbol' in (post-)Kantian thought, including some of the key positions taken by philosophers and literary writers; and second, an overview of the Anglo-American reception of this debate, both contemporary and modern.[3]

Aesthetic and Intellectual Intuition

Kant distinguishes between intuition ('Anschauung') and concept ('Begriff'), which relate respectively to sensibility ('Sinnlichkeit') and understanding ('Verstand'), as two stems of human cognition. The distinction is a vital one for post-Kantian philosophy. Kant bases his two-stem theory on the premise that the manifold of objects given in intuition is cognizable only in the logical form of synthetic combination, whereas concepts produced by the understanding are distinguishable by the analysis of meanings. According to this model, sensibility and understanding obey different logics. The question discussed in the wake of Kant's work is how the connection of the two heterogeneous forms of cognition, namely conceptual and intuitive, may be grounded in one subject. Kant himself had claimed their unitary apperception in a 'besondern Actus der Synthesis des Mannigfaltigen' [special act of the synthesis of the manifold].[4]

In the debate surrounding the theory of the two stems, two problem-solving strategies emerge. These attempts involve a rehabilitation of different formulations of *intuitive cognition*. One prominent option is to determine a connection between concept and intuition in the field of aesthetics. In particular, thinkers such as Johann Gottfried Herder, Friedrich Schiller, Johann Wolfgang von Goethe, and F. W. J. Schelling further developed the Kantian idea of 'symbol'. For this purpose Kant's understanding of symbol as a creative achievement of the productive imagination[5] was transformed, step by step, into the notion that the symbol is constitutive for cognition — as both Goethe and Schelling would emphatically argue. Accordingly, the concept of *aesthetic intuition* is of especial importance.

Another path towards a solution diverges more clearly from Kant. In the context of the systematizing philosophy of German Idealism, the attempt is made to unite concept and intuition in the notion of a higher *intellectual intuition* ('intellektuelle Anschauung').[6] Intellectual intuition does not consist in reference to an intelligible object, but in an activity of philosophical reflection that is itself transparent: intellectual intuition involves the immediate presence of the I to itself, prior to and independently of any sensory content. In Johann Gottlieb Fichte's account, it basically consists in the inclusion of the conceptual in intuition.[7] Meanwhile G. W. F. Hegel, distancing himself from the appeal to intellectual intuition, asserts the reverse in his philosophy of absolute knowing: the intuition is sublated in concept. By this time it is in any case apparent that the means of representation afforded by discursive types of cognition alone are not sufficient to achieve such foundational syntheses.

Kant explains the unity of the manifold of intuition, which makes it possible to link together all experiences to form one single experience, by means of the above-mentioned foundational principle of the original synthetic unity of apperception. Transcendental apperception is for Kant the 'oberste Grundsatz im ganzen menschlichen Erkenntnis' [highest principle in the whole sphere of human cognition].[8] This theory presents post-Kantian philosophy and natural science with the challenge of providing a critical answer to the following question: can knowledge of unity be propositional knowledge at all? The foundational philosophies of Karl Leonhard Reinhold and the early Fichte answered this question in the affirmative; the subsequent formations of the transcendental idealism of Fichte and Schelling answered it with a decisive 'no'. The latter systems — critically adapting Spinoza's notion of a *scientia intuitiva* — assign the cognition of cognition to intellectual intuition. In their different ways, Herder, Goethe and Hegel advanced theories that link intuition and concept in various possible forms of intuitive thought. The more or less subtle differences between these writers have major implications for our topic. Hegel, for instance, explicitly criticizes the principles that (as he sees it) guide Goethe's research in natural science (*Naturforschung*) as a false type of immediacy, disregarding the work of conceptual distinction: 'denn aus der Anschauung kann man nicht philosophieren' [for one cannot philosophize from intuition]. For Hegel, intuition must also be conceptualized in thought and must not be elevated above reflection.[9] Goethe for his part tries to profile a specific form of judgment through intuitive perception which, as opposed to the mere inductions of empiricism or the mere deductions of the speculative philosophy of nature, should inform the method of research.

Viewed from this background, the systems of philosophy in German Idealism, the heuristic method of the early philosophy of science, and the Romantic project of an encyclopaedia can all be considered as modes of presentation that extend propositional knowledge, with the help of non-propositional cognition, to a cognition of unity and totality.[10] It is evident that what we are accustomed to term 'classical German philosophy' may be appropriately interpreted only by taking into account its literary forms and its interaction with both science and poetry.

Theorization of the Symbol

A constellation of writers around 1800, especially in Jena and Weimar, redefined and debated the concept of the symbol[11] in the realm of aesthetics. A major controversy, however, centred on the question of whether a symbolic object or work of art merely refers to something outside itself (some paraphrasable content, in the case of a written text), or whether it may be said to participate in what it signifies, for instance as a part within a whole.[12]

As the discourse on the symbol develops, there occurs a movement from the analysis of linguistic signs (which by virtue of being linguistic are subject to the control of specific rules) to the interpretation of images in nature and art, inexhaustible in their great fullness of meaning. In this context it becomes important to distinguish symbol from allegory. Allegory is seen as a sign that points beyond itself, equipped with an abundance of possible meanings: structurally, to employ an allegory is to mean more than one explicitly says or shows. Symbol, on the other hand, is considered in the philosophical, art–theoretical, *naturphilosophische* and theological discussion around 1800 as an exemplary object, with which the meaning of an abstract sign can be demonstrated sensuously. In this sense a symbol is: (i) an object given to the senses, which demonstrates an idea; (ii) an individual that is at the same time representative for a totality of individuals of a particular kind or type and to that extent is a 'particular', i.e. a part of a whole which makes that whole present;[13] (iii) owing to its cognitive function of illustrating and bodying forth, the symbol is not an object that is simply given, but rather is bodied forth by the creative working of the imagination.[14] The concept of symbol is thus characterized by the facets of intuition–guided demonstration, making–present and creativity.

In Kant's terminology, a concept which only reason can think but which does not relate to an object of intuition is an 'idea'. Symbolic presentation makes it possible to construct analogies of an idea in the realm of sensuous intuition. From what was in Kant's work a heuristic category of analogical thought, the notion of the symbol develops, step by step, into a concept that in Schelling is constitutive for cognition. In his *Lectures on the Philosophy of Art*, Schelling differentiates three terms: schema, allegory and symbol. The terms alone make clear what he is trying to achieve: nothing less than the systematic unification of Kant's theory of the different ways in which concepts may be related to objects with Goethe's (and Johann Heinrich Meyer's) distinction between allegory and symbol.[15] The latter distinction was prepared not least by the reflections on aesthetic autonomy offered by Karl Philipp Moritz.[16] Goethe, however, uses the term 'symbol' for the first time in a new sense, to denote the representation of self-referential aesthetic signs. He makes the symbol a unit of sense whose abundance of meaning in principle exceeds the resources of linguistic communication and which is no longer the representative of something else, but is rather the original object of intuitive contemplation.

For Schelling, then, the symbol is the 'synthesis' of schema and allegory, 'wo weder das Allgemeine das Besondere, noch das Besondere das Allgemeine bedeutet, sondern wo beide absolut eins sind' [where neither the universal means the particular nor the particular the universal, but rather where both are absolutely one].[17] In Schelling's view schema and allegory deploy signs in a referential network of references, such that meaning can be attributed to them. Schema follows the semantics of subsumption of particular objects under general concepts; allegory in a certain sense reverses the direction of meaning and lets the object point beyond itself. Allegory and schema are forms of representation. Symbol, on the other hand, does not stand as a reference to something else, and in the strict sense has no meaning at all: for meaning, according to Schelling's way of thinking, is a relationship for which a direction is constitutive. Allegory and schema are accordingly characterized by a basic gap between the subjective apprehension of an object and the latter's objectivity. In the case of the symbol, for Schelling, this division disappears. He considers symbols to be subject-objects, which exemplarily present to the cognizing subject in the form of an object of experience the Absolute as the identity surpassing all experience of subject and object. Schelling constructs art as the medium of the Absolute and emphasizes that the use of symbols in art presupposes that its content is the history of the gods.[18]

Goethe later distances himself from such a metaphysical symbol-concept and its Romantic extrapolations, when he speaks of the 'sehr üble Folgen, daß man das Symbol, das eine Annäherung andeutet, statt der Sache setzt [...] und sich auf diesem Wege aus der Darstellung in Gleichnißreden verliert' [very bad consequences from positing the symbol, which intimates an approximation instead of the thing and in this way loses the description in parables].[19] Goethe — addressing his objection to Heinrich Steffens's 1806 *Grundzüge der philosophischen Naturwissenschaft* — complains of the dissolution of the epistemological difference between the symbol and that which is symbolized. Here he diagnoses a tendency of Romantic research in natural science, which betrays a lack of scientific self-awareness. In seeking an alternative both to a speculation that is completely alienated from experience and to a methodologically restricted empiricism, Goethe sketches out the idea of a morphological theory of experience. His concept of morphology aims to perceive nature as a whole in its parts and in its parts as a whole.[20]

Schelling, with his symbol-theory, develops an effective definition of the relationship between aesthetic and intellectual intuition. Philosophy makes the formal postulate of a basic unity or identity, but cannot demonstrate that unity as something real — neither in nature, which constantly repeats itself, nor in human history, which is never complete, nor in itself. If the doctrine of postulates introduces intellectual intuition as a requirement of theoretical philosophy, this is affirmed through aesthetic intuition as its external organ.[21] Art as an 'organ' and 'document' of philosophy becomes indispensable for the task of doing philosophy at all. Schelling's concept of aesthetic intuition stands, like Goethe's concept of the symbol, in the tradition of Baumgarten's *perceptio praegnans* and Kant's 'aesthetic idea'[22] — an influential concept that may be traced into the analytical aesthetics of the twentieth century. Nelson Goodman's concept of metaphorical exemplification can be associated with the traditional concept of the symbol: notwithstanding important differences from the aesthetic discourses around 1800, Goodman's theory of symbols makes use of the distinction between denotative reference (as predominates in the sciences) from exemplificatory reference (which is especially important for the arts).[23]

Friedrich Schlegel does not share the categorial distinction between symbol and allegory that Goethe and Schelling try in different ways to set up. He develops forms of dialectic in order to conceive the historical totality of a world that endlessly progresses in a perennial process of *Bildung* (i.e. formation and transformation), and is never completed. In a hermeneutic-critical process he advocates starting with the historically conditioned individual, in order to gain a view of the historical whole. For him symbol and allegory are different modes of presentation, through which the finite is posited and comprehended as appearance of the infinite. Totalizing the finite, the dialectical figure of irony at once marks and surpasses the limits of finite cognition.

In his *Lectures on Aesthetics*, Hegel continues Goethe's critique of allegory as a mode of representation that does only imperfect justice to the concept of art. At the same time, however, Hegel downgrades emphatic symbol-concepts such as those of Goethe and Schelling and rejects Schlegel's form and use of irony. For Hegel, unlike Schelling, the symbolic form of art does not constitute the embodiment of the unity of finite and infinite: rather it is the first and thus imperfect development of the content of the spirit out of nature, which remains entangled in ambiguity. Symbols are, Hegel argues, essentially ambiguous; they are non-arbitrary signs, but they lack the congruence of form ('Gestalt') and meaning ('Bedeutung'). Moreover, Hegel emphasizes the 'Zweifelhaftigkeit des Symbolischen' [doubtfulness of the symbolic] in mythology and art.[24] The symbol does not announce itself *as* a symbol — a problem that Schiller had already addressed in his correspondence with Goethe regarding symbolic objects.

Thus art can no longer simply be judged through the concept of symbolism. To a considerable extent, Hegel's position with respect to the symbol corresponds to the symbol-concept developed by his former colleague at Heidelberg, Georg Friedrich Creuzer, a central figure of the Romantic movement whose influence extended far into the realm of classical scholarship. In Creuzer's view, set out in his *Symbolism and Mythology of the Ancient Peoples, Especially the Greeks*, the incongruence between essence and form is characteristic for the symbol.[25] Creuzer therefore consistently focuses on the aspect of the sacred, linking this with the claim that he was setting the symbol-discussion back to the original meaning of the word.[26] Symbolic presentation bodies forth (for our intuition) and communicates the 'momentary totality': 'In einem Augenblicke und ganz gehet im Symbol eine Idee auf, und erfaßt alle unsere Seelenkräfte' [In a moment, and completely, an idea arises in the symbol and seizes our entire vital spirits].[27] Moritz, too, had maintained that the highest form of beauty would arise in an instantaneous intuition of the whole of nature, which the work of art represents exemplarily.[28] The conception of the symbol as 'idea embodied' is fundamental for the Romantic notion of the religious symbol. According to Creuzer, myths can be deduced from symbols. Myths, by pointing to these archetypes, fulfil the function of providing a poetic explanation of phenomena that are inaccessible to discursive description. In this way, Creuzer takes up the Neoplatonic concept of myth from Plotinus and Proclus. All mythology is essentially symbolic: but myths cannot, just as Moritz and Schelling had already emphasized, be interpreted allegorically.

It becomes apparent that the post-Kantian symbol-concepts we have surveyed so far involve very different arguments and cannot be easily assimilated to one another. In terms of methodology, a reconstruction of the history of the specific problems is required, one that attends carefully to the formations of individual theories, their development and their interactions with other concepts. Not only Hegel but also Goethe emerges as an important critic of the entire discussion. Emphatic symbol-concepts do not necessarily aim at knowledge of the absolute (in the metaphysical or theological sense), but may rather be directed toward examining different forms of the universal in the particular — in the realms of philosophy, research in natural science, art, mythology and religion. Such claims, again, do not inevitably reflect confidence in (as Wordsworth put it) 'How exquisitely the individual Mind / [...] to the external World / Is fitted'.[29] For these symbol-concepts in their very ambition and diversity at the same time reflect a crisis in the model of reality, which by the end of the eighteenth century had become strongly apparent, and led to the decentralization of the cognizing subject. This upheaval may be described as a crisis of sign-systems and a loss of the metaphysical wholeness upon which the mimetic model of art had relied. The controversies emerge from the upheaval in epistemology and endeavour to cope with it: aesthetic theory becomes *ab initio* a central indicator of problem facing, shaping and solving. The discussions surrounding the justification of allegory, just as much as the ambition to privilege the symbol, constitute an attempt reflexively to come to terms with this experience of crisis. The theoretical and artistic-political preoccupation with the notion of a 'natural sign' centred on establishing a language of art that would be self-explanatory without cultural background knowledge and without learned commentary — a language, in other words, that would be accessible to immediate intuition, presenting meaning before the spectator's very eyes. Despite the emphatic nature of such a model, a considerable uncertainty and even embarrassment frequently lies behind it.

The silhouettes of Philipp Otto Runge, of which we present two examples on the front and back covers of this book, elegantly illustrate this double-edged aspect of the symbol-discourse. They display the artist's reflexive engagement with his representation, which stimulates the viewer to imagination. Runge's work uses the method of formal abstraction and reduction, playfully transforming the inherited language of images to create new dimensions of symbolic imagination. The dog barking at the moon is a simple scene, a pose clearly and humorously presented, with the additional suggestion in the dog's upturned muzzle of an aspiration toward heavenly things.[30] Yet there remains a conspicuous distance between dog and full moon, between perceiving subject transfixed by lunar light and the famous 'Romantic object' behind the clouds which pass by. In what sense could the two ever correspond with each other? Could the dog raising its eyes to the sky even be emblematic for human longing? Or does the use of an animal as subject mischievously undermine prevalent claims that the human being alone partakes in networks of symbolic signification?

The Janus-face of the symbol-discourse, which by invoking enormous explanatory power constantly fended off the fear that it could be the last resort of an illusion-ridden humanity, persists in the wider European and American debate. The modes of argumentation reflect various problem-solving strategies of cultural modernity, which is characterized by a plurality of competing forms of aesthetic world view.

The International Debate: Transmission, Transformation, Controversy

The symbol-conceptions of those movements conventionally designated by the umbrella-terms Enlightenment, Weimar Classicism, Jena Romanticism and German Idealism are received and echoed beyond Germany by philosophers, literary writers and artists; such transmissions begin early and continue into the so-called symbolist movement.[31] They gain entry into the Anglo-Saxon world above all via the mediation of Henry Crabb Robinson, Samuel Taylor Coleridge and Thomas Carlyle.

As a student at the University of Jena, Robinson attended Schelling's 1802–03 lecture series on the Philosophy of Art. Probably in collaboration with his friend Fritz

Schlosser, a more enthusiastic follower of Schelling than Robinson was himself, the Englishman compiled detailed notes from these lectures. This preparation proved fruitful when Robinson was called upon to tutor two illustrious visitors to Weimar, Benjamin Constant and Madame de Staël, in Weimar in 1804.[32] Finding his French auditors disposed to dismiss the aspirations of Schelling's thought, Robinson began his private lecture 'On the Philosophy of Schelling' by admitting that the central concept of intellectual intuition 'is the Theme of perpetual ridicule'. He expounds it, however, as a notion that is 'in itself reasonable', given that to assert a relation between a subject and an object always involves reliance upon a *sense*: we can only develop a taste for music or painting because we have senses of hearing and sight, for instance. If we also admit that moral judgments are made by means of a 'moral sense', and even that 'Love is pure sense', then the following rhetorical question must also be answered in the affirmative: 'If this be true of all inferior things, can it be otherwise in respect to the highest conception the mind is capable of? If the Universe is not a Sand hill but a System of beings, united into one whole, must there not be a sense to perceive it?'[33]

There is no specific evidence that Robinson shared his notes on Schelling with either Coleridge or Carlyle, though both the latter writers would in future years regularly seek out Robinson's advice on German sources.[34] But Robinson's framing of the problem of intellectual intuition forecasts in a relatively straightforward manner the difficulties that Coleridge was to face in articulating a symbol-theory as a vehicle for his ambitious claims regarding the spiritual possibilities of human knowledge. Robinson's suggestion that there may exist an organ for beholding the essence of the entire universe, though intended as a gloss on Schelling, resembles the more emphatic statement made by Coleridge a few years previously: 'We see our God everywhere — the Universe in the most literal Sense is his written language'.[35] Such a fideistic approach to reading the book of nature was, however, vulnerable to strong sceptical objections, as David Hume had made clear in his *Dialogues Concerning Natural Religion* (first published posthumously in 1779). In Hume's *Dialogues* the character Philo argues that to discern a divine designer in the entirety of his work is to rely upon an illegitimate form of analogy. We have previous experience of works of art, and we habitually compare one with another, but the universe is — by definition — unique. Is it, then, possible to claim that a sublime or beautiful object in nature and art may stimulate our intuition of the divine Absolute? Coleridge struggled to elucidate a symbol-conception that would support a resoundingly affirmative answer, repeatedly confronting the sceptical response that threatened to dissolve this world view into meaninglessness.[36]

Coleridge's symbol-concept, manifesting in many aspects the trace of Schelling's phase of transcendental idealism, bears considerable weight in the system of philosophy to which he aspires above all in writings of the 1820s.[37] That his theory remained fragmentary, that it owed much to German sources, and that he applied it with encyclopaedic ambition in the various contexts of theology, philosophy, literature, politics and science, are features that have alternately exhilarated and exasperated commentators ever since.

Coleridge's polemical approach in his published works certainly courted such controversy. His most famous definition of symbol contrasts it with allegory, a distinction whose essential contours he may have first encountered many years previously in Robert Lowth's distinction between allegory and 'mystical allegory' in *De Sacra poesia hebrorum*. Coleridge writes polemically in 1816:

> Eheu! paupertina philosophia in paupertinam religionem ducit: — A hunger-bitten and idea-less philosophy naturally produces a starveling and comfortless religion. It is among the miseries of the present age that it recognizes no medium between *Literal* and *Metaphorical*. Faith is either to be buried in the dead letter, or its name and honors usurped by a counterfeit product of the mechanical understanding, which in the blindness of self-complacency confounds SYMBOLS with ALLEGORIES. Now an allegory is but a translation of abstract notions into a picture-language which is itself nothing but an abstraction from objects of the senses; the principal being more worthless even than its phantom proxy, both alike unsubstantial, and the former shapeless to boot. On the other hand a Symbol (ὁ ἔστιν ἄει ταυτηγόρικον [which is always tautegorical]) is characterized by a translucence of the Special in the Individual or of the General in the Special or of the Universal in the General. Above all by the translucence of the Eternal through and in the Temporal. It always partakes of the Reality which it renders intelligible; and while it enunciates the whole, abides itself also a living part in that Unity, of which it is the representative.[38]

Coleridge here preserves the elitist tone adopted by Schelling, but adapts it to the context of the British philosophical and theological scene, attacking the reductive 'mechanical philosophy' that he identifies with empiricism. He also retains the conception of the symbol as a synecdoche, a part that points to a whole by virtue of subsisting within it; and he reinforces this point in the Appendix to the same volume when he affirms that 'By a symbol I mean, not a metaphor or allegory or any other figure of speech or form of fancy, but an actual and essential part of that, the whole of which it represents.'[39] Schelling's suggestion that the meanings offered by the symbol glimmer through (*durchschimmern*) the material surface also finds an echo in Coleridge's notion of 'translucence'.[40] The term 'tautegory', which Schelling himself praised Coleridge for coining,[41] continues to play an occasional role in the latter's subsequent works.

If Coleridge's *Statesman's Manual* attracted strong criticism from contemporaries, opposition to its ideological orientation even increased in the late twentieth century. Paul de Man's celebrated essay 'The Rhetoric of Temporality' objects above all to the intimation in the above-quoted passage that the material manifestation of the symbol reveals an 'eternal' substrate. In de Man's view, the Coleridgean symbol is a 'mystification', a denial of the plain fact that all (authentic) human experience occurs in time. De Man then draws on Walter Benjamin's defence of allegory to reverse the Coleridgean hierarchy and demote the symbol.[42] Influential though de Man has been, his preference for allegory (in his view authentically temporal, acknowledging the proper gap between signifier and signified, between composition and interpretation) over symbol (clutching at eternity, falsely conflating signifier and signified, composition and interpretation) reflects the fact that he nevertheless continues to operate within a Coleridgean frame of reference:[43] another reader could well deny his conclusion — 'Symbol cannot be a mystification', retorts one of Coleridge's chief modern champions[44] — but, more importantly, could even see and celebrate precisely the same thing that de Man sees and deplores.[45]

Pressing the deconstructionist-historicist line of critique to its logical conclusion, however, a series of studies by Nicholas Halmi has now raised a more fundamental objection. According to Halmi, not only is the vocabulary of Coleridge's symbol-definitions incompatible with the Christian orthodoxy he nominally defends, but Coleridge also applies the symbol-allegory distinction inconsistently and opportunistically.[46] For Halmi, such incongruities reflect the fact that the 'Romantic symbol' is an ideological construct formed in response to the legacy of semiotic crisis left by the Enlightenment: there is simply *no such thing* as a symbol as Coleridge and other Romantic-period writers define it.

It could well be questioned whether it is legitimate to speak of 'the Romantic symbol', given the great variety of competing as well as mutually supportive conceptions revealed not least in Halmi's own work. The largely author-by-author organization of the present volume presumes that there are substantial, not purely terminological, differences to be reconstructed. For Halmi, on the other hand, the symbol-concepts in this period are indeed reducible to the singular 'Romantic symbol' to the extent that they lack the explanatory power with which they are supposed to be invested, being themselves susceptible of explanation in other, 'genealogical' terms.

Returning to the specific case of Coleridge, however, to understand his symbol-definition as an evaluative attempt to place texts in this or that objective category would be one-sided. It may instead best be read as directing readers' *activity* of interpretation. As Halmi himself puts it, the Coleridgean symbol 'was strictly a theoretical construct, the purpose of which [...] was not to describe objects of perception but to condition the perception of objects.'[47] In particular, Coleridge probably considered the energy of mind required in making the distinction between allegory and symbol to be conducive to a wholesome balance in the interpretation of (sacred) texts.[48] The clue appears in the fact that Coleridge's distinction between symbol and allegory emerges from a complaint about religious faith being either buried in the dead letter or 'usurped' by a counterfeit: this statement reflects the fact that he sought an essentially Anglican medium between the hermeneutic strategies of the Evangelicals and Methodists on the one hand, and the Unitarians on the other.[49] By 1816, Coleridge conceived his own role as that of a poet-prophet attempting to guide a nation he saw as trapped, with respect to the Bible, in the polar extremes of either fundamentalist literalism, or the 'allegorical' claim that particular stories have no value in themselves but must be translated into the modern language of moral responsibility. Coleridge relies on the notion of the symbol to claim that biblical narratives may be read as both embodying instructive meanings and also as self-referentially significant in themselves. In this way, Coleridge pleads for an intuitive, or imaginative, hermeneutic method. Then, drawing on Creuzer, Coleridge eagerly extends the symbol-concept to classical mythography.

The echo of the symbol-debate in Carlyle's *Sartor Resartus* (first published 1833–34), which pretends to record the opinions of the fictional Herr Teufelsdröckh, is clearly ironic — not to say self-ironizing:

> Of kin to the incalculable influences of Concealment, and connected with
> still greater things, is the wondrous agency of *Symbols*. In a Symbol there is
> concealment and yet revelation: here therefore, by Silence and by Speech
> acting together, comes a double significance. [...] In the Symbol proper, what
> we can call a Symbol, there is ever, more or less distinctly and directly, some
> embodiment and revelation of the Infinite; the Infinite is made to blend itself
> with the Finite to stand visible, and as it were, attainable there. By Symbols,
> accordingly, is man guided and commanded, made happy, made wretched.[50]

The note of irony appears most strongly in the combination of vagueness ('*some*
embodiment [...] as it were') with grandiloquent claims regarding the power of
symbols; a deliberately unstable combination that also appears in the uncertainty
over whether symbols are to be discovered 'out there' ('the Symbol proper') or
are mere subjective or even rhetorical constructs ('what we can call a Symbol').[51]
The problem is one that Schiller had already posed in his epistolary discussions
with Goethe.

In the American Transcendentalist reception of Coleridge, the impetus of his
symbol-concept to imaginative biblical interpretation remains important.[52] At
the same time, writers such as Ralph Waldo Emerson and Henry David Thoreau
combined Coleridge's theoretical symbol-concept with his legacy as a nature
poet: according to the view of nature itself as a symbol, what is beyond nature is
revealed through nature. 'I am thankful that this pond was made deep and pure for
a symbol', writes Thoreau in his description of Walden Pond. Thoreau nevertheless
preserves a Carlyle-like note of scepticism regarding what, exactly, we may read in
such a symbol: he suggests that there is no purely transcendent realm, for 'Here or
nowhere is our heaven'.[53]

While Thoreau emphasized the simple dimension of the symbol-concept,
especially its use in a return to a natural life, inheritors of the debates examined in
the present book have often stressed instead the complexity of networks of symbols
within civilized society. 'No longer in a merely physical universe, man lives in a
symbolic universe', writes Ernst Cassirer. 'Language, myth, art, and religion are
parts of this universe. [... Man] has so enveloped himself in linguistic forms, in
artistic images, in mythical symbols or religious rites that he cannot see or know
anything except by the interposition of this artificial medium.'[54] Cassirer provides
a modern approach to the symbol-discussion around 1800 in his philosophy of
culture. His close relation to the European debates surveyed above appears not least
in his explanation of the concept of 'symbolische Prägnanz' [symbolic pregnancy].[55]
This is a strong reminder of the long-term persistence of a debate that is by no
means a museum piece of the nineteenth century. The new aspect that Cassirer
introduces is the genuine connection of two traditions: the formal-logical use of
the symbol-concept, taking its orientation from Leibniz; and the aesthetic form of
thought that reaches back to Baumgarten, Kant and Goethe. In this way Cassirer
can make clear that all truly strict thought relies upon 'symbolism and semiotics'.
A specific process by which we gain knowledge in the natural sciences, according
to Cassirer, consists in underlaying signs that were originally purely formal with
specific intuitions. In all sciences there emerges the 'Grundprinzip der Erkenntnis'
[fundamental principle of cognition], 'daß sich das Allgemeine immer nur im

Besonderen anschauen, das Besondere immer nur im Hinblick auf das Allgemeine denken läßt' [that the universal can be perceived only in the particular while the particular can be thought only in reference to the universal].[56]

The Contributions to This Volume

Chapter 1 ('Kant's Transformation of the Symbol Concept') introduces the reader to the history of the concepts of 'symbol' and 'intuition' especially in German thought. Stephan Meier-Oeser demonstrates that Kant objects to the distinction of intuitive and symbolic knowledge which is established in the tradition of Leibniz and Wolff. Kant criticizes the adoption of the word 'symbolic' by modern logicians in a sense opposed to an intuitive mode of representation. Instead of being opposed to intuition symbolic representation is, together with schematic hypotyposis, one of the two modes of intuitive representation. Connected to this regrouping, Kant re-establishes the old sense of the symbolic, characterized by analogy and metaphoricity, as exemplified in his well-known designation of the beautiful as the symbol of the morally good. While both the schematic and symbolic presentations provide a central cognitive function, words (the former paradigm of symbols) do not. Kant describes them on many occasions as mere marks. In contrast to this, however, he is well aware that in language we have many indirect presentations modelled upon an analogy enabling the expression in question to contain 'a symbol for reflection'. Although his appraisal of symbolic presentations and expressions remains finally ambivalent — they are at the same time necessary means for connecting categorical forms and perceptible intuitions and a characteristic of an 'unenlightened' way of thinking — Kant's transformation of the older notion of symbol opened new perspectives for exploring the function of symbols both in language and the arts.

In Chapter 2 ('"Mere Nature in the Subject": Kant on Symbolic Representation of the Absolute'), Jane Kneller continues the focus on Kant's third *Critique*, discussing his definition of symbolic presentation as it occurs both in beautiful art and in the experience of the sublime. She illuminates a vital respect in which the discourse on aesthetics in the *Critique of Judgment* forms a bridge between the epistemology of the first *Critique*, in which knowledge of things-in-themselves is denied, and the categorical imperative of the second *Critique*, according to which knowledge of the moral law is immediate. Kant's symbol-theory, argues Kneller, raises the possibility that our sole noumenal certainty — the moral self-determination within us — may be identified at least in part with the supersensible substrate of nature outside us, a possibility that Romantic writers would eagerly seize upon.

Contemporaneously with Kant, and presumably without any Kantian influence, Moritz elaborated the theory of the inner autonomy of beauty that would become a kind of manifesto for Weimar Classicism and early Romanticism. In Chapter 3 ('"Neither mere allegories nor mere history": Multi-layered Symbolism in Moritz's *Andreas Hartknopf*') Jutta Heinz moves beyond the familiar contours of this theory, analysing the 'whole Moritz' and in particular the novelist: in his semi-autobiographical fiction Moritz employed a variety of strategies of symbolism. In a multileveled reading of *Andreas Hartknopf*, Heinz demonstrates that the work invokes different systems of language and image, whether biblical, masonic or mystical, and concludes that the novel may be understood as an attempt at the mode of 'realistic mythology' of which Schelling would speak in his *Philosophy of Art*.

In Chapter 4 ('Comparative Morphology and Symbolic Mediation in Goethe') Helmut Hühn examines the origins of Goethe's reflections on the symbol in the epistolary debate with Schiller on this topic. He demonstrates the formative connection and the difference between two central ideas in Goethe's work: the theory of comparative morphology, first articulated in 1796, and the theory of symbolic objects and symbolic representation, first developed in 1797. Both ideas, reflecting the close relations between his aesthetic and epistemological studies and his nature-research (*Naturforschung*) around 1800, are based on the method of intuition (*Anschauung*). Both aim at a sensuous mediation of the particular and the general, which Goethe regards as a necessary correction of abstract intellectual approaches, and both are means of apprehending reality and media of human communication. Tracing the developments and orientations of these concepts, Hühn shows that in response to Schiller's transcendental critique of Goethe's emphasis on symbolic objects, Goethe integrated an acknowledgement of the central role of the perceiving subject in his morphology.

Historians of philosophy have only relatively recently reconstructed Friedrich Schlegel's highly original role in problematizing the above-mentioned search for a single, foundational principle from which philosophy should set out. Related to his insight into the need to posit a plurality of foundational principles in a dynamic relationship of movement, he rather exceptionally de-emphasizes the distinction between allegory and symbol, as Jan Urbich reveals in Chapter 5 ('Friedrich Schlegel's Symbol-Concept'). In an examination of scattered statements in Schlegel's published fragments and notebooks, Urbich explicates his symbol-concept as the epistemological medium to establish a set of relations between the finite and the infinite by means of the poetic work of art. Symbolic representation becomes the objective consciousness of the possibilities for transgressing the boundaries of definite presentation, while at the same time it instantiates the reflection of its own limitations. Schlegel's emphasis on the self-reflexive elements of the symbol corrects naive theological doctrines of the presence of the absolute without erasing what Schlegel regards as the justified claim of aesthetic realization to exceed finite bounds.

Chapter 6 ('Bread, Wine and Water: Hegel's Distinction between Mystical and Symbolical in *The Spirit of Christianity and its Fate*'), examines another text from the formative decade of the 1790s. Cecilia Muratori brings to light a little-known, subtle and yet crucial terminological distinction made by Hegel long before his explicit deflation of the symbol-concept. Hegel describes Jesus's actions at the Last Supper, when he forced a new nature onto objects (the bread and wine), as 'mystical'; whereas John the Baptist's action of immersing the disciples into water is 'symbolical', being based on a simple physical feeling. Although, as Muratori explicates, Hegel's distinction is not without ambiguities, the power associated with Christ's 'mystical' action will inform Hegel's subsequent, nuanced account of the enthusiasm of certain mystics.

In the next two chapters, James Vigus considers the two principal early mediators of German aesthetic theory. Chapter 7 ('"All are but parts of one stupendous whole"? Henry Crabb Robinson's Dilemma') contextualizes a manuscript translation which Robinson made of Moritz's 'On the Plastic Imitation of the Beautiful'. Vigus emphasizes that the translator's Unitarian religious background enabled him to sympathize — a certain sceptical self-awareness notwithstanding — with Moritz's aspiration to construct a theodicy on the basis of the symbolic functioning of the autonomous productions of genius. Chapter 8 ('The Spark of Intuitive Reason: Coleridge's "On the Prometheus of Aeschylus"') revisits Coleridge's controversial concept of the tautegorical symbol in the context of ancient mythology. Reconstructing the argument of Coleridge's 1825 essay, Vigus suggests that the fire-bringing god provides Coleridge with a more effective symbol of the intuitive, morally based activity of the human mind than he could find in the creation account of Genesis.

In Chapter 9 ('Emerson's Exegesis: Transcending Symbols'), Jeffrey Einboden traces several twists in Emerson's conception of the symbol, focusing especially on the role of Coleridgean symbol-theory in the American's momentous transition in the 1830s from Unitarian minister to founder of Transcendentalism. Increasingly committed to the notion of the tautegorical symbol, Emerson comes to see boundless potential in reading symbolic meanings in the forms of nature (to adapt the words of the young Coleridge in 'Frost at Midnight') rather than merely in the equivocal objects in Christian ritual. Yet Emerson's eventual questioning of this emphatic symbol-concept is, in a sense, representative of the movement frequently discerned in the present volume between enthusiastic affirmation and sceptical doubt.

In Chapter 10 ('Pointing at Hidden Things: Intuition and Creativity'), Temilo van Zantwijk provides an analytic approach to the concept of intuition as it is used in classical philosophy. He takes the term 'intuition' to refer to our faculty to grasp non-extensional (and non-intensional) mereological objects like 'organisms', 'continua', 'persons' or 'totalities'. Intuition also means the construction of such objects by the mind and the self-awareness of the mind in conveying cognitive acts. These systematic assumptions, ultimately derived from Spinoza, inform van Zantwijk's account of Schelling's theory of 'aesthetic intuition': this theory is based on the distinction between intuition and imagination, the latter being the faculty to represent individuals not definitely determinable by concepts and propositions.

Taking up the thread of Goodman's analytic aesthetics, Gottfried Gabriel argues in Chapter 11 ('Aesthetic Cognition and Aesthetic Judgment') for the cognitive value of art — defending, in other words, the possibility of aesthetic cognition. He draws a line from Baumgarten's idea of the 'perceptio praegnans' via Kant's 'aesthetic idea' to Goodman's concept of exemplification and, by implication, from continental to analytic aesthetics. Gabriel identifies the cognitive value of art with the ability of the particular to make things present; this ability semantically corresponds to the indeterminacy and conceptual ineffability of works of art.

Finally, Nicholas Halmi contributes an afterword to the book, reflecting on the current status of research on symbol-concepts.

Notes to the Introduction

1. Umberto Eco, 'Vom offenen Kunstwerk zum Pendel Foucaults', *Lettre International*, 5 (1989), 38–42 (pp. 40, 41); quoted from Christoph Bode, *The Novel: An Introduction*, trans. by James Vigus (Oxford: Wiley-Blackwell, 2011), p. 228.
2. Andrew Bowie, 'Romantic Aesthetics and the Ends of Contemporary Philosophy', in *Das Neue Licht der Frühromantik. Innovation und Aktualität frühromantischer Philosophie*, ed. by Bärbel Frischmann and Elizabeth Millán-Zaibert (Paderborn: Schöningh, 2009), pp. 213–24 (p. 213).
3. For full English-language histories of the development of philosophy after Kant, see Dieter Henrich, *Between Kant and Hegel: Lectures on German Idealism*, ed. by David S. Pacini (Cambridge, MA, and London: Harvard University Press, 2003); Frederick Beiser, *The Fate of Reason: German Philosophy from Kant to Fichte* (Cambridge, MA, and London: Harvard University Press, 1987). For further explanation of technical terms in Kantian philosophy, see Howard Caygill, *A Kant Dictionary* (Oxford: Blackwell, 1995).
4. Immanuel Kant, *Kritik der reinen Vernunft*, in *Kants Gesammelte Schriften*, herausgegeben von der Königlich Preußischen Akademie der Wissenschaften [Akademie-Ausgabe] (Berlin: Walter de Gruyter & Co., 1900 ff.), III, § 17, B 138. ('B' denotes the relation of the second edition of Kant's *Critique of Pure Reason*, published in 1787.) With respect to the relation of intuition and concept cf. further 'Preisschrift über die Fortschritte der Metaphysik' (1791), in Akademie-Ausgabe, XX, 325.
5. *Critique of the Power of Judgment* (1790), § 59: 'On beauty as a symbol of morality'. Symbolization here means the heuristic operation of indirect presentation of a concept of reason by means of an analogy.
6. In the realm of aesthetics, a conception of a 'Totalvorstellung' [total representation] or 'Totaleindruck' [total impression], distinguished from intellectual intuition, appears in authors such as Friedrich Schiller, Friedrich Hölderlin und Alexander von Humboldt. This develops from the old distinction between 'perceptio totalis' and 'perceptio partialis': cf. Alexander Gottlieb Baumgarten, *Metaphysica Metaphysik* [1739, 1757]. Historisch-kritische Ausgabe, trans. and ed. by Günter Gawlick and Lothar Kreimendahl (Stuttgart-Bad Cannstatt: Frommann-Holzboog 2011), p. 272 f. (§ 514); Georg Friedrich Meier, *Anfangsgründe aller schönen Wissenschaften*, 3 vols (Halle: Carl Hermann Hemmerde, 1748–50), II (repr. 1755), 11–13 (§ 260).
7. Cf. Kant's critique of those authors who claim intellectual intuition as an aim of philosophy: 'Von einem neuerdings erhobenen vornehmen Ton in der Philosophie' (1796). Akademie-Ausgabe, VIII, 387–408 (p. 389).
8. *Kritik der reinen Vernunft*, B 135.
9. Georg Wilhelm Friedrich Hegel, *Enzyklopädie der philosophischen Wissenschaften*, II, § 246, Zusatz, in *Werke*, vol. IX, edited by Eva Moldenhauer and Karl Markus Michel (Frankfurt am Main: Suhrkamp, 1986), p. 21. Compare Immanuel Kant, *Kritik der reinen Vernunft*, B 75: 'Gedanken ohne Inhalt sind leer, Anschauungen ohne Begriffe sind blind' [intuitions without concepts are blind].
10. For a detailed presentation of this view, see Gottfried Gabriel, Helmut Hühn and Temilo van Zantwijk, 'Heuristik im Spannungsfeld von Wissenschaft und Poesie', in *Ereignis Weimar-Jena. Kultur um 1800*, ed. by Olaf Breidbach (Munich: Fink, forthcoming 2013).
11. The aptness of this concept to achieve the unification of intuition and concept is in a way suggested by its etymology: the Greek 'symballein' originally signifies to throw together or unify; 'symballesthai' indicates bringing into harmony. See further Walter Müri, 'ΣΥΜΒΟΛΟΝ. Wort- und sachgeschichtliche Studie', in id., *Griechische Studien. Ausgewählte wort- und sachgeschichtliche Forschung zur Antike*, ed. by Eduard Vischer (Basel: Reinhardt, 1976), pp. 1–44. For a bibliography of the history of the term, see the anthology *Symbol. Grundlagentexte aus Ästhetik, Poetik und Kulturwissenschaft*, ed. by Frauke Berndt and Heinz J. Drügh (Frankfurt am Main: Suhrkamp, 2009), pp. 12–13 (note 11).
12. Cf. the following thorough accounts: Bengt Algot Sørensen, *Symbol und Symbolismus in den ästhetischen Theorien des 18. Jahrhunderts und der deutschen Romantik* (Copenhagen: Munksgaard, 1963); Michael Titzmann *Strukturwandel der philosophischen Ästhetik 1800–1880. Der Symbolbegriff als Paradigma* (Munich: Fink 1978); Andreas Kubik, *Die Symboltheorie bei Novalis. Eine ideengeschichtliche*

Studie in ästhetischer und theologischer Absicht (Tübingen: Mohr Siebeck, 2006); Nicholas Halmi, *The Genealogy of the Romantic Symbol* (Oxford: Oxford University Press, 2007).

13. In the context of rhetoric, this symbol concept is therefore readily identifiable with synecdoche and metonymy; cf. Halmi, *The Genealogy of the Romantic Symbol*, esp. pp. 3, 128 f.

14. On the creativity of the aesthetic imagination, see Dietmar H. Heidemann, 'Kann Erkenntnis kreativ sein? Die produktive Einbildungskraft in der Ästhetik und Erkenntnistheorie Kants', in *Kreativität* (XX. Deutscher Kongress für Philosophie, 26.–30. September 2005, Sektionsbeiträge vol. 1), ed. by Günter Abel (Berlin: Universitätsverlag der TU Berlin, 2005), pp. 565–76.

15. Cf. Johann Wolfgang von Goethe, 'Über die Gegenstände der bildenden Kunst' (1797), in *Goethes Werke. Hrsg. im Auftrage der Großherzogin Sophie von Sachsen*. Abteilung I–IV, 133 vols (Weimar, 1887–1919), Abt. I, vol. XLVII, pp. 91–95; cf. 'Ruysdael als Dichter'. WA I, 48, p. 168. See also Peter-André Alt, *Begriffsbilder. Studien zur literarischen Form der Allegorie* (Tübingen: Niemeyer 1995); Christian Scholl, *Romantische Malerei als neue Sinnbildkunst. Studien zur Bedeutungsgebung bei Philipp Otto Runge, Caspar David Friedrich und den Nazarenern* (Munich and Berlin: Deutscher Kunstverlag, 2007), pp. 251 ff. On the difficulties of Kant's concept of schematism, see Paul Guyer, *Kant* (London: Routledge, 2006), p. 86.

16. The opposite of allegory for Moritz is beauty as inner perfection, in the sense of completeness. For the early discourse of aesthetic autonomy see Karl Philipp Moritz, 'Über die Allegorie' (1789), in *Werke in zwei Bänden*, ed. by Heide Hollmer and Albert Meier, 2 vols (Frankfurt am Main: Deutscher Klassiker Verlag, 1997), II, 1008–11; and 'Versuch über die Vereinigung aller schönen Künste und Wissenschaften unter dem Begriff des in sich selbst Vollendeten' (1785), in *idem*, pp. 943–49; after reading 'Über die bildende Nachahmung des Schönen' (1788; in *idem*, pp. 958–91), Schiller sceptically comments, 'Was mir und einem jeden Schriftsteller misfallen muß, ist die übertriebene Behauptung, daß ein Produkt aus dem Reiche des Schönen ein vollendetes Rundes Ganze seyn müsse' [What must dissatisfy me and any writer is the exaggerated claim that a product from the realm of beauty has to be a complete, round whole]. Letter to Caroline von Beulwitz, 3–6 January 1789, in *Werke. Begründet von Julius Petersen, fortgeführt von Lieselotte Blumenthal und Benno von Wiese*, ed. by Norbert Oellers et al. (Weimar: Hermann Böhlaus Nachfolger, 1943 ff.) XXV, 177.

17. Friedrich Wilhelm Joseph Schelling, *Philosophie der Kunst* (1802–03), in *Sämmtliche Werke*, ed. by Karl Friedrich August Schelling, Stuttgart (Augsburg: Cotta, 1856–61), I/ 5, p. 407.

18. Cf. Ibid., Introduction, p. 370; § 42, p. 414 ff.; Karl Philipp Moritz, *Götterlehre oder mythologische Dichtungen der Alten* (Berlin: Unger, 1791).

19. Letter from Goethe to Wilhelm von Humboldt, 22 August 1806. Quoted from Uwe Pörksen, 'Goethes Kritik naturwissenschaftlicher Metaphorik und der Roman *Die Wahlverwandtschaften*', in *Jahrbuch der Schiller-Gesellschaft*, 25 (1981), 285–315 (p. 297, note 41).

20. Cf. Olaf Breidbach, *Goethes Naturverständnis* (Paderborn: Schöningh, 2011).

21. Cf. Temilo van Zantwijk, 'Ästhetische Anschauung. Die Erkenntnisfunktion der Kunst bei Schelling', in *Der Körper der Kunst*, ed. by Johannes Grave and Reinhard Wegner (Göttingen: Wallstein, 2007) pp. 132–61. Idem, 'Das Ereignis Weimar-Jena als Symbol einer geistigen Welt', in *Anna Amalia, Carl August und das Ereignis Weimar*, ed. by Hellmut Th. Seemann (Göttingen: Wallstein, 2007), pp. 118–31.

22. Cf. Gottfried Gabriel, 'Baumgartens Begriff der "perceptio praegnans" und seine systematische Bedeutung', in *Aufklärung. Interdisziplinäres Jahrbuch zur Erforschung des 18. Jahrhunderts und seiner Wirkungsgeschichte*, 20 (2008), Themenschwerpunkt: Alexander Gottlieb Baumgarten, ed. by Alexander Aichele and Dagmar Mirbach, pp. 61–71.

23. Cf. Gottfried Gabriel, 'Kontinentales Erbe und analytische Methode. Nelson Goodman und die Tradition', *Erkenntnis*, 52 (2000), 185–98.

24. Hegel, *Werke*, XIII, 397 ff.

25. Friedrich Creuzer, *Symbolik und Mythologie der alten Völker, besonders der Griechen*, 2 vols (Leipzig, Darmstadt: Leske, 1810–12), here cited in the second edition (Leipzig, Darmstadt: Leske, 1819), I, 57 f. (§ 29).

26. Cf. *Friedrich Creuzer 1771–1858. Philologie und Mythologie im Zeitalter der Romantik*, ed. by Frank Engehausen, Armin Schlechter and Jürgen Paul Schwindt (Heidelberg: Verlag Regionalkultur 2008); Christoph Jamme, '"Göttersymbole". Friedrich Creuzer als Mythologe und seine

philosophische Wirkung', *Heidelberger Jahrbücher*, 51 (2008), 487–98; Halmi, *The Genealogy of the Romantic Symbol*, pp. 164–67.

27. Creuzer *Symbolik*, I, 70 f. (§ 35); by contrast, the allegorical is conceived as a discursive representation progressing temporally through a series of moments.

28. Cf. Moritz, 'Versuch einer Vereinigung aller schönen Künste und Wissenschaften unter dem Begriff des in sich selbst Vollendeten' (1785), *Werke*, II, 943–49 (p. 945 f.); 'Über die bildende Nachahmung des Schönen' (1788), *Werke*, II, 958–91 (p. 973); Sabine M. Schneider, *Die schwierige Sprache des Schönen. Moritz' und Schillers Semiotik der Sinnlichkeit* (Würzburg: Königshausen & Neumann, 1998).

29. *The Excursion* (1814), Preface.

30. Modern artists like Joan Miró (*Dog Barking at the Moon*, 1926. Oil on canvas, 28 3/4 x 36 1/4 inches. Philadelphia Museum of Art) and Paul Klee (*Howling Dog*, 1928. Oil on canvas, 17 1/2 x 22 3/8 inches. The Minneapolis Institute of Arts) adopt the motive.

31. Cf. René Wellek, 'Symbol and Symbolism in Literature', in *Dictionary of the History of Ideas*, ed. by Philip Paul Wiener, 5 vols (New York: Scribner, 1973–74), IV, 337–45; Oliver R. Scholz, 'Symbol, 19. und 20. Jahrhundert', in *Historisches Wörterbuch der Philosophie*, ed. by J. Ritter, K. Gründer and G. Gabriel (Basel: Schwabe, 1998), X, col. 723–38; Anca Vlasopolos, *The Symbolic Method of Coleridge, Baudelaire and Yeats* (Detroit: Wayne State University Press, 1983); and with respect to the difference between Goethe and Baudelaire: Paul Hoffmann, 'Goethes "wahre Symbolik" und die "Wälder der Symbole"', in *Von der Natur zur Kunst und zurück. Neue Beiträge zur Goethe-Forschung*, ed. by Moritz Baßler, Christoph Brecht and Dirk Niefanger (Tübingen: Max Niemeyer Verlag 1997), pp. 199–218.

32. For fuller accounts, see Henry Crabb Robinson, *Essays on Kant, Schelling, and German Aesthetics*, ed. by James Vigus (London: MHRA, 2010), esp. pp. 18–25, and James Vigus, 'Zwischen Kantianismus und Schellingianismus. Henry Crabb Robinsons Privatvorlesungen über Philosophie für Mme de Staël 1804 in Weimar', in *Germaine de Staël und ihr erstes deutsches Publikum. Literaturpolitik und Kulturtransfer um 1800*, ed. by Gerhard R. Kaiser and Olaf Müller (Heidelberg: Winter, 2008), pp. 355–92.

33. Henry Crabb Robinson, 'On the Philosophy of Schelling' (1804), in *Essays on Kant, Schelling, and German Aesthetics*, p. 126. In later years, Robinson kept up with the ongoing symbol controversy, noting rather wearily on 29 September 1834, 'Finished *Voß's Antisymbolik*. I have now had enough of Voß.' In Hertha Marquardt, *Henry Crabb Robinson und seine deutschen Freunde*, 2 vols (Göttingen: Vandenhoeck & Ruprecht, 1964–67), II, 585. For a further analysis of Robinson's view of intellectual intuition, see Philipp Hunnekuhl, 'Reconstructing the Voice of the Mediator: Henry Crabb Robinson's Literary Criticism', in *Informal Romanticism*, ed. by James Vigus (Trier: Wissenschaftlicher Verlag Trier, 2012), pp. 61–76.

34. See Ernst Behler, 'Schellings Ästhetik in der Überlieferung von Henry Crabb Robinson', *Philosophisches Jahrbuch der Görres-Gesellschaft*, 83 (1976), 133–83 (pp. 148–51). Robinson's work did, however, have a significant impact on Madame de Staël's presentation of German aesthetics in her bestseller *De l'Allemagne*: see especially Margaret R. Higgonet, 'Madame de Staël and Schelling', in *Comparative Literature*, 38 (1986), 159–80.

35. S. T. Coleridge, *The Collected Works of Samuel Taylor Coleridge*, gen. ed. Kathleen Coburn, 16 vols in 34 (Princeton, NJ: Princeton University Press, 1971–2002), V: *Lectures 1795: On Politics and Religion*, ed. by Lewis Patton and Peter Mann, p. 339.

36. As Ben Brice has argued, 'Kantian aesthetics acted as a kind of "Trojan Horse" through which Coleridge was forced to confront Humean scepticism.' Ben Brice, *Coleridge and Scepticism* (Oxford: Oxford University Press, 2007), p. 83. Nicholas Reid objects, however, that recent Coleridge criticism tends 'to assimilate him to his German sources, in their most sceptical form': Nicholas Reid, 'Why we need the Opus Maximum to understand the Coleridgean Symbol', *The Coleridge Bulletin*, n.s. 38 (Winter 2011), 93–99 (p. 99). For a judicious investigation of Coleridge's German philosophical sources and influences, see Monika Class, *Coleridge and Kantian Ideas in England, 1796–1817* (London: Continuum, 2012).

37. See especially Paul Hamilton, *Coleridge and German Philosophy: The Poet in the Land of Logic* (London: Continuum, 2007), pp. 103 ff. and Nicholas Reid, *Coleridge, Form and Symbol: Or, the Ascertaining Vision* (Farnham: Ashgate, 2006).

38. Samuel Taylor Coleridge, *The Statesman's Manual* (1816), in *The Collected Works of Samuel Taylor Coleridge*, gen. ed. Kathleen Coburn (Princeton, NJ: Princeton University Press, 1971–2002), VI: *Lay Sermons*, ed. by R. J. White (1972), pp. 30–31.

39. Ibid., p. 79.

40. Hazard Adams, *Philosophy of the Literary Symbolic* (Tallahassee: Florida University Press, 1983), p. 73, notes that 'The special is meant in its literal sense of the species that the individual embodies.'

41. Cf. Schelling, *Einleitung in die Philosophie der Mythologie*, Lecture 8, in *Sämmtliche Werke*, ed. by Karl Friedrich August Schelling (Stuttgart, Augsburg: Cotta, 1856–61), II/ 1, p. 196; and Paul Ricœur, *Symbolism of Evil*, trans. from the French by Emerson Buchanan (Boston, MA: Beacon Press 1967), pp. 163 f., 349 f.

42. Paul de Man, 'The Rhetoric of Temporality', in *Blindness and Insight: Essays in the Rhetoric of Contemporary Criticism* (London: Methuen, 1983), pp. 187–228. Benjamin's *The Origin of German Tragic Drama* (trans. by John Osborne; London: NLB, 1977) had in its turn rehabilitated Creuzer's long-discredited interpretative method, enabled by the fact that Creuzer's distinction between allegory and symbol carries much less systematic weight than Coleridge's.

43. A similar observation is made by Christian Moser, 'Sichtbare Schrift, lesbare Gestalten. Symbol und Allegorie bei Goethe, Coleridge und Wordsworth', in *Allegorie. Konfigurationen von Text, Bild und Lektüre*, ed. by Eva Horn and Manfred Weinberg (Opladen and Wiesbaden: Westdeutscher Verlag, 1998), pp. 118–32 (p. 118).

44. Thomas McFarland, 'Involute and Symbol in the Romantic Tradition', in *Coleridge, Keats and the Romantic Imagination: Romanticism and Adam's Dream*, ed. by J. Robert Barth and John L. Mahoney (Columbia and London: University of Missouri Press, 1990), pp. 29–57 (p. 51). McFarland argues (p. 43) that de Man tends to confuse 'symbol' — etymologically and traditionally conceived as a physical thing — with 'rhetoric' and 'figural language'.

45. Thus Douglas Hedley defends the religious import of Romantic symbol-conceptions in *Living Forms of Imagination* (London: T&T Clark, 2008): 'Of course, de Man is quite correct in his conviction that, lying behind the idea of the symbol in the strong Platonic sense of conveying truths and not mere figurative illustrations, is the conviction that matter can body forth the immaterial — it can become an image and give authentic expression to the spiritual' (p. 139).

46. For a condensed account of Halmi's conclusions, see 'Coleridge, Allegory and Symbol', in *The Oxford Handbook of Samuel Taylor Coleridge* (Oxford: Oxford University Press, 2008), pp. 345–58; on the theological unorthodoxy of Coleridge's symbol-conception see chapter 4 of *The Genealogy of the Romantic Symbol*, esp. pp. 124–32; on Coleridge's opportunism in applying the allegory–symbol distinction to different areas of investigation, 'Coleridge's Most Unfortunate Borrowing from A. W. Schlegel', in *British and European Romanticisms: Selected Papers from the Munich Conference of the German Society for English Romanticism*, ed. by Christoph Bode and Sebastian Domsch (Trier: Wissenschaftlicher Verlag Trier, 2007), pp. 131–42.

47. Halmi, *The Genealogy of the Romantic Symbol*, p. 1.

48. To say this need not be to follow McFarland's artificial insistence on the 'theological primacy' of Coleridge's symbol-concept ('Involute and Symbol', p. 42). Coleridge aimed to extend symbolic readings beyond biblical and mythological texts, too: in his marginalia to G. W. Tennemann's *Geschichte der Philosophie* he challenges a future scholar to arrange Tennemann's quotations in two columns, one explaining 'the Sense which the words would bear, *if* the Philosopher, from whom the Dogma is extracted, had been exclusively a *Categoric* or Verstandsphilosoph: while in an opposite Column should be given the Sense, which the same words would bear, if we suppose him to have used them as Symbols of Ideas.' This passage make especially clear that Coleridge conceives the symbol as being generated at the point of conjunction between authorial intention and the reader's interpretation. Samuel Taylor Coleridge, *The Collected Works of Samuel Taylor Coleridge*, XII: *Marginalia*, ed. by George Whalley and H. J. Jackson, 6 vols (Princeton, NJ: Princeton University Press, 1980–2001), V, 692.

49. See Daniel Fried, 'The Politics of the Coleridgean Symbol', *Studies in English Literature*, 46.4 (Autumn 2006), 763–79, esp. pp. 770 f.; James C. McKusick, 'Symbol', in *The Cambridge Companion to Coleridge*, ed. by Lucy Newlyn (Cambridge: Cambridge University Press, 2002), pp. 217–30 (pp. 223–24) and the further bibliography provided by McKusick. Joel Harter

makes the symbol central to a reading of Coleridge's theology in *Coleridge's Philosophy of Faith* (Tübingen: Mohr Siebeck, 2011); on the politics of Coleridge's symbol-concept see pp. 61f.

50. Thomas Carlyle, *Sartor Resartus: The Life and Opinions of Herr Teufelsdröckh* (London: Chapman and Hall, 1869), Book 3, Chapter 3 ('Symbols'), pp. 212–13.

51. M. Jadwiga Swiatecka, *The Idea of the Symbol: Some Nineteenth-Century Comparisons with Coleridge* (Cambridge: Cambridge University Press, 1980), argues that for Carlyle, 'the idea of concealment is obviously primary — an emphasis absent from Coleridge' (p. 86); but this conclusion depends on Swiatecka's questionable understanding of an affirmative 'German Idealist influence' to which Coleridge supposedly remained truer than Carlyle.

52. For a full discussion, see Patrick J. Keane, *Emerson, Romanticism, and Intuitive Reason: The Transatlantic 'Light of All Our Day'* (Columbia: University of Missouri Press, 2005).

53. Henry David Thoreau, *Walden* (1854), quoted in McKusick, 'Symbol', p. 225.

54. Ernst Cassirer, *An Essay on Man: An Introduction to a Philosophy of Human Culture*, in *Gesammelte Werke* [Hamburger Ausgabe], vol. XXIII, ed. by Birgit Recki (Hamburg: Felix Meiner, 2006), p. 30.

55. Cf. Ernst Cassirer, *Philosophie der symbolischen Formen III. Phänomenologie der Erkenntnis*, part II, ch. 5, in *Gesammelte Werke* [Hamburger Ausgabe], vol. XIII, ed. by Birgit Recki (Hamburg: Felix Meiner, 2002), pp. 218–33.

56. *Philosophie der symbolischen Formen I. Die Sprache*, in Ernst Cassirer *Gesammelte Werke* [Hamburger Ausgabe], vol. XI, ed. by Birgit Recki (Hamburg: Felix Meiner, 2001), p. 16.

CHAPTER 1

Kant's Transformation of the Symbol-Concept

Stephan Meier-Oeser

Traditional Ambiguities of the Notions of 'Symbol' and 'Intuition'

It is conventional wisdom that Kant's *Critique of the Power of Judgment* is 'one of the important source texts for all Romantic theories of art'.[1] For with Kant, who marks an 'important climax in the history of symbol theory',[2] begins the career of the notion of symbol within aesthetics,[3] so that — if Romantic aesthetics can be condensed into the single word 'symbol'[4] — Kant's third *Critique* 'made romanticism possible'.[5]

Symbol and intuition: the two basic notions that mark the focus of the present volume are loaded with a variety of conceptual implications that have accrued to them from the long history of their use in philosophical language. An assessment of Kant's conception of these central notions of eighteenth-century epistemology and of the mode and limitation of their impact on Romantic-period aesthetics, therefore, has to take its point of departure from a closer look at their older *Begriffsgeschichte*. For it is only against this deeper historical background that both the terminological decisions Kant makes in some respects and his seeming undecidedness in some others may become sufficiently intelligible.

Already in ancient times the notions of symbol and intuition are affected by some fundamental ambiguities. Etymologically, the Greek noun 'symbolon' derives from the verb 'symballein' (συμβάλλειν), which most literally signifies 'to throw together', but was used in a wide range of meanings including those of 'to connect', and 'to collect', 'to compare' and 'to bring together mentally', 'to conjecture' (from the Latin *conicere*) and 'to meet (or agree) with something or someone'.

Under these circumstances it is not surprising that later on the term 'symbol' takes on a number of meanings which are partly overlapping and partly contrasting. It may stand, inter alia, not only 1) for the sign in general but also — even though in different theoretical contexts — for the two mutually exclusive classes of 2) the arbitrary linguistic sign and 3) that special kind of natural sign, which, in contrast to mere conventional signs, is founded upon analogy between the sign and the signified.[6]

While the 'symbol' in the sense of a linguistic sign based on a social agreement amongst the members of a speaking community goes back to Aristotle, its opposite conception as an analogy-based allegorical sign has its roots in the Stoic interpretation of mythical texts,[7] and later on acquired a fundamental importance for the late antique and medieval tradition of symbolic theology. Whereas in the former case the classification of a sign as 'symbolic' indicates its stipulated or conventional mode of signifying (θέσει καὶ συμβολικῶς)[8] and thus refers to the relation between the sign users, in the latter case it refers to the relation of analogy that holds between the sign and its significate, especially between corporeal signs and spiritual significates.[9] Since late antiquity, a characteristic feature of this analogy-based symbol was deemed to be its non-discursive mode of signifying.[10] Hence, in the Middle Ages a speech could be called symbolical because in it — as Alanus of Lille explained by a somewhat outlandish etymology — 'the whole is comprehended at once' ('locutio [...] symbolica [...] dicitur a "sin", quod est simul, et "olon", quod est totum, quia in tali locutione simul totum comprehenditur').[11]

No less affected by ambiguity is the term 'intuition' (intuitus, intuitio), the Latin translation of the Greek epibole (ἐπιβολή), which was coined as a philosophical term by the Epicureans to characterize an instantaneous grasping (ἀθρόα ἐπιβολή) of the entire object in contrast to a merely partial conception of it (κατὰ μέρος). In the course of the Late Antique adoption of Hellenistic philosophemes the term epibole was semantically modified by making it the opposite of discursive thought (διεξοδικὸς λόγος).[12] This provided leeway for ambiguity (or diversification), given that while epibole in Epicurean philosophy was originally used to mark visual sense perception it later became primarily or even, as in some Neoplatonic authors like Plotinus, exclusively a constitutive feature of intellectual cognition.

In the scholastic tradition the corresponding Latin term intuitus as well as the adjective 'intuitive' qualify both sensible and intellectual cognition (intuitus mentis). Besides its opposition to discursive cognition (viz. deductive reasoning and inference), intuitive cognition, due to a distinction successfully introduced by Duns Scotus in the fourteenth century, enters into antithesis to what is called 'abstractive cognition'. The distinction of cognitio intuitiva and cognitio abstractiva, a subject of many medieval debates, has received various interpretations. Commonly, however, intuitive cognition in this context is understood as a cognition the object of which is attained immediately in itself or, in the case of sense perception, as present to the cognizer in time and space; whereas abstractive cognition attains its object only indirectly through a representing form or medium (in aliquo medio repraesentativo) like a phantasm, as for instance in the case of memory and imagination. While according to this terminology, on the one hand, every discursive cognition, relying on sign operations in one way or another, is an abstractive cognition, there are, on the other hand, instances of abstractive cognition (viz. remembrance and imagination) which are not discursive. This dissymmetry results from the criterial diversity concerning the mode in which intuitive cognition is contradistinct to discursive and abstractive cognition respectively. Whereas the former discrimination of intuitive from discursive cognition regards its temporal structure of immediately compassing the object at once in its entirety (simul totum), the distinction of intuitive from abstractive cognition refers to the immediacy of presenting the object in itself. Insofar, therefore, as according to scholastic terminology, cognitio abstractiva abstracts from the immediate presentiality of the object rather than from its particularity, intellection is usually described as intuitive cognition and imagination as abstractive cognition.

Leibniz's Distinction of *cognitio intuitiva* and *cognitio symbolica*

In late seventeenth- and eighteenth-century epistemology the ambiguities which traditionally adhere to the notions of symbol and intuition are still effective and become particularly apparent or even multiplied in the framework of the various topical distinctions between forms of knowledge labelled as symbolic, intuitive, discursive, and abstract cognition.

Of pivotal importance for the conceptual history of the two notions of intuition and symbol in the philosophy of enlightenment are Leibniz's 1684 *Meditationes de cognitione, veritate et ideis*, where he delineates a dichotomically structured hierarchy of modes of cognition. Based on Descartes but ultimately in direct confrontation with Cartesian epistemology, Leibniz here distinguishes in the first instance between obscure and clear cognition (*cognitio obscura — clara*) and then divides clear cognition in turn into confused and distinct cognition (*cognitio confusa — distincta*); the latter of which again is subdivided into inadequate and adequate cognition (*cognitio inadaequata — adaequata*) on the one hand, and into symbolic and intuitive cognition (*cognitio symbolica — intuitiva*) on the other. The most perfect of these is (or rather: would be) an adequate intuitive cognition (*cognitio adaequata intuitiva*),[13] i.e. a distinct and instantaneous (*à la fois*) conception of a complex notion together with all its partial notions.[14] According to Leibniz, however, such an intuitive or pure intellection (*pura intellectio*), which Descartes conceived of as an essential feature of the human mind warranting its independence from and superiority to the realm of sensibility and imagination, is a mere limit-concept. For he regards the pure form of intuitive cognition as hardly ever accessible to the human intellect[15] — and then, if at all, only with regard to the most simple objects or notions.[16]

It is obvious that Leibniz's distinction between intuitive and symbolic cognition is closely related to the conceptual history of these terms. This becomes especially evident when Leibniz defines intuitive cognition — which he considers a borderline case hardly ever given — by the ancient criterion of *simul totum*, i.e. as simultaneously conceiving all constitutive moments of an object or concept. Nevertheless it is not the negation of the *simul totum* that characterizes symbolic in contrast to intuitive cognition, but rather — and here the scholastic determination of abstractive cognition as a 'cognitio in aliquo medio repraesentativo' comes into effect — the substitution of the cognitive total presence of the object by an intuitively cognizable sign.

Provided that the simultaneity of cognition is what essentially gives the evidence of an object's unity,[17] the incapacity of the limited human intellect to comprehend the content of any more complex concept other than successively makes it necessary that in the process of reasoning the complex concept of the thing itself is substituted by an instantaneously conceivable sensible sign (or by an imagination of it), always supposing that a detailed explication of its meaning could be given if needed. Leibniz, therefore, maintains that human knowledge of complex objects or notions is always symbolic, i.e. performed in the medium of signs.[18] His doctrine of symbolic cognition, claiming a necessary commitment of intellectual thought to the sensible and thus 'corporeal' medium of signs, has as its metaphysical basis his system of pre-established harmony of body and soul which he formulates in direct opposition to the Cartesian substance dualism and the intellectual intuitionism implied therein. For it is, as Leibniz underlines, an immediate consequence of that harmony that by 'a wonderful economy of nature' abstract ideas are always associated with sensible characters.[19]

In line with this Leibniz emphasizes the fundamental epistemic function of language and, more generally, the dependency of thinking on the use of signs; for 'Omnis Ratiocinatio nostra nihil aliud est quam characterum connexio; et substitutio. Sive illi characteres sint verba; sive notae, sive denique imagines' [all our reasoning is nothing but a process of connecting and substituting characters which may be words or other signs or images].[20] Thus, 'Cogitationes fieri possunt sine vocabulis [...] At non sine aliis signis' [thinking can take place without words [...] but not without some other signs].[21] Even if Leibniz took the signs applied in symbolic cognition as arbitrary signs,[22] the possibility and validity of symbolic knowledge is ultimately founded upon the principle of proportionality or analogy according to which the elementary signs of symbolic knowledge may be chosen arbitrarily provided that the internal relations between these signs correspond to the relations that exist between the things signified.[23]

Wolffianism and its Critics: The Linguistic Reinterpretation of Symbolic Cognition

Leibniz's distinction between symbolic and intuitive cognition and the epistemological theory connected to it became, especially through its propagation by Christian Wolff and his school, one of the main issues of German enlightenment epistemology. Wolff, avowing the massive impact of Leibniz's *Meditationes de cognitione* on his conception of the powers of human understanding,[24] explains the opposition of intuitive and symbolic cognition by giving the following example:

> Wenn ich an einen Menschen gedencke, der abwesend ist und mir sein Bild gleichsam vor Augen schwebet; so stelle ich mir seine Person selbst vor. Wenn ich aber von der Tugend diese Worte gedencke: Sie sey eine Fertigkeit seine Handlungen nach dem Gesetze der Natur einzurichten; so stelle ich mir die Tugend durch Worte vor.[25]

> [When I think of a man who is absent, and his image, as it were, hovers before my mind's eye, I represent his person himself; but when I think of virtue these words: that it is an ability to conform one's acts to the natural law, I represent virtue through words.]

Unlike in the scholastic language regime, imaginative presentation is characterized as a mode of intuitive cognition. For according to Wolff and his school, we 'represent things either in themselves, or through words or other signs. [...] The first cognition is called intuitive; the latter figurative cognition.'[26] Our cognition, therefore, is intuitive '[...] wenn wir uns die Begriffe oder Abbildungen der Dinge selbst vorstellen [...]' [when we represent the concepts or images of the things themselves],[27] or when we '[...] eine Sache, indem wir sie uns vorstellen, [...] durch etwas denken, was sie an sich selbst ist' [think a thing on presenting it to ourselves through something that it is in itself];[28] symbolic in contrast, 'when we represent to ourselves, instead of the things, only their signs, e.g. the words by which we designate them.'[29] Words, says Wolff, are therefore 'der Grund von einer besonderen Art der Erkäntniß [...], welche wir die figürliche nennen' [the basis of a special kind of knowledge [...] which we call the figurative].[30] Taking into account the emphasis put on the constitutive function that language has for any abstract thinking or any thinking of abstract objects, it comes as no surprise that Wolff in this context refers to the venerable topos of thinking as 'internal speech'.[31] Wolff maintains that '[...] so bald wir uns entweder einen allgemeinen Begriff von einer Art Dinge [...] formiren, oder auch nur etwas deutliches mercken [geschieht es, dass] wir von der anschauenden Erkäntniß zu der figürlichen schreiten, oder zu uns selbst reden, oder wenigstens die dazu nöthige[n] Worte gedencken' [as soon as we either form a general idea [...] or even attend to something distinct, we proceed from intuitive to symbolic cognition and speak to ourselves, or at least remember the words that are necessary for this].[32] Thus, all distinct general cognition is symbolic cognition. For 'if what we comprehend to be common to several things could not be designated by means of words', claims Georg Bernhard Bilfinger, an early propagator of Wolffian philosophy, 'we would only be able to form very few and hardly other than obscure and confused general ideas.'[33] Along the same lines Friedrich Christian Baumeister declares:

> Sensibus cognoscimus res praesentes, quae *cognitio* dicitur *intuitiva*. At intellectus in cognoscendis notionibus universalioribus, iisque distincte formandis, versatur, quod, nisi per verba, fieri non potest, quae *cognitio* dicitur *symbolica*, quae ab intellectu seiungi non potest. [...] abstractarum notionum nulla distincte formari potest, nisi verborum adminiculis.[34]

> [Through the senses we grasp the things present, and this *cognition* is called *intuitive*. The intellect, however, is concerned with cognizing more general notions and with forming them distinctly, which is possible only by means of words; this *cognition* is called *symbolic* and cannot be separated from the intellect. [...] No distinct cognition of abstract notions can be formed without the support of words.]

In this sense Johann Heinrich Lambert claims that 'unsere allgemeine oder abstrakte Erkenntniß' is 'durchaus symbolisch' [our general or abstract cognition is thoroughly symbolic].[35] The passages quoted are representative particularly — though not exclusively[36] — for early and mid eighteenth-century thought. They evince some important conceptual shifts in standing out against the traditional scholastic notion of *cognitio abstractiva* as well as Leibniz's version of symbolic knowledge. The central moments of the complex conceptual shuffle are the following:

(1). The traditional scholastic distinction of intuitive and abstractive cognition is replaced by the distinction of intuitive and symbolic cognition.

(2). This process includes a) a transformation or reinterpretation of abstractive cognition into abstract cognition, and b) an amalgamation of the latter with symbolic cognition. While in the scholastic tradition *cognitio abstractiva* was characterized by being mediated through signs rather than by the moment of generality, here the former is taken as the basis of the latter: general, i.e. abstract cognition is seen as possible only in the form of a cognition through signs.

(3). In close connection to these conceptual changes, the notion of *cognitio intuitiva*, due to the refusal of the possibility of an intellectual intuition and an *intellectus purus*, is reinterpreted in such a fashion that it now encloses (in contrast to the scholastic tradition) imaginative presentation but (in contrast to the Cartesian tradition) precludes intellectual cognition.

The result of that amalgamation of the thus modified conceptions of symbolic and abstract cognition is the commonly shared conviction that general or abstract cognition is possible only as symbolic cognition. Besides the frequently repeated claim that symbolic cognition — as Leibniz maintained — is founded upon signs in general, there is a strong tendency predominant in the Wolffian school to restrict symbolic cognition to thinking in words: as Bilfinger claims, 'omnis cognitio universalis symbolica est, symbola autem communia voces sunt [...]' [all general knowledge is symbolic, but the common symbols are words].[37] The Wolffian Andreas Boehm therefore underlines the 'miraculous support' symbolic knowledge provides for any operation of the intellect.[38] The view that any higher cognitive function strictly depends on the use of signs in general and language in particular is a common conviction the diffusion and prevalence of which within eighteenth-century epistemology can hardly be overemphasized.

The most elaborate exposition of the theory of *cognitio symbolica* was provided by Johann Heinrich Lambert in his *Semiotik, oder die Lehre von der Bezeichnung der Gedanken und Dinge* [*Semiotics, or the doctrine of the signification of thoughts and things*], published in 1764 as the second volume of his *Neues Organon*. The leading idea of Lambert's *Semiotik*, which examines various sign systems (such as language, musical notes, maps, chemical symbols, algebraic signs, etc.) with regard to their scientificity ('Wissenschaftlichkeit'), is Leibniz's principle of proportionality, i.e. the analogy that exists between the relations among things and the relations among signs. For it is this proportionality or constant relation of relations which guarantees 'daß die Theorie der Sache und die Theorie ihrer Zeichen mit einander verwechselt werden können' [that the theory of things and the theory of signs are interchangeable] in which he sees 'die letzte Vollkommenheit der Zeichen' [the ultimate perfection of signs].[39] For the very function as well as the scientific use of symbolic cognition consists 'in reducing the theory of things to the theory of signs, i.e. in exchanging the dim consciousness of concepts with an intuition, sensation, and a *clear* presentation of signs.'[40] While the ideal of symbolic cognition is marked by the system of algebraic signs, the general rule is provided by any well-formed spoken language.

The theoretical foundation of any abstract reflection upon the use of signs, however, has its problematical flipside, particularly when it is connected to the view that words are what makes up the most common and most important class of signs for symbolic cognition. Leibniz and Wolff had already warned against the dangers of an uncritical or incautious use of symbolic cognition which occurs '[...] indem wir leere Wörter, mit denen kein Begriff verknüpfet ist, für Erkänntniß halten, und Wörter für Sachen ausgeben' [if we regard empty words with which no concept is connected as knowledge and pass off words as things].[41]

While Leibniz and Wolff did not consider the misuse of language as a principal argument against its fundamental importance for human knowledge, Kant is — particularly in his early writings — much more sceptical about the epistemic function of language. But Kant was not the first to oppose the Wolffian concept of symbolic cognition. Before him, Christian August Crusius criticized the current conception of symbolic knowledge as a cognition 'da man eine Sache [...] durch Worte denket' [where one is thinking a thing [...] through words]. Focusing on the common reduction of symbolic cognition to thinking in internalized linguistic signs he claims 'daß die Gewohnheit, die Begriffe mit Worten zu verbinden [that the practice of connecting concepts with words] is totally different from symbolic cognition proper.[42] Words, according to Crusius, are 'nichts anders als Zeichen der Begriffe [...], welche nur zu besserer Nutzung der Begriffe damit verbunden wurden, in den Begriffen selbst aber nichts verändern' [nothing but signs of our concepts that have been connected to them only for the sake of using concepts better, but do not change anything in the concepts themselves]. Hence, he points out — in fact directly against Wolff's proposition that words are 'the basis of a special kind of knowledge'[43] — that 'auch die Gewohnheit Worte mit seinen Begriffen zu verbinden, keine besondere Art der Erkenntniß ausmachen könne' [the practice of connecting words with conceptions cannot constitute a special kind of knowledge]. 'Denn es wäre sonsten eben so, als wenn man eine Blume in einem Garten deswegen zu einer besondern Classe rechnen wolte, weil ein Pflock mit einer Nummer darbey stehet, und als wenn man deswegen das Blumenreich in zwey Reiche eintheilen wolte, nemlich in dasjenige, wo Pflöcker mit Nummern dabey stehen, und wo keine dabey stehen' [For otherwise it would be as though one were to put a flower in the garden in a special class simply because a post with a number is standing beside it, and thus were to divide the realm of flowers into two, viz. into that where posts with numbers stand beside them, and that where they don't].[44]

Symbolic cognition, therefore, as Crusius holds in contrast to the prevailing conviction of the mid-eighteenth century, cannot be based on words: for words, in his view, are nothing but an 'ein äusserliches Hülfsmittel der Erkenntniß' [an external accessory of knowledge]. For regardless of the unquestionable utility words may have for our abstract thinking, 'the concepts we have do not become others by the use of words'.[45] Just as it is possible to have the same thought in different languages we may have 'thoughts without words'.[46] Crusius contrasts intuitive and symbolic cognition such that the latter is conceived of as one where the thing is thought 'durch etwas, welches wegen eines gewissen Verhältnisses gegen dieselbe geschickt ist, ein Zeichen derselben abzugeben' [through something that, due to a certain relation it bears to a certain thing, is apt to function as a sign for it].[47] Such a relation can be either logical or, as it is mostly the case, causal, viz. 'when causes and their properties are represented through their effects' or vice versa.[48] The merely arbitrary association of words and objects, however, never suffices to provide the basis for that epistemic function connected to symbolic signs.

Kant's Transformation of the Symbol

Symbolic cognition vs. language

In this point the early Kant agrees with Crusius. Although fully acknowledging the important role signs play within the sphere of arithmetic, he strictly rejects the idea that its methodological principle of substituting things or concepts by signs could ever be instantiated in the medium of linguistic signs and via that medium be transferred to philosophical issues.[49] For 'the procedure of philosophy' is, as he points out in his *Inquiry concerning the distinctness of the principles of natural theology and morality*, 'completely different' from that of mathematics.[50] The whole of arithmetic is based the rule-governed use of operational signs. Here

> [...] werden zuerst anstatt der Sachen selbst ihre Zeichen mit den besondern Bezeichnungen ihrer Vermehrung oder Verminderung, ihrer Verhältnisse u.s.w. gesetzt und hernach mit diesen Zeichen nach leichten und sichern Regeln verfahren durch Versetzung, Verknüpfung oder Abziehen und mancherlei Veränderung, so daß die bezeichneten Sachen selbst hiebei gänzlich aus den Gedanken gelassen werden, bis endlich beim Beschlusse die Bedeutung der symbolischen Folgerung entziffert wird.

> [are posited first of all not things themselves but their signs, together with the special designations of their increase or decrease, their relations etc. Thereafter, one operates with these signs according to easy and certain rules, by means of substitution, combination, subtraction and many kinds of transformation, so that the things signified are themselves completely forgotten in the process, until eventually, when the conclusion is drawn, the meaning of the symbolic conclusion is deciphered.][51]

Philosophical knowledge, in contrast, cannot be achieved by means of rule-governed operations on a set of signs. For 'Die Zeichen der philosophischen Betrachtung sind niemals etwas anders als Worte, die weder in ihrer Zusammensetzung die Theilbegriffe, woraus die ganze Idee, welche das Wort andeutet, besteht, anzeigen, noch in ihren Verknüpfungen die Verhältnisse der philosophischen Gedanken zu bezeichnen vermögen' [the signs employed in philosophical reflection are never anything other than words that can neither show in their composition the constituent concepts of which the whole idea, indicated by the word, consists; nor are they capable of indicating in their combinations the relations of the philosophical thoughts to each other].[52] Whereas mathematical signs function as 'sinnliche Erkenntnißmittel' [sensible means of cognition],[53] enabling mathematics to regard its objects and its universal knowledge 'under signs [or 'in signs']'[54] in concreto', philosophy always regards its universal knowledge 'in abstracto, as existing alongside signs'.[55]

While the signs used in mathematics guarantee that 'in' or 'under' them each step of a proof or demonstration can be known 'mit derselben Zuversicht, wie man dessen, was man mit Augen sieht, versichert ist' [with the degree of assurance characteristic of seeing something with one's own eyes] (so that, in this respect, these signs are intuitive as well as symbolic),[56] 'Dagegen helfen die Worte, als die Zeichen der philosophischen Erkenntniß, zu nichts als der Erinnerung der bezeichneten allgemeinen Begriffe' [the only help which words, construed as the signs of philosophical cognition, afford is that of reminding us of the universal concepts which they signify]. In philosophy, therefore (unlike mathematics), it is at all times necessary to be immediately aware of their significance, or rather, as Kant actually says: 'Man muß ihre Bedeutung jederzeit unmittelbar vor Augen haben' [it is necessary to have their signification immediately before one's eyes].[57] In other words, philosophical reflection prerequisites to have 'the thing itself before one's [mind's] eye' without being able 'to avail oneself of that important device which facilitates thought and which consists in handling individual signs rather than the universal concepts of the things themselves.'[58]

Even if the repeated recourse to 'things before one's eyes' might seem to suggest that Kant would see philosophical comprehension as some kind of intellectual intuition in contrast to the symbolic cognition of mathematics, the opposite is the case. For the formula does not refer to the Leibniz criterion of *cognitio intuitiva*, viz. to the instantaneity or simultaneity (*simul totum*) but rather to the immediacy of cognizing the object or concept in itself instead of in a representing medium. Philosophical cognition essentially consists in contemplating complex abstract concepts immediately in themselves by discursively analysing their characteristic marks or partial notions.

While the operational signs utilized in arithmetic establish a cognition that is both intuitive and symbolic — so that, according to Kant, in contrast to the common contemporary view, intuitive and symbolic cognition do not stand in negative contradistinction to each other — philosophical cognition, like any cognition of reason, is neither intuitive nor symbolic but rather discursive. Not intuitive, for Kant, like many authors of the Leibnizo-Wolffian school,[59] denies the possibility of an intellectual intuition (*intellectuelle Anschauung*), claiming that since our nature is so constituted 'that intuition with us never can be other than sensuous',[60] '[t]here is (for man) no intuition of what belongs to the understanding':[61] thus because there is no intellectual intuition of the supersensible that 'would conceive and exhibit the object immediately and at once' ('den Gegenstand unmittelbar und auf einmal fassen und darstellen würde'), 'the discursive understanding must [...] bestow much labour on the resolution and composition of its conceptions.'[62] Not symbolic, because the only signs used in philosophical reflection are words or characters which however, in contrast to the Wolffian school where they are conceived of as the most frequently used and most important kind of symbols, for Kant are not symbols at all.[63]

Thus, the early Kant does not deny the existence of symbolic cognition, but takes it as strictly limited to the mathematical sphere of quantities. Outside this area the prerequisite condition of cognitive immediacy rules out any possibility of reducing the knowledge of things to the knowledge of signs which Lambert had propagated as the methodological kernel of symbolic cognition. Abstract philosophical reflection, according to Kant, cannot be performed in or 'replaced by the transposition of signs in accordance with rules, the representation of the things themselves being replaced in this procedure by the clearer and the easier representation of the signs' ('so daß man die Vorstellung der Sachen selbst in diesem Verfahren mit der kläreren und leichteren der Zeichen vertauschte').[64] Words, therefore, contrary to what the majority of Wolffian philosophers took for granted, cannot function as a compensation of the lack of intuition. And yet, to procure a device that may substitute the missing direct intuition is in fact all the more necessary within the framework of Kant's critical philosophy in which the theoretical design of this device is intimately correlated with Kant's 'new' conception of the symbol.

Kant's conception of symbol is primarily known from the prominent § 59 of his *Critique of the Power of Judgment* where the beautiful appears as 'the symbol of the morally good'. It is with reference to this context when Todorov claims that '[u]ntil 1790, the word "symbol" had a very different meaning from the one it was to acquire in the romantic era'.[65] What is true of the academic philosophy, especially of the Wolffian school, however, is not quite correct with regard to Kant. For here the concept of symbol is closely connected to some core problems of his critical philosophy and therefore has long been on the philosophical agenda.

Symbol not opposed to intuition

It is well known that according to Kant's *Critique of Pure Reason* conceptions without content are empty while intuitions without conceptions are blind, so that it is 'eben so nothwendig, seine Begriffe sinnlich zu machen (d.i. ihnen den Gegenstand in der Anschauung beizufügen), als seine Anschauungen sich verständlich zu machen (d.i. sie unter Begriffe zu bringen)' [as necessary for the mind to make its conceptions sensuous (that is, to join to them the object in intuition), as to make its intuitions intelligible (that is, to bring them under conceptions)].[66] Human cognition is possible only as a connection of sensible intuitions and intellectual concepts. Kant therefore is confronted with the problem of explaining how to pure concepts of the understanding, which 'can never be encountered in any intuition',[67] a corresponding intuition may nevertheless be given a priori, and, even more, how a 'concept [...] which only reason can think, and to which no sensible intuition can be adequate' may be 'supplied with an intuition'.[68]

From what has been said it is clear that with Kant the lack of a direct sensible intuition of intelligible objects can neither be superseded, contrary to the Cartesian tradition, by an intellectual intuition, nor can it, in contrast to the Wolffian version of symbolic cognition, be compensated by linguistic signs (i.e. words). With Kant, the function of substituting the non-given or even principally impossible direct intuition for the purpose of providing a concept with objective reality[69] is rather provided by an activity of the judgment. Borrowing a rhetorical term that since ancient times is closely related to the concept of ἐνάργεια [evidence], Kant calls this activity *hypotyposis* or — in reference to Cicero's characterization of hypotyposis as 'sub oculos subiectio'[70] — as 'subiectio sub adspectum' [submission to inspection]. Kant's utilization of the term 'hypotyposis' must be considered well thought out. For here, on a pivotal systematic point, which is closely related to the long-discussed issue of the epistemic function of mental images and linguistic signs, the term refers to a procedure of establishing intuitivity, presentiveness and vividness ('Anschaulichkeit') in a non-imagist or non-iconic medium.[71] At the same time this use of a highly charged rhetorical term is, as David Wellbery has rightly pointed out, 'rather surprising in view of Kant's rejection of oratorical art [...], for it amounts to a massive expansion of the domain of rhetoric', insofar as Kant 'effectively conceives even our normal perception and designation of the world as a rhetorical (in the sense of "presentational") operation'.[72]

In his *Critique of Pure Reason* Kant presents a 'Stufenleiter' of modes of repre- sentation that can be seen as a counter-model to the arrangement of perceptions and cognitions of Leibnizo-Wolffian school:[73] cognition (*cognitio*), he declares, 'is either an *intuition* or a *concept* (*intuitus vel conceptus*). The former is immediately related to the object and is singular; the latter is mediate, by means of a mark, which can be common to several things. A concept is either an *empirical* or a *pure* concept, and the pure concept, insofar as it has its origin solely in the understanding (not in a pure image of sensibility), is called *notio*. A concept made up of notions, which goes beyond the possibility of experience, is an *idea* or a concept of reason.'[74] While intuitions are always required to verify the reality of our concepts, the different kinds of concepts are related to different modes of intuition: 'If the concepts are empirical, the intuitions are called examples: if they are pure concepts of the understanding, the intuitions go by the name of schemata.'[75] Even if it is impossible to verify the objective reality of ideas, symbols — or symbolic exhibitions — are required in order to 'provide the concept with meaning through the presentation of an object for it'.[76]

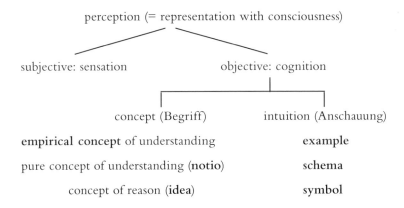

According to Kant's *Critique of the Power of Judgment*, 'intuitive representations can be divided into the schematic and the symbolic kinds of representation. Both are hypotyposes, i.e., presentations (*exhibitiones*): not mere characterizations, i.e., designations of the concepts.'[77] Kant, as Halmi has pointed out, 'rejecting the usage of the Leibnizo-Wolffian school, was the first philosopher of the Enlightenment to identify symbolism exclusively as an intuitive, in contradistinction to discursive, mode of representation.'[78] Kant therefore explicitly criticizes 'the adoption of the word symbolic by modern logicians in a sense opposed to an intuitive mode of representation', in which he sees a 'wrong use of the word and subversive of its true meaning: for the symbolic is merely a species of the intuitive',[79] because 'all hypotyposis (presentation, subjectio sub adspectum) as a rendering in terms of sense', is either schematic or else symbolic, as where the concept is one to which no sensible intuition can be adequate.[80]

Symbol as an analogy-based model for reflection

Even if in the *Critique of Pure Reason* the schema is introduced as a 'procedure for providing a concept with its image',[81] Kant underlines that 'the schema is to be distinguished from an image'. Instead of being a pictorial representation of the object itself it rather is a 'representation of a method for representing', i.e. a 'representation of a general procedure of the imagination for providing a concept with its image'. Kant explains this thus: in order to endow my concept of the number five with an image or intuition, I may appropriately 'place five points in a row'. But 'if I only think a number in general, which could be five or a hundred, this thinking is more the representation of a method for representing a multitude [...] in accordance with a certain concept than the image itself.'[82] Instead of being an image, the schema rather is a rule or, as Wellbery rightly terms it, a 'rule cluster' for the intuitive actualization of a non-intuitive concept,[83] i.e. a method or 'procedure for providing a concept with its image'.[84] This also holds for the symbol. Even if Kant, especially in his anthropological writings, several times brings the *symbolic representations* in close connection to images,[85] the symbol is not founded on a likeness between the representamen and the represented object but rather on analogy which — for Kant — 'does not signify (as is commonly understood) an imperfect similarity of two things, but a perfect similarity of relations between two quite dissimilar things.'[86]

Schema and symbol are not images. Like the schema, the symbol, too, functions as a model providing a rule of how to reflect on a certain non-sensible object, even if it does so merely according to rules of analogy. Kant can therefore present the symbol as a kind of schema, distinguishing between the 'real' or 'transcendental schema' and the symbolic 'schematism according to analogy',[87] in which the concept is supplied with an intuition such that the procedure of judgment 'is merely analogous to that which it observes in schematism'. Thus, what in this case agrees with the concept is not an intuition but merely a rule for the procedure of reflecting and making judgments about the object, so that the agreement consists merely in the form of reflection, and not in the content.[88] In this way, a monarchical state can be represented as a living body when it is governed by constitutional laws,[89] but as a mere machine (such as a handmill) when it is governed by an individual absolute will. In both cases the representation is merely symbolic. For even if there is certainly neither a 'likeness between a despotic state and a handmill' nor between a republic or a monarchical state and the human body on the one hand, there surely is one 'between the rules of reflection upon both and their causality'.[90] And it is also in this way that the claim that the 'beautiful is the symbol of the morally good' has to be understood.

This foundation of the symbol upon analogy (with which Kant reinforces an aspect of Leibniz's genuine conception of symbolic cognition)[91] marks a fundamental difference between Kant's and Crusius's conception of symbolic cognition. Crusius classifies a cognition as symbolic if a cause and its nature is represented through its effect or vice versa ('wenn man sich die *Ursachen und deren Beschaffenheit* durch ihre Wirkungen vorstellet; oder wenn man sich das, was eine Wirkung ist, durch seine Ursachen vorstellet').[92] Kant, however, declares (somewhat opaquely): 'Das Symbol einer Idee [...] ist eine Vorstellung des Gegenstandes nach der Analogie, d.i. [nach] dem gleichen Verhältnisse zu gewissen Folgen, als dasjenige ist, welches dem Gegenstande an sich selbst, zu seinen Folgen beygelegt wird' [The symbol of an idea [...] is a representation of the object by analogy, i.e., by the same relationship to certain consequences as that which is attributed to the object in respect of its own consequences].[93] What at first sight may look quite similar is in fact fundamentally different. This becomes clear when Kant exemplifies his claim: we may conceive of organized things in nature in relation to their cause as we present a clock in relation to its human maker, viz. in a relation to causality in general which is the same in both cases. In such a symbolic cognition of God as the creator of things the intrinsic character or nature ('innern Beschaffenheit') of the subject that has this relation and these effects remains unknown, as Kant remarks apparently with reference to Crusius. For we cannot exhibit it in itself, we can only exhibit the relation.[94] This indirect mode of representation is a characteristic feature of symbolic exhibition. Even though there is no such thing as intellectual intuition, the symbol, as its functional surrogate, is both intellectual and intuitive, albeit not directly: Kant describes it as an 'indirect intuition' ('indirecte anschauung')[95] and again as 'indirectly intellectual' ('indirecte intellectual').[96]

The ambivalence of the symbolic

Kant's account of symbolic cognition and the epistemic value of symbols in general remains ambivalent: even the label 'symbolic cognition' which Kant himself adopts several times[97] is problematic insofar as it presupposes that 'the name of cognition may be given to what only amounts to a mere mode of representation' ('Vorstellungsart').[98] Symbolic representation, exhibition or hypotyposis of the supersensible provides 'kein theoretisches Erkenntniß, aber doch ein Erkenntniß nach der Analogie' [no theoretical cognition, but merely a cognition by analogy].[99] It has to be noted that in such a 'cognition by analogy', even if analogy may imply 'a perfect similarity of relations',[100] the object itself will remain unknown or will be merely cognized in the mode of 'as if'. Thus, Kant's fairly traditional-looking statement that 'all our knowledge of God is merely symbolical' ('so ist alle unsere Erkenntnis von Gott bloß symbolisch'),[101] has to be spelled out more fully: in cognizing God as the creator of the world, we must not 'attribute to the Supreme Being any properties in themselves' but rather 'limit our judgment merely to the relation which the world may have to a Being whose very concept lies beyond all the knowledge which we can attain within the world.'[102] We are therefore 'compelled to consider the world *as if* it were the work of a Supreme Understanding and Will' ('die Welt so anzusehen, *als ob* sie das Werk eines höchsten Verstandes und Willens sei'), which simply means 'that a watch, a ship, a regiment, bears the same relation to the watchmaker, the shipbuilder, the commanding officer, as the world of sense [...] does to the unknown, which I do not hereby cognize as it is in itself [...]. In this way '[t]he expression suited to our feeble notions is, that we conceive the world *as if* it came, as regarding its existence and internal plan, from a supreme reason.'[103] The mode of 'as if', therefore, not only characterizes the way in which the object is represented or 'cognized' but also the epistemic status of such a quasi-cognition.

As important as it is with Kant to take both the schema and the symbol as kinds of intuitive presentation, it is no less important to clearly distinguish them from each other. For confounding symbolic with schematic hypotyposis necessarily results in that epistemic error of ascribing objective reality to what is merely a functional analogon which Kant criticizes as 'dogmatic anthropomorphism'[104] or 'mysticism'.[105] In exhibiting ideas that belong to pure reason, 'it is *enlightenment* to distinguish the symbolic from the intellectual [...], the temporarily useful and necessary shell from the thing itself' ('das Symbolische vom Intellectuellen [...], die zwar einige Zeit hindurch nützliche und nöthige Hülle von der Sache selbst zu unterscheiden, ist Aufklärung').[106] While Kant holds on the one hand that the symbol 'is only a means to promote the intellection', and as such 'serves only the immediate cognition of the understanding, *but with time it must fall away*', he says in the same breath that 'where intuition is not immediately allowed to us, there we must help ourselves by analogy with symbolic cognition.'[107] In all these cases enlightenment cannot consist in overcoming the symbolic elements of thought, for without them all ideas would be without content. Here enlightenment must rather consist in sharpening the consciousness about the irreducible *as if*-status of our knowledge of objects that lie beyond the sphere of sensible intuition. This awareness of the *as if*-mode of thinking and speaking about ideas of reason that Kant terms characterizes as 'symbolic anthropomorphism'[108] is the only way to avoid the epistemic problems connected to both dogmatism and Hume's scepticism. Kant's philosophy, therefore, as Erich Adickes and, more recently, Heiner Bielefeldt have rightly pointed out, has to be taken essentially as an 'as-if philosophy'[109] (albeit not in the sense of Hans Vaihinger) according to which 'whenever it comes to representing ideas of reason, all claims of objectifying knowledge must be transformed into the mode of a conscious "as if".'[110]

The 'as if'-analogy in which for instance 'the pure judgment of taste [...] stands to the moral judgment'[111] not only governs the relation of aesthetics and moral philosophy but also allows Kant — notwithstanding his sharp rejection of physico-theology — to talk of the 'Chiffreschrift [...], wodurch die Natur in ihren schönen Formen figürlich zu uns spricht' [cypher in which nature speaks to us figuratively in its beautiful forms] and say that the beautiful modifications of light and sound are 'gleichsam eine Sprache, die die Natur zu uns führt, und die einen höhern Sinn zu haben scheint' [as it were a language in which nature speaks to us and which has the semblance of a higher meaning].[112]

While the various aspects and different interpretations that have attached to the ambiguous notion of symbol over its long *Begriffsgeschichte* were to a large extent already present in Leibniz's theory of symbolic cognition, in which the symbol is taken as a sign in the broadest sense, so that the symbol embraces words, images and other signs, within the Wolffian school it was almost completely reduced to the algebraic and linguistic sign. In the development of Kant's conception of the symbol a complex and somewhat paradoxical movement is apparent. Starting his early examination of the current theory of symbolic cognition by contrasting the mathematical symbols with the words used in philosophy, Kant, with his specific transformation of the concept of the symbolic characterized (like that of symbolic theology)[113] by intuitivity, non-discursivity, and analogy, opposes the Wolffian tendencies of reducing symbolic cognition to a procedure of substituting concepts by words.

Viewed against the background of the longstanding tradition of explaining human cognition and thinking through the two paradigmatic models of image and speech, Kant's doctrine of schematic and symbolic exhibition (*hypotyposis*) is particularly interesting insofar as it provides an alternative to the inveterate conviction that any representations must be either linguistic (or else 'propositional') or imagistic (or else 'pictorial')[114] and, thus, consist of either words or images. According to Kant the symbol, just like the schema, is irreducible to either of these sign classes; it is neither linguistic nor pictorial in the proper sense. And yet, the symbolic hypotyposis is, as Kant points out in the famous § 59 of his *Critique of the Power of Judgment*, intimately related to or even partly identical with words, which in turn are now conceived of as both linguistic and pictorial. The ambivalent assessment of the symbol is hereby transferred to language. Already in his anthropological lectures dating from the 1770s Kant had pointed out that 'the use of signs is a thing of great importance'. While there are, one the one hand, certain signs — viz. characters or words — the function of which, as Kant maintained, merely consists in reproducing thoughts, there are, one the other hand, certain other signs — viz. symbols or poetic images — which 'die Sache und den Mangel der Begriffe ersetzen sollen' [function to substitute the things and to compensate the lack of concepts].[115] Still in the *Critique of the Power of Judgment* Kant holds (just as in his earlier writings) that words are, on the one hand, 'merely designations of concepts [...] devoid of any intrinsic connection with the intuition of the object', and therefore are signs the sole function of which is 'to afford a means of reinvoking the concepts according to the imagination's law of association'.[116] And yet, Kant, now taking up some observations made by John Locke,[117] Leibniz,[118] and others,[119] claims in the very same textual context that '[o]ur language is full of [...] indirect presentations, in accordance with an analogy, where the expression does not contain the actual schema for the concept but only a symbol for reflection.'[120] Kant exemplifies this by pointing to the fact that

> So sind die Wörter Grund (Stütze, Basis), Abhängen (von oben gehalten werden), woraus Fließen (statt Folgen), Substanz (wie Locke sich ausdrückt: der Träger der Accidenzen) und unzählige andere nicht schematische, sondern symbolische Hypotyposen und Ausdrücke für Begriffe nicht vermittelst einer directen Anschauung, sondern nur nach einer Analogie mit derselben, d.i. der Übertragung der Reflexion über einen Gegenstand der Anschauung auf einen ganz andern Begriff, dem vielleicht nie eine Anschauung direct correspondiren kann.[121]

[the words ground (support, basis), to depend (to be held up from above), to flow from (instead of to follow), substance (as Locke puts it: the support of accidents), and numberless others, are not schematic, but rather symbolic hypotyposes, and express concepts without employing a direct intuition for the purpose, but only drawing upon an analogy with one, i.e., transferring the reflection upon an object of intuition to quite a new concept, and one with which perhaps no intuition could ever directly correspond.]

And even if Kant still in his 1798 *Anthropology* (just like in his earlier anthropological writings)[122] claims that words are not symbols, but 'accompany the concepts merely as guardians (*custodes*) in order to reproduce the concept when the occasion arises',[123] in the very same context he then clearly underlines the fundamental cognitive function of language. For he now characterizes language — in a way that does not fit well with the charge of his total neglect of language brought by Herder, Hamann, Reinhold and others — as 'the greatest instrument for understanding ourselves and others.'[124]

The fundamental epistemic function that Kant ascribes to symbolic representations in metaphysics, moral, theology, politics, aesthetics and jurisprudence, is reflected in language. In jurisprudence, for instance, as Kant notes, the term 'right' ('Recht *rectum*') refers to 'was einer Regel gemäs ist' [what is compliant to a rule],[125] so that 'the technico-practical concept of the right and straight is used as a symbol of the moral and practical'.[126] But the ambivalent appraisal of the cognitive function of the symbolic is also clearly reflected in Kant's highly ambivalent assessment of language. Just as the symbolic exhibition, functioning in the cognitive process as a means to compensate our lack of intuition, is assessed ambivalently with regard to its function, the symbolic expression of language both compensates and indicates the lack of concepts. For 'Wer sich immer nur symbolisch ausdrücken kann, hat noch wenig Begriffe des Verstandes [he who can only express himself symbolically still has only a few concepts of understanding], so that even the admired eloquence of Homer and Ossian essentially is 'blos [...] Mangel an Mitteln, ihre Begriffe auszudrücken' [nothing but poverty in concepts and, therefore, also in the words to express them].[127]

Due to the manifold and massive ambiguities in Kant's theory of the symbolic it is hardly surprising that also its impact on contemporary and later symbol theories has been highly ambivalent. On the one hand, certain aspects of Kant's critical assessment of the symbol reappear (for example) in Fichte's claim that symbolic cognition is 'gar nicht Erkenntniß des Kopfes sondern bloßes Organ' [by no means a cognition of the head but rather a mere organon],[128] or in Hegel's retaining the view that the symbolic is a characteristic feature of an early stage in the development of art and culture. On the other hand there are, not least through the mediation of Goethe, who was particularly attracted to the analogy Kant saw between art and nature and between the aesthetic and teleological judgement,[129] a number of fundamental concordances between the Kantian and the Romantic symbol concepts, such as the determination by intuitability, non-discursiveness, and indirectness,[130] and its characterization as 'expression of the inexpressible'.[131] And yet, when Kant laid out the analogy between nature and art as well as the basic logic of the symbolical in general in the weakest possible mode of *as if*, this was incompatible with the Romantic 'rejection of analogically for ontologically based symbolism'.[132]

Even if symbolic presentation, rather than being cognition in the strict sense, is 'a substitute for cognition, an accommodation to its impossibility in the face of the limits of the faculty of understanding', it is not to be identified 'with the tradition of apophatic theology'.[133] For when Kant explicitly calls 'symbolization' 'eine Nothülfe für die Erkenntnis des Übersinnlichen' [an expedient for concepts of the super-sensible] his notion of the symbol is — mutatis mutandis — more or less the resumption of the symbol-concept underlying the tradition of symbolic theology. But even this 'reveals how distant his concept of the analogical symbol' still is 'from the Romantic concept of the synecdochical symbol'; or, at least, from all those interpretations of the symbol which, due to 'the Romantic project of re-enchanting the world', imagined 'the meaning of objects to inhere in their physical presence'.[134] But even if one could say with Todorov that Romantic aesthetics may be condensed into the single word 'symbol',[135] it is nonetheless possible that there is more than only one single Romantic concept of symbol.

Notes to Chapter 1

1. David E. Wellbery, 'The Transformation of Rhetoric', in *The Cambridge History of Literary Criticism*, vol. v: *Romanticism*, ed. by Marshall Brown (Cambridge: Cambridge University Press, 2000), pp. 185–202 (p. 191).

2. Andreas Kubik, *Die Symboltheorie bei Novalis. Eine ideengeschichtliche Studie* (Tübingen: Mohr Siebeck, 2006), p. 52.

3. Oliver R. Scholz, 'Symbol II', in *Historisches Wörterbuch der Philosophie*, ed. by J. Ritter, K. Gründer, and G. Gabriel (Basel: Schwabe, 1998), x, col. 723–38 (col. 723).

4. Cf. Tzvetan Todorov, *Theories of the Symbol* (Ithaca, NY: Cornell University Press, 1982), p. 198.

5. *Continental Aesthetics: Romanticism to Postmodernism: An Anthology*, ed. by Richard Kearney and David M. Rasmussen (Hoboken, NJ: Wiley-Blackwell, 2001), p. 3.

6. Cf. Stephan Meier-Oeser, 'Symbol I', in *Historisches Wörterbuch der Philosophie*, ed. J. Ritter, K. Gründer, and G. Gabriel (Basel: Schwabe, 1998), x, cols 710–23.

7. Jean Pépin, *Mythe et allégorie* (Paris: Aubier, 1958), pp. 125–72.

8. Proklos [Proclus], *Procli Diadochi In Platonis Cratylum commentaria* 56, ed. by Giorgio Pascuali (Leipzig: Teubner, 1908; repr. Stuttgart: Teubner, 1994), pp. 24, 22.

9. Cf. Albert the Great, *Super Dionysium de caelesti hierarchia*, Opera omnia 36/1, ed. by P. Simon and W. Kübel (Münster: Aschendorff, 1993), pp. 70–72: 'Symbolum [...] dicitur hic similitudo corporalis spiritualia repraesentans, licet quaelibet similitudo symbolum possit dici'.

10. Cf. Porphyry, 'Vita Pythagorae' 36, in *Opuscula selecta*, ed. by August Nauck (Leipzig: Teubner, 1886), p. 38.

11. Alanus ab insulis, 'Expositio super symbolum apostolicum et Nicenum', prol., *Textes inédits*, ed. by Marie-Thérése d'Alverny (Paris: J. Vrin, 1965), p. 84.

12. Cf. Theo Kobusch, 'Intuition', in *Historisches Wörterbuch der Philosophie*, ed. by J. Ritter, K. Gründer and G. Gabriel (Basel: Schwabe, 1976), IV, col. 524.

13. Gottfried Wilhelm Leibniz, *Meditationes de cognitione, veritate, et ideis*, in *Sämtliche Schriften und Briefe* (Berlin: Akademie Verlag, 1923 ff. [= A]), VI, 4, 585–86.

14. Ibid., p. 588; cf. *Discours de Métaphysique* § 24, A VI, 4, 1568,7–10: '[...] quand mon esprit comprend à la fois et distinctement tous les ingrediens primitifs d'une notion, il en a une connoissance *intuitive* [...].'

15. Cf. G. W. Leibniz, *Aus und zu Malebranche, De la recherche de la verité*, A VI, p. 1815: 'Non puto ullam esse intellectionem puram, sine aliquo responsu in corpore. [...] Non nisi intellectus purus

verum circulum percipit. Puto nullam a nobis ideam percipi veri circuli, sed nos habere tantum ejus cognitionem caecam sive suppositivam.'

16. G. W. Leibniz, to Michael Gottlieb Hansch, 25 July 1707, in *Opera omnia*, ed. by Louis Dutens, vol. 2, 1 (Geneva: Fratres de Tournes, 1768), p. 223: '[...] pura Intellectio, quae veritatis nexum uno mentis ictu perspicit: quod Deo in omnibus competit, nobis tantum in simplicibus datum est.'

17. G. W. Leibniz, *De arte combinatoria*, A VI, 1, p. 170: 'Unum autem esse intelligitur, quicquid uno actu intellectus s. simul, cogitamus [...].'

18. G. W. Leibniz, *Meditationes de cognitione*, A VI, 4, p. 588.

19. G. W. Leibniz, *Nouveaux Essais* I, 1, § 5, A VI, 6, p. 77: '[...] c'est par une admirable Oeconomie de la nature, que nous ne saurions avoir des pensées abstraites, qui n'ayent point besoin de quelque chose de sensible, quand ce ne seroit que des caracteres tels que sont les figures des lettres et les sons; quoiqu'il n'y ait aucune connexion necessaire entre tels caracteres arbitraires, et telles pensées.'

20. G. W. Leibniz, *De modis combinandi characteres*, A VI, 4, p. 922.

21. G. W. Leibniz, *Dialogus* A VI, 4, p. 22: 'Cogitationes fieri possunt sine vocabulis [...] At non sine aliis signis.'

22. G. W. Leibniz to Jean Gallois (1672) Konzept B, A II, 1, p. 228 f.: 'Notae [...] symbolaque arbitraria sunt, sive sint verba, sive characteres [...].'

23. Cf. *Dialogus*, A VI, 4, p. 24: '[...] etsi characteres sint arbitrarii, eorum tamen usus et connexio habet quiddam quod non est arbitrarium, scilicet proportionem quandam inter characteres et res; et diversorum characterum easdem res exprimentium relationes inter se.' Cf. *Quid sit idea*, A VI, 4, p. 1370: 'Exprimere aliquam rem dicitur illud in quo habentur habitudines, quae habitudinibus rei exprimendae respondent.'

24. Cf. Christian Wolff, *Vernünftige Gedanken von den Kräften des menschlichen Verstandes und ihrem richtigen Gebrauche in Erkenntnis der Wahrheit* (1712), ed. by Hans Werner Arndt, in Chr. Wolff, *Gesammelte Werke*, ed. by Jean École et al. (Hildesheim: Georg Olms, 1965 ff. [= Works]), sect. 1, vol. 1, p. 109. For Wolff and his school see Matteo Favaretti Camposampiero, *Conoscenza simbolica. Pensiero e linguaggio in Christian Wolff e nella prima età moderna* (Hildesheim, NY: Olms, 2009).

25. Chr. Wolff, *Vernünftige Gedancken von Gott, der Welt, und der Seele des Menschen* § 316, Works, sect. 1, vol. 2, p. 173.

26. Ibid.; cf. *Psychologia empirica* § 289, Works, sect. 2, vol. 5, p. 204: 'Quodsi cognitio nostra terminatur actu, quo verbis tantum enunciamus, quae in ideis continentur, vel aliis signis eadem repraesentamus, ideas vero ipsas verbis aut signis aliis indigitatas non intuemur; *cognitio symbolica* est.'; cf. Johann Wilhelm Golling, *Theses philosophicae de cognitione symbolica et intuitiva* (Altdorf: Meyer, 1725), p. 4: 'Philosophi solicite distinguunt inter [...] repraesentationes, quae rem ipsam praesentem nobis exhibitam intuentur, et eam quae mediantibus quibusdam aliis rebus, cognoscendae rei destinatis, in animo excitantur. Illam Intuitivam, hanc Symbolicam vocant.'

27. Johann Christoph Gottsched, *Erste Gründe der gesamten Weltweisheit*, erster Theil (Leipzig: Barnhard Christoph Breitkopfen, 1733), p. 493.

28. Christian August Crusius, *Weg zur Gewißheit und Zuverläßigkeit der menschlichen Erkenntnis* (Leipzig: Gleditsch, 1747), p. 347.

29. Cf. Friedrich Christian Baumeister, *Institutiones metaphysicae* § 562 (Wittenberg and Zerbst, 1774; first published 1738), p. 379: 'Cum rem nobis immediate repraesentamus, ita ut illam coram intueamur, tum illa cognitio dicitur *intuitiva*. Cum vero res nobis, vel per verba, vel per alia quaecunque signa, nobis sistimus, dicitur illa cognitio *cognitio symbolica*.' J. Chr. Gottsched, *Erste Gründe*, p. 493: '[...] wann wir uns statt der Dinge, nur ihre Zeichen, z.E. die Wörter, womit man sie benennet, vorstellen.'

30. Chr. Wolff, *Vernünftige Gedancken von Gott, der Welt, und der Seele des Menschen* § 316, Works, sect. 1, vol. 2, p. 173.

31. Cf. Stephan Meier-Oeser, 'Wort, inneres / Rede, innere', in *Historisches Wörterbuch der Philosophie*, ed. by J. Ritter, K. Gründer, and G. Gabriel (Basel: Schwabe, 2004), XII, cols. 1037–50.

32. Cf. Wolff, *Vernünftige Gedancken von Gott* § 322, Works, sect. 1, vol. 2, p. 178. Cf. *Psychologia empirica* § 284, Works, sect. 2, vol. 5, p. 202: '[...] nos tacite nobismetipsis loqui, quando de rebus cogitare intendimus.'

33. Georg Bernhard Bilfinger, *Dilucidationes philosophicae* (Tübingen: Cotta, 1725), p. 267: 'Symbolicam cognitionem praecipue inservire cognitioni generali. Nisi enim vocibus designari posset id, quod in pluribus rebus commune deprehendimus: Ideas generales paucissimas, & vix alias, quam obscuras aut confusas nancisci nobis liceret.'

34. Friedrich Christian Baumeister, *Elementa philosophiae recentioris* (Leipzig: Gleditsch, 1747), pp. 257–58.

35. Johann Heinrich Lambert, *Neues Organon*, vol. 2: *Semiotik* § 17 (Leipzig: Wendler, 1764), pp. 12–13.

36. See for instance Peter Villaume who still in the third edition of his popular *Practical logic for young people who do not want to study* (*Practische Logik für junge Leute, die nicht studieren wollen* (1787, third edition Leipzig 1819, p. 87) defines symbolic concepts as 'Begriffe, die wir uns nicht eigentlich vorstellen, sondern nur durch Worte fassen können' [concepts we do not represent intrinsically but rather can grasp only through words].

37. G. B. Bilfinger, *Praecepta logica* (Jena: Marggraf, 1742), p. 87.

38. A. Boehm, *Metaphysica* (Giessen: Krieger, 1767), p. 275: 'Notiones facilius distinctiusque formantur in cognitione symbolica, quam intuitiva, item judicia & ratiocinia. Quare cum hae tres sint omnes intellectus operationes: *Omnes intellectus operationes mirifice juvat cognitio symbolica*.'

39. J. H. Lambert, *Neues Organon*, vol. 2: *Semiotik* § 23, p. 16.

40. Ibid. § 24, p. 16: '*Die Theorie der Sache auf die Theorie der Zeichen* reduziren, will sagen, das dunkle Bewußtseyn der Begriffe mit der anschauenden Erkenntniß, mit der Empfindung und *klaren* Vorstellung der Zeichen verwechseln.'

41. Chr. Wolff, *Vernünftige Gedancken von Gott, der Welt, und der Seele des Menschen* § 320, Works, sect. 1, vol. 2, p. 177. Cf. G. W. Leibniz, *Vocabula*, A VI, 4, p. 63, 16–19.

42. Chr. A. Crusius, *Weg zur Gewißheit und Zuverlässigkeit der menschlichen Erkenntnis* (Leipzig: Gleditsch, 1747), p. 347.

43. Wolff, *Vernünftige Gedancken von Gott, der Welt, und der Seele des Menschen* § 316, Works, sect. 1, vol. 2, p. 173.

44. *Weg zur Gewißheit*, p. 389.

45. Ibid. p. 389 f.: '[...] die Begriffe, die wir haben, werden doch durch die Worte an sich keine andern, sondern die Worte setzen nur die denkende Kraft in den Stand dieselben besser zu gebrauchen [...]'.

46. Cf. ibid, pp. 390–91: 'Daß die Worte die Art der Erkenntniß innerlich nicht afficiren, kan man auch schon daraus abnehmen, weil wir in verschiedenen Sprachen einerley denken können [...]. Daher ist es auch unläugbar, daß wir Gedanken ohne Worte haben können. Dieses gilt nicht nur von den unmittelbaren Empfindungs-Ideen [...] Man findet es auch im Nachsinnen, wenn man auf abstracte Ideen kommt, vor welche man allererst einen Namen suchet, weil sie noch keinen haben, oder da man denselben nicht weiß. Daher solte man auch nicht einmal sagen, daß wir die Sachen durch Worte dächten. Wenigstens muß man es nicht anders als also meinen, daß wir die Begriffe der Sachen mit den Begriffen der Worte als Zeichen verbinden.'

47. Ibid., p. 347.

48. Ibid., p. 348: 'Es ist also die anschauende Erkenntniß diejenige, da man sich ein Ding durch dasjenige vorstellet, was es an sich selbst ist. Die symbolische Erkenntniß aber ist diejenige, da man sich ein Ding nicht durch dasjenige vorstellet, was es an sich selbst ist, sondern durch andere Begriffe, welche fähig sind, Zeichen von jenen abzugeben, z.E. wenn man sich die Ursachen und deren Beschaffenheit durch ihre Wirkungen vorstellet; oder wenn man sich das, was eine Wirkung ist, durch seine Ursachen vorstellet; wenn man sich das, was in einem Dinge beständig ist, durch die möglichen Veränderungen seines Zustandes vorstellet; oder wenn man eine Sache durch Verhältnisse gegen andere, oder negativisch, durch dasjenige, was sie nicht ist, gedenket.'

49. Cf. Brigitta-Sophie von Wolff-Metternich, *Die Überwindung des mathematischen Erkenntnisideals. Kants Grenzbestimmung von Mathematik und Philosophie* (Berlin and New York: de Gruyter, 1995), esp. pp. 17–35.

50. Immanuel Kant, *Untersuchung über die Deutlichkeit der Grundsätze der natürlichen Theologie und der Moral. Inquiry concerning the distinctness of the principles of natural theology and morality*, in Kant, *Theoretical Philosophy, 1755–1770*, trans. by David Walford and Ralf Meerbote (Cambridge: Cambridge University Press, 1992), p. 251.

51. Kant, *Inquiry concerning the distinctness*, p. 250. *Untersuchung über die Deutlichkeit der Grundsätze der natürlichen Theologie und der Moral* (1764), in *Kant's Gesammelte Schriften*, ed. by Preußische Akademie der Wissenschaften (Berlin: Akademie-Verlag, 1900– [= Akademie-Ausgabe]) vol. 2: p. 278.

52. Ibid, p. 251; *Untersuchung über die Deutlichkeit*, Akademie-Ausgabe 2:278–79:

53. Kant, *Inquiry concerning the distinctness*, p. 265; Akademie-Ausgabe 2:291.

54. Kant, *Inquiry concerning the distinctness*, p. 265; Akademie-Ausgabe 2:292.

55. 'die Mathematik [betrachtet ...] ihre allgemeine Erkenntniß unter den Zeichen in concreto, die Weltweisheit aber neben den Zeichen noch immer in abstracto'. Kant, *Inquiry concerning the distinctness*, p. 265; Akademie-Ausgabe 2:291.

56. For the criterion of the symbolic sign precisely in allowing to cognize the objects 'in' or 'under the sign'. Cf. Kant, *Lectures on Metaphysics*, trans. by Karl Ameriks and Steve Naragon (Cambridge: Cambridge University Press, 1997), p. 56: '[...] cognition is symbolic where the object is cognized *in the sign*, but with discursive cognition the signs are not symbols [symbola] because I do not cognize the object in the sign but rather the sign produces only the representation of the object for me.' *Vorlesungen über Metaphysik*, Akademie-Ausgabe 28:238: 'Die Erkenntniß ist symbolisch, wo der Gegenstand in dem Zeichen erkannt wird; aber bei der discursiven Erkenntniß sind die Zeichen nicht symbola, indem ich in dem Zeichen nicht den Gegenstand erkenne, sondern das Zeichen mir nur die Vorstellung von dem Gegenstande hervorbringt.'

57. Kant, *Inquiry concerning the distinctness*, p. 265; Akademie-Ausgabe 2:291–92.

58. Translated after: Kant, *Theoretical Philosophy, 1755–1770*, p. 251; Kant, *Untersuchung über die Deutlichkeit*, Akademie-Ausgabe 2:279: 'Daher man bei jedem Nachdenken in dieser Art der Erkenntniß *die Sache selbst vor Augen haben muß* und genöthigt ist, sich das Allgemeine in abstracto vorzustellen, ohne dieser wichtigen Erleichterung sich bedienen zu können, daß man einzelne Zeichen statt der allgemeinen Begriffe der Sache selbst behandele.' Italics added.

59. Cf. e.g. Samuel Christian Hollmann who saw pure intellection as a pure fiction (*purum figmentum*). *Philosophiae rationalis quae Logica vulgo dicitur editio auctior et emendatior* (Göttingen, 1767; first edition 1746), pp. 129–30: '[...] multi, nescio quem, *intellectum purum* sibi hic effingant, quo & res immateriales, & conceptus universales [130] atque abstractos, *absque omni conceptu materiali* se sibi repraesentare videntur. Purum enim, *intellectus* ille *purus*, putumque figmentum est [...].'

60. Kant, *Kritik der reinen Vernunft*, Akademie-Ausgabe 3:74.

61. Cf. Kant, *On the form and principle of the sensible and the intelligible World*, in *Theoretical Philosophy, 1755–1770* (1992), p. 389; *De mundi sensibilis atque intelligibilis forma et principiis dissertatio pro loco* (1770) Akademie-Ausgabe 2:396: 'Intellectualium non datur (homini) intuitus, sed nonnisi cognitio symbolica, et intellectio nobis tantum licet per conceptus universales in abstracto, non per singularem in concreto.' In in this passage the opposition between *intuitus* and *cognitio symbolica* is only a relative one, in the sense that '*symbolum* is an *indirect* intuition'; cf. *Entwürfe zu dem Colleg über Anthropologie aus den 70er Jahren*; Akademie-Ausgabe 25:710.

62. Kant, *Von einem neuerdings erhobenen vornehmen Ton in der Philosophie (On a newly arisen superior tone in philosophy)* [1796], Akademie-Ausgabe 8:389.

63. Cf. Kant, *Lectures on Metaphysics* (1997), p. 56: '[...] the word table is no symbol, but rather only a means for producing the representation of the understanding through association': Akademie-Ausgabe 28:238. Cf. *Entwürfe zu dem Colleg über Anthropologie aus den 70er Jahren*, Akademie-Ausgabe 25:710: 'Words are not symbola, because they don't provide a picture [Bild]'. Cf. *Anthropologie in pragmatischer Absicht*, Akademie-Ausgabe 7:191.

64. Kant, *Inquiry concerning the distinctness* (1992), p. 251. *Untersuchung über die Deutlichkeit*, Akademie-Ausgabe 2:279.

65. Tzvetan Todorov, 'The Romantic Crisis', in *Theories of the Symbol*, trans. by Catherine Porter (Ithaca, NY: Cornell University Press, 1982), pp. 147–221 (p. 200).

66. *Critique of Pure Reason*, ed. and trans. by Paul Guyer and Allen W. Wood (Cambridge: Cambridge University Press, 1998), p. 193–94; B 176, Akademie-Ausgabe 3:75.

67. *Critique of Pure Reason* (1998), p. 271; Akademie-Ausgabe 3:134.

68. Kant, *Critique of Judgment*, transl. by Werner S. Pluhar (Indianapolis, IN: Hackett Publishing

Company, 1987), p. 226; Akademie-Ausgabe 5:531.

69. Cf. Kant, *Welches sind die wirklichen Fortschritte, die die Metaphysik seit Leibnizens und Wolfs Zeiten in Deutschland gemacht hat?* [*What real progress has metaphysics made in Germany since the time of Leibniz and Wolff?*], Akademie-Ausgabe 20:279.

70. Cicero, *De orat.* 3, 53, 202; cf. Quintilian, *Inst. orat.* 9, 2, 40.

71. The German philosophical tradition had absorbed the old definition of hypotyposis, which in Micraelius's very popular *Philosophical Lexicon* is described as '[...] narrationis evidentia, qua rem oculis in sermone ita subjicimus, ut non narrari, sed geri videatur' [evidence of a speech by which we place a thing in speaking in such a way before our eyes, that it does not seem to be told, but rather to actually take place]. Johannes Micraelius, *Lexicon Philosophicum Terminorum Philosophis Usitatorum* (Jena: Freyschmid, 1653), col. 507. Cf. Pietro Perconti, *Kantian Linguistics: Theories of Mental Representation and the Linguistic Transformation of Kantism* (Münster: Nodus Publikationen, 1999), p. 33.

72. David E. Wellbery, 'The Transformation of Rhetoric', in *The Cambridge History of Literary Criticism*, vol. V: *Romanticism*, ed. by Marshall Brown (Cambridge: Cambridge University Press, 2000), pp. 185–202 (p. 193).

73. Kant, *Kritik der reinen Vernunft* B377, Akademie-Ausgabe 3:249–50: 'Die Gattung ist *Vorstellung* überhaupt (*repraesentatio*). Unter ihr steht die Vorstellung mit Bewusstsein (*perceptio*). Eine Perception, die sich lediglich auf das Subject als die Modification seines Zustandes bezieht, ist *Empfindung* (sensatio), eine objective Perception ist *Erkenntniß* (*cognitio*). Diese ist entweder *Anschauung* oder *Begriff* (*intuitus vel conceptus*). Jene bezieht sich unmittelbar auf den Gegenstand und ist einzeln, dieser mittelbar, vermittelst eines Merkmals, was mehreren Dingen gemein sein kann. Der Begriff ist entweder ein *empirischer* oder *reiner Begriff*, und der reine Begriff, so fern er lediglich im Verstande seinen Ursprung hat (nicht im reinen Bilde der Sinnlichkeit), heißt *Notio*. Ein Begriff aus Notionen, der die Möglichkeit der Erfahrung übersteigt, ist die *Idee* oder der Vernunftbegriff.' See also below.

74. *Critique of Pure Reason* (1998), p. 399, with bold type replaced by italics.

75. *Kritik der Urteilskraft* § 59, Akademie-Ausgabe 5:351.

76. *Anthropologie in pragmatischer Hinsicht*, Akademie-Ausgabe 7:191; *Anthropology from a Pragmatic Point of View*, in *Anthropology, History and Education*, ed. and trans. by Robert B. Louden and Günter Zöller (Cambridge: Cambridge University Press, 2007), pp. 227–429 (p. 298).

77. *Kritik der Urteilskraft* § 59, Akademie-Ausgabe 5:351; *Critique of the Power of Judgment*, ed. and trans. by Paul Guyer and Eric Matthews (Cambridge: Cambridge University Press, 2000), p. 226.

78. Nicholas Halmi, *The Genealogy of the Romantic Symbol* (Oxford: Oxford University Press, 2007), p. 63.

79. *Kritik der Urteilskraft*, Akademie-Ausgabe 5:351. Cf. *Anthropologie*, Akademie-Ausgabe 7:191.

80. Cf. *Kritik der Urteilskraft*, Akademie-Ausgabe 5:351.

81. Kant, *Critique of Pure Reason*, p. 273; Akademie-Ausgabe 3:135.

82. *Critique of Pure Reason*, p. 273, Akademie-Ausgabe 3:135.

83. David E. Wellbery, 'The Transformation of Rhetoric', p. 192.

84. *Critique of Pure Reason*, p. 273, Akademie-Ausgabe 3:135.

85. Cf. *Anthropologie Collins*, Akademie-Ausgabe 25:126.

86. *Prolegomena zu einer jeden künftigen Metaphysik*, Akademie-Ausgabe 4:357. *Prolegomena to Any Future Metaphysics*, ed. and trans. by James W. Ellington, 2nd edn (Indianapolis, IN: Hackett Publishing Company, 2001), p. 91.

87. *Welches sind die wirklichen Fortschritte*, Akademie-Ausgabe 20:332.

88. *Kritik der Urteilskraft* (*Critique of the Power of Judgment*), Akademie-Ausgabe 5:351; cf. Simon Swift, *Romanticism, Literature and Philosophy: Expressive Rationality in Rousseau, Kant, Wollstonecraft and Contemporary Theory* (London: Continuum, 2006), pp. 65–66; cf. Alison Ross, 'Natural Beauty as Symbolic and Analogical Relation to Ideas', in *The Aesthetic Paths of Philosophy: Presentation in Kant, Heidegger, Lacoue-Labarthe, and Nancy* (Stanford, CA: Stanford University Press, 2007), pp. 28–29.

89. Cf. Kant, *Vorlesungen über die Metaphysik*; *Lectures on Metaphysics* (1997), p. 56: '[...] the human body can serve as a symbol of a republic in which all members constitute a whole'; Akademie-

Ausgabe 28:238: 'So kann zum Symbol einer Republik der menschliche Körper dienen, in welchem alle Glieder ein Ganzes ausmachen.'

90. Kant, *Critique of the Power of Judgment* (2000), p. 226.

91. Cf. note 23.

92. See note 48, italics added.

93. *Welches sind die wirklichen Fortschritte*, Akademie-Ausgabe 20:280; *What Real Progress Has Metaphysics Made in Germany since the Time of Leibniz and Wolff?*, in Kant, *Theoretical Philosophy after 1781*, ed. by Henry Allison and Peter Heath (Cambridge: Cambridge University Press, 2002), p. 370.

94. Ibid. (italics added).

95. Kant, *Entwürfe zu dem Colleg über Anthropologie*, Akademie-Ausgabe 15:710: 'Die Anschauung wird nicht dem symbolischen, sondern der Erkentnis durch Begriffe entgegengesetzt. Die symbolische Vorstellung dient vielmehr zur Anschauung. [...] Symbolum ist eine indirecte anschauung.'

96. Kant, '*Metaphysik* L', Akademie-Ausgabe 28:238, *Lectures on Metaphysics* (1997), p. 56: 'A cognition of the understanding which is indirectly intellectual and is cognized through the understanding, but is produced through an analogy of sensible cognition, is a symbolic cognition, which is opposed to logical cognition, just as the intuitive is to the discursive. The cognition of the understanding is symbolic if it is indirectly intellectual and is produced through an analogy of sensible cognition, but is cognized through the understanding.'

97. Cf. *De mundi sensibilis atque*, see note 61; *Lectures on Metaphysics* (Akademie-Ausgabe 8:238: see note 96); *Kritik der Urteilskraft*, Akademie-Ausgabe 5:353, see note 104; *Anthropology from a Pragmatic Point of View* (2006), p. 84, see note 127.

98. *Kritik der Urteilskraft* (*Critique of the Power of Judgment*) § 59, Akademie-Ausgabe 5:353.

99. *Welches sind die wirklichen Fortschritte*, Akademie-Ausgabe 20:280.

100. See note 86.

101. *Kritik der Urteilskraft*, Akademie-Ausgabe 5:353.

102. *Prolegomena to any Future Metaphysics* (2001), p. 91.

103. Ibid. Italics added.

104. Cf. *Kritik der Urteilskraft*, Akademie-Ausgabe 5:353: 'If one may call a mere mode of representation (Vorstellungsart) cognition (Erkenntniß) [...] then all our cognition of God is merely symbolic; and one who takes it, with the properties of understanding, will, and so forth, which only evidence their objective reality in beings of this world, to be schematic, falls into anthropomorphism.'

105. Cf. *Kritik der praktischen Vernunft* (*Critique of Practical Reason*) Akademie-Ausgabe 5:70, where Kant warns against 'the mysticism of practical reason, which turns what served only as a symbol into a schema, that is, proposes to provide for moral concepts actual intuitions'.

106. *Anthropologie in pragmatischer Hinsicht*, Akademie-Ausgabe 7:192; *Anthropology from a Pragmatic Point of View*, ed. by Louden (2006), p. 85.

107. Kant, *Lectures on Metaphysics* (1997), p. 56, italics added; Akademie-Ausgabe 28:238: 'Das Symbolum ist nur ein Mittel, die Intellection zu befördern; es dient nur der unmittelbaren Verstandeserkenntniß; *mit der Zeit muß es aber wegfallen*. [...] Wo uns also die Anschauung nicht unmittelbar erlaubt ist; da müssen wir uns per analogiam mit der symbolischen Erkenntniß behelfen.'

108. *Prolegomena*, AA 4:357.

109. Cf. Heiner Bielefeldt, *Symbolic Representation in Kant's Practical Philosophy* (Cambridge: Cambridge University Press, 2003), p. 35; cf. Erich Adickes, *Kant und die Als-Ob-Philosophie* [*Kant and the As-If-Philosophy*] (Stuttgart-Bad Cannstatt: Frommann, 1927).

110. Bielefeldt, *Symbolic Representation*, p. 35.

111. *Kritik der Urteilskraft* (*Critique of the Power of Judgment*) § 42, Akademie-Ausgabe 5:301.

112. *Kritik der Urteilskraft* (*Critique of the Power of Judgment*) § 42, Akademie-Ausgabe 5:302; cf. A. Ross, 'Natural beauty as symbolic and analogical relation to ideas' (2007), p. 31: 'According to Kant nature in its beautiful products displays itself *as if* it were art, *as if* it were beautiful intentionally, and thus presents a purposiveness without a purpose.' Italics added.

113. Cf. Porphyry, note 10.

114. Cf. Stephan Meier-Oeser, 'Sprache und Bilder im Geist. Skizzen zu einem philosophischen Langzeitprojekt', *Philosophisches Jahrbuch der Görres-Gesellschaft*, 111 (2004), 312–42.

115. *Anthropologie Collins*, Akademie-Ausgabe 25:126.

116. *Kritik der Urteilskraft* § 59, Akademie-Ausgabe 5:352: 'Bezeichnungen der Begriffe durch begleitende sinnliche Zeichen, die gar nichts zu der Anschauung des Objects Gehöriges enthalten, sondern nur jenen nach dem Gesetze der Association der Einbildungskraft, mithin in subjectiver Absicht zum Mittel der Reproduction dienen'.

117. John Locke, *Essay concerning Human Understanding*, ed. by P. H. Nidditch (Oxford: Clarendon Press, 1975), p. 403.

118. Cf. Leibniz, *Nouveaux Essais*, AA VI, 6: 275–79.

119. The forgotten metaphoricity of language and its cognitive role is e.g. underlined in Christian Garve, 'Betrachtungen einiger Verschiedenheiten in den Werken der ältesten und neuern Schriftsteller, insbesondere der Dichter', in *Neue Bibliothek der schönen Wissenschaften und der freyen Künste*, vol. 10 (Leipzig: Dyck, 1770), p. 21: 'Es sind zwar in allen Sprachen die Wörter für die Dinge aus der unsichtbaren und geistigen Welt, ihrem Ursprung nach Metaphern. Aber dieser Ursprung ist bey uns vergessen, die Metapher wird nicht mehr bemerkt. Bey den alten war eben diese Metapher das einzige Mittel sich den Begriff entweder selbst zu formiren oder ihn andern verständlich zu machen.'

120. *Kritik der Urteilskraft* § 59, Akademie-Ausgabe 5:352, *Critique of the Power of Judgment* (2000), p. 226.

121. *Kritik der Urteilskraft* § 59, Akademie-Ausgabe 5:352.

122. Cf. *Entwürfe zu dem Colleg über Anthropologie*, Akademie-Ausgabe 15:710: 'Wörter sind nicht *symbola*, denn sie geben kein Bild ab' ('Words are not symbols, for they give no image').

123. *Anthropologie in pragmatischer Hinsicht*, Akademie-Ausgabe 7:191.

124. *Anthropologie in pragmatischer Hinsicht*, Akademie-Ausgabe 7:192.

125. Kant, *Vorarbeiten zur Einleitung in die Rechtslehre* (*Preparatory Work on the Doctrine of Right*), Akademie-Ausgabe 23:255.

126. Ibid., p. 256: 'Der technisch-practische Begrif des Rechten und Geraden wird [...] zum Symbol des moralisch-practischen gebraucht und in der That ist in der Rechtsbeurtheilung etwas Analogisches mit der Mathematik sowohl was die pünctliche Angemessenheit zur Regel als auch die Gleichheit des Maaßes betrift [...].'

127. Kant, *Anthropologie in pragmatischer Hinsicht*, Akademie-Ausgabe 7:191; *Anthropology from a Pragmatic Point of View* (2006), p. 84.

128. Johann Gottlieb Fichte, *Vorlesungen über Logik und Metaphysik* [*Lectures on Logic and Metaphysics*], 1797, § 361, in *Gesamtausgabe der Bayerischen Akademie der Wissenschaften*, vol. IV, 1, ed. by Reinhard Lauth and Hans Gliwitzky (Stuttgart-Bad Cannstatt: Friedrich Frommann Verlag, 1977), p. 247.

129. Cf. Halmi, *The Genealogy of the Romantic Symbol*, p. 93.

130. In a short text *Über die Gegenstände der bildenden Kunst* [*On the Objects of Plastic Art*], written in 1797, Goethe notes: 'if the symbolic points to something else beyond representation, it will always do so indirectly'; cf. Todorov, *Theories of the Symbol*, p. 199.

131. Cf. Todorov, ibid., p. 189.

132. Cf. Halmi, *The Genealogy of the Romantic Symbol*, pp. 93–94.

133. Cf. Halmi, *The Genealogy of the Romantic Symbol*, p. 64.

134. Cf. ibid., p. 102.

135. Todorov, *Theories of the Symbol*, p. 198.

CHAPTER 2

'Mere Nature in the Subject': Kant on Symbolic Representation of the Absolute

Jane Kneller

In the chapter entitled 'Von dem Grunde der Unterscheidung aller Gegenstände überhaupt in Phaenomena und Noumena' [On the ground of the distinction of all objects in general into phenomena and noumena] in the *Kritik der reinen Vernunft*, Kant 'solves' the problem of our inability to represent the world as it is '*an sich*' (in itself, or noumenally) by simply affirming its status as 'problematic' for us.[1] Indeed, throughout the first *Critique* he argues that nature as we know it consists of nothing beyond what we can possibly experience, which is an ordered network of phenomena constituted by concepts of the human understanding and shaped by the forms of human sensory intuition, space and time, a priori, from *whatever* it is that is first given to the mind. The concept of nature beyond or behind possible experience is for our cognition a boundary notion only.

It does not follow from this, however, that neither Kant's ethics nor aesthetics offer a positive solution to the problem of representation of that which is beyond concepts of the understanding. In this paper I argue that the 'supersensible' ('das Übersinnliche'), as Kant also calls it, has ontological significance in both. In his ethics it is more than a mere postulate for practical reasoning, and in his aesthetics more than a mere formal analogy between symbolic empirical object and rational idea.[2] To that end I begin with a brief sketch of Kant's views on the positive sense in which we cognize the world as actors in it, and then re-examine aspects of both Kant's first *Critique* account of representation of the absolute in ideas of reason and his third *Critique* supplement to that in terms of aesthetic ideas. Finally I examine the way in which his account of symbolic representation constitutes a positive answer to the question of how to represent the supersensible to sense.

The Moral Absolute

Kant's moral theory is an objectivist account of a universe of agents and their action that itself represents an aspect of human experience beyond the limits of our cognition of nature as described in the first *Critique*. There, Kant limits the domain of what *is* the case to the realm marked out by the laws of human understanding —

laws that determine a priori and so without exception what *can possibly be the case* in physical nature. This leaves, Kant famously says, an 'empty space' to be determined by a theory of pure practical reason about what *ought to be the case*.[3] The boundaries of the newly cleared space are determined by concepts of practical, rather than theoretical reason, and the argument of the second *Critique* populates this space with the objects constituted by precepts of the pure will — practical laws governing the choices of a free will. Because they are not dependent on the forms of sensible intuition (space and time), the moral agents and actions that inhabit the realm of practical reason are not physical objects. But they are real nonetheless; indeed Kant refers to them as 'Erkenntnisse' (cognitions), a term that he typically uses to refer to objects of possible experience as determined by the categories and concepts of the understanding:

> [...] da es in allen Vorschriften der reinen praktischen Vernunft nur um die Willensbestimmung, nicht um die Naturbedingungen (des praktischen Vermögens) der Ausführung seiner Absicht zu thun ist, die praktischen Begriffe *a priori* in Beziehung auf das oberste Princip der Freiheit sogleich Erkenntnisse werden und nicht auf Anschauungen warten dürfen, um Bedeutung zu bekommen, und zwar aus diesem merkwürdigen Grunde, weil sie die Wirklichkeit dessen, worauf sie sich beziehen, (die Willensgesinnung) selbst hervorbringen, welches gar nicht die Sache theoretischer Begriffe ist.[4]

> [Since in all precepts of the pure practical reason it is only a question of the determination of the will and not of the natural conditions (of practical ability) for achieving its purpose, it thereby happens that the practical concepts *a priori* in relation to the supreme principle of freedom *immediately become cognitions, not needing to wait upon intuitions* in order to acquire a meaning. This occurs for the noteworthy reason that they themselves produce the reality of that to which they refer (the intention of the will) — an achievement which is in no way the business of theoretical concepts.][5]

For Kant, our cognition of the *physical* world is never direct in this sense of producing the object of which it is aware. Cognition of nature always requires (spatio-temporal) intuitions which are spontaneously mediated by the understanding's ordering principles a priori. Thus in the passage just quoted, Kant says that our experience of physical objects, including ourselves, depends on what are 'nur Gedankenformen' ('only forms of thought').[6] His point here is not that physical objects are therefore less real than the objects of our moral judgments. After all, our experience of ourselves as acting subjects, i.e., as *freely choosing agents* among other free agents is also determined by conditions a priori. But the conditions of practical reasoning, which Kant calls 'elementary practical concepts which determine the free faculty of choice' ('die Bestimmung einer freien Willkür'),[7] differ from the categories of the understanding insofar as they are immediately known to us by the very fact that we *consciously* legislate them for ourselves. Actions we perform based on a concept of what we want and how we ought to go about getting it require that we consciously follow a rule that we find within our own capacity to reason. So long as we choose to dwell within it by being morally reflective, the moral aspect of the universe is, so to speak, open to our gaze.[8]

For Kant, the fact that our experience of the world of nature around us is always limited, i.e., determined by the means we have for representing it to ourselves, entails that we cannot have knowledge of the way things are in themselves, or absolutely. But unlike many of his contemporaries and younger cohort, Kant appears not to be particularly bothered by this fact. This is explained largely by the complementary view that our capacity for moral judgment makes possible a priori an entirely different sort of knowledge. Although the actions we choose occur *in* space and time, they are not entirely *of* space and time, because they are initiated by our own capacity for practical reasoning. As moral agents under the moral law we are free beings and initiators of causal chains in the physical world. The products of our freedom, i.e. of our rational self-legislation, are of our own intentional making, and as such we are aware of them as they are in themselves: as of *our own creation*. No wonder then, that Kant finds 'the moral law within' sublimely awesome: no sceptical argument can touch it. This *is* metaphysical knowledge of our own reason in action: to the degree that I will an action freely in accordance with the moral law 'in me', I have to that degree acted absolutely, creating an absolutely new act-object in the moral universe. The creator knows her own creation directly.

It is well known that Kant purchased this unconditional knowledge of the moral absolute by mortgaging our direct access to *any other aspect* of the absolute. Yet at the end of the second *Critique* he includes the starry heavens above alongside the moral law within as the twin pinnacles of human experience. Our *natural* human longing and striving for this other absolute, the absolute of human nature, is something that Kant recognizes and pays tribute to over and over again in the Critical philosophy. Yet scholars have mostly failed to appreciate that Kant's theory of the cognitive partitioning of human experience opened up the possibility of *a kind of cognition* of the absolute in nature *outside* as well as within the subject. It is in his theory of aesthetic reflection that the possibility of a certain intuitive access to nature in the object via nature in the subject is explored and incorporated into the critical system. For Kant, the moral law comes to immediate awareness through a kind of inner intuition (variously described by him as recognition, reverence, or a feeling of respect for our own moral self-legislation). The story of how and what we come to intuitively grasp about the starry heavens above us is complicated and less developed, but its outlines can be found in his views on the nature of symbolic aesthetic representation.

Representing the Absolute

To understand Kant's theory of symbolic representation and its role in our awareness of the 'absolute' in nature, it is necessary to examine briefly the first *Critique* discussion of the notion of the absolute as expressed by transcendental ideas. In Section 2 of the first book of the 'Transcendental Dialectic' ('Von den transscendentalen Ideen') Kant provides an extended discussion of the absolute, and introduces concepts that express it. These concepts he says, are of an 'absolute' in the widest meaning of the term, namely the concept 'von der Notwendigkeit eines Dinges in aller Beziehung (auf alles Mögliche)' [of the necessity of a thing in every relation (to everything possible)].[9] Such concepts refer to the absolute totality of conditions that necessarily stands behind all cognition: 'Sie sind Begriffe der reinen Vernunft; denn sie betrachten alles Erfahrungserkenntniß als bestimmt durch eine absolute Totalität der Bedingungen. Sie sind nicht willkürlich erdichtet, sondern durch die Natur der Vernunft selbst aufgegeben und beziehen sich daher nothwendiger Weise auf den ganzen Verstandesgebrauch' [They are concepts of pure reason because they regard all experiential cognition as determined through an absolute totality of conditions. They are not arbitrarily invented, but are given through the nature of reason itself and relate therefore necessarily to the entire use of the understanding].[10]

In other words, the idea of the absolute is a particular kind of representation, namely an 'Idee' or 'transcendentaler Vernunftbegriff' [transcendental concept of reason] that serves as a guide for acquiring further knowledge of the physical world but does not contribute directly to our cognition of it. For Kant, these concepts are ideas which, originating in the intellect rather than experience, posit as necessary the *absolutely unconditioned* in any series or system in nature.[11] The 'absolute' that they represent is thus inaccessible to human experience, but it is nevertheless of great importance, for Kant claims here that transcendental ideas of the absolute *are capable* of linking our moral ideas of an absolute to the speculative claims of reason: 'Zu geschweigen, daß sie vielleicht von den Naturbegriffen zu den praktischen einen Übergang möglich machen und den moralischen Ideen selbst auf solche Art Haltung und Zusammenhang mit den speculativen Erkenntnissen der Vernunft verschaffen können' [Not to mention that they perhaps make possible a transition from the concepts of nature to practical concepts and in this way can generate support for the moral ideas themselves and connection with the speculative cognitions of reason].[12]

In order to distinguish these transcendental ideas clearly from other kinds of representations, Kant begins this section of the 'Transcendental Dialectic' with an account of what a representation in general is, laying out the various species, from the most simple and immediate consciousness of something (perception of self or other things) to the transcendental ideas, which are complexes of purely rational concepts originating in the mind a priori:[13] *Representation* (*Vorstellung*), he tells us, is a completely generic term for any product of mental activity:

> Die Gattung ist *Vorstellung* überhaupt (*repraesentatio*). Unter ihr steht die Vorstellung mit Bewusstsein (*perceptio*). Eine *Perception*, die sich lediglich auf das Subject als die Modification seines Zustandes bezieht, ist *Empfindung* (*sensatio*), eine objective Perception ist *Erkenntniß* (*cognitio*). Diese ist entweder *Anschauung* oder *Begriff* (*intuitus vel conceptus*). Jene bezieht sich unmittelbar auf den Gegenstand und ist einzeln, dieser mittelbar, vermittelst eines Merkmals, was mehreren Dingen gemein sein kann. Der Begriff ist entweder ein *empirischer* oder *reiner Begriff*, und der reine Begriff, so fern er lediglich im Verstande seinen Ursprung hat (nicht im reinen Bilde der Sinnlichkeit), heißt *Notio*. Ein Begriff aus Notionen, der die Möglichkeit der Erfahrung übersteigt, ist die *Idee* oder der *Vernunftbegriff*.[14]

> [The genus is *representation* in general (*repraesentatio*). Under it stands the representation with consciousness (*perceptio*). A *perception* that refers to the subject as a modification of its state is a *sensation* (*sensatio*); an objective perception

is a *cognition* (*cognitio*). The latter is either an *intuition* or a *concept* (*intuitus vel conceptus*). The former is immediately related to the object and is singular; the latter is mediate, by means of a mark, which can be common to several things. A concept is either an *empirical* or a *pure concept*, and the pure concept, insofar as it has its origin solely in the understanding (not in a pure image of sensibility), is called *notio*. A concept made up of notions, which goes beyond the possibility of experience, is an *idea* or concept of reason.][15]

This 'Stufenleiter' (stepwise ordering) of various species and subspecies of representation is introduced in order to emphasize that Kant's technical use of the term 'idea' designates a highly complex species of representation used to refer to metaphysical absolutes like God, human freedom, and eternity, that is, ideas that involve 'die absolute Totalität der Synthesis auf der Seite der Bedingungen (es sei der Inhärenz oder der Dependenz oder der Concurrenz)' [the absolute totality of synthesis of conditions (be it of inherence, dependence, or concurrence)],[16] which is to say that these ideas represent *in thought* but not in intuition, the absolute or *an sich* versions of what we can know only in a conditioned way via intuition and concepts. Spatio-temporal representations of substances, causes and causal interactions are 'demonstrable' (*demonstrabel*) in Kant's terms because they can be exhibited (ostended) in space and time.[17] Their purely rational counterparts are 'notions' that stand at the heart of both speculative and practical metaphysics.[18]

The account of representation Kant sets out in the *Stufenleiter* passage of the first *Critique* is both assumed and enlarged in the third *Critique*, where rational ideas play a crucial role in his overall theory of aesthetic reflection and creativity. Indeed they are mentioned in the very first section of the 'Critique of Aesthetic Judgment', where he introduces another kind of representation, an *aesthetic* representation, as the basis of judgments of beauty (taste). An *aesthetic representation* is one that occurs, Kant says, when *any* representation, including even a purely rational idea, awakens in the subject a feeling of pleasure or displeasure 'wodurch gar nichts im Objecte bezeichnet wird, sondern in der das Subject, wie es durch die Vorstellung afficirt wird, sich selbst fühlt' [by means of which nothing at all in the object is designated, but in which the subject feels itself as it is affected by the representation]: 'wenn die gegebenen Vorstellungen gar rational wären, würden aber in einem Urtheile lediglich auf das Subject (sein Gefühl) bezogen, so sind sie sofern jederzeit ästhetisch' [Even if the given representations were rational, if they were related in a judgment solely to the subject (its feeling), then they are to that extent always aesthetic].[19] Kant thus extends his notion of a subjective representation, or sensation, to include a sensory intuition of one's own inner state of feeling, (i.e., pleasure or displeasure) aroused by reflecting upon a given representation. The representation of the feeling of being affected by another representation, *even a rational concept*, is an *aesthetic* representation.

He further divides aesthetic representations into those that represent the feeling of immediate stimulus/response pleasures, and pleasures produced by the satisfaction of a desire for an object (either a conditional or unconditional good). They are then contrasted with a third kind of aesthetic representation, namely that of the pleasure we take in the beautiful. The representation of beauty is of a pleasure taken in the representation of an object in nature apart from mere sense gratification or any personal or moral interests.[20] All three are aesthetic because they involve the immediately experienced, self-conscious sensory awareness of a pleasure (or pain), but clearly representations of beauty cannot be the mere sensations which Kant, in the 'Stufenleiter' passage, categorizes as subjective perceptions by contrast with objective perceptions or 'cognitions'. To be sure, here in the third *Critique* he reiterates the view that they are about feelings, and that aesthetic representations contribute nothing to cognition:

> Ein regelmäßiges, zweckmäßiges Gebäude mit seinem Erkenntnißvermögen [...] zu befassen, ist ganz etwas anders, als sich dieser Vorstellung mit der Empfindung des Wohlgefallens bewußt zu sein.[21]

> [To grasp a regular, purposive structure with one's faculty of cognition [...] is something entirely different from being conscious of this representation with the sensation of satisfaction.]

However, the three kinds of aesthetic representations he introduces 'fail to cognitively grasp' in importantly different ways. In the case of judgments about mere gratification states, the pleasure represented is immediate, but also fleeting and private: it is merely about one individual's state at one time, and it can make no claims to the agreement of others or even of the individual herself at a different time. Representations of the good refer us to pleasure taken in obtaining a desired object and so are in this sense 'objective' even though they involve precepts of reason that do not directly involve the understanding. Representations used in judgments about the beautiful are not objective in this way, but neither are they *merely fleeting*, subjective representations. In judgments of the beautiful,

> [...] wird die Vorstellung gänzlich auf das Subject und zwar auf das Lebensgefühl desselben unter dem Namen des Gefühls der Lust oder Unlust bezogen: welches ein ganz besonderes Unterscheidungs- und Beurtheilungsvermögen gründet, das zum Erkenntniß nichts beträgt, sondern nur die gegebene Vorstellung im Subjecte gegen das ganze Vermögen der Vorstellungen hält, dessen sich das Gemüth im Gefühl seines Zustandes bewußt wird.[22]

> [the representation is related entirely to the subject, indeed to its feeling of life, under the name of the feeling of pleasure or displeasure, which grounds an entirely special faculty for discriminating and judging that contributes nothing to cognition but only holds the given representation in the subject up to the entire faculty of representation, of which the mind becomes conscious in the feeling of its state.]

In other words, we call something beautiful when its sensory representation is 'held up to the entire faculty of representation' with no purpose except to play with it in imagination. 'Beauty' refers both to our pleasure in reflection and also to the sensory form of the object whose representation in us is well suited for this reflective free play that gives rise to a pleasurable 'Lebensgefühl' and makes us conscious of the lively power of our minds in general.

Far from being a merely subjective sensation, 'beauty' is an extremely complex representation of nature both within the subject and outside it. To call an object beautiful is to represent it as something outside us whose representational form within us arouses and sustains the free play of our imagination and understanding, exhilarates us and makes us pleasurably aware of our cognitive faculties and the world outside us in an entirely new way.

Aesthetic Ideas

> Man kann überhaupt Schönheit (sie mag Natur- oder Kunstschönheit sein) den Ausdruck ästhetischer Ideen nennen [...].[23]

Beauty in nature and in art, Kant says, is the expression of *aesthetic ideas*, and aesthetic ideas, he says, are the 'Stoff' [material] of aesthetic reflection. Aesthetic ideas appear for the first time in the third *Critique* as yet another kind of representation, specifically an *Idee* in the technical sense introduced in the *Stufenleiter* passage. Yet, as we saw, the idea of reason or transcendental idea introduced there is a complex of pure rational concepts that refer to a completed set of conditions and therefore to a whole that is in itself unconditioned. Concepts like the soul, the whole of the universe, and God are examples of such concepts that originate only in the understanding, not in experience. They are not 'demonstrable' — they could never be exhibited in intuition.[24] Aesthetic ideas are also complexes of representations, but by contrast with rational ideas they are not combinations of pure concepts. Rather, they are representations that introduce to the mind a cornucopia of intuitive content gleaned from cognition (objective experience). Precisely because they are made up of intuitive representations that do not originate solely in the understanding, they are capable of demonstration in experience. They are not, on the other hand, capable of being adequately conceptualized, i.e., unified under a single concept.

> [...] unter eine *ästhetischen Idee* aber verstehe ich diejenige Vorstellung der Einbildungskraft, die viel zu denken veranlaßt, ohne daß ihr doch irgend ein bestimmter Gedanke, d.i. Begriff, adäquat sein kann, die folglich keine Sprache völlig erreicht und verständlich machen kann. — Man sieht leicht, daß sie das Gegenstück (Pendant) von einer *Vernunftidee* sei, welche umgekehrt ein Begriff ist, dem keine *Anschauung* (Vorstellung der Einbildungskraft) adäquat sein kann.[25]

> [by an *aesthetic idea* I understand that representation of the imagination that occasions much to think about without any determinate thought, that is, concept, being adequate to it, so that as a consequence no language can fully capture it or make it fully comprehensible. One easily sees that it is the counterpart to an *idea of reason*, which conversely, is a concept to which no *intuition* (representation of the imagination) can be adequate.]

In other words, rational ideas are representations in which we *think* something that is beyond our capacity to sense or feel. Aesthetic ideas are representations in which we sense and feel something that is beyond our capacity to articulate.

It seems somewhat odd to say that these two kinds of ideas are complementary, since aesthetic ideas do not appear to be ideas at all. Elsewhere Kant says that aesthetic concepts are merely representations without a concept,[26] and several passages in the third *Critique* also emphasize that the aesthetic idea is not a unified single representation, but is rather a collection or play of intuited representations that can be reflectively attached to another concept in order to allow us to explore new ways to make sense of it.[27] Yet these complex collections of aesthetic representational content are still *ideas*, because, like rational ideas, they 'at least strive for something that lies beyond the bounds of experience, and hence try to approach an exhibition of rational concepts (intellectual ideas), and thus these concepts are given a semblance of objective reality.'[28]

Even more important, Kant says that aesthetic ideas are *ideas* because, like their rational counterparts, their content exceeds the capacities of cognition. Rational ideas are intellectual representations that strain to reach cognition of an absolute, unconditioned reality solely through the intellect. They can only strive but never attain it since human cognition is always sensibly intuited. On the other hand, aesthetic ideas are empirical, intuitive representations that aim for cognition of the absolute solely by arousing inner intuitions so diverse and far-ranging that they exceed the capacity of the understanding to expound them. Both are *ideas* because they strive, each from its own side of cognition, to represent that which is unrepresentable for finite beings whose intellects are discursive (concept driven) and whose form of intuition is sensible.[29]

Kant then suggests that when brought together, aesthetic and rational ideas might yield something that pushes back the limitations of both, making the rational idea something we can feel, on the one hand and lending rational structure and purpose to a mere free play of imaginings on the other. Because an aesthetic idea 'occasions so much thinking that it can never be comprehended in a determinate concept' it actually enlarges it:

> [...] mithin den Begriff selbst auf unbegränzte Art ästhetisch erweitert: so ist die Einbildungskraft hiebei schöpferisch und bringt das Vermögen intellectueller Ideen (die Vernunft) in Bewegung.[30]

> [thereby the presentation aesthetically expands the concept itself in an unlimited way, and the imagination is creative hereby and sets the faculty of intellectual ideas (i.e., reason) into motion.]

Although neither rational nor aesthetic ideas alone refer to objective features of the natural world, contemplating these features via aesthetic ideas allows us to imagine new intuitive content for otherwise uncognizable concepts of reason.

Since aesthetic attributes 'geben eine ästhetische Idee, die jener Vernunftidee statt logischer Darstellung dient' [yield an aesthetic idea, that serves that idea of reason in place of logical presentation], Kant claims that aesthetic ideas can serve as *exhibitions* of a rational idea.[31] For example: our rational idea of the *summum bonum* or highest good is conceptually no more than the rational idea of a completely well-ordered social system in which every individual's moral virtue is apportioned with happiness in the same degree.[32] The idea itself is purely formal and tells us nothing about how exactly such a society would look, how it would be instituted, or what it would be like to live in it. A strong imagination however, might form an aesthetic idea to portray this rational idea by reflecting upon an empirical representation that is structurally similar to the idea in some way, and that at the same time gives rise to any number of other associated ideas, concepts, and images. Freely reflecting upon these other relations and affinities expands our thinking about the idea of a perfectly well-ordered state lending life and meaning to the bloodless original idea. The same may hold for all rational ideas, including the central Enlightenment and Kantian triumvirate of freedom, God and immortality. Kant's own example is a poem by Frederick the Great, in which the enlightened Prussian monarch uses the aesthetic idea of a serene sunset to enliven the rational idea of cosmopolitanism. The aesthetic idea at work here is used as what Kant calls an *aesthetic attribute*, i.e., it is a sensory representation attributed *symbolically* to the rational idea of the cosmopolitan attitude toward life for the purpose of evoking and transferring feelings aroused by a serene sunset to the reader's imagined end-of-life experience.

Kant's theory of aesthetic ideas holds out the hope that artistry can bring the moral absolute (which, as we saw, is the only absolute of which we are directly aware in inner intuition) into imaginative connection with the apparently amoral world of nature that we inhabit. He suggests that the activity of imagining a moral world fully embodied in nature is theoretically possible for any human being, given time and leisure to do so. How successfully this is done is another matter, however, hinging on the degree of the individual's power of imagination. The artist, as an individual gifted with a powerful capacity to imagine aesthetic ideas and also a talent for expressing them,[33] is thus uniquely situated to turn these ideas into objects of art that can in turn inspire others to envision them, believe in their possibility, and work for their actualization.[34]

Of course, Kant does not think for a moment that artistic genius is more likely than ordinary cognition to care about rational *moral* concepts, or even rational concepts at all in choosing its reflective materials. Indeed, he is inclined to think of artistic virtuosi as typically more self-promoting than most people, and hence less likely to care about moral issues in their art.[35] Whatever the merits of his views on artistic temperament, though, the point holds that for Kant, *if* so motivated, artistic genius can portray virtue and other rational ideas in an aesthetic form that serves to enliven and hence expand our conception of morality. The entire process depends on contingencies: a naturally creative imagination and the conditions under which to exercise it. However, Kant is quite committed to the view that when those conditions obtain, imagination can indeed be a powerful and transformative force in human experience.[36] All human beings have the capacities requisite for 'taste', i.e., imaginative creative reflection, and Kant believes that under circumstances that afford some leisure time, human beings have a natural inclination to exercise it, as the phenomenon of daydreaming proves.[37] Given that on his theory all human beings have the ability to imaginatively restructure nature as it is given to us into something surpassing nature, while some human beings are capable, in addition, of actualizing these imaginative restructurings as art objects *within* nature, then Kant's aesthetics at least approaches a theory of aesthetic representation of the absolute.

Symbolic Representation

'Die Realität unserer Begriffe darzuthun, werden immer Anschauungen erfordert.'[39]

[To establish the reality of our concepts, intuitions are always required.]

In the penultimate section of the 'Critique of Aesthetic Judgment' Kant emphasizes once again that all cognition, be it empirical or pure a priori, *requires* intuition. Thus, he reminds us, rational ideas derived from pure concepts a priori can never by themselves be demonstrated to be objectively real. The objective reality of empirical concepts is demonstrated empirically, by pointing to examples, whereas pure concepts can be demonstrated only by the existence of spatio-temporal schemata that are formally homogeneous with pure concepts and hence make possible their application to experience. No such schemata are available for rational ideas, since by their very definition they refer to that which exceeds the boundaries of space and time. And yet the point of § 59, 'Von der Schönheit als Symbol der Sittlichkeit' [On Beauty as the Symbol of Morality] is that rational ideas *can* be made intuitive through a process he calls symbolic hypotyposis. 'Hypotyposis', Kant says, is the 'Vorstellungsart' [type of representation] of exhibiting a purely rational concept in sensibility. Such exhibition, or 'Versinnlichung' may be one of two sorts, depending on the kind of a priori representation to be made sensible: it is either a schematic or a symbolic representation.[39] Schematic representation is the process described in the first *Critique*, wherein the imagination fits pure intuitions a priori to pure concepts of the understanding, and this synthesis a priori establishes the objective reality of these concepts. Symbolic hypotyposis, on the other hand strives to make an idea of reason empirically manifest in sensation.

The rational idea, like the pure concept of understanding, is an a priori function of the human mind. But since the rational idea by its very nature is '*übersinnlich*' ('supersensible', that is to say, it is about an unconditioned absolute that is beyond any possible spatio-temporal experience), there is no way to schematize it. It does not follow, however, that these ideas cannot in *some* way be linked to intuitions. Bringing intuition to these ideas is accomplished, Kant says, by a process analogous to schematizing concepts for cognition. The key to that process is the use of a symbol, i.e., an aesthetic idea used to represent the content of the rational idea by guiding our contemplation of it. In other words, schematic hypotyposis *determines the objects* of ordinary cognition, and symbolic hypotyposis *contemplates the possibility of objects* of extraordinary cognition.

The process of symbolic representation involves a 'double function'. That is, Kant says, reflective judgment first must find the aesthetic idea (the concept of a sensible object that will serve as the rule or guide for reflection) and second, it must transfer the rule for reflecting upon that manifold sensible intuition to reflection upon the rational idea. The resulting reflection does not of course, determine the rational idea, bringing the object of that idea into existence, but it does represent it in sensibility in a variety of new ways. The better the aesthetic idea, the more possibilities it presents for imagining the rational idea. Kant's own example is not particularly profound, but it illustrates the process: a handmill serves as a useful symbol for our creative (and in this case critical) reflection upon the various kinships it has with a despotic state, e.g., the production of forced and uniform outputs.

Great artistry could find more productive and inspiring symbols, and that is precisely Kant's definition of genius.[40] But Kant does *not* hold that symbolic processes are rare or even particularly difficult. Indeed, precisely because they are so common, he believed they merit far more study than they had thus far received:

> Dies Geschäft ist bis jetzt noch wenig auseinander gesetzt worden, so sehr es auch eine tiefere Untersuchung verdient [...]. Unsere Sprache ist voll von der-gleichen indirecten Darstellungen nach einer Analogie, wodurch der Ausdruck nicht das eigentliche Schema für den Begriff, sondern bloß ein Symbol für die Reflexion enthält.[41]

> [This business has not been worked on much so far, as much as it deserves deeper investigation [...]. Our language is full of such indirect exhibitions according to an analogy, where the expression does not contain the actual schema for the concept but contains merely a symbol for our reflection.]

The examples he gives to illustrate the ubiquity of symbols in everyday language are indeed basic: 'Grund' (ground) for the notion of a support or basis; 'Abhängen' (to depend) for hanging from something else, etc. These terms are used in everyday parlance symbolically, where they are

> symbolische Hypotyposen und Ausdrücke für Begriffe nicht vermittelst eine directen Anschauung, sondern nur nach einer Analogie mit derselben, d.i. der Übertragung der Reflexion über einen Gegenstand der Anschauung auf einen ganz andern Begriff, dem vielleicht nie eine Anschauung direct correspondiren kann.[42]

> [symbolic hypotyposes and expressions for concepts not by means of a direct intuition but only by analogy to one, that is, by a transfer of our reflection on an object of intuition to an entirely different concept, to which perhaps no intuition can ever directly correspond.]

Significantly, Kant states the view that reflective transference through symbols may be considered cognition:

> Wenn man eine bloße Vorstellungsart schon Erkenntniß nennen darf (welches, wenn sie ein Princip nicht der theoretischen Bestimmung des Gegenstandes ist, was er an sich sei, sondern der praktischen, was die Idee von ihm für uns und den zweckmäßigen Gebrauch derselben werden soll, wohl erlaubt ist): so ist alle unsere Erkenntniß von Gott bloß symbolisch [...] .[43]

> [If a mere way of representing something may already be called cognition (which I think is permissible if this cognition is a principle, not for the theoretical determination of what the object is in itself, but for the practical determination of what the idea of the object ought to be for us and the purposive use of it), then all our cognition of God is merely symbolic.]

Kant mentions symbolic cognition of God in order to warn against confusing symbolic hypotyposis, which *is* a form of cognition, with *hypostasis*, which is not. The latter is the fallacy of regarding symbolic representation of a rational idea as schematic, thus anthropomorphizing the idea.[44] He discusses the psychological process of hypostasizing in the 'Ideal of Pure Reason' in the first *Critique*[45] as an invalid move from the claim that nothing can be an object of our sensory experience unless we presuppose the totality of all empirical reality, to the claim that all things in general must be a unified totality. Thence he says we infer that this totality is a *thing*, an *ens realissimum*, and again fallaciously conclude that it must be an intelligence, and personify it. While the whole process amounts to invalid reasoning, it is a pervasive psychological one that is urged upon us by the nature of reason itself. It is not inescapable, however, nor is it altogether noxious. Kant holds that these psychological fictions are part of a gradual progression in human reason that eventually leads to a clearer understanding of the nature of reason itself.[46] On the other hand he also rejects 'deism' as a kind of arid abstractionism that precludes the 'practical cognition' of God for moral purposes.[47] Cognition of the rational idea of God by symbol, however, is considered a valid form of knowledge, because it presents something real in our experience in a way that neither a hypostasized fiction nor an empty abstraction can. Like moral judgment, aesthetic symbolic reflection produces the reality of that to which it refers, but here what is created is the product of imagination in cooperation with reason: a demonstration or exhibition in symbolic intuition of what the idea of the highest reality ought to be for us.[48]

Representing the Absolute in Nature

Kant's mention of God in the discussion of symbolic hypotyposis is intended to illustrate his more general point that aesthetic ideas, when used as symbols, can serve to make rational ideas intuitive for us, and that in such cases symbolic representations may be considered cognitions. Since Kant's view that symbolic representation of rational ideas can be cognitive must also include rational ideas about the absolutely unconditioned in nature, then it appears that there is after all a way in which an intuition of the absolute is possible. Symbolizing a rational idea, like choosing an action, creates an object for us. Instead of bringing an action into being, however, *symbolization creates an end toward which we should strive*. It 'determines what the idea of the object ought to become for us and for our purposive employment of it.' Of course, to symbolically represent moral absolutes still does not amount to representing outer nature as it is in itself intuitive for us. Kant argues that we might use concretely rendered moral ideas (he calls them 'ideals') like perfect moral virtue to intuit our own subjective ends.[49] But how would symbolic representation ever manage to make outer nature *beyond the human*, intuitive for us?

    An answer is suggested by the fact that, from the outset, Kant holds that rational ideas can themselves be material for aesthetic reflection, and by his own examples of artistic symbolism. We saw Kant's account of how symbolic representation works to evoke feelings about the supersensible in his discussion of the poem by Frederick the Great. After describing the king's use of a natural attribute (a sunset) to enliven the rational moral idea of cosmopolitanism, Kant adds that, conversely, a rational idea may be used as an aesthetic attribute to make the supersensible *in nature* intuitive:

> Andererseits kann sogar ein intellectueller Begriff umgekehrt zum Attribut
> einer Vorstellung der Sinne dienen und so *diese letztere durch die Idee des*

> *Übersinnlichen beleben*; aber nur indem das Ästhetische, was dem Bewußtsein des letztern subjectiv anhänglich ist, hiezu gebraucht wird.[50]

> [On the other hand, even an intellectual concept may serve conversely, as an attribute of a presentation of sense and thus *animate that presentation by the idea of the supersensible*; but we may use for this only the aesthetic element that attaches subjectively to our consciousness of the supersensible.]

A rational idea, in other words, can be an aesthetic attribute or symbol of a natural object or event. Reflection upon a rational idea can also arouse in us a vast array of feelings (in the case of virtue of 'sublime and calming feelings, and a boundless outlook toward a joyful future')[51] that may be transferred to the rational idea of the supersensible substrate of *all* nature. Just as nature symbolism might arouse feelings in us that expand our understanding of rational moral concepts like virtue, the rational ideas of morality, directly intuitable by us in feelings of respect, may be used to arouse feelings that help expand our conception of nature. So long as we recognize these as universally valid *feelings* only, thereby avoiding hypostasizing (anthropomorphizing) the nature in question, we have before us a new understanding of nature.

Herein lies the key to a Kantian account of the representation of the absolute nature beyond human reason that is the complement to the expansion of our conception of the moral law within through symbolic representations. Kant's theory allows that non-anthropomorphized but symbolic reflections may expand our cognition of the starry heavens above by enlivening our conception of them in ways that merely formal intellectual ideas of unconditioned absolutes alone could never do.

For Kant, this enlivening is more than mere aestheticizing or toying with the idea of the supersensible. In the experience of beauty he says, judgment is self-legislating: 'die Urteilskraft/ giebt in Ansehung der Gegenstände eines so reinen Wohlgefallens ihr selbst das Gesetz, so wie die Vernunft es in Ansehung des Begehrungsver-mögens thut [...]' [concerning objects of such pure liking the power of judgment legislates to itself, just as reason does regarding the power of desire]:

> [...] und sieht sich sowohl wegen dieser innern Möglichkeit im Subjecte, als wegen der äußern Möglichkeit einer damit übereinstimmenden Natur auf etwas im Subjecte selbst und außer ihm, was nicht Natur, auch nicht Freiheit, doch aber mit dem Grunde der letzteren, nämlich dem Übersinnlichen, verknüpft ist, bezogen, in welchem das theoretische Vermögen mit dem praktischen auf gemeinschaftliche und unbekannte Art zur Einheit verbunden wird.[52]

> [and because the subject has this possibility [for aesthetic self-legislation] within it, while outside it there is also the possibility that nature will harmonize with this possibility, judgment finds itself referred to something that is *both in the subject itself and outside it, something that is neither nature nor freedom and yet is linked with the basis of freedom, the supersensible*, in which the theoretical and the practical power are in an unknown manner combined and joined into a unity.]

Precisely because his theory of ordinary cognition requires that we cannot know what nature is in itself, Kant's theory of the symbol opens the possibility that what we *can* immediately know *an sich*, namely our moral self-determination, is identified with, or at least a part of, the supersensible substrate of nature *outside us*. No wonder, then, that it is that which is mere nature in us, the supersubstrate of all the powers of genius and subjectivity in general, that unlocks the door to that which lies at the heart of nature outside us.[53]

Conclusion

Two comments can be made by way of assessing Kant's theory of the symbol discussed here. First, it is, after all, not 'apophatic' nor simply 'a substitute for cognition, an accommodation in the face of the limits of the faculty of understanding'.[54] His theory of the symbol was indeed placed within the framework of his overall Critical theory, so that what he allows to be cognition in the third *Critique* strains against the narrower definitions of the first. But this extension of the notion of the cognitive already occurs, as discussed at the beginning of this essay, with his elaboration of the details of practical reasoning. Moral judgments are objective, and as I hope to have shown, in a different way, at the end of the 'Critique of Aesthetic Judgment' Kant has argued that reflective judgment too can expand our cognition of ourselves and nature.

This is not to say that Kant's theory was a *romantic* theory of the symbol, but simply that it is not so utterly removed from the romantic identification of the sensible and supersensible. This identification can be found in Kant's theory, but only as a 'perhaps'. It is there in Kant's conception of 'what may be considered the supersensible substrate of humanity'. The point can be made again by reference to Halmi's analysis: 'Under the dualistic premises [...] of Kantian aesthetics, the aesthetic idea or symbol had no objective reality, but only the subjective appearance of objective reality [... it] could not be "natural".'[55] Yet what Kant's complicated account of representation in general leads him to suggest is that an idea of reason creatively represented by an aesthetic symbol can serve to expand and enlarge cognition. It does so by making intuitive the underlying nature of both our own subjectivity and the world outside us. The source of this creativity is subjective, but it is *nature in the subject* — neither practical nor theoretical reason — but rather the underlying, supersensible nature that grounds both.

Notes to Chapter 2

1. *Kritik der reinen Vernunft*, A 254/B 310–A 256/B 312. All references to the first *Critique* are to the pagination of the first and second editions as provided in *Kants gesammelte Schriften*, herausgegeben von der Königlich Preußischen Akademie der Wissenschaften (Berlin: Walter de Gruyter & Co., 1900–), III. All references to Kant's other works are also to the 'Akademie Ausgabe', indicated by volume number and page.
2. This is a view widely shared by scholars and best developed recently by Nicholas Halmi in *The Genealogy of the Romantic Symbol* (Oxford: Oxford University Press, 2007), pp. 63 ff.
3. *Kritik der reinen Vernunft*, B xxi.
4. *Kritik der praktischen Vernunft*, V: 65–66.
5. Emphases added.
6. Ibid., V: 65.
7. Ibid., V: 65.
8. By contrast, the world of physical nature is known to us only indirectly. The principal functions

that shape it are always unselfconsciously involved in our uptake of what is given in intuition, and these a priori functions become clear to us only by a philosophical inquiry into what conditions are necessary and jointly sufficient for any human experience whatsoever. This is not to say that we are never aware of the process of cognition. Kant's view is that the most fundamental of all principles of understanding, the synthetic unity of apperception expressed in the proposition 'I think' must be *capable* of accompanying all my representations (*Kritik der reinen Vernunft*, B 131, § 16). That is, self-consciousness must always be possible for me. But it is by no means necessary that I am always aware of my own cognitive processes.

9. *Kritik der reinen Vernunft*, A 325/ B 382.
10. *Kritik der reinen Vernunft*, A 327/ B 384.
11. *Kritik der reinen Vernunft*, A 326/ B 382–83.
12. *Kritik der reinen Vernunft*, A 329/ B 386.
13. I will use the English 'representation' in Kant's generic sense to translate his use of the term 'Vorstellung'. In some instances there are legitimate reasons for using the English 'presentation' instead, but most translations of Kant's works use 'representation' and reserve 'presentation' for Kant's use of the term 'Darstellung'. In any event, since in the third *Critique* Kant himself refers to the symbol as a kind of 'Vorstellung' and refers to a symbolic 'Vorstellungsart' (type of representation), I follow Kant in adhering to the language of 'Vorstellung'.
14. *Kritik der reinen Vernunft*, A 320/ B 376–77.
15. Translation from *Critique of Pure Reason*, trans. and ed. by Paul Guyer and Allen W. Wood (Cambridge: Cambridge University Press, 1998), pp. 398–99, with words in bold type replaced by italics.
16. *Kritik der reinen Vernunft*, A 336/ B 393.
17. *Kritik der Urteilskraft*, V: 343, and also *Logik*: IX: 71, 110.
18. *Kritik der reinen Vernunft*, B 395n.
19. *Kritik der Urteilskraft*, V: 204.
20. See ibid., V: 205–09, §§ 3–4: aesthetic representations that refer to the subject's immediate pleasure when a bodily desire is gratified, and those that refer to pleasure in obtaining a desired good both involve an interest in obtaining the object. Although the former is merely subjective and the latter makes reference to the concept of a definite object or action, both types of representation are about a pleasure that the subject takes in the *existence* of something.
21. Ibid., V: 204.
22. Ibid., V: 204.
23. Ibid., V: 320, § 51.
24. Ibid., V: 343. Kant's example of intuitive demonstration here is of an anatomist who explains the concept of the eye discursively, but then 'demonstrates' or exhibits it by proceeding to dissect one, to literally show what he means.
25. Ibid., V: 314.
26. See the Dohna-Wundlacken Logic lecture transcript: XXIV: 753; trans. by Michael Young (Cambridge: Cambridge University Press, 1992), p. 486.
27. See for instance *Kritik der Urteilskraft*: V: 314–15.
28. At ibid., V: 315, Kant says that aesthetic attributes yield aesthetic ideas: the process, Kant elaborates, works when imaginative 'Nebenvorstellungen' ('supplementary representations', or 'aesthetic attributes') allow us to see by analogy certain 'implications of the concept, and its affinity with others.' These *aesthetic attributes* 'stellen [...] etwas anderes vor, was der Einbildungskraft Anlaß giebt, sich über eine Menge von verwandten Vorstellungen zu verbreiten, die mehr denken lassen, als man in einem durch Worte bestimmten Begriff ausdrücken kann; und geben eine ästhetische Idee [...]' [represent something different, something that prompts the imagination to spread over a multitude of kindred presentations that arouse more thought than can be expressed in a concept determined by words. These attributes yield an aesthetic idea].
29. See Kant's 'Comment I' at the end of § 57 on the two kinds of ideas, rational and aesthetic: ibid., V: 342.
30. Ibid., V: 314–15, § 49.
31. Ibid., V: 315.
32. See the *Critique of Practical Reason* (V: 106–19; 123–32) for Kant's definition of the idea, his

incorporation of it into the categorical imperative, and his argument that the postulation of God is required by it.

33. *Kritik der Urteilskraft*, V: 344.

34. If genius is disposed to put its talent to use in the service of expressing aesthetic ideas for a moral idea, it can, for instance, embody what Kant calls the aesthetic ideal of beauty: the visual expression of moral ideas. He speaks of this in detail in section 17 of 'Critique of Aesthetic Judgment' (ibid., V: 231–36), but also clearly has this in mind when discussing the nature of poetic genius of all sorts.

35. Ibid., V: 298–99, § 48.

36. See ibid., V: 314: 'Die Einbildungskraft (als productives Erkenntnißvermögen) ist nämlich sehr mächtig in Schaffung gleichsam einer andern Natur aus dem Stoffe, den ihr die wirkliche giebt' [The imagination (as a productive faculty of cognition) is very mighty when it creates, as it were, another nature out of the material that actual nature provides].

37. 'Wir unterhalten uns mit ihr, wo uns die Erfahrung zu alltäglich vorkommt; bilden diese auch wohl um: zwar noch immer nach analogischen Gesetzen, aber doch auch nach Principien, die höher hinauf in der Vernunft liegen (und die uns eben sowohl natürlich sind als die, nach welchen der Verstand die empirische Natur auffaßt); [...] nach welchem [dem Gesetze der Association] uns von der Natur zwar Stoff geliehen, dieser aber von uns zu etwas ganz anderem, nämlich dem, was die Natur übertrifft, verarbeitet werden kann' [We use imagination to entertain ourselves when experience strikes us as overly routine. We may even restructure experience; and though in doing so we continue to follow analogical laws, we also follow principles which reside higher up, namely in reason (and which are just as natural to us as those which the understanding follows in apprehending empirical nature) [...] for although it is under [the law of association] that nature lends us material, yet we can process that material into something quite different, namely, into something that surpasses nature. Such representations of the imagination we may call ideas] (V: 314).

38. Ibid., V: 351, § 59.

39. Ibid., V: 351–52.

40. Ibid., V: 344.

41. Ibid., V: 352.

42. Ibid., V: 352–53.

43. Ibid., V: 353.

44. Ibid., V: 353.

45. *Kritik der reinen Vernunft*, A 580/ B 608 ff.

46. See, e.g., the discussion at *Kritik der reinen Vernunft*, A 589/B 617–A 590/B 618.

47. See also *Kritik der reinen Vernunft*, V: A 631/B 659–A 634/B 662.

48. See 'Critique of Aesthetic Judgment': *Kritik der Urteilskraft*, V: 353: 'die Urteilskraft/ giebt in Ansehung der Gegenstände eines so reinen Wohlgefallens ihr selbst das Gesetz, so wie die Vernunft es in Ansehung des Begehrungsvermögens thut [...]' [concerning objects of such a pure liking judgment legislates to itself, just as reason does regarding the power of desire].

49. Kant is quite explicit about this in § 17 of the 'Critique of Aesthetic Judgment' when he discusses artistic renderings of the human form as the ideal of beauty. Moreover, there is clearly an important role for the natural absolute in Kant's value theory. Reason naturally takes an interest, he says, whenever nature shows any sign of being compatible with our moral purposes and for this reason we have a moral intellectual interest in the beautiful forms that appear as if designed for the free play of our cognitive faculties. We care about this because any sign at all is enough to give us hope and prevent reason giving up dutiful action in the face of apparently insurmountable odds. See § 42: V: 300. I discuss this issue at length in *Kant and the Power of Imagination* (Cambridge: Cambridge University Press, 2007); see especially chapters 2 and 3.

50. V: 316, emphasis added.

51. V: 316.

52. V: 353, emphasis added.

53. V: 344.

54. Halmi, pp. 63–64. See also pp. 61–63.

55. Halmi, p. 63.

CHAPTER 3

'Neither mere allegories nor mere history': Multi-layered Symbolism in Moritz's *Andreas Hartknopf*

for Manfred Engel

Jutta Heinz

Scholarship on the development of Classical and Romantic concepts of imagery has long since recognized Karl Philipp Moritz as playing a key role.[1] Above all, there has been a focus on his reliance on allegory (in contrast to Winckelmann)[2] and his concept of beauty in art as an autonomous purpose in itself.[3] Time and time again, however, the use of imagery in his (few) literary texts has evoked controversy — above all in the twin but by no means identical novels *Anton Reiser* and *Andreas Hartknopf*. According to the subtitles, one is a 'psychological novel', the other an 'allegory'. But apparently neither is an autonomous work of art that would match the theory: rather, one is the progeny of Moritz's 'Erfahrungsseelenlehre' [doctrine of experiential psychology], and the other is — what, actually? A self-contradiction?[4] A negative example, i.e., of precisely that which you should not do? A relapse into aesthetic heteronomy? Or have we simply not yet found the right 'Gesichtspunkt' [viewpoint] for reading it? As Moritz never tired of emphasizing, finding the correct viewpoint is a hermeneutically irrecoverable act itself — as in *Bestimmung des Zwecks einer Theorie der schönen Kunst*, for example:

> [J]edes schöne Kunstwerk, als ein für sich bestehendes Ganze zu betrachten, ist es nöthig, in dem Werke selbst den *Gesichtspunkt* aufzufinden, wodurch alles Einzelne sich erst in seiner nothwendigen Beziehung auf das Ganze darstellt, und wodurch es uns erst einleuchtet, daß in dem Werke weder etwas überflüßig sey, noch etwas mangle.[5]

> [For every beautiful work of art, to be seen as a whole that exists for itself, it is necessary to locate a *viewpoint* through which all individual elements are represented in their necessary relationship to the whole; and through which it becomes evident to us that there is neither anything superfluous, nor anything missing.]

In the following analysis of *Andreas Hartknopf*, I would like to sketch a 'viewpoint' for Moritz's use of symbolism that will also shed new light on his novel. In order to do so, it is necessary above all to take the 'entire' Moritz into account, always to consider him even in the context of purely aesthetic questions as the teacher of experiential psychology and self-observer; as linguist and grammarian; and finally, in his (still much less examined) role as a pedagogue.[6] What should not be forgotten, however well justified the rejection of purely biographical accounts may be, is the intermittently severe depression (or melancholia, to use the language of his time), which was so central to Moritz's person, and the resulting existential threat to his identity. This life-defining problem directly stimulated the personal questions underlying Moritz's work: how is something like a constant, personal identity, both self-consistent and unreliant on mood or situation, possible?[7] How do I master my melancholy moods and their life-threatening consequences? How can I regain vital activity after the depressive depths of apathy? It is possible to reformulate these questions in semiotic terms: how can I shape my relationship to my environment so as to achieve the closest possible connection between the internal and the external, my self and my world? How can I surround myself with as many significant signs and meanings as possible so that they keep the ever-threatening loss of self and meaning in check? How can I achieve congruency between my 'Geist' [spirit] as my internal sense of experience, and the 'Buchstabe' [letter] as my external appearance and agency, in my life and person?

In this respect, Moritz in his analytical as well as his literary writings is always concerned with self-therapy, too. As an introspective observer of his own self, he felt and recognized his own pathological symptoms, and as an experiential psychologist, he struggled for a psychological explanation. As a pedagogue, he proposed prophylactic educational precepts that were to quell depression from the very beginning, at the very core of personality. Throughout the course of his life, he searched for a positive counterbalance to emptiness and abstraction in mystical or aesthetic experiences;[8] 'aesthetic' in the sense of art as a model for an entirely self-contained form of existence that is in tune with the universe and nature, purposed as art for its own sake, and immortal — indestructible by time or death. In all of his writings, Moritz attempts to achieve for himself in the work of art a relatively stable identity and productive attitude towards life. Hence the more conceptual, as well as figurative, connections that can be made between the internal and the external, the more personal stability one has:[9] 'Jedes denkende Wesen ist also ein *Vereinigungspunkt* des rundumher Zerstreuten' [Every thinking being is thus a *point of coalescence* for everything scattered around it].[10] The answers to the predicament that Moritz diagnoses illuminate each other complementarily from various perspectives, so to speak; but they must be perceived from a point in the middle.

'Neither mere allegories nor mere history': The Symbol-Concept of *Götterlehre*

For this reason, Moritz's symbol-concept should not be derived from his aesthetic writings alone; it has many different layers and aspects that interact with one another and are by no means mutually exclusive.[11] Moritz himself sketched an exemplary model of this multi-layered symbolism in one of his most influential writings, the *Götterlehre*, which was published in the same year as the second *Andreas Hartknopf* novel. It had a strong influence on the Romantics in their search for a new mythology. In the proposed 'Gesichtspunkt für die mythologischen Dichtungen' [viewpoint for mythological fictions], the totality of Greek mythology is regarded as the language ('Sprache') of the imagination ('Phantasie'), which fulfils at the same time the requirements of a beautiful work of art: it is created through the process of isolation ('aus dem Zusammenhange der wirklichen Dinge herausgehoben' [extracted from the connection of real things]), and now subsists as a purpose in itself ('gleichsam eine Welt für sich' [a world in itself]).[12] This mythology thereby avoids metaphysical terms and abstractions and attempts instead, despite its unworldliness, 'ihre Bildungen an Zeit und Ort zu knüpfen' [to connect its images to time and place]. 'Sie ruht und schwebt gern über der Wirklichkeit' [It touches upon and hovers above reality], but without striving to reach its 'Nähe und Deutlichkeit' [immediacy and clarity].[13] It is much more about a close relationship between the imagination and reality: mythology is neither 'leeres Traumbild' [an empty vision], i.e. pure fancy, nor 'bloßes Spiel des Witzes' [a mere play of intelligence], i.e. pure artwork. Instead, it gains a certain 'weight' ('Gewicht') through its relationship to an early human history (and prehistory) that is considered real. This 'weight' prevents its 'Auflösung in bloße Allegorie' [dissolution into mere allegory].[14] Mythology therefore requires from the outset the most literal reading possible, one which excludes each and every figurative meaning and, above all, takes into account the inner coherency of the whole. But in addition, a figurative-allegorical meaning is then *also* possible. Moritz explains using Saturn as an example:

> Auf diese Weise ist nun Saturnus bald ein Bild der alleszerstörenden Zeit, bald ein König, der zu einer gewissen Zeit in Latium herrschte. Die Erzählungen von ihm sind weder bloße Allegorien noch bloße Geschichte, sondern beides zusammengenommen und nach den Gesetzen der Einbildungskraft verwebt.[15]

> [In this way, Saturn is at once an image of the apocalypse and a king who ruled at a certain time in Latium. His narratives are neither mere allegories nor mere history, but rather both taken together and interwoven according to the laws of the imagination.]

Here, then, Moritz exclusively opposes 'bloße Allegorien' [mere allegories] — but he does not forbid allegory as an artistic device. Likewise with the external purposes of poetry: they should not outweigh internal self-purpose, but poetry must of course still teach 'Lebensweisheit' [worldly wisdom] and thereby fulfil pedagogical and therapeutic functions.[16]

According to this model, every work of art can be read at first literally and then understood as a (to some degree biographically or historically real) story; it is granted a kind of existential weight. The second step is to investigate its figurative meaning; and at this stage, it is above all important to explore its internal aesthetic coherence.[17] I will now demonstrate this kind of multileveled reading using the example of *Andreas Hartknopf*. The first step is to take into account the concrete autobiographical references, the reflections on language, as well as the psychological and pedagogical concepts treated in the novel.[18] Second, I will analyse the various figurative 'guises' ('Einkleidungen'), the biblical references, as well as the references to mysticism and freemasonry. And finally, I will focus on the genuinely aesthetic aspects of the text, as well as its specific form. In doing so, I will trace the construction of the imagery, which is neither exclusively symbolic nor exclusively allegorical, neither purely natural nor purely conventional; it is polysemous in terms of its different levels of meaning and diverse readership. At the same time, I will test and reflect upon the application of the theoretical discussions of contemporaries, as well as Moritz's own semiotics.

The guiding thread running through this multileveled reading is the motto that Moritz prefixes to the novel. Its leitmotif-like occurrence in the text suggests that we should at the very least test it out as the sought-after, central 'viewpoint' that discloses all of the interrelations of the artwork: 'Der Buchstabe tötet, aber der Geist macht lebendig' [the letter brings death, but the Spirit gives life].[19] This well-known biblical quotation, from the Second Epistle of Paul to the Corinthians (3. 6), leads us directly to the core of the text. It refers to how God's word reaches the world: through writings and stone tablets (in other words, through 'letters') or through the behaviour and the hearts of men in whom his 'spirit', his higher meaning, lives. The dualism of 'spirit' and 'letter' in the novel, as it is already in the biblical quotation itself, is complexly nuanced; I will therefore point out the specific variations on the individual planes of imagery.[20]

Dingsymbole [personal emblems], Psychological Cures and Descriptive Names: Autobiography, Psychology and Grammar

I have already referred to the autobiographical background of the novel. Since it has a completely different literary form, *Andreas Hartknopf* may be seen as a continuation of *Anton Reiser* only in an abstract sense: for example, individual figures have concrete models in other texts,[21] or the novel evokes childhood memories which Moritz has depicted elsewhere.[22] In close relation to this, we can recognize a first kind of symbolism: while looking into a well, a dark, early-childhood memory causes 'in dessen Bilde gleichsam, alle die folgenden unzähligen Bilder seiner Seele zusammen' [the myriad of images of Hartknopf's soul to surge together all at once].[23] The narrator can convey this in a certain way in that he makes the individual, symbolic image once again a general allegory 'des Ländlichen, des Altertums, und der simplen Natur' [of the pastoral, ancient times, and of simple Nature]. He subsequently allows for the consideration that such *Dingsymbole* (personal emblems) will be 'freilich immer bei einem jeden wieder andre' [of course always different for everyone].[24] The *Dingsymbol* can indeed provide a 'dark' experience of identity over time, but it is not limitlessly universal; instead, it is to be understood as highly intersubjective.[25]

In addition to these specific childhood memories, Hartknopf shares with his author a manic–depressive personality structure (not to the extent of pathological disorder, but rather a generally melancholic *Weltanschauung*): his 'fürchterlichsten Stunden' [most dreadful hours] are characterized by 'Zeichen der gänzlichen Leerheit, der Selbstermangelung, des dumpfen Hinbrütens, der Teilnehmungslosigkeit an allem' [signs of complete emptiness, of self-lack, of dull brooding, and of general apathy].[26] Significantly, however, Hartknopf finds both his melancholic and enthusiastic moods mirrored in the natural environment surrounding him. The author interprets this explicitly as an asset: Hartknopf carries with him a 'certain harmony' of the soul with the 'surrounding nature',[27] so that all external changes are faithfully reflected in his soul: a spruce forest or a turf moor could, for example, bring about death, chaos and emptiness; a sunrise, on the other hand, could cause exaltation and exuberance.[28] In contrast, exactly the opposite occurs with other people: the narrator tells us that Hartknopf experiences an 'ewige Dissonanz aller äußern Umstände mit seinen innern Wünschen und Bestrebungen' [eternal dissonance between all external circumstances and his inner wishes and endeavours].[29] It is perhaps not pure speculation to say that we see here one of many, partial self-portraits of Moritz himself: in Hartknopf, the author has created a complementary, alternative sketch of himself, in both his positive and negative aspects.

This concept of a life in harmony with oneself and nature — at both its highest and lowest moments — includes the metaphors of 'Lebenstext' [life as text], as well as 'Lebenslampe' [life as lamp], the 'Lebensfaden' [web of life][30] or the predetermined 'Laufbahn' [path of life].[31] Discursively, however, this kind of coherence can never be obtained: 'Lieber Vetter, unser ganzes Leben und Sein drängt sich in ein großes Wort zusammen, aber ich kann es nicht buchstabieren' [Dear cousin, our entire life and being is compressed together in one, great word; only I cannot spell it].[32] It is therefore all the more important to listen to the 'Worte des Lebens' [words of life] in one's own soul and to feel the 'Takt' [rhythm] in oneself. This results in man's only assurance, that of his own existence: 'Vetter, *wir sind* ist das höchste, was wir sagen können' [cousin, *we are* is the highest thing that we can say];[33] or transposed into a mystical mode of speaking: 'Das Sein ist der Stift in dem Wirbel. Ohne Mittelpunkt ist kein Cirkel, ohne Sein kein Haben' [Being is the anchor in the storm. There is no circle without a central point, no possessing without being].[34] In this ontological model, every man is a single word, but one that only the Creator can spell; his entire life is an attempt to vest this perceived and experienced existence in deeds and his own creations, to give it a 'spirit', and to make it ascertainable to other men. For it is this 'spirit' (Geist) that Moritz is getting at; he celebrates its development and progress in many of his writings as the highest purpose of man.[35]

The 'Lied an die Weisheit' [song to wisdom] that closes the first part praises the immortality of the 'spirit' in contrast to the transience of all physical being. Hartknopf's maxim for life, 'resignation', ought to be understood in this context — but not by any means as a rejection of life. Rather it is a prerequisite for the free development of the individual: only he who recognizes death as 'ultima linea rerum',[36] as the last line of the first part of the novel significantly states, can lead his life free of fear and therefore wisely and cognizantly.

This old philosophical wisdom is presented in the novel with great consistency — in Hartknopf's martyrdom, and also for example as the educational precept of the innkeeper Knapp: 'Diesem von Kindheit auf seiner Seele fest eingeprägten Bilde des Todes, verdankt er den sichern und ruhigen Genuß, all der Freuden seines Lebens' [He owes the confident and calm pleasure, all of the joys of his life, to the image of death engraved on his soul since childhood].[37] For all intents and purposes, 'memento mori'[38] functions just like the ancient precept *carpe diem*; it invokes here, as in many other of Moritz's writings, a consciousness of the moment, the present hour, the here and now. Alongside *carpe diem*, further maxims from classical dietetics of the soul appear as well, such as the basic values represented by Knapp: 'Gesundheit, Zufriedenheit, und Arbeit' [health, contentment and occupation].[39] On the other hand, the development of the 'letter' as opposed to the 'spirit' is conducted with the utmost caution: the son of the innkeeper Knapp was allowed to learn the alphabet only 'da er zehn Jahre alt war' [once he was ten years old], and not until he was fourteen years old should he pronounce the name of God.[40] According to this pedagogy, much of which concords with Rousseau, the 'spirit' comes first, and then only later, after one has reached advanced physical and spiritual maturity, the 'letter'.

In this respect, the antagonism between 'letter' and 'spirit' is also related to the fundamental problem of contemporary anthropology and experiential psychology, i.e. the *commercium* of body and soul. Andreas Hartknopf, along with his brother in 'spirit', Kersting, possesses the ability to carry out psychological treatments in order 'den Leib des Menschen durch die Seele zu heilen' [to heal the body of man through the soul] — as performed on the novel's narrator, for example.[41] The body is in this context clearly the materially definable 'letter'; the sign or the symptom that has in some way become estranged from the 'spirit', the human soul, so that both have become disharmonious. And just as the body can be healed through the soul, so can the soul be healed through the body. This is why the eponymous hero of the novel is necessarily, and with equal seriousness, a priest as well as a blacksmith,[42] and why he senses the proximity of gallows (bodily death) and the cross (spiritual resurrection) at the hangman's hill in Gellenhausen; this is why his maxim for life is not only 'ich will, was ich muß' [I want what I must],[43] i.e. resignation, but also 'ich muß, was ich will' [I have to do what I want], i.e. agency.[44] It is not despair and passivity that are associated with the submission to irrational strength (of nature, as well as malicious men), but rather the essential duty to educate oneself, to realize one's personal talents and abilities. Hartknopf experiences his greatest happiness accordingly in the 'Gefühl seiner Kraft' [feeling of his strength] or in the 'Gefühl der erweiterten Ichheit' [the feeling of enhanced ego-ness].[45] Body and soul, death and life are connected in this novel just as closely as 'letter' and 'spirit'; neither exists without the other. Rather, each gains its meaning and value through the complementary, but not dualistically determined relationship to the other:

> *Hartknopf* lehrte mich die Nacht lieben ohne den Tag zu scheuen, und den Tag ohne die Nacht zu scheuen. — Finsternis und Licht — Tod und Leben — Ruhe und Bewegung — mußten in sanfter Mischung sich ineinander verschwimmen.[46]

> [*Hartknopf* taught me to love the night without dreading the day, and the day without shying away from the night. Darkness and light, death and life, stillness and motion: all must blur together in a soft blend.]

Ultimately, the same model appears in the reflections on language and grammar that permeate the entire text. The diametrically opposed relationship of dead 'letter' and living 'spirit' also yields the relationship between the vitalizing word of God, as creation, and the deadening word of man (for example, of 'Satan *Hagebuck*' or of the catechizing sexton Ehrenpreiß);[47] the relationship between music as the

'Sprache der Empfindungen' [language of sentiments] and the verbal language of ideas;[48] between body-language and written language.[49] Incidentally, as with the accordance of outer and inner nature, it also holds true that such a linguistic harmony can indicate both good and bad: thus the great 'Halleluja' at the celebration must fail, 'weil es zu einer gesuchten, *veranstalteten* Scene bestimmt war' [for it was fixed as part of a sought-after, *organized* event].[50] If one does not express the word of creation for its own sake, for the sake of its inner purpose and being, then it becomes only an external simulation.

The text reserves a special role for the relationship between 'spirit' and 'letter' for the characters' names in the text. They are not only already recognizable superficially as descriptive names that allow for the concurrence of person as 'spirit' and the name as 'letter' (as with the beautiful soul Sophie Erdmuthe, the tenant Heil, the sexton Küster, or the sexton Hagebuck), but they also have additional, allegorical meanings. This is relatively easy to see in the rector Emeritus, whose first name, Elias, refers to the biblical prophet and combatant of the cult of Ba'al.[51] The title figure is somewhat more difficult: 'Andreas' is not only a common, everyday name (on a literal level), but also stands for outstanding courage and virtue in Greek (the name, in other words, expresses as a natural sign exactly what the name-holder is). In addition, Andreas (Andrew) is the first apostle of Christ; and he died, like Hartknopf, a martyr's death on the cross. The surname adds yet further layers of meaning: Hartknopf, whose name translates literally as 'hard button', is 'von oben bis unten zugeknöpft' [buttoned up from top to bottom].[52] Hartknopf is compared with a diamond beneath a hard pebble — and this too may be seen as a reference to the 'spirit'–'letter' dualism.[53] His hardness is manifest not only in his unaccommodating and straightforward character, but also in his professional activity as a blacksmith. When, on the other hand, a multiple 'charging' of a name is impossible because it refers to a real historical person, the heightened referentiality can take the place of the enhanced imagery. There was indeed a Johann Adam Kersting who was an authority on horse medicine. In this case, conversely, the reality authenticates the fiction; the 'letter' of the name receives 'spirit' not only through allegorical meaning, but also through a lived life. On the level of language, as well, the relationship between 'spirit' and 'letter' is not to be determined partially, in favour of one or the other. Rather, music and verbal language enhance each other like melody and text, and the recurring metaphor for word as the 'guise' ('Kleid') of the thought indicates, too, that a designation can be fitting or unfitting.

The Bible, Mysticism and Freemasonry: Allegorical Systems of Imagery

The life that is indeed lived, in all its literal, biographical readability, as well as its psychological expressibility and its verbal representability, makes up the text's first level of meaning. Above this first level appear further, figurative levels of representation in the novel that are classifiable within various systems of imagery. The most prominent among these is without a doubt the reference to Christianity, which is established by countless quotations from and allusions to the Bible. Writing to Goethe, Moritz himself characterized the novel as 'wilde Blasphemie' [crazed blasphemy],[54] and critics have interpreted it as a 'parodistische Kontrafaktur zur christlichen Passionsgeschichte' [parodic contrafactum to the Passion of Christ].[55] It does indeed seem more plausible to me to read Hartknopf as a disciple or prophet of an awaited Messiah, who would then no longer exhibit all of Hartknopf's aesthetic and worldly deficits.[56] But what then did Moritz mean by 'wilde Blasphemie'? I think that this phrase gives us a hint about the general concept of the novel: not only does the reference to freemasonry serve as a 'guise' for 'bisher noch zu sehr verkante Wahrheiten' [truths that have until now been too greatly underestimated] (as Moritz himself explains in another statement), but the reference to Christianity represents ultimately only one of many 'guises'.[57] The Bible, like any other mythology, is in this context to be read as a 'language of the imagination' [Sprache der Phantasie]. This relegates the Bible, like mythology, not entirely to the realm of fiction, but rather to the realm of a dark prehistory of humankind that must be brought to life by imagination and re-translated for contemporary readers. But for this reason — and this was enough to fulfil known contemporary criteria for blasphemy — the Bible is on the same level as mythology.[58]

This process may be illustrated most effectively with the Genesis creation narrative, which Moritz extols in many other writings as the ontological and semiotic paradigma *par excellence*.[59] The creation narrative displays an exemplary act of revival through the word, which calls being to life — characteristically through an entire series of existential, fundamental dualisms according to the model of light and darkness[60] — and grants it a 'spirit'. Hartknopf then acuminates this for his model of the 'Viereinigkeit' [quadrinity].[61] The novel demonstrates anew a positive and negative variation of such a process of ensoulment through the word: while Hartknopf's first sermon about the quadrinity is interrupted by the wooden dove falling onto the pulpit — which at the same time cogently expresses the discord between the congregation and the preacher — it is this very sermon that turns out to be the best when repeated in front of the kindred spirits Sophie Erdmuthe and her brother. Its aesthetic perfection as work of art and well-ordered whole are proven to the narrator in that not only the congenial beauty of similarly tempered souls, but also the 'brutality' of the farmers,[62] oriented only towards sensuality, comes to light through its beauty. Both are, however, the effects of the perfect harmony of a work of art.

One variation of this biblical allegory displays the dealings with mysticism that are integrated into the novel through the figure of Herr v. G.; and which Moritz frequently struggled with as a result of his childhood experiences.[63] In this context, Herr v. G. represents an extreme position. He wants to exclude everything having to do with the body from religion, even nature and its 'Fülle' [abundance];[64] on the other hand, he trusts 'innern Worte' [inner words] alone.[65] In this sense, Herr v. G. and Hartknopf constitute a contrasting pair in the novel that is represented with various figurative dualisms:

> Der Herr v. G. [...] war für das Leichte, Auflodernde, Himmelanstrebende. — Hartknopf war für das Schwere, sich niedersenkende, in sich selbst ruhende [...]. Und doch trafen beide immer in gewissen Punkten zusammen. — Dann war es, als ob sie sich über einem Abgrunde die Hände reichten.[66]

[Herr v. G. was for everything light, burning, heaven-aspiring. — Hartknopf
was for everything heavy, sinking, self-contained [...]. And yet both always
came together at a certain point. — Then it was as if they reached and joined
hands across an abyss.]

Both are ultimately pursuing the same goal: a re-vitalization of the 'letter' through
the 'spirit'; only they do so in different, individual ways. Hartknopf's means of
doing so is depicted as broader, more all-embracing, for he is capable of integrating
a greater 'abundance' of phenomena.[67] Nonetheless, mystical experience is presented
here, as elsewhere in Moritz's work, with its own importance as a structural analogy
to aesthetic experience and philosophy. This is shown, for example, in the depiction
of a night-time encounter of the narrator with Andreas Hartknopf, who portrays
this not only as a religious conversion experience, but specifically as a spiritual
rebirth according to the Pietist model: 'Ich lernte die große Weisheit: *des Alles im
Moment. Ich ward zum neuen geistigen Leben geboren*' [I learned the great wisdom:
everything in the moment. I was born into a new, spiritual life].[68] The entire scene
is once again depicted as an analogy to the creation narrative and ends eventually
with the narrator's invocation of the *Unsagbarkeitstopos* [topos of unutterability]
through the narrator and the biblical quotation about 'spirit' and 'letter'. Connected
with this is the transition from the discursive 'Sprache des Verstandes' [language
of understanding] to music as the 'Sprache der Empfindungen' [language of
sentiments], when Hartknopf picks up the flute and 'übersetzt' [translates] his
teachings.[69] In this example it is possible to follow almost microscopically how the
various levels of language and image intertwine in the novel.

The third system of language and image that the novel invokes is that of
freemasonry.[70] Certain masonic symbols serve as the means of spontaneous and
wordless understanding of the insiders in the novel,[71] but they are at the same
time in a more comprehensive sense symbols of life and natural signs — just like
Hartknopf's orientation towards the sun, which I will examine in more detail in
the following section. At the same time, the model of a refined 'großen Geister-
republik' [great republic of spirits],[72] like that of the freemasons, stands for a
spiritual community that includes living contemporaries, as well as certain literary
works: Hartknopf finds them in equal measure in Wieland's *Musarion*, in Homer's
epics, in Horace's *Epistles*, in Rousseau's *Emile*.[73] Literary works of art, too, make
possible the survival of the spiritual individual over time, if only through 'erhabnen
Egoismus' [sublime selfishness],[74] and they thus prevent the depressing loss of self
and solipsistic isolation: 'Er fand sich wieder, wohin er blickte' [he found himself
again, wherever he looked].[75] For the same reason, friendship as social and spiritual
confraternity is valued more highly than love. On the other hand, a negative
counter-image exists, as well: the equally like-minded and committed community
of misguided, 'Afterweisen, der Weltreformatoren, der Hagebucks' [common
sages, do-gooders, Hagebucks],[76] who not only wallow in reformatory fantasies,
but also fail to maintain a grip on reality, in contrast to the blacksmith Hartknopf
or his freemasonic friends Elias and Kersting. Indeed, here Moritz thematizes
the moral neutrality of a 'Gleichlaut der Gemüter' [consonance of dispositions]
quite explicitly:[77] not only do the sublime freemasonic figures of the text work

harmoniously, but also the smarmy sexton Ehrenpreiß and the former priest von Ribbeckenau. This is also a 'consonance' ('Gleichlaut') of 'tones' ('Töne'), even if it is not perceived as beautiful, but rather a form of 'grobe Selbstzufriedenheit' [crude self-satisfaction].[78]

Living Images, Guises and Curtains: The Criticism of Allegory and its Justification

Altogether, Christianity, mysticism and freemasonry are equivalent in terms of their function in the novel: they are systems of images and signs that reveal their historical conventionality and are made once again relevant for life. In the process, they do not by any means lose their allegorical quality, nor the closely related capacity for multiple meanings: the single 'letter', the conventional sign, once again contains the living 'spirit', without entirely losing its value as a sign. This process is thematized at an aesthetic level again and again in the novel, as Moritz seizes upon and at the same time tests his central concepts.

Thus the concept of the 'Metaphysische Schönheitslinie' [metaphysical line of beauty],[79] for example, is evoked at two different places in the novel. Hartknopf reflects in the very first scene on his misadventure with the ditch:

> Dies führte ihn zu tiefsinnigen Betrachtungen über die gerade und über die krumme Linie, und in wie fern die gerade Linie gleichsam das Bild des Zweckmäßigen in unsern Handlungen sei, indem die Tätigkeit der Seele den kürzesten Weg zu ihrem Ziele nimmt — die krumme Linie hingegen das Schöne, Tändelnde und Spielende, den Tanz, das Spazierengehen bezeichnet.[80]

> [This led him to reflect deeply on the straight line and the winding line, and to what degree the straight line was more or less the image of purposefulness in our actions: the activity of our soul takes the shortest route to its objective. The winding line, on the other hand, designates all that is beautiful, blithe and playful, dancing and taking walks.]

The line of beauty is here explicitly consigned to the realm of aesthetic phenomena, while the straight line is reserved for the purposeful activity of the soul, i.e. ultimately that which Hartknopf, the priest and the blacksmith rely upon. Therefore, Hartknopf is clearly not an artist, nor will he ever become one. However, as he stands at the crossroads of his life and has to make a decision whether to court Sophie Erdmuthe or to wander further, he does not allow himself to be guided by this realization and thus makes the wrong decision: he chooses the 'krummen Fußweg' [winding path] to the town and not the 'gerade Straße' [straight road],[81] and so drifts away from his life-task, his character, and his call to action:

> Für ihn war die breite Heerstraße, welche vom Aufgange bis zum Niedergange die Länder durchschneidet, die von den Menschen nach ihren Zungen und Sprachen benannt sind

> [For him, it was the wide Heerstraße, which from beginning to end, sunrise to sunset, cut through those countries named by man according to their tongues and languages].[82]

This short sentence compacts a series of images that are closely tied to the central

issue of the text, as well as interwoven with each other: Hartknopf follows the
sun (an important freemasonic symbol) on his life journey from West to East, in
other words anti-cyclically from decline to rise. Thus the road not only connects
people to one another (it is, after all, a Heerstraße, not a one-lane footpath), but
also traverses various language areas — just as the text itself 'speaks' in various
'languages' and systems of images. In contrast, the winding footpath 'vollendete
und verlor' [completed and lost] itself. This is undoubtedly a mark of aesthetic
quality and an ideal of identity, for it reflects 'das in sich selbst vollendete ruhige
Leben' [a peaceful life that is complete in itself].[83] However, such aesthetic quality
is granted only to Sophie, who, as a beautiful soul, already embodies 'himmlische
Weisheit' [heavenly wisdom] on earth.[84]

Indeed Hartknopf himself is similarly depicted as being essentially stable and
in harmony with nature; but his destiny is altogether oriented towards expansion,
influence, and activity in continually renewed contexts. It is his purpose to work
as a doctor of souls. This is shown not only in the case of the narrator, but also
with the Carthusian monk, the ultimate trial of Hartknopf's philosophy: 'Wenn es
eine wahre Weisheit gibt, so muß sie lehren, wie man auch als Kartäusermönch,
sobald man es einmal ist, auf seine Weise glücklich sein kann' [If there is such a
thing as true wisdom, it must teach how each man can be happy in his own way
— even as a Carthusian monk, once you have become one].[85] The Carthusian
monk is a particular challenge for Hartknopf's psychological cures because he
may be considered, as a result of his living cut off from all social contacts and
human communication, a 'lebendiges Bild des Todes' [living image of death].[86]
Hartknopf's therapy applies his steadfast maxim of resignation: the monk must
learn to love his fate. Hence comes his freedom, which in turn makes possible an
impartial perception of the self, without fear of death, and the configuration of
one's own inner being as a substitute for failed, external activity. Just as with the
spiritual rebirth of the narrator, an exemplary creation occurs here through healing
— in the blasphemous style characteristic for the text and in allusion to the creation
narrative: 'und Hartknopf sahe an, alles, was er hervorgebracht hatte, und siehe da
es war sehr gut' [and so Hartknopf looked at all that he had made, and he saw that
it was very good].[87]

Hartknopf's pedagogical-therapeutic mission clearly has a greater value than the
aesthetic shaping of a lifestyle in the novel. Still, this mission profits from his own,
also aesthetic, wholeness and the ever more closely tied connections to his life-text:
'Jemehr Zusammenhang, jemehr Wahrheit — jemehr Ordnung, jemehr Licht' [the
more coherency, the more truth; the more order, the more light],[88] as the emeritus
succinctly puts it. Hartknopf is therefore fully capable of aesthetic creations. He
would have become a great musician (on occasion he composes verses), but his real
talent is rhetorical: his tool is the word, brought to life by the 'spirit' in as many
ways as possible.[89] Therefore, the novel, too, as Hartknopf's 'life-text', cannot round
itself out to the classical, symbolic harmony of the internal and external, but rather
has to rely more strongly on external rhetorical means — like those of the allegory
that Moritz dismissed in his 'pure' aesthetic theory. The 'letter' of the novel can
interact harmoniously with its 'spirit' if the 'letter' be expressed in its individuality,

which is, in this case, to be prioritized over its beauty: 'Das Gleichnis hinkt!' [the comparison is lame!], says Hartknopf. The emeritus replies, 'Laß er es hinken!' [Let it limp!].[90] This is most certainly not a maxim from the classicist aesthetics of beauty, just as an old, limping poodle is no 'beautiful' symbol. But it is a very vivid sign.

Moritz's theoretical criticism of allegory in *Über die Allegorie* is based above all on the claim that allegory draws the beholder's attention away from the inner coherence of the artwork; for it points to external, conventional meanings of signs that are not inherent to the work of art itself. As already implied, this does not systematically exclude allegory as an artistic device; but it may only 'dally' ('umgaukeln') about the artwork; 'nur gleichsam an seinem äußersten Rande spielen' [only more or less play on its outermost edges]. If allegory is limited to this subordinate function, it can even be 'beautiful'.[91] Moritz argues along quite similar lines in *Die große Loge* regarding symbols for freemasonry; they are 'schöne Einfassungen großer Gedanken' [beautiful encapsulations of great thoughts][92] and indispensable as 'Kleid' [guise] for thoughts: for 'ohne das Wort wäre der Gedanke nichts' [thoughts would be nothing without words].[93]

Finally, the *Grammatische Wörterbuch der deutschen Sprache* offers a third under-standing of allegory in the entry 'Allegorie, Gleichnißrede, Bildrede'. Allegory consists of pursuing a 'bildlicher Ausdruck' [figurative expression]: 'Diese Gemählde sind gleichsam durchsichtige Vorhänge, durch welche man die Gegen-stände wahrnimmt, die uns dargestellt werden sollen' [these paintings are more or less transparent curtains, through which one perceives the objects that are being presented].[94] Encapsulations, guises, curtains: allegory, in the broadest sense of the basic mode of figurative speech, contributes decisively to the process of interconnecting and interweaving 'nackten Gedanken' [naked thoughts] as tightly as possible and thereby of strengthening aesthetic coherence. [95] Crucial here is the criterion of continuation, as mentioned in the *Wörterbuch*, which the leitmotif-like structure of *Andreas Hartknopf* brings clearly to the fore. Certain images appear again and again at various different levels and so structure the text. Thus, on the lowest level, the sun (as part of nature) is omnipresent and serves as a signpost for Hartknopf's personal life journey; at the next level, the sun is an image of enlightenment, as well as a conventional symbol for freemasonry; at the next, it plays a significant role in the first act of the creation narrative. The sun is most intimately interwoven with its opposite: the night and darkness as complementary parts of the original creation. Yet night and darkness also have equivalents in Hartknopf's character and his story. Ultimately, all other creatures arise from day and night, light and darkness; and not only in the Mosaic creation narrative, but also in the novel, which can be understood as an allegory of the creation narrative that has been re-translated into life. In this way, the original allegory is 'stripped' of its conventional character, and then traced back to its possible basis as a 'natural sign'.

On the Use of Multi-layered Symbolism: Forms of Comparison

Even the most superficial reading of *Andreas Hartknopf* makes clear that Moritz did not produce a prototype of an autonomous work of art as prescribed by classical theory. However, the reasons for his choice of the widely criticized 'allegory' as the large-scale form for the novel should now be somewhat easier to determine.[96] First, there are reasons of a personal nature. It is no coincidence that Moritz often cites Goethe in his aesthetic writings at decisive points: Goethe, the brother blessed by fortune, the (in Schiller's terms) naive poet who can intuitively create beauty, for it is already inherent to his universal genius.[97] Moritz, on the other hand, is sentimentally conflicted,[98] to the point of pathology — and his literary works, so different from one another, demonstrate this as well; an old, one-eyed poodle can only be good for lame comparisons. This conflict defines the forms of representation of the text, not only in its thoroughly dualistically constructed symbolism, but also in the choice of literary means in the first place: next to enthusiastic sentiment is bitter satire; moments of deep tragedy are relieved by outbreaks of bizarre comedy;[99] songs alternate with prose, metaphysical reflections follow invocations of unutterability. The harmony that can be thereby achieved is either a positive one (the congruency of beautiful souls, as musical harmony) or a negative one (the congruency of base souls, as dissonance). What can in one instance be an aesthetic repetition and 'replicated appeal' [vervielfältigte[r] Reiz][100] (Hartknopf's sermon in Ribbeckenäuchen) is in another instance merely a dull monotony and 'bland recurrence' [einförmige Wiederkehr].[101]

For this novel, ultimately more important than 'objective' [objektive] beauty is consistent individuality, understood as situative appropriateness of content and artistic means. For this reason various kinds of figurative language also appear: personal *Dingsymbole* (wells, drawbridges); complex 'living images' (the Carthusian monastery); descriptive names as models for an ideal language; conventional systems of signs that serve the solidarity of a social community (the symbols for free-masonry); pseudo-mythological stories based on systems of images (the Bible, above all the creation narrative); non-figurative imagery (mysticism, for example with its circle symbolism). Altogether, none of these phenomena may be apprehended or differentiated in any concrete terms; rather, they refer semiotically to boundaries between various kinds of images — boundaries which are only clear in theory, always blurred in practice.[102] They are different types of allegorical comparisons ('Gleichnißrede'), with different scopes of interpretation and various claims to validity, most comprehensive when an image may be read on several different levels (for example, the sun,[103] or the name 'Andreas Hartknopf').[104]

One advantage of such multi-layered symbolism[105] is its differentiated appeal to the audience. Moritz refers to this consideration twice. Thus he justifies the immersion in mysticism with the claim that 'zarte Gemüther' [tender souls] find relief in such 'mysticism without physics'; but such a paradoxical effect should also be taken seriously and investigated in terms of psychology.[106] In the case of *Andreas Hartknopf*, he ultimately legitimizes the above-mentioned 'guise', the 'freemasonic' guise, in stating that the author wants to 'gewisse bisher noch zu sehr verkannte Wahrheiten, auch unter die Classe von Menschen, [...] verbreiten [...], denen diese Einkleidung nun einmal lieb ist, und welche ihre Begriffe vom Guten und Schönen an Bilder zu knüpfen sich einmal gewöhnt haben' [promulgate certain truths that were up until now too little known, even to the class of people [...] to whom this dressing is dear, and who have become used to tying their notions of the good and the beautiful to images].[107] In terms of symbolism, one must address children differently from adults; mystics differently from freemasons, learned readers differently from the unlearned readers — at least if one wants to be, in the interest of 'truth', as thoroughly understood as possible; that is, if the work of art is to deliver worldly wisdom.[108]

A particular organizational structure in the form of a repeated circle results from the artistic devices of the continuing allegory and multi-layered symbolism. Again and again, Moritz emphasizes the necessity of a self-contained centre as a 'Vereinigungspunkt' [point of unification] for a stable identity and for the recognition of truth.[109] The paradigm for such a centre is God, who is without physical extension, but in whom everything exists side by side in any given moment: 'Alles ist bei ihm ineinander Nichts außereinander' [In him, everything is interwoven; nothing is dispersed].[110] The temporal order of succession is thus only a result of the limited 'Fassungskraft' [mental capacity] of the human 'spirit'.[111] The epistemological as well as the aesthetic ideal, the greatest coherence imaginable, would be the simultaneity of all being in a great circle. In the end, Moritz attempts to approach such simultaneity in *Andreas Hartknopf*: chronology is abandoned in the representation, even if a life path (that is in itself circular) would be easy to reconstruct and to outline chronologically. The text circles tightly and extensively around its title character, who appears from the most varied perspectives and appears refracted through highly diverse narrative techniques and styles.[112] Above all, the continuing allegories and the interwoven discourses on images under the auspices of the dualism of 'spirit' and 'letter' create coherency: from this viewpoint, Hartknopf's entire life appears to be the continued attempt to spell the 'great word' [große Wort] of human existence in new creations and rebirths.[113] However, he himself is only Andreas: the precursor, the first disciple of the coming genius, one who does not have to subject himself to the arduousness of allegory and of the fourfold exegesis. Only the genius can create a great, ideally beautiful work of art, using his almost unlimited human apprehension and an inner being that is not only widely developed, but also focused on a central point.

In this respect, *Andreas Hartknopf* marks not just the transition from the didactic late Enlightenment to classical, autonomous aesthetics and symbolism: it becomes at the same time a model for kindred authors like Jean Paul, who develops his own concept of 'humour'. It is also a forerunner of the Romantic project of a 'new mythology'.[114] This is perhaps most evident in Schelling's philosophy of art, which explicitly recognizes Moritz's accomplishments. Schelling's understanding that mythology is the 'höchstes Urbild der poetischen Welt' [highest archetype of the poetic world],[115] one which is only to be grasped with imagination and which constitutes a 'totality', owes much to the *Götterlehre*.[116] However, Moritz's influence is also to be found more subtly in the approach to different concepts of imagery — schematism, symbol and allegory — which Schelling had systematically distinguished from one another in his *Philosophie der Kunst*. While schematism reveals something specific through something general, and allegory does the opposite (something general is revealed through something specific), the symbol incorporates both: the specific and the general become identical (as in art or organicism). However, despite Schelling's stringency in the abstract definitions, the boundaries between those kinds of imagery are fluid, for allegory may be thought of as a particular kind of symbol: 'Aber eben deswegen ist auch alles Symbolische sehr leicht zu allegorisieren, weil die symbolische Bedeutung die allegorische [...] in sich schließt' [but because of this, everything that is symbolic is also very easy to allegorize, for symbolic meaning [...] implies an allegorical one].[117] Schelling, as Moritz, cites mythology as an example, especially the work of Homer: 'Der Zauber der homerischen Dichtung und der ganzen Mythologie ruht allerdings mit darauf, daß sie die allegorische Bedeutung auch als *Möglichkeit* enthält' [the magic of Homeric poetry and all of mythology rests upon the inclusion of allegorical meaning also as *possibility*].[118] Moritz's *Andreas Hartknopf* may also be understood as an attempt at such 'realistische Mythologie' [realistic mythology]:[119] neither mere allegories nor mere history.

Translated by Kathleen Singles

Notes to Chapter 3

1. Cf. for example, Achim Geisenhanslüke, *Der Buchstabe des Geistes. Postfigurationen der Allegorie von Bunyan zu Nietzsche* (Munich: Wilhelm Fink Verlag, 2003), p. 47: 'Winckelmann, Moritz und Goethe markieren die wichtigsten Stationen auf dem Weg der Dichtungstheorie im 18. Jahrhundert von der Allegorie zum Symbol' [Winckelmann, Moritz and Goethe represent the most important stations from allegory to symbol in the poetic theory of the eighteenth century].

2. Cf. Günter Niklewski, *Versuch über Symbol und Allegorie (Winckelmann — Moritz — Schelling)* (Erlangen: Palm & Enke, 1979).

3. Geisenhanslüke is quite right: he points out that Moritz never had a clear, differentiated definition of symbol, and for this reason, it is not possible to contrast allegory and symbol. The antonym of allegory is not so much 'innere Vollkommenheit' [inner perfection] as 'das Schöne'. But even this, however, is not consistent; at a different point, Moritz grants allegory the possibility of beauty (see below).

4. See, for example, Geisenhanslüke, *Der Buchstabe des Geistes* (p. 56): 'Daß Moritz' Ästhetik des Schönen wiederum auf ihre eigene Weise auf die Allegorie zurückgeht, zeigt sich in seinem Roman *Andreas Hartknopf*: "der Buchstabe tötet, aber der Geist macht lebendig", lautet das paulinische Motto, das Moritz seinem Roman voranstellt, um das Ideal des Schönen am Buchstaben der Allegorie scheitern zu lassen. So weist der widersprüchliche Umgang mit der Allegorie in Moritz' theoretischem und literarischem Werk zugleich auf die Doppelbödigkeit der Abwertung der Allegorie im 18. Jahrhundert hin' [The novel *Andreas Hartknopf* shows that Moritz's aesthetics of the beautiful refers back to allegory in its own way: "the letter brings death, but the Spirit gives life" is the Pauline motto that Moritz presents in his novel in order to allow the ideal of the beautiful to fail due to the "letter" of the allegory. In this way the contradictory handling of allegory in Moritz's theoretical and literary work portends the ambiguity of the devaluation of the allegory in the eighteenth century]. Other analyses see *Hartknopf* as, for example, the 'ersten symbolischen Roman der deutschen Literatur' [first symbolic novel in German literature] (Langen), or as a 'sehr persönliche Form allegorischer Symbolik' [very personal form of allegorical symbolism], or a 'säkularisierten Evanglienbericht' [secularized evangelical testimony] (Schrimpf); cf. the research report in Karl Philipp Moritz, *Werke in zwei Bänden*, ed. by Heide Hollmer and Albert Meier, 2 vols (Frankfurt am Main: Deutscher Klassiker Verlag, 1997–99), I: *Dichtungen und Schriften zur Erfahrungs-Seelenkunde* (from now on cited with the siglum DSE), p. 1126 ff.

5. In Karl Philipp Moritz, *Schriften zur Ästhetik und Poetik*, ed. by Hans Joachim Schrimpf (Tübingen: Niemeyer, 1962; from now on cited with the siglum S), p. 122.

6. Because of the limited space here, this will be presented primarily in the endnotes. Cf. the work of Barbara Thums, who also points to the fact that, in the work of Karl Philipp Moritz, the 'Gleichursprünglichkeit von empirischer Wissenschaft und Ästhetik' [simultaneous origination of empirical science and aesthetics] contribute to this agglomeration; also in this context, the 'Grenzen zwischen Fakt und Fiktion, zwischen Gesundheit und Krankheit' [boundaries between fact and fiction, between health and sickness] must be newly defined. Barbara Thums, *Aufmerksamkeit. Wahrnehmung und Selbstbegründung von Brockes bis Nietzsche* (Munich: Fink, 2008), p. 219.

7. Cf. for example, the many statements in *Beiträgen zur Philosophie des Lebens* (anonymous 1780; in Karl Philipp Moritz, *Werke in drei Bänden*, ed. by Horst Günther, 3 vols (Frankfurt a.M.: Insel Verlag, 1981; from now on cited with the siglum W and by volume number): the writer (who might very well be identified as Moritz) feels 'in der Seele eine beständige Ebbe und Flut' [a constant ebb and flow in his soul] (W 3, p. 8) or a 'Sturm' [storm] (p. 22), and desires nothing more than psychological balance and a soul that serves as a 'heiterer Spiegel' [bright mirror] (p. 83); he wrestles for 'Herrschaft über die Gedanken' [mastery of his thoughts] (p. 11), which control him instead; he finds idleness the worst condition (p. 24) and constantly refers to the necessity of using his rare good moods productively; he is already addressing the basic principle of resignation (p. 14). Various descriptions of depressive moods can be found in *Fragmenten aus dem Tagebuch eines Geistersehers* (1787), as well: Moritz writes about a 'kranken Phantasie' [sickly imagination] (W 3, p. 275) and swears by the healing powers of activity and movement as therapy (cf. p. 276). The basic life-principle of resignation and the healing power of moderation are also described (cf. p. 311). The particular closeness of this text to *Andreas Hartknopf* may also be seen through the fact that the opening episode seems to be a model for the latter novel (cf. p. 321 ff.), and the figure Knapp is prefigured by the pedagogue Sonnenberg; the fragmentary structure reveals further similarities.

8. On the therapeutic effects of art, cf. *Versuch einer Vereinigung aller schönen Künste und Wissenschaften unter dem Begriff des in sich selbst Vollendeten* (1785): 'Während das Schöne unsre Betrachtung ganz auf sich zieht, zieht es sie eine Weile von uns selber ab, und macht, daß wir uns in dem schönen Gegenstande zu verlieren scheinen; und eben dies Verlieren, dies Vergessen unsrer selbst, ist der höchste Grad des reinen und uneigennützigen Vergnügens, welche uns das Schöne gewährt' [in drawing our attention entirely to itself, the beautiful draws our attention for a while also away from ourselves; we seem to lose ourselves in the beautiful object. And this loss, the forgetting of ourselves, is the highest degree of pure and unselfish pleasure that the beautiful grants us] (S, p. 5).

9. Cf. for example, the description of a successful day in *Beiträge zur Philosophie des Lebens*: 'Ich habe doch heute einmal die ganze Wonne des Daseins empfunden — als ich alles, was ich um mich her erblickte, in mich hineindachte, und es gleichsam mit mir selber verwebte' [Once today I felt the entire delight in being, as I tried to understand everything that I saw around me and interwove it, so to speak, with myself] (W 3, p. 69).

10. *Versuch einer kleinen praktischen Kinderlogik* (W 3, p. 446).

11. Sabine Schneider has already drawn attention to the 'multidimensionality' of Moritz's central terms; she concentrates, however, on the aesthetic aspects. Sabine Schneider, *Die schwierige Sprache des Schönen. Moritz' und Schillers Semiotik der Sinnlichkeit* (Würzburg: Königshausen & Neumann, 1998), p. 73.

12. Karl Philipp Moritz, *Götterlehre oder Mythologischen Dichtungen der Alten*, W 2, p. 611. In Mark Boulby's translation: 'the fictions of mythology must be regarded as a language of the imagination. As such, they comprise so to speak a world of their own and are separate from the totality of real things'. Mark Boulby, *Karl Philipp Moritz: At the Fringe of Genius* (Toronto, Buffalo and London: University of Toronto Press, 1979), p. 194.

13. Ibid.

14. Ibid.

15. Ibid., p. 623.

16. Ibid., p. 613.

17. Given the dominant, intertextual reference to the Bible, one might also consider the old model

of fourfold exegesis; cf. also Michael Voges, *Aufklärung und Geheimnis. Untersuchungen zur Vermittlung von Literatur- und Sozialgeschichte am Beispiel der Aneignung des Geheimbundmaterials im Roman des späten 18. Jahrhunderts* (Tübingen: Max Niemeyer Verlag, 1987), p. 513. Ulrike Morgner takes a similar approach in that she suggests an anthropological, aesthetic and semiotic means of interpreting the first part: see *'Das Wort aber ist Fleisch geworden'. Allegorie und Allegoriekritik im 18. Jahrhundert am Beispiel von Karl Philipp Moritz' 'Andreas Hartknopf. Eine Allegorie'* (Würzburg: Königshausen & Neumann, 2002), chapters 4.1–4.3. According to the anthropological interpretation, the title figure himself is a personification of his teaching; the 'allegory' in the title would in this case not refer to the text, but rather to its protagonist (cf. p. 125). According to the aesthetic interpretation of the text, Hartknopf's character and behaviour simultaneously personify Moritz's basic aesthetic principles (cf. p. 134); for example, on the basis of the aesthetic topos of development and destruction. And lastly, the semiotic interpretation allows for the identification of Hartknopf with the *logos*, with a focus on the word as sign (cf. p. 148); here, for example, the relationships between language and music or between orality and literality serve as evidence. However, for Morgner these three different kinds of interpretation are not to be seamlessly combined; rather, they open for the reader a multiplicity of perspectives on the text.

18. On the central role of pedagogy in this novel, cf. also Voges, *Aufklärung und Geheimnis*, p. 495.

19. AH, p. 520.

20. On the relationship between 'spirit' and 'letter' on the one hand, and symbol and allegory on the other, cf. Christoph Brecht: 'Die Macht der Worte. Zur Problematik des Allegorischen in Karl Philipp Moritz' *Hartknopf*-Romanen', in *Deutsche Vierteljahrsschrift für Literaturwissenschaft und Geistesgeschichte*, 64 (1990), 624–51: 'Die Dialektik von Geist und Buchstabe in ihrer wechselseitigen Abhängigkeit ist das eigentliche Thema des Moritzschen Erzählens' [the dialectical relationship between spirit and letter in their mutual dependency is the real subject matter of Moritz's narration] (p. 650); altogether, the Hartknopf novels can be seen as 'semiotische Experimentalromane' [semiotic experimental novels] (p. 632). For Ulrike Morger, Hartknopf himself has become an incarnation of the 'letter' of his own teaching (*'Das Wort aber ist Fleisch geworden'*, p. 7). Morgner's comprehensive study offers a nuanced contextualization of Moritz in the allegory-critical discourse of the eighteenth century, as well as a detailed analysis of the first part of the *Hartknopf* novels.

21. For example, the horse veterinarian Johann Adam Kersting (1727–1784), or the professors whom Hartknopf meets at the academy in Erfurt; his experiences with the philanthropist from Dessau in early 1778 and at Berlin's *St.-Johannes-Loge zur Beständigkeit*.

22. Cf. *Erinnerungen aus den frühesten Jahren der Kindheit* (DSE, p. 821).

23. AH, p. 549. At this point, an exemplary identity-building process is described, centring diverse aspects around a common middlepoint — this time a figurative centre.

24. Ibid.

25. On the identity-forming function of memory, cf. for example Moritz's *Beiträge zur Philosophie des Lebens*: 'Dies Gefühl meines Daseins, o Erinnerung, ist bloß dein Werk. Ohne dich, wie zerstückt, wie abgerissen, wäre das Leben, aber du reihest seine Augenblicke zusammen, wie auf eine Perlenschnur, daß keiner davon verloren geht [This feeling of my being, oh memory, is your work alone. Without you, life would seem fragmented, broken; but you arrange all moments together, as on a thread of pearls, so that none are lost] (W 3, p. 19). On the well as a 'symbolic object', whose symbolic value may be traced back to allegorical tradition, cf. Morgner, *'Das Wort aber ist Fleisch geworden'*, pp. 59 f.

26. AH, p. 621.

27. AH, p. 559.

28. The similar representation of the symbolic experience of nature in Goethe's *Werther* shows that this, however, can be a rather projective operation.

29. AH, p. 559.

30. AH, p. 554.

31. AH, p. 657.

32. AH, p. 540.

33. AH, p. 541.

34. AH, p. 599. A similar notion can be found in *Kinderlogik* (cf. W 3, p. 435).
35. Cf., for example, *Fragmente aus dem Tagebuch eines Geistersehers*: the purpose of nature is the 'Erhöhung der Denkkraft und die Veredlung des Geistes' [increase in the strength of thought and the ennoblement of the spirit] (DSE, p. 709).
36. AH, p. 600 f.
37. AH, p. 571.
38. AH, p. 572.
39. AH, p. 564.
40. AH, p. 573.
41. AH, p. 529.
42. The relationship between priest and blacksmith may be interpreted in many ways: literally speaking, Hartknopf did indeed learn both professions. Intellectually speaking, both professions stand for his physical ('leibliche') and his spiritual ('geistliche') birth (AH, p. 573); this is further illustrated by the mention of the mythological name 'Thubalkain' (AH, p. 574), the first ancestor of the blacksmith. The pairing gains existential-symbolic character lastly through the specific functions of the blacksmith and of the priest: the blacksmith realizes his creative work by imparting to it an 'unförmlichen Masse Bildung und Form' [unstructured measure of composition and form] and so is able 'eine Schöpfung neuer Wesen zusammenzuzwängen' [to achieve a creation of a new essence] (ibid.); similarly, Hartknopf as a priest cures various people whose inner being has been thrown out of balance, and he helps them to achieve a spiritual rebirth.
43. AH, p. 522.
44. AH, p. 525. A nearly identical phrase can be found in *Fragmenten aus dem Tagebuch eines Geistersehers* (cf. DSE, p. 748 f.)
45. AH, pp. 525, 557.
46. AH, p. 584.
47. AH, pp. 601, 624 f.
48. AH, p. 587.
49. Cf. A particularly original image: 'Der Händedruck hatte etwas Erhabenes, Nerven- und Seelenerschütterndes, und eine überzeugende Kraft, die mehr als der bündigste Syllogismus wirkte' [the handshake had something sublime, vibrations of nerve and soul, and a persuasive strength that had a greater effect than the most binding syllogism] (AH, p. 553) — which, in addition to the literal meaning, can also refer of course to the freemasonic handshake as a secret sign. For a comprehensive account of the related antagonism between natural and conventional signs in historical context, cf. Schneider, *Die Schwierige Sprache des Schönen*.
50. AH, p. 649.
51. In the text: of the gangs of do-gooders and of cosmopolitans, cf. AH, p. 525.
52. AH, p. 521.
53. Ibid.
54. To Goethe, 7 June 1788; cited from: AH, p. 1116.
55. See Horst Günther in his commentary on W 1, p. 590.
56. One could, quite speculatively, even see Hartknopf's own son (together with Sophie Erdmuthe), who was then raised by the foster father Kersting/Joseph, in this role.
57. Cf. Moritz's explanation of the novel in *Staats- und Gelehrtenzeitung des Hamburgischen unparteiischen Correspondenten*, which also emphasizes the reference to the audience and therefore the pedagogical-therapeutic intention (DSE, p. 1116 f.); see below.
58. Of course, this thought is not particularly revolutionary for the time; the blasphemous character of *Hartknopf* is revealed rather by the specific, individual, anti-dogmatic translation references, such as the famous quadrinity ('Viereinigkeit'), or the reinterpretation of the Last Supper.
59. Cf. for example, *Versuch einer kleinen praktischen Kinderlogik* (1786), which manifests many parallels to the novel (W 3, p. 441). In *Fragmenten aus dem Tagebuch eines Geistersehers*, the creation narrative is recommended as elementary reading for children (cf. W 3, p. 285).
60. Further dualisms in this context are: the inner and outer world of man, world and language, order and chaos, heaven and earth, body and 'spirit', destruction and construction, and in addition, the moral dualism of truth and falsehood, good and bad, and the anthropological dualism of motion and stillness, to culture and nature.

61. Cf. AH, p. 610.

62. AH, p. 617.

63. For more on Moritz's position on mysticism, cf. also his fragmentary text 'Über Mystik' (1789), in which he characterizes mysticism as a form of 'Metaphisik ohne Physik' [metaphysics without physics] (DSE, p. 897). Mysticism is completely non-figurative and non-empirical, but still has an undoubtedly strong appeal and strong effect on certain people; it must therefore be examined in terms of psychology. Cf. Bernhard Fischer on the relationship between mysticism and other aesthetic experience in Moritz's work: 'Kunstautonomie und Ende der Ikonographie. Zur historischen Problematik von "Allegorie" und "Symbol" im Winckelmanns, Moritz' und Goethes Kunsttheorie', *Deutsche Vierteljahrsschrift für Literaturwissenschaft und Geistesgeschichte*, 64 (1990), 247–77 (p. 259); Fischer also understands mysticism as a kind of system of language that can be applied to aesthetic experience.

64. AH, p. 623.

65. AH, p. 634.

66. AH, p. 623.

67. Hartknopf describes his own position on mysticism as follows: 'denn er konnte die Mystik wohl leiden, bis auf den Punkt hin, wo sie das menschliche Wissen ausschließet und für Torheit achtet. — Hartknopf hatte sehr viel Achtung für alles menschliche Wissen, es mochte sich aufwärts oder abwärts erstrecken; am liebsten war es ihm aber, wann es von der Ceder bis zum Ysop reichte' [for he could tolerate mysticism up until the point at which it excludes human knowledge and regards it as a folly. Hartknopf had great respect for human knowledge, whether it reached outwards or upwards; preferably, he would have it reach from the cedar to the hyssop] (AH, p. 632). Cedar and hyssop are not only particularly sonorous words that span the range of the alphabet. They also stand for the animals and plants, and therefore also the breadth of creation, with which Hartknopf has a particular relationship (in contrast to the mystics, with their fixation on the 'spirit', who kick an old poodle to death). They are, of course, ultimately a hidden reference to the Bible, as well: King Solomon wrote poetically of trees, 'from the cedar that is in Lebanon to the hyssop that grows out of the wall' (1 Kings 4. 33). In the Bible, the hyssop is also said to be a medicinal herb.

68. AH, p. 584.

69. AH, p. 586.

70. Cf. also the depiction of freemasonry in *Fragmente aus dem Tagebuche eines Geistersehers*: 'Als Bild betrachtet aber ist sie das schicklichste Symbol, um eine große edle uneigennützige Tätigkeit zu bezeichnen, wobei wir nicht uns selber zum Mittelpunkte machen, sondern außer uns ins Ganze wirken' [considered as an image, it is the most apt symbol that could be used to represent a great, noble, selfless activity; rather than making ourselves the focus, we seem to be outside of ourselves, part of the whole] (W 3, p. 309). For Moritz's position on freemasonry and his own freemasonic activities, cf. E. M. Batley: 'Masonic Thought in the Work of Karl Philipp Moritz: Sheen or Substance?', *London Germanic Studies*, 6 (1998), 121–46.

71. Thus Hartknopf exchanges the password 'humanitas' with Kersting (AH, p. 506). For the relationship of the *Hartknopf* novels to the literature of the secret societies of that time, cf. Voges, *Aufklärung und Geheimnis*, esp. ch. 3, III, which conceptualized a 'zunehmend ästhetisch realisierte Esoterik in pädagogischer Absicht' [ever more aesthetically realized esotericism with pedagogical intent] (p. 474) in the novel. Decisive for the structure of the novel is the figure of 'sinnstiftenden Verbergens' [meaningful concealment] (ibid.). Voges lists the exact references to the language of freemasonic rituals in detail (p. 517).

72. AH, p. 590. On Moritz's own membership of the Berlin's *St.-Johannes-Loge zur Beständigkeit*, cf. Voges (1987), p. 476 f.

73. AH, p. 591.

74. Ibid.

75. AH, p. 592.

76. AH, p. 595.

77. AH, p. 614

78. AH, p. 615.

79. Thus the title of an essay by Moritz, written in 1793.

80. AH, p. 525.
81. AH, p. 637.
82. AH, p. 637 f.
83. AH, p. 638.
84. AH, p. 645. As such, she embodies a human ideal of blissfulness that Moritz describes in his *Kinderlogik*: 'Das höchste Ziel seiner Wünsche ist *häusliche Zufriedenheit, verbunden mit dem ungestörten Genuß der schönen Natur*' [the highest goal of his desires is *domestic contentment, connected with the unhindered enjoyment of beautiful Nature*] (W 3, p. 470).
85. AH, p. 595.
86. AH, p. 592.
87. AH, p. 597.
88. AH, p. 555.
89. Cf. AH, p. 587 f., where Hartknopf's musical talent is first described, and then consequently his relationship to poetry, which he uses precisely 'wozu sie eigentlich da ist, zur Veredlung und Erhebung des Geistes, zur Beruhigung der Leidenschaft' [for its intended purpose: the ennoblement and exaltation of the spirit, the taming of passion] and as 'Seelenarzenei' [medicine for the soul] (AH, p. 589).
90. AH, p. 562.
91. S, p. 114.
92. W 3, p. 326.
93. Ibid., p. 325.
94. For more on the ancient tradition of this definition of allegory as 'metaphora continua' cf. Morgner, p. 21 f. Similar definitions may also be found in the eighteenth century, in Adelung's *Grammatisch-Kritischen Wörterbuch* or from Gottsched (cf. ibid.).
95. The prominence of the weaving metaphor has been explored above all by Barbara Thums, who also established the reference to genius. Barbara Thums, 'Das feine Gewebe der Organisation. Zum Verhältnis von Biologie und Ästhetik in Karl Philipp Moritz' Kunstautonomie und Ornamenttheorie', *Zeitschrift für Ästhetik und Allgemeine Kunstwissenschaft*, 49.2 (2004), 237–60 (p. 243).
96. It is also worth noting, as Hollmer and Meier do in their commentary (cf. DSE, p. 1136), that Moritz's writings on aesthetics were produced mostly after the first part of *Andreas Hartknopf* and parallel to the second.
97. Cf. for example, the above-cited series Wieland, Homer, Horace, Rousseau, Mendelssohn, Lessing, and in the same breath, the repudiation of Young (AH, p. 462). Significantly, the texts named (*Musarion*, Horace's epistles, *Emile*, *Phaidon*, *Nathan the Wise*) can all be understood as texts of wisdom in a broad sense, or as pedagogical texts. They all reveal an intention similar to that of *Hartknopf.*
98. Like the authors Klopstock and Young, who are treated rather negatively in the novel, being accused of a certain artificial, staged sensibility; see, for example, the passage in which the narrator watches the sunset with Klopstock and is therefore criticized by Hartknopf (cf. AH, p. 581 f.).
99. Note a metafictional reflection in the text: 'Warum sind die Anekdotenbücher so voll von komischen Predigergeschichten? [...] Kömmt es nicht daher, weil man einen gewissen angenommenen feierlichen Ernst schon voraussetzt, mit dem das geringste Komische weit mehr, als im gemeinen Leben absticht?' [Why are the books of anecdotes so full of strange preacher stories? [...] Does it not come as a result of one's assuming a certain, affected, ceremonial seriousness, with which even the slightest comic moment stands out much more than in everyday life?] (AH, p. 649). Through a staging of their profession, the preachers effectuate the opposite. Mark Boulby, too, characterizes the novel as a 'weird melting pot of a variety of traditions and of several styles': *Karl Philipp Moritz*, p. 227.
100. AH, p. 617.
101. AH, p. 657.
102. Morgner, too, insists (p. 41) that the boundaries between allegory and symbol were by no means carefully delineated around the end of the eighteenth century, nor are they today: 'Insofern steht ein modernes, symbolisches Verständnis von Kunst, sofern sich ihre Deutungsoffenheit

aus alternativen Lesarten konstruiert, in der Tradition der Allegorese, denn an die Stelle des drei- oder vierfachen tritt der mehrfache, aber nicht unbegrenzte Schriftsinn. Der Unterschied von Allegorie und Symbol wäre dann kein qualitativer, sondern ein quantitativer' [In this sense, there is a modern, symbolic understanding of art; its interpretive openness is constructed by various different readings, in the tradition of allegoresis. For instead of three or four meanings, we get multiple (but not unlimited) possibilities for meaning. The difference between allegory and symbol would be then not qualitative, but quantitative]. Mark Boulby makes a similar statement about the *Hartknopf* novels: 'The line between allegory and symbolism is being crossed here at many points' (*Karl Philipp Moritz*, p. 239).

103. Cf. also the commentary of Hollmer and Meier (DSE, pg. 1142).

104. If we follow the model of the fourfold exegesis of the Bible in distinguishing a literal, an allegorical, a moral, and an anagogical meaning: first, on the literal level, the novel is the story of a concrete individual in a concrete, physical reality; next, it is an allegorical representation of biblical stories and fundamental ideas, in which Hartknopf may be typologically related to Christ or the disciple Andrew; on the moral level, it conveys wisdom; on the anagogical level, it is the proclamation of an imminent aesthetic, one that is truer to the ideal of the beautiful and is thereby connected to another life ideal as represented by Sophie.

105. Schrimpf, for example, has already pointed out the similar diversity of topics and genres: 'Er ist ein Freimaurerroman, ein Pastorenroman, ein Schwärmer- und Ketzerroman; er ist aber dazu ein pädagogischer, ein empfindsamer, ein satirischer und humoristischer Roman' [It is a freemasonic novel, a clerical novel, a fanciful and heretical novel; but it is also a pedagogical, sentimental, satirical and humorous novel] (cited in DSE, p. 1127).

106. *Über Mystik* (DSE, p. 897).

107. Cited in DSE, p. 1117.

108. This is a realization that can also be found, for example, in Lessing's *Erziehung des Menschengeschlechts*.

109. Cf. in particular *Der letzte Zweck des menschlichen Denkens. Gesichtspunkt* (1786).

110. *Kinderlogik*, W 3, p. 445.

111. Cf. the formulation in the rhapsodic rendering of Hartknopf's sermon: 'Ist es die Fassungskraft nicht selbst, die sich erweitern muß, um das Edle aufzufassen?' [is it not mental capacity itself that must be furthered in order to grasp what is noble?] (AH, p. 618).

112. Voges makes a similar point, p. 517: 'Die episodenhafte, parataktisch reihende Struktur der *Hartknopf*-Romane erweist sich bei näherem Hinsehen als eine lakonisch gefügte Kette bedeutender Bilder' [the episodic, paratactically arranged structure of the *Hartknopf* novels proves itself upon closer inspection to be a laconically assembled chain of meaningful images].

113. Sabine Schneider also speaks of a 'Projekt der Resemiotisierung' [project of resemiotization], 'das den Bruch zwischen Zeichen und Dingen zu kitten und diese somit wieder in eine wesentliche Beziehung zueinander zu bringen hätte' [that bridges the gap between signs and things, and so was to have re-established a meaningful relationship between them] (p. 73).

114. For more on Moritz's influence on the artists and thinkers of his time, also through his lectures at the academy, which were attended for example by Tieck and Wackenroder, as well as the Humboldt brothers: cf. Boulby, *Karl Philipp Moritz*, pp. 207–23.

115. Friedrich Wilhelm Joseph Schelling, *Philosophie der Kunst*, in *Texte zur Philosophie der Kunst*, ed. by Werner Beierwaltes (Stuttgart: Reclam, 1982), p. 176. For more on Schelling's adaptation of Moritz's *Götterlehre*, cf. Boulby, *Karl Philipp Moritz*, p. 196: 'Schlegel's dependence is a good example of the influence of what was to be its author's best-known book. The *Götterlehre* soon became a standard text in schools, and was reprinted ten times in the course of the next seventy years'.

116. Ibid., p. 183.

117. Ibid., p. 194.

118. Ibid., p. 195.

119. Ibid., p. 211.

CHAPTER 4

Comparative Morphology and Symbolic Mediation in Goethe

Helmut Hühn

Two forms of thought are equally fundamental for Goethe the naturalist ('Naturforscher') and Goethe the poet: morphology and symbolism. They are both important patterns of orientation in the world and of interpretation of the world, whose role throughout the Goethean oeuvre can hardly be overestimated. The beginnings of Goethe's morphology date back to his co-operation with Herder in the 1780s, while the first traces of his discovery and reflection of the symbolic may be found in his 1797 correspondence with Schiller. In what follows, I shall explore the relationship between these two fundamental forms of thought, their similarities and convergences as well as their differences and divergences. I will proceed in four steps. First, I shall outline Goethe's morphological thinking as it presents itself in the mid-1790s, following a decade of intense study and practice on Goethe's part. My focus will be on a note made in 1796 in which he develops the methodological principle ('Grundsatz')[1] of his morphology. With this in mind, I shall secondly look at the epistemological 'primal scene' of Goethe's theory of the symbol. In August 1797, on a journey to Switzerland, he made a stop in Frankfurt, his native town, where he suddenly became aware of a new form of object perception and object experience which so struck him that he immediately set to discussing it in a letter to Schiller. The central categories of his theory of the symbol, viz. intuition ('Anschauung'), representation ('Repräsentation') and totality ('Totalität'), appear as early as this Frankfurt letter, prefiguring the characteristic way in which Goethe was to conceive the relationship between the universal ('das Allgemeine') and the particular ('das Besondere') into his late work: as a dialectics, that is, not of nature but of history. For the symbolic objects mentioned by Goethe in this letter are genuinely historical: Frankfurt's marketplace and the site ('Raum') where his grandfather Textor's house had stood before being reduced to a pile of rubble ('Schutthaufen')[2] by the French bombardment. Just as morphology allows us to orientate ourselves in nature and even to conceive creative Nature herself, symbolism provides us with a basic guide to human history. In a third step I shall explain Schiller's critique of the Goethean conception of symbolic objects. It is not confined to the category of intuition, since Schiller makes it very clear that symbolic objects reveal themselves neither to immediate intuition nor, for that matter, to intuition alone but that they acquire their meaning only through an act of interpretation. Acknowledging the role of this interpretative act, and thereby of the fundamental contribution of the interpreting individual, did, however, entail serious problems not only for Goethe's as-yet sketchy theory of the symbol; it subsequently also led to modifications (which can only be hinted at in the present paper) in his morphology. Fourthly and lastly, I propose to ask in which way the thought forms of morphology and symbolism can contribute to the cognizability and representation of totality and how they may become relevant for a reflection on the unity of historical events.

The 'Principle' of Morphological Thinking

As we can see from his essay *Der Versuch als Vermittler von Object und Subject* (1793), Goethe's study of nature entered a methodological phase in the 1790s. He was now able to explicate his intuitions by coining the word 'morphology' in 1796.[3] With this new concept, he presented the results of a long thought process.[4] 'Morphology' was the comparative study of the forms or shapes of organisms ('Gestalten'), and in particular of their formation and transformation. Whereas in 1796 Goethe conceived it as a universal science of nature, he later reduced its scope within the field of natural history,[5] while on the other hand extending it beyond that field to cover the history of literature, art and science. The conception of morphology as a universal science of nature figures in a letter to Schiller dated 12 November 1796, where Goethe, freshly returned from the Ilmenau mine, writes:

> Durch die unmittelbare Berührung mit den Gebürgen und durch das Voigtische Mineralienkabinet bin ich diese Zeit her wieder in das Steinreich geführt worden. Es ist mir sehr lieb, daß ich so zufälligerweise diese Betrachtungen erneuert habe, ohne welche denn doch die berühmte *Morphologie* nicht vollständig werden würde. Ich habe diesmal diesen Naturen einige gute Ansichten abgewonnen, die ich gelegentlich mittheilen werde.[6]

> [Thanks to the direct contact with the mountains and to Voigt's mineral cabinet I have since been re-introduced to the realm of rocks. I am very glad that I have thus by chance been able to renew these reflections without which the famous morphology would, after all, not reach completion. This time, I have gained some good insights into these natures, which I shall impart to you in due course.]

Goethe's reference to 'the famous morphology' makes it as clear as does Schiller's prompt reply ('Ich freue mich, wenn Sie mir Ihre neuen Entdeckungen für die Morphologie mittheilen' [I am looking forward to receiving your news about the new discoveries you have made in morphology])[7] that we are dealing here with a key word ('Kennwort')[8] which evokes a whole context being discussed by the two authors. The compound noun 'morphology' hearkens back to the Greek language and philosophy. Aristotle had defined *morphê* as the shape of a sensible thing. In an oft-quoted example given in his *Metaphysics*, Aristotle explains the difference between *morphê* and *eidos*:[9] a smith makes a brazen circle, where the brass is the matter, the geometrical figure of the circle the *eidos* and the circle the *morphê*.[10]

Morphê is thus the shape of the *synholon*, of the concrete thing or concrete whole. In the process of forging, according to Aristotle, the *eidos* or intelligible form, which pre-exists, emerges in a specific materiality.

Goethe conceived his morphology as a science of metamorphosis and of type. He thought that the *Gestalten* of organisms were modifications of the archetype ('Urbild') of each group or type of organisms, type being for him not merely a mental construct but a real principle adhered to by Nature when bringing about organisms. Type is apprehended by a specific form of intuition, viz. a constant interaction between empirical and ideating intuition.[11]

The process of formation of the organisms — paradigm of a dynamic whole — is characterized by continual transformation. *Gestalt* is a transitory, developing form. The naturalist must therefore aspire to a form of knowledge that can cope with this dynamics of *formation through transformation*. He must not cling to a single isolated *Gestalt* but ought to become aware of the succession of *Gestalten* as a whole. While the individual *Gestalt* is accessible to empirical intuition where, as Goethe puts it, we use our 'bodily eyes' ('leibliche Augen'), the transition from one changeable *Gestalt* to another is captured by the 'mind's eyes' ('geistige Augen')[12] which operate genetically and at the same time synoptically and integratively. Only by detaching ourselves from the individual empirical *Gestalten* while simultaneously remaining sensually faithful to them can we productively intuit the idea which manifests itself in the process of formation; to know the idea means to comprehend its whole process of development. The idea in Goethe differs essentially from the Platonic idea in that it is not timeless: it appears in time as a sensibly perceptible shape. Goethe therefore changed the Platonic concept of idea in an important way.[13] In the context of his morphology he also framed a particular conception of time, according to which time manifests itself sensually in the metamorphoses of the *Gestalten*.

Methodologically speaking, Goethe usually proceeds from the particular in his quest for the whole to which this particular belongs, or of which it is a part. He refuses to neglect the particular in favour of what philosophical tradition calls 'abstraction'. As Schiller succinctly put it in an early characterization of Goethe's thinking: 'Sie nehmen die ganze Natur zusammen, um über das Einzelne Licht zu bekommen, in der Allheit ihrer Erscheinungsarten suchen Sie den Erklärungsgrund für das Individuum auf' [You look at nature as a whole in order to illuminate its individual parts: within the fullness of nature's manifestations you seek explanations for individual entities].[14] The guiding hermeneutical principle of this morphological approach is that the individual empirical *Gestalten* that appear in the course of the process of formation are not contingent and that by their succession we can cognize the basic shape or idea ('Idee') — which Goethe in 1798 also termed the 'pure phenomenon' ('reines Phänomen')[15] — thereby knowing the explanation for each transitory *Gestalt*. For Goethe, this research method of intuitive knowledge was a compromise between empiricist induction on the one hand and the deductive efforts of a speculative natural philosophy on the other. Schiller called this procedure a 'rational empiricism' ('rationelle Empirie');[16] Hegel later spoke of a 'sinnigere[s] Naturanschauen' [more meaningful way of intuitively perceiving nature] and of a vivid contemplation of nature.[17] It was Hegel, however, who also pointed out to

Goethe that intuition must not be ranked above reflection: one cannot philosophize from intuition.[18]

The morphological approach in Goethe is an instrument with which to acquire knowledge of the wholeness or totality. Through it, the integrity of the organism's process of formation becomes evident, as does the necessity of each specific appearance. At the same time, the metamorphic process imparts to us an intuitive perception of self-creative Nature (*natura naturans*): for Goethe meant not simply to describe the metamorphosis of plants but to demonstrate, on this basis, the metamorphosis of the whole of nature,[19] its constant alteration, in which man himself, being a creature of nature as well as of knowledge, is involved.[20] The morphological contemplation of nature as conceived by Goethe is therefore always, by implication, an attempt at human self-knowledge. The unity of nature is seen as a unity in time, as the evolution of an organic whole which comprises the human world. As his note from 1796 makes clear, Goethe at this time explicitly included man in nature's succession of *Gestalten*. He describes an ontological principle which he has been following instinctively for a long time: all that is expresses itself, presents itself, explicates itself in such a way that the 'inner' becomes visible and takes shape in the 'outer'. This ontological principle gives substance to Goethe's concept of living intuition and illustrates his faith in the basic perceptibility of the world. It is one of his well-known tenets that there is nothing like contemplation with the living eye.

With his principle of morphology, Goethe affirms that it is the essence itself which appears and that, consequently, appearance is not a mere delusion but a manifestation of what is real for the 'outer' as well as the 'inner sense' ('äußerer/innerer Sinn').[21] Goethe's thinking in 1796 was primarily ontological, not transcendental. Nevertheless, he adopted the Kantian terminology according to which the 'outer sense' is that property of the mind whereby we represent to ourselves objects as outside us, and all as in space, while the 'inner sense' enables us to represent inner states (which include the representation of external objects) in their temporal relations.[22] In his note, Goethe envisages a peculiar interlocking of the inner and the outer, characteristic not only of his morphology but also later to be taken up — structurally, at least — in his conception of the symbol. He deliberately correlates the self-manifestation of that which is with the individual's cognition of such self-manifestation. The morphological approach relies on the inner sense as a temporal sense, which in the dynamic succession of *Gestalten* is able to apprehend creative Nature herself. Morphology can thus be described as an attempt at understanding temporal Nature through a living participation in her creative spirit of productivity.

On the basis of this principle, Goethe established the possibility of a morphological semiotics of Nature: all things natural appear as what they are, while in this self-manifestation simultaneously referring to Nature as a whole. That is, roughly, where matters stood in morphology at the time when Goethe, in a discussion with Schiller, began to develop his concept of the symbolic.

The Beginnings of Symbolism

In 1797, Goethe made intense preparations for a journey that was meant again to take him to Italy but in the event, owing to Napoleon's Italian campaign and the disturbances occasioned by it, had to be broken off in Switzerland. It was on this journey, stopping over in his native Frankfurt, that he developed a new form of object perception which can also be described as a new form of aesthetic perception ('ästhetische Wahrnehmung').[23] Goethe had intended to appreciate through immediate experience ('unmittelbare Erfahrung') the different natural-historical, geographical, economic and political conditions he encountered on his trip; he wanted to study and know the particular in its complex mediatedness. Nevertheless, his attitude towards empirical knowledge was at that time highly ambivalent. On the one hand, he feared the 'millionenfache Hydra der Empirie' [million-headed hydra of empiricism],[24] the overkill of experience and the profusion of empirical data which, given their multiplicity, disorder and heterogeneity, threatened to make all perception of totality impossible, causing him to lose sight of the whole for the details. On the other hand, he sought, in an unprecedented manner, to empirically saturate sober observation, in the hope that this saturation would in itself provide a theory capable of organizing the wealth of phenomena.[25] In his letter to Schiller, composed in Switzerland on 14 October 1797, he wrote: 'Man erfährt wieder bey dieser Gelegenheit daß eine vollständige Erfahrung die Theorie in sich enthalten muß' [On this occasion one observes again that a complete experience must contain its theory in itself].[26] He therefore developed new forms of 'diversification' ('Vermannichfaltigung')[27] as well as of collecting and filing his experimental procedures. Having returned to Frankfurt for the first time in many years, he was surprised to find that certain objects produced 'sentimental' experiences in him. The word 'sentimental' is used here by Goethe in the twofold sense of a 'sentimental journey' evoking feelings and sensations, and of Schiller's 'sentimental poet' who is moved by certain objects to experience mental processes, ideas and reflections. Goethe says expressly that these symbolic objects had come to him in his 'calm and cold manner of observing or mere watching' ('ruhigen und kalten Weg des Beobachtens, ja des bloßen Sehens'),[28] that he had not been in a poetic mood ('poetische Stimmung')[29] and that symbolic objects cannot by any means become poetic ones without prior transformation. He emphasizes that (I quote from a previous letter written in Frankfurt):

> Für einen Reisenden geziemt sich ein skeptischer Realism; was noch idealistisch an mir ist, wird in einem Schatullchen, wohlverschlossen, mitgeführt wie jenes undenische Pygmäenweibchen.[30]

> [For a traveller, a sceptical realism is fitting. Whatever idealism I still have is carried with me, locked in a little strongbox like the famous undine female pigmy.]

Now where do the affects evoked by these objects come from? Goethe, observing himself even as he observes the phenomena, explains to Schiller:

> Ich habe daher die Gegenstände, die einen solchen Effect hervorbringen,

genau betrachtet und zu meiner Verwunderung bemerkt daß sie eigentlich symbolisch sind, das heißt, wie ich kaum zu sagen brauche, es sind eminente Fälle, die, in einer charakteristischen Mannigfaltigkeit, als Repräsentanten von vielen andern dastehen, eine gewisse Totalität in sich schließen, eine gewisse Reihe fordern, ähnliches und fremdes in meinem Geiste aufregen und so von außen wie von innen an eine gewisse Einheit und Allheit Anspruch machen. Sie sind also, was ein glückliches Sujet dem Dichter ist, glückliche Gegenstände für den Menschen, und weil man, indem man sie mit sich selbst recapitulirt, ihnen keine poetische Form geben kann, so muß man ihnen doch eine ideale geben, eine menschliche im höhern Sinn, das man auch mit einem so sehr mißbrauchten Ausdruck sentimental nannte, und Sie werden also wohl nicht lachen, sondern nur lächeln, wenn ich Ihnen hiermit zu meiner eignen Verwunderung darlege, daß ich, wenn ich irgend von meinen Reisen etwas für Freunde oder für's Publicum aufzeichnen soll, wahrscheinlich noch in Gefahr komme empfindsame Reisen zu schreiben.[31]

[I have therefore looked carefully at the objects which produce such an effect and noticed with amazement that they are really symbolic, i.e., as I barely need to mention, they are eminent cases which stand as representatives, in characteristic multiplicity, of many others and enclose within themselves a certain totality; they demand a certain sequence, excite in my mind similar and unfamiliar instances, and therefore lay claim to a certain unity and universality from the outside and the inside. They therefore constitute what is a fortunate subject matter for the *poet*, namely, fortunate objects for *mankind*. And since by recapitulating them with oneself, one cannot give them a *poetic* form, they must be given an *ideal* form, a *human* one in a higher sense — what one used to call with a much misused expression 'sentimental'. You will therefore probably not laugh if I declare to you herewith my own amazement that I might run the danger of writing sentimental journeys, if I am to write anything of my travels for friends or the public.]

Symbolic objects, then, are 'eminent cases', standing out from others. In the same letter, Goethe gives two instructive examples of what he means:

Bis jetzt habe ich nur zwey solcher Gegenstände gefunden: den Platz auf dem ich wohne [sc. der Roßmarkt schräg gegenüber der Hauptwache], der in Absicht seiner Lage und alles dessen was darauf vorgeht in einem jeden Momente symbolisch ist, und den Raum meines großväterlichen Hauses, Hofes und Gartens, der aus dem beschränktesten, patriarchalischen Zustande, in welchem ein alter Schultheiß von Frankfurt lebte, durch klug unternehmende Menschen zum nützlichsten Waaren- und Marktplatz verändert wurde. Die Anstalt ging durch sonderbare Zufälle bey dem Bombardement zu Grunde und ist jetzt, größtentheils als Schutthaufen, noch immer das doppelte dessen werth was vor 11 Jahren von den gegenwärtigen Besitzern an die Meinigen bezahlt worden.[32]

[Up to now I have found only two such objects: the place where I am staying [i.e. Roßmarkt diagonally opposite Hauptwache], which is symbolic with regard to its location and everything that happens there every moment; and the site of my grandfather's house with its yard and garden, which some intelligent and enterprising people transformed from the most limited patriarchal estate, in which an old mayor of Frankfurt had lived, to a very useful place for selling goods and food. The establishment went to pieces during the bombardment

under strange circumstances, but even as a pile of rubble it is still twice as
valuable as what the present owners paid to my family eleven years ago.]

Hence it emerges that, with symbolic objects, we are no longer in the sphere of
nature but have entirely moved to the field of social and historical experience.
Goethe lived with his mother at Roßmarkt (Horse Market), which presented him
with the opportunity to experience a real metropolis (as compared with Weimar)
as well as the deep historical change it had recently witnessed. The square itself did
not belong to the historical centre of the city, which had evolved into a commercial
hub. The circumstances of the time had strongly affected the city. The French
bombardment that had taken place the year before[33] had laid in ruins, among other
buildings, the house of Goethe's grandfather Textor (which is specifically paid
tribute to as a *lieu de mémoire* in *Dichtung und Wahrheit*),[34] although in economic
terms, it was more valuable, having been converted into a marketplace. Goethe's
use of words such as 'place' and 'site' makes it clear that symbolic objects are not
simply real objects at hand. They are objects of perception, i.e. constellations and
configurations that can be experienced by the senses but cannot, by virtue of their
characteristic multiplicity ('charakteristische Mannigfaltigkeit'), be subsumed under
a specific concept or category. Symbolic objects, being intuitive objects, obey the
logic of part and whole; they do not, like discursive concepts, conform to the logic
of subordination and superordination.

It must be pointed out that the concept of the manifold, or of multiplicity,
mentioned in the letter originates from Goethe's morphology. There, the manifold
Gestalten of natural organisms evolve from the unity of disposition.[35] Put differently,
their multiplicity is already present in the unity of disposition, which in its turn is
present in the multiplicity of *Gestalten*. It must, however, be equally pointed out
that no analogy exists between the morphological multiplicity of organisms and
the multiplicity of symbolic objects. The latter, in their phenomenal individuality,
render a certain state of affairs intuitively perceptible — they bring something to
light which is the case. Being complex, specific objects, they do not directly refer
to a universal idea. Their symbolic quality is, after all, not purely synecdochical but
rather of a metonymic kind. They are therefore not representative in the way of *pars
pro toto*, where an example is selected to stand for the whole, but act, as Goethe says,
'as representatives of many others', because in them some state of affairs of a higher
universality shines through. A symbolic object, for Goethe, refers primarily to other
'eminent cases'; it is the 'Symbol vieler tausend ander[er] Fälle' [symbol of many
thousands of similar cases].[36] This has not been sufficiently taken into account by
students of Goethe's conception of the symbol. It also presents a marked structural
contrast to the metaphysical conception developed by Friedrich Wilhelm Joseph
Schelling in his *Philosophie der Kunst*.[37] The referential structure outlined by Goethe
in his letter is the following: a specific object, i.e. a meaningful individual entity,
refers to a thousand other individuals, and it is only through their 'neighbourly'
reciprocal way of referring that together they refer to some higher universality. In
this sense, the symbolic representation can be said to be of an indirect nature, which
also implies that the universal is not simply 'enclosed' in the particular. Like Kant's
'aesthetic idea' ('ästhetische Idee [...] die viel zu denken veranlaßt'), Goethe's symbolic

object occasions 'much thought'[38] and requires the use of reflective judgment ('reflektierende Urteilskraft'). The 'characteristic multiplicity' of objects signifies wealth[39] and complexity but explicitly rules out metaphysical totality. For Goethe, only conditioned totalities can be interpreted as symbols. What does this mean? We need to distinguish between a totality that forms part of a more comprehensive totality and a totality that cannot be conceived of as such a part because it is defined as comprehensiveness itself, or totality as such. The first might be called a relative or conditioned totality, while the latter would be absolute or unconditioned totality. Now unconditioned totality cannot become an object of consciousness in the same way as can the partial or conditioned totalities. For consciousness can position itself vis-à-vis a conditioned totality but not the unconditioned one of which it is itself a part.[40] Goethe's symbolism is rooted in the tradition of criticism of metaphysics. From the very outset, he kept the symbolic thought form apart from the idea of a metaphysical, universalistic manner of reference espoused by Schelling in Jena, who thought of art as a sensual representation of the Absolute.[41] For Schelling, symbols are subject-objects: intuitive, or eidetic, images that, starting from an exemplary object of experience, reveal to the subject of cognition the Absolute as the experience-transcending identity of subject and object.

According to Goethe the subject, with the help of its inner sense, will recapitulate the meaning of the symbolic objects.[42] This review of objects will always only lead to a certain limited totality, limited not least because of the subject involved. This limited totality is gradually constructed in the wake of the perceptual experience and is not itself an object of immediate intuition. '[D]aß ein "Schutthaufen" doppelt so viel wert ist wie "vor elf Jahren" ein vollständiges Haus, kann nur *gegen* alle Anschauung richtig sein' [The idea that a 'pile of rubble' is twice as valuable as the intact house was 'eleven years ago' can only hold true *against* all intuition], Heinz Schlaffer rightly observes in his Marx-inspired critique of Goethean classical aesthetics.[43] Yet the sequence-mediated synthesis of unity and multiplicity, described by Goethe as early as his *Versuch* of 1793 as a method of his science of nature, is not reconstructed accurately enough by Schlaffer. This is why Schlaffer fails to appreciate the specific process of experience triggered by the intuition of symbolic objects. As we have seen above, symbolic objects demand 'a certain sequence', they excite 'similar and unfamiliar instances' in the contemplating mind and 'therefore lay claim to a certain unity and universality'. This means that the sequence of representations is more than a sequence of subjective, arbitrary associations. The subject, affected by the objects of perception, goes back to its own past experiences, remembers similar and dissimilar instances and can, through this work of reflection, muster and deepen its present experiences. That 'a certain [...] universality' is achieved by reflecting upon the object's 'characteristic multiplicity' does, however, never imply a claim on the part of the contemplating subject to know the comprehensive totality.

To sum up the argument, the epistemological 'primal scene' of Goethe's theory of the symbol makes clear three things. First, the meaning of symbolic objects is not simply given in their intuition, nor is their intuition wholly devoid of concepts, since Goethe tells us that he worked through his apodemic plan in

Frankfurt,[44] a catalogue of phenomena to observe he had drawn up in order to be able to systematically focus on complex relationships like those between nature and culture. Second, symbolic objects can exemplify (a certain) universality only indirectly and by way of mediation. Third, the universality thus re-presented commands only 'a certain' unity and 'a certain' totality. It is not the totality of an all-encompassing whole but the limited totality of a structure or relationship of which the intuiting and reflecting individual becomes aware. Reconstructing the relationship of the universal and the particular with a view to symbolic objects leads us to acknowledge the limits of symbolic visualization ('Veranschaulichung') as well as of symbolic re-presentation ('Vergegenwärtigung'). Symbolic objects do not merely refer to some absent entity, they re-present what is through their specific *Gestalt*.[45] In this way they do not simply mean something, they actually are what they mean. Still, the symbol and the symbolized, being and meaning do not entirely coincide for Goethe. Symbolic objects are 'fortunate objects for mankind'[46] in that subject and object co-operate, as it were, in the act of cognition. The subject draws from the object of perception whatever the latter exemplifies, and reflects upon it. The object therefore opens up the subject's own world anew and helps the subject to have a new experience of itself. Hence, the experience of symbolic objects leads us not into the 'empirical breadth of the world' ('empirische Weltbreite')[47] but deepens our understanding of the world.[48] How did Schiller react to these views?

Schiller's Critique

The 'sentimental phenomenon' ('sentimentale Phänomen')[49] acting on Goethe in Frankfurt was appraised very differently by Schiller, who in his reply strictly refers to the concept of sentimental poet framed by himself in his *Ueber naive und sentimentalische Dichtung*. According to this concept it is not the objects themselves which affect the subject in the way described by Goethe, nor is it emotion which gives rise to reflection but, on the contrary, reflection which engenders emotion:

> Dieser [sc. der sentimentalische Dichter] *reflektirt* über den Eindruck, den die Gegenstände auf ihn machen und nur auf jene Reflexion ist die Rührung gegründet, in die er selbst versetzt wird, und uns versetzt. Der Gegenstand wird hier auf eine Idee bezogen, und nur auf dieser Beziehung beruht seine dichterische Kraft.[50]

> [He (the sentimental poet) reflects on the impression which objects make on him, and the emotion into which he himself is transposed and into which he transposes us is based only on that reflection. The object is related here to an idea and its poetic strength rests only on this relationship.]

This is how Schiller had put it in his famous treatise from 1795. In his response to Goethe he explains that Goethe's experience originates from the human need to appropriate the world in its depth through sentiment; it ultimately is

> ein Effekt des poetischen Strebens, welches, sey es aus Gründen die in dem Gegenstand, oder solchen, die in dem Gemüth liegen, nicht ganz erfüllt wird. Eine solche poetische Forderung, ohne eine reine poetische Stimmung und ohne einen poetischen Gegenstand scheint Ihr Fall gewesen zu seyn [...].[51]

[an effect of poetic strivings which are not quite fulfilled, either for reasons that lie in the object or for those that lie in the mind. Such a poetic demand without a pure poetic mood and without a poetic object seems to have been your case.]

Schiller then turns to the crucial difference between Goethe and himself, viz. the issue of the generation of meaning. To him as a trained Kantian it was obvious that the object's meaning is established by the subject. The object is not symbolic in itself: it becomes symbolic only when a subject apprehends it as a symbol by means of its faculty of ideas:

> Nur eins muß ich dabei noch erinnern. Sie drücken sich so aus, als wenn es hier sehr auf den Gegenstand ankäme, was ich nicht zugeben kann. Freilich der Gegenstand muß etwas *bedeuten*, so wie der poetische etwas *seyn* muß; aber zulezt kommt es auf das *Gemüth* an, ob ihm ein Gegenstand etwas bedeuten soll, und so däucht mir das Leere und Gehaltreiche mehr im Subject als im Object zu liegen. Das Gemüth ist es, welches hier die Grenze steckt, und das Gemeine oder Geistreiche kann ich auch hier wie überal nur in der Behandlung nicht in der Wahl des Stoffes finden. Was Ihnen die zwey angeführten Plätze gewesen sind, würde Ihnen unter andern Umständen, bei einer mehr aufgeschloßenen poetischen Stimmung jede *Strasse, Brücke*, jedes *Schiff*, ein *Pflug* oder irgend ein anderes mechanisches Werkzeug vielleicht geleistet haben.[52]

> [I must point out just one more thing. You express yourself in such a way that one must think that the important thing is the object. I cannot grant you that. Of course, the object must *signify* something, just as the poetic subject matter must *be* something. But ultimately it is a matter of the *mind* whether an object means something; thus methinks the empty or the substantial quality lies more in the mind than in the matter. It is the mind which creates the limit. As always, I can find the common or the substantial only in the treatment, not in the choice of subject matter. Those two places you mentioned which were so important to you could have been substituted, under other circumstances and in a more poetic mood, by any *street, bridge, boat, plough* or any other mechanical tool.]

Taken together, this points less to the subtle difference ('zarte Differenz') to which Goethe was to play it down later,[53] than to a fundamental contrast between the two poets. In Goethe's conception, the symbolic meaning falls on the side of the object. The contemplated object, in manifesting its meaning, allows us to capture a historical reality. The object reveals itself, its meaning and thereby a historical context that in a specific way becomes visible in it and, through this visibility, accessible to reflection as well. For Schiller, on the other hand, the symbolic meaning lies not in the object but is brought forth by the subject: '[d]er Bedeutungsreichtum des Objektes' [the object's richness in meaning] turns out to be 'eine Funktion der Bedeutungsfülle des Subjektes' [a function of the subject's richness in meaning].[54] For each object there is the possibility of being perceived in various different ways. Schiller's critique has many implications which cannot be elaborated upon here. If, for example, meaning is ultimately assigned to objects by the subjects, then the problem of the intersubjective and cultural dimensions of symbolization immediately arises. Can every object become symbolic? Can an object be assigned totally different meanings by different subjects? How can subjects communicate about the meanings assigned by them, and what are the bases and conditions of their assignments?

As for the 'sceptical realism' ('skeptische Realism') to which Goethe subscribed in 1797, it seems to lend itself to ontological hypostasizations. Goethe's early conception of the symbol is certainly not without such hypostasizations, and it substantially lacks an intersubjective dimension. The morphological conception of reality on the one hand and the claim to visibleness on the other also formed the basis of that defining opposition of symbol and allegory which Goethe, upon his arrival in Switzerland, together with Johann Heinrich Meyer started developing in the field of the theory of representation in art.[55] Had he by then already seen through Schiller's critique with all its implications, he would probably not have been able to dismiss the allegorical form of representation in the fine arts with such conviction. Radicalizing Meyer's ideas, Goethe in effect accused the allegorical forms of representation in the fine arts of 'destroying whatever interest there is in the representation, driving the mind back, so to speak, into itself and depriving its eyes of that which is actually being represented' (daß sie 'das Interesse an der Darstellung selbst zerstören und den Geist gleichsam in sich selbst zurücktreiben und seinen Augen das, was wirklich dargestellt ist, entziehen').[56] The deprecation of the allegory and the appreciation of the symbol need to be seen against the backdrop of a fundamental crisis of the semiotic systems around 1800.[57] It then becomes clear that the Goethean 'sceptical realism' with its assumption is by no means free of all idealization: for it is an idealization in all but name when objects are declared totalities in themselves whose meaning is self-evident. Herder's 'natural symbols' ('Natursymbole'),[58] put forward against the Kantian conception of a faculty of imagination which symbolically represents the ideas of reason by means of an analogy, follow the same logic of idealization, though this cannot be pursued in any detail here. Schiller's criticism did affect Goethe, who could not help noticing that the tension between 'Natur und der unmittelbaren Erfahrung' [nature and immediate experience],[59] which he thought to have successfully overcome — with the help of symbolic objects — even in the field of human history, presented itself anew.

The Methodological Potential of the Two Forms of Thought

The morphological and the symbolic forms of thought embrace both art and nature. They belong closely together, given that Goethe developed the symbolic point of view from the morphological one. In 1796 he had found the basis of both thought forms in the principle that all that is shows and manifests itself in phenomena accessible to intuition. The poet and the naturalist alike in Goethe adhered to this principle right into his late years. Already in the 'primal scene' of his theory of the symbol, the natural context to which scholars have long restricted their interpretations was actually transcended: it was a genuinely historical experience that Goethe touched upon in 1797 with regard to Frankfurt's Roßmarkt and the site of his grandfather's estate. The historical changes identified by him in his native town did not follow an evolutionary growth pattern but were of a revolutionary origin, and so could not and cannot be reduced to a natural type of development. The symbolic 'objects', viewed as particularly telling cases, exemplify a general historical transformation that takes place in each moment of (contemporary) history and is, in all its complexity, conspicuous to any individual who is familiar with the sites in question and is at the same time able to look at them with fresh eyes — as if it were for the first time. Only one who is familiar with these objects can form a morphological sequence of development in his mind's eye and detect a historical universality in this metamorphic process. The idea of 'eminent cases' points to the way in which Goethe conceived of the relationship of the individual, the particular and the universal. The individual in itself cannot illustrate ('veranschaulichen') a universal. What is individual becomes, symbolically conceived, a particular which thanks to its quality of 'eminent case' refers to many other cases: it is now a 'symbol of many thousands of similar cases'. The universal establishes itself and becomes knowable via this very process whereby one case refers to a thousand others. Only through symbolic mediation will the particular entity reveal to us a supra-individual universal. This universal can be perceived only in the particular, in the 'eminent cases'.

With his morphology and the symbolic, Goethe thus appreciated two forms of intuitive knowledge which allow us to explore relations and to search for 'family resemblances' (Wittgenstein) by starting from the particular. Goethe distrusted all abstracting, hypostasizing generalization and sought to keep faith with the individual phenomena, even when transcending them towards totality, by staying within the limits of experience. The two forms of thought, morphology and symbolism, have themselves been developed in the context of a historical situation, viz. the one characterized by the names of the two towns of Jena and Weimar.[60] Could morphology and symbolism, if methodologically combined, help to conceive of the unity of this historical event?

Both forms of thought proceed from the empirical multiplicity and from thence search for unity and interrelatedness. The morphological approach, by a comparative procedure, joins together partial occurrences or events whose existence can be empirically proved. Speaking of partial events necessarily presupposes their integration into some process. The morphological approach enquires into their structural similarities and dissimilarities and also into their different relations and contexts. The symbolic approach helps to envisage the partial events as 'eminent cases' in a historical configuration, events which stand for themselves while at the same time referring to each other in the way of a metonymic symbolism. No partial event can claim an absolute meaning, but each has a specific meaning. If understood in the sense of Schiller's critique, the symbolic approach also makes clear that even well-documented, verifiable historical events are not simply given but have to be established in the context of an interpretation of a superior whole. Schiller is acutely aware that the historian could not operate without the heuristic of a regulative idea.[61] The subject of symbolic cognition is essentially involved in the realization of cognition. Morphological comparison too, when applied to complex historical events as suggested by Goethe, refers us to the subjects of cognition: the patterns of morphology must themselves be epistemically justified, for they depict the subjects' attempts at organizing and interpreting the wealth of phenomena.[62] The morphological and the symbolical order of things is not given but made, the cognition of reality an interminable process.

Translated by Katrin Grünepütt

Notes to Chapter 4

1. 'Morphologie. Ruht auf der Überzeugung daß alles was sey sich auch andeuten und zeigen müsse. [...] Das unorganische, das vegetative, das animale das menschliche deutet sich alles selbst an, es erscheint als was es ist unserm äussern und unserm inneren Sinn. Die Gestalt ist ein bewegliches, ein werdendes, ein vergehendes. Gestaltenlehre ist Verwandlungslehre. Die Lehre der Metamorphose ist der Schlüssel zu allen Zeichen der Natur' [Morphology rests on the conviction that everything that is must also manifest and show itself. [...] The inorganic, the vegetable, the animal, the human, all manifests itself, appears as what it is, to our outer and inner sense. Form is something mobile, that comes into being and passes away. The science of form is the science of transformation. The doctrine of metamorphosis is the key to all of Nature's signs]. Johann Wolfgang von Goethe, *Morphologie* [1796]. In *Goethes Werke*, ed. by commission of the Grand Duchess Sophie von Sachsen. Sections I–IV, 133 vols in 143 (Weimar, 1887–1919; photomechanical reprint Munich, 1987), II, 6, p. 446. All references to Goethe are to this edition, henceforth under the abbreviation WA (i.e. Weimarer-Ausgabe).
2. Letter to Schiller, 16 and 17 August 1797. WA IV, 12, pp. 243–47 (p. 246).
3. In his diary entry for 25 September 1796 (WA III, 2, p. 48), written during a stay in Jena, Goethe used the term for the first time.
4. Cf. Dorothea Kuhn, 'Goethes Morphologie. Geschichte — Prinzipien — Folgen', in *Typus und Metamorphose. Goethe-Studien*, ed. by Renate Grumach (Marbach am Neckar: Deutsche Schillergesellschaft, 1988), pp. 188–202 (p. 196).
5. Cf. Goethe, 'Betrachtung über Morphologie überhaupt'. WA II, 6, pp. 292 f.
6. Letter to Schiller, 12 November 1796. WA IV, 11, p. 260.
7. Letter from Schiller to Goethe, 13 November 1796. In *Werke. Begründet von Julius Petersen, fortgeführt von Lieselotte Blumenthal und Benno von Wiese*, ed. by Norbert Oellers et al. (Weimar: Hermann Böhlaus Nachfolger, 1943–), vol. 29, p. 4. All references to Schiller are to this edition, henceforth under the abbreviation NA (i.e. Nationalausgabe).
8. Kuhn, 'Goethes Morphologie', p. 197.
9. Aristotle, *Metaphysics* VII, 8, 1033 b.
10. Cf. Georg Picht, *Aristoteles' 'De anima'* (Stuttgart: Klett-Cotta, 1987), pp. 274–77.
11. Cf. Joachim Schulte, 'Chor und Gesetz. Zur "morphologischen Methode" bei Goethe und Wittgenstein', in Joachim Schulte, *Chor und Gesetz. Wittgenstein im Kontext* (Frankfurt am Main: Suhrkamp, 1990), pp. 11–42.
12. Goethe, Nacharbeiten und Sammlungen. WA II, 6, p. 172: the 'mind's eyes' see 'wie Gestalt in Gestalt sich wandelt' [how *Gestalt* changes into *Gestalt*]; see also Letter to J. S. M. D. Boisserée, 24 November 1831 (WA IV, 49, p. 152); Letter to Schultz, 1 September 1820 (WA IV, 33, p. 185).
13. Cf. Helmut Hühn, '"Epídosis eis hauto". Zur morphologischen Geschichtsbetrachtung bei Johann Gustav Droysen', in *Morphologie und Moderne. Goethes 'anschauliches Denken' in den Geistes- und Kulturwissenschaften seit 1800*, ed. by Jonas Maatsch and Thorsten Valk (Berlin and New York: de Gruyter, 2012).
14. Letter from Schiller to Goethe, 23 August 1794. NA 27, p. 25. Translations into English draw upon: *Correspondence between Goethe and Schiller, 1794–1805*, trans. by Liselotte Dieckmann (New York: Peter Lang, 1994). See Goethe, 'Der Versuch als Vermittler von Object und Subject'. WA II, 11, p. 31: 'In der lebendigen Natur geschieht nichts, was nicht in einer Verbindung mit dem Ganzen stehe' [Nothing happens in living nature that does not bear some relation to the whole]; Johann Wolfgang von Goethe, *Scientific Studies*, ed. and trans. by Douglas Miller (New York: Suhrkamp, 1988), p. 15.

15. Goethe, *Erfahrung und Wissenschaft* (1798). WA II, 11. pp. 38–41 (p. 38).
16. See Goethe's Letter to Schiller, 21 February 1798. WA IV, 13, p. 72.
17. Georg Wilhelm Friedrich Hegel, *Enzyklopädie der philosophischen Wissenschaften* (1830), Einleitung, in *Werke*, ed. by Eva Moldenhauer and Karl Markus Michel, vol. 9 (Frankfurt am Main: Suhrkamp, 1970), p. 9.
18. *Enzyklopädie* § 246. *Werke* vol. 9, p. 21; § 345, ibid., p. 392; cf. the Introduction to the present volume, p. 3.
19. Cf. Olaf Breidbach, *Goethes Metamorphosenlehre* (Munich: Fink, 2006), p. 122.
20. Cf. Goethe, 'Ganymed' (WA I, 2, p. 80): 'Umfangend umfangen!' [Embracing, embraced!].
21. 'Paralipomena'. WA II, 6, p. 446.
22. See Immanuel Kant, *Kritik der reinen Vernunft* B 37. Akademie-Ausgabe vol. 3, pp. 51 f.
23. Cf. Frauke Berndt and Heinz J. Drügh (eds.), 'Einleitung', *Symbol. Grundtexte zur Ästhetik, Poetik und Kulturwissenschaft* (Frankfurt am Main: Suhrkamp, 2009), pp. 21–37 (pp. 28 f.).
24. Letter to Schiller, 16 and 17 August 1797. WA IV, 12, p. 247.
25. For the changes that occurred in Goethe's thinking in 1797 see Stefan Blechschmidt, *Goethes lebendiges Archiv. Mensch — Morphologie — Geschichte* (Heidelberg: Winter, 2010), pp. 11–24.
26. WA IV, 12, p. 326. Cf., however, his letter to Schiller from 12 August 1797, where he sets the 'Sattheit der Empirie' [richness of experience] against totality ('Totalität'): WA IV 12, p. 234.
27. 'Der Versuch als Vermittler von Object und Subject'. WA II, 11, p. 32 (where he speaks of following every single experiment through its variations); 'Verbindung objectiver und subjectiver Versuche'. WA II, 1, p. 148.
28. Letter to Schiller, 16 and 17 August 1797. WA IV, 12, p. 243.
29. Ibid., pp. 243 f.
30. Letter to Schiller, 12 August 1797. WA IV, 12, p. 231.
31. Letter to Schiller, 16 and 17 August 1797. WA IV, 12, p. 244.
32. Ibid., pp. 245 f.
33. Cf. the draft ('Concept') of Goethe's letter to K. A. Böttiger, 16 August 1797. WA IV, 12, p. 240.
34. *Dichtung und Wahrheit, Erster Theil*. WA I, 26, pp. 55 ff.
35. See Goethe's elegy 'Die Metamorphose der Pflanzen'. WA I, 1, pp. 290–92 (p. 291).
36. Letter to Schiller, 16 and 17 August 1797. WA IV, 12, p. 246.
37. For the notion of an absolute representation in art ('absolute Kunstdarstellung') see Friedrich Wilhelm Joseph Schelling, *Philosophie der Kunst* § 39. In *Sämmtliche Werke*, ed. by Karl Friedrich August Schelling (Stuttgart, Augsburg: Cotta, 1856–61), vol. I, 5, pp. 406–13 (p. 411); *System des transscendentalen Idealismus*, ibid., I, 3, p. 625.
38. Immanuel Kant, *Kritik der Urteilskraft* § 49 (Akademie-Ausgabe vol. 5, p. 314): 'unter einer ästhetischen Idee aber verstehe ich diejenige Vorstellung der Einbildungskraft, die viel zu denken veranlaßt, ohne daß ihr doch irgend ein bestimmter Gedanke, d.i. Begriff, adäquat sein kann, die folglich keine Sprache völlig erreicht und verständlich machen kann' [By an aesthetic idea I understand that representation of the imagination which occasions much thought, without however any definite thought, i.e. any concept, being capable of being adequate to it; it consequently cannot be completely compassed and made intelligible by language]: *Critique of Judgment*, trans. by J. H. Bernard (Amherst, NY: Prometheus, 2000), B 192 f.
39. Goethe, like Kant, stands in the tradition of Alexander Gottlieb Baumgarten's concept of *perceptio praegnans*.
40. For a discussion of this problem cf. Axel Hutter, 'Hegels Philosophie des Geistes', in *Hegel-Studien*, 42 (2007), 81–97 (p. 86).
41. For the problem of constructing a uniform concept of symbol see the Introduction to the present volume.
42. For Goethe's methodology see his 'Der Versuch als Vermittler von Object und Subject'. WA II, 11, p. 21: 'Sobald der Mensch die Gegenstände um sich her gewahr wird, betrachtet er sie in Bezug auf sich selbst, und mit Recht' [As soon as man becomes aware of objects in his environment he will relate them to himself, and rightly so].
43. Heinz Schlaffer, *Faust Zweiter Teil. Die Allegorie des 19. Jahrhunderts* (Stuttgart: Metzler, 1989), pp. 18 f.
44. Cf. Goethe's letter to Schiller, 9 August 1797. WA IV, 12, p. 216.

45. Cf. Gottfried Gabriel, 'Bestimmte Unbestimmtheit — in der ästhetischen Erkenntnis und im ästhetischen Urteil', in *Das unendliche Kunstwerk. Von der Bestimmtheit des Unbestimmten in der ästhetischen Erfahrung*, ed. by Gerhard Gamm and Eva Schürmann (Hamburg: Philo, 2007), pp. 141–56, esp. pp. 145 f.

46. Goethe, Letter to Schiller, 16 and 17 August 1797. WA IV, 12, p. 244.

47. Letter to Schiller, 29 July 1797. WA IV, 12, p. 209.

48. See Letter to Schiller, 16 and 17 August 1797. WA IV, 12, p. 246.

49. Schiller, Letter to Goethe, 7 and 8 September 1797. NA 29, p. 127.

50. Schiller, *Ueber naive und sentimentalische Dichtung*. NA 20, p. 441; for the English translation cf. *On the Naive and Sentimental in Literature*, trans. by Helen Watanabe-O'Kelly (Manchester: Carcanet, 1981).

51. Letter to Goethe, 7 and 8 September 1797. NA 29, p. 127.

52. Ibid.; cf. with respect to Schiller's concept of poetical symbolization, letter to Goethe, 31 August 1794. NA 27, p. 32: 'Mein Verstand wirkt eigentlich mehr symbolisierend, und so schwebe ich wie eine ZwitterArt, zwischen dem Begriff und der Anschauung [...]' [My understanding works more in a symbolizing way, and so I hover like a hybrid between concept and intuition].

53. Cf. Goethe, [Mein Verhältniß zu Schiller]. WA I, 42.2, p. 146; Bengt Algot Sørensen, *Symbol und Symbolismus in den ästhetischen Theorien des 18. Jahrhunderts und der deutschen Romantik* (Copenhagen: Munksgaard, 1963), p. 105.

54. Rüdiger Safranski, *Goethe und Schiller. Geschichte einer Freundschaft* (Munich: Hanser, 2009), p. 199.

55. See Johann Heinrich Meyer, 'Über die Gegenstände der bildenden Kunst', in Johann Wolfgang von Goethe, *Sämtliche Werke nach Epochen seines Schaffens*, ed. by Karl Richter et al., 20 vols in 33 (Munich: Hanser, 1985–98), vol. 6.2, pp. 27–68.

56. Goethe, 'Über die Gegenstände der bildenden Kunst'. WA I, 47, p. 95.

57. See the Introduction to the present volume.

58. For Herder's doctrine of the natural symbol which signifies by virtue of its inherent qualities cf. Herder, *Kalligone*, III, 4, in *Werke in zehn Bänden*, vol. 8, ed. by Hans Dietrich Irmscher (Frankfurt am Main: Deutscher Klassiker Verlag, 1998), p. 952; ibid., p. 956: '*Jedes Ding bedeutet*, d. i. es trägt die Gestalt dessen was es *ist*; die darstellendsten, ausdrückendsten, prägnantesten sind also die *Natursymbole*' [*Every thing signifies*, i.e. it bears the *Gestalt* of that which it *is*; whence the natural symbols are those that represent most, express most and are the most meaningful].

59. Goethe, Letter to Schiller, 16 and 17 August 1797. WA IV, 12, pp. 246 f.

60. In a cross-disciplinary collaboration conbining approaches from the humanities, cultural studies and natural sciences, the special research project 'SFB 482: The Weimar-Jena Phenomenon: Culture around 1800' (finalized 2010) explored the uniquely productive and intensive communication and interaction that took place in and between Weimar and Jena around 1800. The aim of the research was to examine the interrelation of Enlightenment, Classicism, Idealism and Romanticism so characteristic for the phenomenon Weimar-Jena.

61. Cf. Friedrich Schiller, 'Was heisst und zu welchem Ende studiert man Universalgeschichte?' (1789), in NA 17, pp. 359–76 (p. 373).

62. Taking his lead from Goethe's insight, Novalis develops the idea of a morphological order of knowledge: cf. Friedrich von Hardenberg [Novalis], *Das Allgemeine Brouillon* (1798/99), in *Schriften*, ed. by Paul Kluckhohn and Richard Samuel (Stuttgart: Kohlhammer, 1960), vol. 3, p. 452 (Nr. 967): 'Göthische Behandlung der Wissenschaften — mein Project' [Goethean treatment of the sciences — my project]. Cf. Jonas Maatsch, '*Naturgeschichte der Philosopheme*'. *Frühromantische Wissensordnungen im Kontext* (Heidelberg: Winter, 2008), pp. 219 ff.

CHAPTER 5

Friedrich Schlegel's Symbol-Concept

Jan Urbich

'There's a crack in everything
That's how the light gets in'

LEONARD COHEN

Cornerstones of Friedrich Schlegel's Theory of Poetry

Friedrich Schlegel's poetology, like early German Romantic philosophy and aesthetics in general, participates in the claims which are linked with the highest possible position of art in the idealistic systems elaborated by Schiller, Schelling, Hegel and Solger. In Hegel's words: 'Als ein Mittelglied zwischen dem reinen Gedanken, der übersinnlichen Welt, und dem Unmittelbaren, der gegenwärtigen Empfindung, [...] versöhnt die Kunst [...] Begriff und [...] Natur' [As a bond between the pure thought, the extrasensory world, and the immediate, present sensation, art reconciles concept and nature].[1] Still more emphatically than Hegel, the young Schelling asserts: 'Die Kunst bringt den *ganzen Menschen*, wie er ist, dahin, nämlich zur Erkenntnis des Höchsten, und darauf beruht der ewige Unterschied, und das Wunder der Kunst' [Art takes the whole person, as he is, to the knowledge of the highest, and on that the eternal difference, and the miracle of art is based].[2] A philosophical 'Liebhaberei fürs Absolute' [amateur enthusiasm for the absolute][3] as the understanding that 'alles Filosofieren muß bey einem absoluten Grunde endigen' [all philosophy has to end on an absolute ground][4] is concentrated in the following statement of Schelling, which brings in its wake an epistemological consequence that becomes the foundation of most of early Romantic thought: 'Jeder ist von Natur getrieben, ein Absolutes zu suchen; aber indem er es für die Reflexion fixiren will, verschwindet es ihm. [...] Es ist nur da, inwiefern ich es nicht habe, und inwiefern ich es habe, ist es nicht mehr' [Everybody is driven by nature to search for the absolute; but as soon as he wants to fix it by reflection, it disappears. [...] It is only there when I do not have it; and when I have it, it is not there].[5] The romantic 'Sehnsucht nach dem Unendlichen' [longing for the infinite] is often misunderstood.[6] It is based on the paradoxical notion — inspired by Kant's theory of 'regulative ideas' — that the completion of all knowledge and being in the absolute must necessarily be sought for, while at the same time it cannot be made present within the space of the finite mind: '*Erkennen* bedeutet schon ein *bedingtes* Wissen. Die Nichterkennbarkeit des Absoluten also eine identische Trivialität' [To know already means to have limited knowledge. The unknowability of the absolute is thus an identical triviality].[7] The problem becomes more complicated for the early Romantics owing to the differences between the various media by which one might hope to grasp the absolute, reflected in the difference between the activity of knowing and the presentation of knowledge: 'Das reine Denken und Erkennen des Höchsten kann nie adäquat dargestellt werden' [The pure thinking and knowledge of the highest can never be represented adequately] — a principle that Schlegel calls the 'Prinzip der relativen Undarstellbarkeit des Höchsten' [principle of the relative unrepresentability of the highest].[8] The assignment of poetry is linked closely to that principle: 'Der Sinn für Poesie hat viel mit Mystizism gemein. [...] Er stellt das Undarstellbare dar' [The sense for poetry has a lot in common with mysticism. [...] It represents the unrepresentable].[9]

Early Romantic poetics therefore persistently revolves the possibility and the form of an 'indirect representation' of the 'only negatively knowable absolute',[10] through processes which annihilate the finiteness of all determinations, using both the logic of form and the figural or semantic techniques of art — including irony, wit, and so on.[11] The finiteness of the significant elements must be exceeded by the aesthetic network of expressions; but the illusion of the prevailing 'symbol'-concept which simply identifies the finite and the infinite in symbolic representation must be avoided. Thereby the temporality of an infinite aesthetic dynamics becomes the microcosmic image of the infinite within the finite.[12] The negativity of its permanent transgression of every closed, determined finiteness without its ever becoming positively infinite provokes (in the wake of Lessing's *Laokoon*) the search for the inner form of temporality that marks the aesthetic space of poetry. The absolute as the Beyond of intentionality and consciousness[13] enters into view in early Romantic poetics through the infinity and inexhaustibility of the poetic meaning which is produced by works of literary art.[14] Subsequent to Kant's theory of 'aesthetic idea'[15] (and in opposition to Karl Philipp Moritz's notion that meaning is suspended within the beauty of poetic works),[16] then, the constitutional semantic ambiguity of poetic works becomes understood as the indirect expression of the epistemological and ontological unease that blurs the clear distinction between the finite and the infinite.

Friedrich Schlegel is above all concerned with how to set nature and poetry in a specific relation. His basic intuition is therefore 'enthusiastic', in a sentimental, pantheistic sense,[17] emphasizing the unity, wholeness and ontological harmony of the universe within the plurality and diversity of nature. Early Romantic thought considers the organic dynamics and harmonic interplay of nature as the expression of the eternal, divine 'creative principle' to be the basis and creative power of poetic activity: 'Die Natur hat Kunstinstinkt' [Nature has an instinct for art], and Novalis asserts that it would be '[ein] Geschwätz, wenn man Natur und Kunst unterscheiden will' [idle to want to distinguish between nature and art].[18] The *natura naturans* becomes the substance of poetic creativity — for the infinite harmonic productivity and beauty of its forms of expression as well as for the organic unity und inner necessity of its works[19] — and ensures at the same time in its Spinozistic harmony the translatability of its elements into every possible relation of expression.

Early Romantic thought longs to understand everything from language to poetry in analogy to nature:[20] 'Im Universum der Poesie aber selbst ruht nichts, alles wird und verwandelt sich und bewegt sich harmonisch' [In the universe of poetry nothing rests, everything becomes and changes and moves harmoniously].[21] Only as 'genetische Nachamung' [genetic imitation] is poetry alive and romantic.[22] Rejecting the Aristotelian concept of 'mimesis' (as set out in Charles Batteux's 'Les beaux arts réduits à un même principe' of 1746, which posits art as imitation of reality), Novalis as well as Friedrich Schlegel emphasize the autonomous law and self-reflexivity of art, which only imitates nature by reproducing analogically its infinite power to produce ('natura naturans'):[23] it creates forms and sets everything in harmonic dynamics within the medium of the 'nous' (spirit). This infinitely creative natural force is at work in nature and art at different levels of power. This notion enables Schlegel to redefines the tradition of the 'genius'. It ensures at the same time the relation of art to the 'absolute', which represents itself in poetry without being representable by knowledge or poetry at all: 'Das Wesen der höhern Kunst und Form besteht in der *Beziehung aufs Ganze*' [The essence of art and form is its relation to the whole].[24]

In the *Lectures on Transcendental Philosophy* that Schlegel delivered in Jena (1800–01), the relation to the whole of the creative natural power which articulates itself in poetry within the limits of aesthetic representation is founded in a logic of expression of the 'absolute'. Here for the first time Schlegel's central thought concerning the term 'symbol', which explains the participation as well as the distance of the poetic representation to the infinite, is expressed clearly:

> *Warum ist das Unendliche aus sich herausgegangen und hat sich endlich gemacht?* — das heißt mit andren Worten: *Warum sind Individua?* Oder: *Warum läuft das Spiel der Natur nicht in einem Nu ab, so daß also gar nichts existirt?* Die Antwort auf diese Frage ist nur möglich, wenn wir einen Begriff einschieben. Wir haben nämlich die Begriffe *eine, unendliche Substanz* — und *Individua*. Wenn wir uns den Übergang von dem einen zu den andern erklären wollen, so können wir dies nicht anders, als daß wir zwischen beyden noch einen Begriff einschieben, nämlich den Begriff *des Bildes* oder *Darstellung, Allegorie* (εἰκών). Das Individuum ist also ein *Bild der einen unendlichen Substanz*. (Man könnte dies auch ausdrücken: Gott hat die Welt hervorgebracht, um sich selbst darzustellen.)

> [*Why has the infinite gone out of itself and made itself finite?* — that is, in other words: *Why are individua?* Or: *Why isn't the whole game of nature executed in just a single moment, so that nothing exists at all?* The answer to this question is only possible if we insert a term. That is to say, we have the terms *one, infinite substance* — and *individua*. If we want to explain to ourselves the transfer from one to the other, we cannot do this except by inserting one more term, namely that of the *image* or *representation, allegory* (*eikon*). The individual, then, is an *image* of the *one, infinite substance*. (One could also express this in the following way: God has produced the world to represent himself.)][25]

The curtailed, indirect and somehow broken image — 'Welt im verringerten Maasstabe [world in reduced size][26] — which marks the energetic centre of the lively, individual image, is denominated by the term 'allegory' to indicate its relation to the infinite. In the 'Wesen des Geistes [...], sich selbst zu bestimmen und im ewigen Wechsel aus sich herauszugehn und in sich zurückzukehren' [being of the spirit [...] to determine itself and to go out and return to itself in everlasting movement], a movement in which 'die unbeschränkte Fülle neuer Erfindung, durch die allgemeine Mitteilbarkeit und durch die lebendige Wirksamkeit aufs herrlichste offenbart' [the unrestricted fullness of new invention is most splendidly revealed by the universal mediacy and vivid potency], there emerges the unity of a common harmonic productivity between the finite and the infinite, by which both mirror each other as elements of a divine relation without erasing their difference.[27] Far from being eradicated, indeed, their difference constitutes precisely the impulsion to move continuously towards each other and to represent each other in themselves as that image of their common harmonic striving which Schlegel calls the 'spirit of love'. With this phrase Schlegel alludes to the platonic conception of 'eros' as everlasting striving, which figures the very harmony of its elements as an inability to bring each other to the completion of non-differential identity. 'Nie wird der Geist, welcher die Orgien der wahren Muse kennt, auf dieser Bahn bis ans Ende dringen, oder wähnen, daß er es erreicht: denn nie kann er eine Sehnsucht stillen, die aus der Fülle der Befriedigungen selbst sich ewig von neuem erzeugt' [The spirit which has experienced the orgies of the true muse will never penetrate to the end of this road, or attain the delusion of having reached it: for it can never allay a longing that eternally generates itself anew from the fullness of fulfilments itself].[28] Schlegel here assimilates a concept from Aristotle that describes the fulfilment of an infinite movement in which deficiency and fulfilment are identical within the dynamics of their mediation, because this movement is at the same time completed in every moment of its infinite striving.[29] This open dialectic of absence and fulfilment, of dynamic restriction and self-transcendence, by which the irreducibly positive quality of aesthetic indirectness, limitation and negativity is conceived, plays a central role in Schlegel's theory of the artwork and at the same time informs his theory of symbol and allegory. The concept of the inner infinity of the artwork as effect of its aesthetic composition is enhanced by the idea of a 'medium of art':[30] 'Darum sind alle Werke Ein Werk, alle Künste Eine Kunst, alle Gedichte Ein Gedicht. Denn alle wollen ja dasselbe, das überall Eine, und zwar in seiner ungeteilten Einheit. Aber eben darum will auch jedes Glied in diesem höchsten Gebilde des menschlichen Geistes zugleich das Ganze sein' [This is why all works of art are just One work, all arts just One art, all poems just One poem. For everything wants the same, that which is everywhere One in its undivided unity. But therefore every element in this highest unity of the human mind wants to be the unity itself].[31] For Schlegel, poetic works of art are linguistic structures of expression, which are not primarily determined by the substance of their content, but rather by the special formal, individual, self-reflexive, autonomous order of their formation.[32]

In the richness of the relations of its elements, in the interplay of contrast and reconciliation, in the liveliness of its inner movement of meaning and structure, as Schlegel explains paradigmatically in his philosophical review of Goethe's *Wilhelm-Meister*, the artwork creates an individual organic internal harmony which becomes at the same time the basis of its transcendence into the universal. The individual unity of the work preserves itself precisely in the resistance mounted by the greatest possible internal differentiality against the effort to unify. This unity, as a kind of an abridged image of art itself, therefore depends upon the whole 'medium of art' as a final unity that all works of art aim for. In its inner completion, the individual artwork recapitulates a unity which it actually lacks in its own individuality, yet at the same time exhibits in a lower and abridged form. Symbolically, the aesthetic completion of the formation of the work of art points to an absence that is at the same time fulfilled; organically, the whole is present in the single work in such a way that its absence is no longer mere absence. The 'external' means by which the single work of art may be raised to that complete unity of art that is already smouldering in the artwork is 'criticism', understood as a completion of the individual disposition of the artwork. It is here that Walter Benjamin's concept of criticism has its origins.[33] The internal structures of the work of art that make this kind of ontological criticism possible are the symbol and the allegory.

Symbol and Allegory in Schlegel's System of Poetry

By what means can the individual work of art, with its constitutively self-reflexive dimension, simultaneously relate to the whole of art? '[D]urch dasselbe, wodurch überall der Schein des Endlichen mit der Wahrheit des Ewigen in Beziehung gesetzt und eben dadurch in sie aufgelöst wird: durch Allegorie, durch Symbole, durch die an die Stelle der Täuschung die Bedeutung tritt, das einzige Wirkliche im Dasein, weil nur der Sinn, der Geist des Daseins entspringt und zurückgeht aus dem, was über alle Täuschung und über alles Dasein erhaben ist' [By the same means by which everywhere the appearance of the finite is connected with the truth of the eternal and so is dissolved into the eternal: by allegory, by symbols, through which the appearance is replaced by the meaning itself, the only real thing in existence because only the meaning, the spirit of existence arises and returns from that which is elevated above all deceit and above all existence].[34] The self-transcendency of the work of art as a result of its internal unity that relates the limited sign and the unlimited meaning without erasing one side, is bound to the reflexive self-relation that Walter Benjamin has called the 'Reflexionsmedium' [medium of reflection]: '[Die] höhere Kunst [...] ist selbst Natur und Leben und schlechthin eins mit diesen; aber sie ist die Natur der Natur, das Leben des Lebens, der Mensch im Menschen" [The higher art is itself nature and life und utterly one with both; but it is the nature of nature, the life of life, the human in the human being].[35] Schlegel coined the term 'Transzendentalpoesie' in order to describe the constitutive function of self-reflexivity of poetic works of art, which represent 'das Produzierende mit dem Produkt' [the producer along with the product] and are 'überall zugleich Poesie und Poesie der Poesie' [always simultaneously poetry and the poetry of poetry];[36] so that the work of art hovers 'auf den Flügeln der poetischen Reflexion in der Mitte' [at the midpoint on the wings of poetic reflection], 'diese Reflexion immer wieder potenzieren und wie in einer endlosen Reihe von Spiegeln vervielfachen' [raising that reflection over and over again to a higher power and multiplying it in an endless row of mirrors].[37] For Schlegel, at this time a follower of Fichte, it is only this structure that guarantees the spiritual nature of art: 'Sinn, der sich selbst sieht, wird Geist' [Meaning that becomes aware of itself is spirit].[38]

The levels of self-relation that are realized in poetic representations and that dynamize their ironic movements are also counter-forces to the bare symbolic identity of being and meaning. While they turn the non-identity of consciousness as form of the difference of the sides of reflection into the constitutive fact of aesthetic representation and aesthetic meaning, at the same time they prevent the closure of the aesthetic process of meaning and guarantee that every work of art in its very unity and closure initiates a movement of opening the finite to the infinite. The distance between the signifier and the signified, in which the relation of reflection as well as the concept of aesthetic form is grounded, not the thing-like unity of both, becomes the meta-logic of poetic representation. The self-reflexivity and intransitivity of the romantic concepts of art and language[39] express allegorically a model of the relation of being and meaning: the thing-like closeness of poetic language, its ontic aspect is inseparably bound to forms of reference and difference, in other words to the reflexive aspect of signifying. Being and meaning do not form an identity in the symbol as Moritz's or Goethe's symbol-conception posits. The reflexive non-identity of signs and meaning that neither issues in the extreme of the thing-like identity of both nor in purely arbitrary, purely differential sign-like non-identity propels the inner force of Romantic representation: 'Jedes Kunstwerk ist eine Anspielung aufs Unendliche' [Every work of art is an allusion to the infinite].[40]

That also explains why the distinction between 'symbol' and 'allegory' is not a central one in Schlegel's concept of poetics: for the pure and metaphysical difference between being-like identity (symbol) and meaning-like difference (allegory) is invalid. The open space of this difference is filled by different degrees and kinds of poetic 'Hindeutung auf das Höhere, Unendliche' [allusion to the higher, infinite][41] as 'indirectly telling', and by the emphasis on the dynamics of a 'repeatedly different representing' as only possibility to dynamize the unignorable 'Zeichen, Repräsentanten d[er] Elemente die nie an sich darstellbar sind' [signs, representations of elements that cannot be represented as themselves][42] for their infinite approach to the absolute: 'Alle Wahrheit ist relativ Alles Wissen ist symbolisch' [All truth is relative all knowledge is symbolic].[43] In this basic sense, the expressions 'symbol' and 'allegory' are interchangeable for Schlegel, who in fact employs the term 'allegory' far more often. The 'höhere idealische Ansicht der Dinge' [higher idealistic view of things] as 'Wesen der Poesie' [essence of poetry], in which the individual entity becomes 'Zeichen, Mittel zur Anschauung des Ganzen' [sign, means to the view of the whole][44] is defined as follows: 'Alle Schönheit ist Allegorie. Das Höchste kann man eben, weil es unaussprechlich ist, nur allegorisch sagen' [All beauty is allegory. The highest can only be represented allegorically because it is itself inexpressible].[45] In any case, Schlegel uses the term 'allegory' in a more homogeneous way, always related to the idea of 'alluding to' or 'indirectly representing' the infinite. Allegorically, the infinite appears in poetic representation, because the finite negates itself and thereby opens up the space of a figurative and semantic otherness without completely filling it in a positive sense,[46] even if finite representation and infinite absolute are tied together by numerous internal, organic relations in a more than only sign-like arbitrariness: '[A]lles hat [...] eine eben so tiefe als unendlich reiche Bedeutung und allseitige Beziehung' [Everything has a deep as well as infinitely rich meaning and relation to every other].[47]

The term 'symbol' in Schlegel is far more vague and ambiguous than the term 'allegory', which suggests the likelihood that he uses it in a less strict manner. On the one hand, Schlegel uses 'symbol' in the sense of 'arbitrary sign' (as in the subsequent analytic tradition), often referring to an object as 'bloß symbolisch' [merely symbolic].[48] Connected with this meaning is the use of 'symbolic' as external, rhetorically shaped form of linguistic expression.[49] On the other hand, Schlegel uses the term 'symbolic' to describe the special aesthetic logic of artistic meaning in a work of art which also pertains language as such: 'Die modernen Sprachen sind symbolischer in d[er] Wortartung besser beziehungsvoller, reicher, bedeutender' [the modern languages are more symbolic, in their word-formation better, more allusive, richer, more meaningful].[50] And thirdly, the most common use of 'symbolic' in Schlegel describes a *partly motivated* relation between sign and meaning which is not a relation of identity but rather of metonymic continuity[51] as a relation of expression between the whole of something and its parts.[52] In this context the term 'symbol' denotes the organic harmony of nature that refigures the whole as 'verkürztes Bild' [abbreviated image] within its parts. Furthermore, this use of the term 'symbol' preserves the 'secret' of the relations between the constituent elements and the whole, the finite and the infinite: for 'symbolic' signifies the *traces of relations*[53] (such as analogy or metonymy) that can be made visible through represented objects but cannot be fully grasped conceptually and therefore express by the miracle of distance between sign and meaning the secret of hidden unity of all being.

We have seen that for Schlegel the blurring of the distinction between 'symbol' and 'allegory' is based on the denial of the abstract unity of being and meaning in some versions of the symbol-concept around 1800 (such as Schelling's) in order to elaborate the idea of an open interplay between being and meaning as 'symbolic'.[54] This interplay fundamentally roots every relation between the finite and the infinite, goes through the movement of harmony between spirit and nature and reveals itself in the various levels of the work of art in an intensified way. It is always Schlegel's purpose to conceptualize the movement *between* meaning and being as a fundament that cannot be derived any further; in other words, neither one of the two parts of this relation may be grasped as a single, fundamental principle for the other. The only presence of the absolute lies in the symbolic (that is to say allegorical) relation within the work of art and thereby in the relation to the absolute via the interplay of sign and meaning, meaning and being. Therefore, Walter Benjamin's development of the term 'Reflexionsmedium' [medium of reflection] to describe the concept of the absolute in Schlegel seems legitimate. Rethinking the paradigm of symbolic presence also as a theological pattern, this reflexive theory of symbolical difference *and* unity of being and meaning gains a specific meaning that was unfolded by Schlegel in his collection of fragments entitled *Ideen* [Ideas]. The allegorical, ironical, symbolical movement of the work of art is seen as a keeping-open for the completely exterior intrusion of the divine that can be prepared by the work of art but not procured by it.[55] Exactly in that sense the later Paul Ricœur had deintentionalized the term 'symbol' against its culturalization by Ernst Cassirer: 'Symbole des Heiligen [...] bezeichnen [...] den Einschlag der Realität in die Kultur, einer Realität, welche die Bewegung der Kultur nicht enthält; sie sprechen vom Absolut-Anderen, vom Absolut-Anderen jener Geschichte' [Symbols of the divine [...] mark [...] the impact of reality in culture, a reality that does not contain the movement of culture; they speak of the absolute-other, the absolute-other of history].[56]

Schlegel's symbol-concept raises an objection against the abstract theological mode of symbol that has been claimed as a general pattern for the so-called *Goethezeit*,[57] while at the same time partaking in the discussions of German Idealism about the relation between mind and world, meaning and being, finite forms of representation and denotation and the infinite that transgresses every one of it. The so-called 'classical' concept of symbol cannot reason the presence of the identity of its different aspects (the general and the particular, the meaning and the being, the finite and the infinite) *as a representational unity*, without considering the constitutional level of difference that emerges from the logic of aesthetic representation itself: to *mean* and *represent* this symbolic identity, the symbolic mode of presentation has to differentiate the identity of being and the non-identity of meaning within itself without erasing one of its counterparts in their difference. Furthermore, the effect of being-like presence in the symbol is not the other *to* meaning but the other *of* meaning: the way in which meaning conveys the insight into the relational and meaningful nature of being itself, its necessity to express itself by meaning as constitutional foundation of the concurrent contrast to meaning. The relational knowledge that every form of identity carries within itself the difference of meaning as reasonable mediation,[58] together with the insight that every difference rests on a ground of unity from which it derives its possibility of relation,[59] is the metaphysical core of Schlegel's concept of symbol. In this way, Schlegel participates in discussions of an axiomatic nature that define the actuality of Early German Romanticism and German Idealism precisely in their blending of the fields of aesthetics and ontology, the theory of aesthetic representation and the theory of knowledge.

Notes to Chapter 5

1. Georg Wilhelm Friedrich Hegel, *Vorlesungen über die Philosophie der Kunst*, ed. by Annemarie Gethmann-Siefert (Hamburg: Meiner, 2003), p. 5. All references to Friedrich Schlegel are to the following critical edition: *Kritische Friedrich-Schlegel-Ausgabe*, ed. by Ernst Behler et al., 35 vols published (Paderborn, Darmstadt, Zürich: Schöningh, 1958–). Henceforth cited using the abbreviation 'KFSA', by volume and page number, and fragment-number where applicable.
2. Friedrich Wilhelm Joseph Schelling, *System des transzendentalen Idealismus*, ed. by Horst D. Brandt and Peter Müller (Hamburg: Meiner, 2000), p. 301.
3. KFSA II, 164 [26].
4. *Novalis. Die Schriften Friedrich von Hardenbergs*, ed. by Paul Kluckhohn and Richard Samuel, 6 vols published (Stuttgart: Kohlhammer, 1960–), II, 269.
5. Friedrich Wilhelm Joseph Schelling, *Fernere Darstellungen aus dem System der Philosophie*, in id., *Ausgewählte Werke*, ed. by Manfred Frank (Frankfurt am Main: Suhrkamp, 1985), II, 77–169 (p. 101).

6. KFSA XVIII, 418 [1168].

7. KFSA XVIII, 511 [64]. See Manfred Frank, 'Unendliche Annäherung'. Die Anfänge der philosophischen Frühromantik (Frankfurt am Main: Suhrkamp, 1997), p. 359. For a survey of critical discussion of the Romantic absolute see Jan Urbich, Darstellung bei Walter Benjamin. Die 'Erkenntniskritische Vorrede' im Kontext ästhetischer Darstellungstheorien der Moderne (Berlin: De Gruyter, 2011), pp. 64–67, 350–59.

8. KFSA XII, 214.

9. Novalis. Die Schriften Friedrich von Hardenbergs, III, 685 [671].

10. Ibid., II, 270 [566].

11. Concerning romantic irony and wit, see Ernst Behler, Frühromantik (Berlin and New York: de Gruyter, 1992), pp. 247–55; Manfred Frank, Einführung in die frühromantische Ästhetik (Frankfurt am Main: Suhrkamp, 1989), pp. 231–307; Martin Götze, Ironie und absolute Darstellung (Paderborn and Munich: Schöningh, 1999), pp. 195–217; Jan Urbich, 'Epoche und Stil. Überlegungen zu zwei Deutungsmustern der Jenaer Frühromantik', in Jena. Ein nationaler Erinnerungsort?, ed. by Jürgen John and Justus H. Ulbricht (Köln and Weimar: Böhlau, 2008), pp. 123–38.

12. See Manfred Frank, Das Problem 'Zeit' in der deutschen Romantik (Paderborn and München: Schöningh, 1990), pp. 22–97; Frank, Einführung in die frühromantische Ästhetik, pp. 262 ff.

13. KFSA II, 153 [47].

14. KFSA II, 215 [297].

15. Immanuel Kant, Kritik der Urteilskraft, ed. by Manfred Frank and Véronique Zanetti (Frankfurt am Main: Suhrkamp, 2001), 664 [B 192–93 (§ 49)].

16. Karl Philipp Moritz, Schriften zur Ästhetik und Poetik, ed. by Hans Joachim Schrimpf (Tübingen: Niemeyer, 1962), p. 95.

17. KFSA VIII, 49.

18. Novalis. Die Schriften Friedrich von Hardenbergs, III, 650 [554].

19. See Ernst Behler's introduction in: KFSA XVIII, pp. xii–xxi.

20. See Tzvetan Todorov, Symboltheorien (Tübingen: Niemeyer, 1995), pp. 163–69.

21. KFSA II, 252 [434].

22. Novalis. Die Schriften Friedrich von Hardenbergs, II, 535 [41].

23. On Schlegel's theory of the 'genetic method' of art and philosophy, see Urbich, 'Epoche und Stil'; Urbich, Darstellung bei Walter Benjamin, pp. 350–59.

24. KFSA II, 414.

25. KFSA XII, 39.

26. Friedrich Hölderlin, 'Anmerkungen zur Antigonä', in id., Theoretische Schriften, ed. by Johann Kreuzer (Hamburg: Meiner, 1998), pp. 101–11 (p. 109).

27. KFSA II, 314.

28. KFSA II, 284–85.

29. Aristotle, Metaphysics, IX, 6–7, 1048b.

30. See Walter Benjamin, Der Begriff der Kunstkritik in der deutschen Romantik, in id., Gesammelte Schriften, ed. by Rolf Tiedemann and Hermann Schweppenhäuser (Frankfurt am Main: Suhrkamp, 1991), I.1, 9–123 (pp. 36–37).

31. KFSA II, 414.

32. See KFSA II, 328.

33. See Jean-Michel Palmier, Walter Benjamin (Frankfurt am Main: Suhrkamp, 2009), pp. 819–46.

34. KFSA II, 414.

35. Ibid.

36. KFSA II, 204 [238].

37. KFSA II, 182–83 [116].

38. KFSA II, 225.

39. See Todorov, Symboltheorien, pp. 169–73, Novalis's famous 'Monologue' (Novalis, Monolog, in id., Werke, ed. by Gerhard Schulz, 2nd edn (Munich: Beck, 1981), p. 426), and KFSA II, 364. See also Jan Urbich, '"Mysterium der Ordnung". Anmerkungen zum Verhältnis von Absolutem und Sprache bei Friedrich Schlegel und Walter Benjamin', in Sprache und Literatur, 1 (2009), 93–111.

40. KFSA XVIII, 416 [1140].

41. KFSA II, 334.

42. KFSA XVIII, 420 [1197].

43. KFSA XVIII, 417 [1149].

44. KFSA II, 323.

45. KFSA II, 324.

46. See KFSA XVIII, 249 [663], KFSA XIX, 5 [26], KFSA XIX, 25 [227], KFSA XIX, 167 [106].

47. KFSA XIX, 242 [319].

48. See KFSA XIX, 219 [142], KFSA XIX, 239 [298], KFSA, XIX 331 [219]. For the use of 'symbol' as 'sign', see KFSA XIX, 24 [215], KFSA XVIII, 138 [195], KFSA XVIII, 290 [1127], KFSA XVIII, 417 [1149], KFSA XVIII, 463 [315], KFSA XVIII, 420 [1197].

49. See KFSA XVIII, 205 [105], KFSA XVIII, 218 [284].

50. KFSA XVIII, 132 [120].

51. See Nicholas Halmi, *The Genealogy of the Romantic Symbol* (Oxford: Oxford University Press, 2007), pp. 16, 25; Paul de Man, 'Allegorie und Symbol in der Frühromantik', in *Typologia litterarum*, ed. by Stefan Sonderegger et al. (Zürich: Atlantis, 1969), pp. 403–27 (p. 406); David Wellbery, 'Rhetorik und Literatur. Anmerkungen zur poetologischen Begriffsbildung bei Friedrich Schlegel', in *Die Aktualität der Frühromantik*, ed. by Ernst Behler and Jochen Hörisch (Paderborn and Munich: Schöningh, 1987), pp. 161–74.

52. See KFSA XVIII, 105 [907], 156 [398], 158 [427], 159 [434], 160 [445], 175 [598], 229 [421], 410 [1084], 578 [157]; KFSA XIX, 126 [381], 135 [452], 212 [195/196].

53. See *Novalis. Die Schriften Friedrich von Hardenbergs*, II, 650 [481].

54. See Manfred Frank, 'Wechselgrundsatz. Friedrich Schlegels philosophischer Ausgangspunkt', *Zeitschrift für philosophische Forschung*, 50 (1996), 26–50.

55. For a detailed account of this concept, see Jan Urbich, ' "Die Kunst geht auf den letzten Messias". Friedrich Schlegels *Ideen*-Fragmente und das Verhältnis von Revolution und Religion', in *Romantik und Revolution. Zum politischen Reformpotential einer unpolitischen Bewegung*, ed. by Klaus Ries (Heidelberg: Winter, 2012), pp. 171–95.

56. Paul Ricœur, *Die Interpretation. Ein Versuch über Freud* (Frankfurt am Main: Suhrkamp, 1974), p. 540. See Jeffrey Andrew Barash, 'Was ist ein Symbol? Bemerkungen über Paul Ricœurs kritische Stellungnahme zum Symbolbegriff bei Ernst Cassirer', *Internationales Jahrbuch für Hermeneutik*, 6 (2007), 259–74.

57. See Hans-Georg Gadamer, *Wahrheit und Methode. Grundzüge einer philosophischen Hermeneutik* (Tübingen: Mohr, 1986), pp. 76–87.

58. See e.g. Georg Wilhelm Friedrich Hegel, *Enzyklopädie der philosophischen Wissenschaften* I (Frankfurt am Main: Suhrkamp, 1986), vol. 8 of *Werke in 20 Bänden*, p. 18.

59. See Hölderlin, *Urteil und Sein*, in id., *Theoretische Schriften*, pp. 7–8.

CHAPTER 6

Bread, Wine and Water:
Hegel's Distinction between
Mystical and Symbolical in
The Spirit of Christianity and its Fate

Cecilia Muratori

The aim of this essay is to suggest an interpretation of Hegel's distinction between
the terms *mystisch* (mystical) and *symbolisch* (symbolical) as presented in *The Spirit
of Christianity and its Fate*.[1] I argue that Hegel's early attempts to deal with the
connection and with the distinction between these terms lead to a very subtle but at
the same time crucial differentiation. Exploring this differentiation — as I will try
to show — will prove further relevant in reconsidering Hegel's later speculations
not only on symbol and symbolism but also on the nature of mysticism.

   While important studies have been dedicated to Hegel's conception of symbol
in the later writings, and above all in the aesthetics,[2] the early interpretation of the
word *symbolisch*, especially in the expression 'symbolic action' (*symbolische Handlung*),
remains to my knowledge still unexplored. Likewise, Hegel's understanding of
mysticism has yet to be investigated in its philosophical depth:[3] this essay takes a
first step towards a detailed reconstruction of Hegel's reflections on the nature of
mysticism, by focussing especially on the expressions 'mystical object' (*mystisches
Objekt*) and 'mystical action' (*mystische Handlung*) in the long text from the Frankfurt
period.[4] A study of the meaning of symbolic and mystical, and in particular of the
difference between a symbolic and a mystical action, could therefore contribute to
revealing the genesis of Hegel's later speculations on the significance of mysticism
in the history of philosophy, and at the same time on the characteristics of a symbol.
In other words, I want to suggest that Hegel begins to elaborate the distinction
between *mystisch* and *symbolisch* in the early writings, and that this distinction
becomes crucial in the later writings, where *mystical* and *symbolical* have developed
into two definite conceptions.[5]

   Indeed, a close reading of selected pages from *The Spirit of Christianity* shows that
Hegel repeatedly focuses on the defining characteristics of the adjectives *mystisch*
and *symbolisch* and in doing so differentiates one from the other. This leads to an
important result: the term *mystical* acquires a meaning of its own, not dependent

on the symbolical and not equivalent to the vague, 'standard' definition given for instance by the Grimm brothers' dictionary, according to which 'mystical' is, in a religious context, simply something obscure.[6] For instance, in his influential work, *Symbolik und Mythologie*, Friedrich Creuzer briefly explains that a symbol can be defined as mystical when it aims at encompassing all meaning, but ends up pointing towards speechless contemplation because of its incapability of expressing everything. This type of symbol — so says Creuzer — is still used in religious contexts, but it requires an explanation to be understood, otherwise it remains utterly mysterious.[7]

Does the word 'mystical', then, refer to a specific range of phenomena, or does it just stand for unclear, obscure? And moreover, is the mystical element in particular only a kind of symbolism, as Creuzer suggested? Can a definite line be drawn to distinguish the mystical from the symbolical, or is the mystical a form of the symbolical? In other words: is 'mystical' a technical term or not? I argue that Hegel reflects precisely on these questions in attempting to define what is mystical and what is symbolical, as he distinguishes Christ's mystical action during the Last Supper from John the Baptist's act of baptizing, a typical symbolical action.

Nevertheless, Hegel's argumentation (as is often the case in the so-called early writings) is not free from incongruities. The terminology seems in a few passages to be dangerously unstable, almost to the point of leading the reader to doubt whether the terms mystical and symbolical are really clearly differentiated, or if they may rather be considered as synonyms. I will come finally to the problems that Hegel's approach seems to leave unresolved in dealing with the characteristics of a symbolical and of a mystical action, and especially to the question of their differentiation from one another. The aim of the following pages is nevertheless to suggest that despite the fact that the terminology presents irregularities, there is still a fundamental distinction between *symbolisch* and *mystisch* emerging in the text. In other words, it is important to recognize the *direction* towards which Hegel's argumentation is evolving. The distinction between mystical and symbolical that Hegel is beginning to draw is not yet completely set in this early work, but it will continue to develop and will play an important role in the later writings.[8] Hegel *moves* towards a differentiation, and *The Spirit of Christianity* reveals only the beginning of this process.

A reconstruction of this whole process would, of course, exceed the space and the aim of this essay, which is in its turn only a first step — but perhaps a useful one if it will prompt reconsideration on the one hand of the relevance of Hegel's early distinction between symbolical and mystical in the context of contemporary theories, and on the other of the originality of Hegel's conception of mysticism, as it starts to emerge around 1800.[9]

I will proceed in two steps: first, I will sketch the meaning of mystical and symbolical action and the role they play in *The Spirit of Christianity*; then I will draw attention to the irregularities in Hegel's argumentation in this text, suggesting possible interpretative solutions. In the conclusion, I will briefly point to the importance of these early conceptions of mysticism and symbolism in the light of the evolution of Hegel's thought.

Mystical and Symbolical Action

Jesus's mystical action: the Last Supper

In *The Spirit of Christianity* the adjectives *mystisch* and *symbolisch* are mainly employed to define two different types of *action*. In other words, they are used in the context of actions being performed, thus defining a movement that is carried out and not something static. While John the Baptist's action of baptizing with water is a symbolic one, Christ's action during the Last Supper (that is: breaking the bread and declaring it his own body, pouring the wine and declaring it his own blood) is a mystical one. The aim of the following remarks will be to explain why this is so, that is, what conceptual difference between the two terms lies behind this distinction. The difference between a symbolical and a mystical action is based on the different way in which the movement of mediation takes place in the two cases.

A long section of *The Spirit of Christianity* is dedicated to the interpretation of the Last Supper, 'die Feier eines Mahls der Liebe' [celebration of a love-feast] through which Jesus marks his departure from his disciples. During the Last Supper the bond of love (*Liebe*) between Jesus and the disciples was revealed, and each action performed during the meal — according to Hegel — was an expression of this love.[10] Love in fact leads to reconciliation (*Versöhnung*) which according to Hegel is the defining characteristic of Jesus's preaching. When Jesus invites his disciples to eat together with him, he seals the bond of friendship with them by the act of sharing the food: the Last Supper is therefore in the first place a 'Zusammenessen der Freundschaft' [common table of friendship].[11] On the other hand, during the meal Jesus performs actions which go beyond the expression of friendship and love in sharing the food. When he breaks the bread and calls it his own body, and when he offers to the disciples the wine, calling it his own blood, he seems to perform a 'religious action', since the love binding master and disciples becomes objective in Jesus himself and in the bread and wine that he handles as if they were his flesh and his blood. Hegel claims that it is therefore difficult to grasp the spirit (*Geist*) of the Last Supper, a meal of love and friendship during which Jesus performs a complex religious action, an action which will be repeated in his memory, becoming in all respects a codified ritual. Indeed these actions cannot yet be defined as a ritual, because Jesus performs them for the first time, but Hegel defines them nevertheless as partly *religious* because they point towards a deeper meaning than just the sealing of friendship through sharing the food. For this reason the definition of the essence of the Last Supper must remain uncertain, its meaning oscillating between the form of a religious ceremony and a representation of love, which makes the participants feel united.[12]

During the Last Supper Christ declares that the bread and wine *are* his body and blood: and this is the starting point in Hegel's argument, which reads as follows:

> Das gemeinschaftliche Nachtessen Jesu und seiner Jünger ist an sich schon ein Akt der Freundschaft; noch verknüpfender ist das feierliche Essen vom gleichen Brote, das Trinken aus dem gleichen Kelche; auch dies ist nicht ein bloßes Zeichen der Freundschaft, sondern ein Akt, eine Empfindung der Freundschaft

selbst, des Geistes der Liebe. Aber das Weitere, die Erklärung Jesu: dies ist mein Leib, dies ist mein Blut, nähert die Handlung einer religiösen, aber macht sie nicht dazu; diese Erklärung und die damit verbundene Handlung der Austeilung der Speise und des Tranks macht die Empfindung zum Teil objektiv.[13]

[The supper shared by Jesus and his disciples is already in itself an act of friendship; but a still closer link is the solemn eating of the same bread, drinking from the same cup. This too is not a mere symbol of friendship, but an act, a feeling of friendship itself, of the spirit of love. But the sequel, the declaration of Jesus that 'this is my body, this is my blood' approximates the action to a religious one but does not make it one; this declaration, and the accompanying distribution of food and drink, makes the feeling partly objective].[14]

The words pronounced by Jesus while indicating the bread and the wine — 'this is my body, this is my blood' — cause a break in the balance: the Last Supper becomes something more than just a festive communal meal, it *tends* towards a religious meaning but without being completely identified with it. The reason for this incomplete identification is that Jesus's sentence and the action of sharing bread and wine work only a partial modification in the perception of the participants. Is it *really* the flesh and blood of Christ that is given to the disciples to eat, or does the bread remain in its essence bread, and the wine, wine? Do the words pronounced by Jesus have the power to transform two objects radically, to change their essence from within?

These are the questions that raise the meaning of the communal meal *almost* to the level of a religious ritual, since love, as a binding feeling between master and disciples, now becomes visible on the scene as embodied in two objects. In this context Hegel introduces, for the first time in the text, the term *mystisch*: the action performed by Jesus is not generically religious, but more precisely it can be called a *mystical* one. The mystical character of this action depends on the way Jesus handles two objects, the bread and the wine, and on the words that he pronounces while showing the objects to the disciples.[15] It is this combination — the sentence pronounced while holding an object — that takes the meaning of the meal beyond the simple feeling of community in love and friendship. The feeling of love uniting the participants becomes visible as Jesus declares that bread and wine are now his flesh and his blood. This mystical transformation is described in the following passage:

Die Gemeinschaft mit Jesu, ihre Freundschaft untereinander, und die Vereinigung derselben in ihrem Mittelpunkte, ihrem Lehrer, wird nicht bloß gefühlt; sondern indem Jesus das an alle auszuteilende Brot und Wein seinen für sie gegebenen Leib und Blut nennt, so ist die Vereinigung nicht mehr bloß empfunden, sondern sie ist sichtbar geworden, sie wird nicht nur in einem Bilde, einer allegorischen Figur vorgestellt, sondern an ein Wirkliches angeknüpft, in einem Wirklichen, dem Brote, gegeben und genossen. Einerseits wird also die Empfindung objektiv, andererseits aber ist dies Brot und Wein und die Handlung des Austeilens zugleich nicht bloß objektiv, es ist mehr in ihr als gesehen wird; sie ist eine mystische Handlung [...].[16]

[Their association with Jesus, their friendship with one another, and their unification in their center, their teacher, are not merely sensed. On the contrary, since Jesus calls the bread and wine, which he distributes to all, his body and blood given for them, the unification is no longer merely felt but has become visible. It is not merely represented in an image, an allegorical figure, but linked to a reality, eaten and enjoyed in a reality, the bread. Hence the feeling becomes in a way objective; yet this bread and wine, and the act of distribution, are not purely objective; there is more in it than is seen; it is a mystical action.][17]

The mystical character of Christ's action is defined by two different moments. First, Christ's love for his disciples takes up a precise form, that of a piece of bread and of wine poured into the chalice: a feeling becomes thereby an object, which can be touched, shared, consumed. And yet there is something more in the objects and in the action of sharing them, something that remains hidden resisting the transformation: in this action — a *mystical* action — there is more than that which is visible.

In other words, Christ's love for the disciples becomes objective, incorporated in two objects (bread and wine): it is no longer something subjective, a feeling (of love and friendship), but takes the shape of something visible, tangible, and even consumable. This is, so to speak, the first step. By the end of the passage quoted, Hegel introduces a second step: the sharing of bread and wine is not purely the sharing of the visible objects, because there is more in them that what we see. Hegel writes further: 'So ist, objektiv betrachtet, das Brot bloßes Brot, der Wein bloßer Wein; aber beide sind auch noch mehr' [Objectively considered, then, the bread is just bread, the wine just wine; yet both are something more].[18] They are indeed the flesh and blood of Christ, that the disciples are invited to consume, not *just* bread and wine. This is why an external spectator, who hadn't heard Christ's words ('This is my body, this is my blood'), could not possibly be aware of this transformation. Through Christ's action bread and wine become mystical objects, which Hegel defines as follows:

> Hier aber werden [...] Wein und Brot mystische Objekte, indem Jesus sie seinen Leib und Blut nennt, und ein Genuß, eine Empfindung unmittelbar sie begleitet; er zerbrach das Brot, gab es seinen Freunden: Nehmet, esset; dies ist mein Leib, für euch hingegeben; so auch den Kelch: Trinket alle daraus; dies ist mein Blut, das Blut des neuen Bundes, über viele ausgegossen zur Entlassung der Sünden.[19]

> [Here, however, bread and wine [...] become mystical objects, for Jesus calls them his flesh and blood, and a pleasure, a feeling, is their direct accompaniment. He broke bread and gave it to his friends: 'Take, eat, this is my body sacrificed for you.' So also when he took the cup: 'Drink all of it; this is my blood, the blood of the new covenant, poured out for many for the remission of their sins.'][20]

It is important to remark that the mystical transformation consists in the fact that the bread and wine are declared to *be* (and not only *represent*) Christ's body and blood.[21] In Christ's hands, bread and wine become mystical objects, their nature transformed from within. And yet the transformation of the object can never be complete — and this is, I argue, the crucial characteristic defining a mystical action. Christ's words created a deep connection between the object and Christ's feeling of love for the disciple: the bread has become the tangible sign of this love. But Christ went even further in declaring that the bread is now not just his love but his own body: he has therefore imposed on the bread a new essence, a new nature, he has undertaken a *mystical* action.

The result is nevertheless deeply unstable. The bread *tends* to become something else — Christ himself, who gives his own body to the disciples as a sign of friendship and love — and yet it remains bread, something that can be touched, seen, and especially eaten. When the disciples eat Christ's body, it is really bread that they are eating. Therefore the consumption of the mystical object sets in motion yet another transformation: Christ's body turns again into bread when it is consumed.

> Das Brot soll gegessen, der Wein getrunken werden; sie können darum nichts Göttliches sein; was sie auf der einen Seite voraus haben, daß die Empfindung, die an sie geheftet ist, wieder von ihrer Objektivität zu ihrer Natur gleichsam zurückkehrt, das mystische Objekt wieder zu einem bloß Subjektiven wird, das verlieren sie eben dadurch, daß die Liebe durch sie nicht objektiv genug wird. Etwas Göttliches kann, indem es göttlich ist, nicht in der Gestalt eines zu Essenden und zu Trinkenden vorhanden sein.[22]

> [The bread is to be eaten, the wine to be drunk; therefore they cannot be something divine. What, on the one hand, they presuppose (namely, the fact that the feeling attached to them almost reverts from their objectivity to their respective nature, the fact that the mystical object becomes a purely subjective thing once more), this, on the other hand, they lose just because love is not made objective enough by them. Something divine, just because it is divine, cannot present itself in the shape of something to eat and drink.][23]

What Hegel describes here is this second movement or transformation (he uses the verb *zurückkehren*, 'to go back', *revert*). Christ's love had not become objective *enough* in the transformation of the object, and the tasting of the bread brings back its nature as food, made of water and flour and quite different from the substance of Christ's flesh. The delicate structure described above — Christ becoming incorporated in an object — breaks down altogether in the moment when the object is consumed, revealing the limits of the transformation.

Christ's mystical action thus sets in motion a precise chain of transformations, which we could sum up as follows: his words operate a radical alteration in the objects he handles, which are declared to turn into his flesh and blood, thus embodying his bond of friendship with the disciples. In the mystical object created in this way, the physical appearance becomes the cover of an inner nature (Christ's body), which is visible only to the disciples attending the ritual. When the disciples eat the mystical object, the balance is broken: what the mouth tastes is bread, and not Christ's flesh. What had become, for a moment, objective, turns again into something subjective, that is the feeling of the disciple in eating a piece of bread declared by Christ to be his own body.[24]

The mystical action can therefore be seen as the impulse to this series of changes; on the other hand the mystical object is defined by the delicate and dynamic structure sketched above, which transforms the object itself in a movement of disappearing and reappearing comprising two different phases: first Christ transfers himself into the object, and then the object re-emerges as such when it is consumed, revealing thereby the inevitable discrepancy between the material of the bread and what it should become — Christ's body. The mystical object is thus the medium of this transformation, the point on which the transformations converge.

Two aspects should be emphasized before considering Hegel's presentation of John's baptism: first, *mystisch* (both in the expressions 'mystische Handlung' and 'mystisches Objekt') is employed to describe a twofold movement. This dynamism, as I will briefly show below, is essential also in Hegel's later accounts of the meaning of *Mystizismus*. Secondly, *mystisch* defines a powerful (almost violent) way of pushing together two extremes that cannot be held together, an effort to merge them into one, like the bread and Christ's body (even if the transformation, as we saw, is not stable).

This complex structure of the mystical action is not present in John's baptism, which is a symbolical, not a mystical action.

John's symbolical action: baptism

Describing John's custom of baptizing, Hegel writes:

> Die Gewohnheit des Johannes (von Jesu ist keine solche Handlung bekannt), die zu seinem Geist Erzogenen in Wasser unterzutauchen, ist eine bedeutende symbolische. Es gibt kein Gefühl, das dem Verlangen nach dem Unendlichen, dem Sehnen, in das Unendliche überzufließen, so homogen wäre, als das Verlangen, sich in einer Wasserfülle zu begraben; der Hineinstürzende hat ein Fremdes vor sich, das ihn sogleich ganz umfließt, an jedem Punkte seines Körpers sich zu fühlen gibt; er ist der Welt genommen, sie ihm; er ist nur gefühltes Wasser, das ihn berührt, wo er ist, und er ist nur, wo er es fühlt; es ist in der Wasserfülle keine Lücke, keine Beschränkung, keine Mannigfaltigkeit oder Bestimmung; das Gefühl derselben ist das unzerstreuteste, einfachste; der Untergetauchte steigt wieder in die Luft empor, trennt sich vom Wasserkörper, ist von ihm schon geschieden, aber er trieft noch allenthalben von ihm; sowie es ihn verläßt, nimmt die Welt um ihn wieder Bestimmtheit an, und er tritt gestärkt in die Mannigfaltigkeit des Bewußtseins zurück. Im Hinaussehen in die unschattierte Bläue und die einfache gestaltenlose Fläche eines morgenländischen Horizontes wird die umgebende Luft nicht gefühlt, und das Spiel der Gedanken ist etwas anders als das Hinaussehen. Im Untergetauchten ist nur Ein Gefühl und die Vergessenheit der Welt, eine Einsamkeit, die alles von sich geworfen, allem sich entwunden hat.[25]

> [John's custom (nothing similar is known to have been done by Jesus) of baptizing by immersion in water those drawn to his spirit is a significantly symbolical one. No feeling is so homogeneous with the desire for the infinite, the longing to merge into the infinite, as the desire to immerse one's self in an amplitude of water. He who plunges into it is confronted by an alien element which at once flows round us on every side and which is felt at every point of the body. He is taken away from the world and the world from him. He is nothing but felt water which touches him where he is, and he is only where he feels it. In the amplitude of water there is no gap, no restriction, no multiplicity or determination. The feeling of it is the simplest, the least broken up. The person who has been immersed comes up into the air again, separates himself from the water, is at once removed from it and yet it still drips from

him everywhere. So soon as the water leaves him, the world around him takes
on determination again, and he comes back strengthened to the multiplicity
of consciousness. Looking out into the unshaded sky and into the simple,
shapeless, plain of an eastern horizon, the air surrounding is not felt, and the
play of thoughts is something different from gazing. In the person who has been
immersed there is only one feeling and forgetfulness of the world, a solitude
which has repelled everything, withdrawn itself from everything.][26]

John's action stimulates a physical sensation: the water completely surrounds the
person who is baptized, giving him or her a perfect sensation of homogeneity,
of immersion in infinity, since the water touches the body on the whole of its
surface. This physical sensation symbolizes the beginning of a new life for the
person baptized. Hegel insists on this word: 'feeling' (*Gefühl*). Feeling the water all
around gives the impression of immersing oneself into something without limits
and without determination or boundaries. The action of baptism consists in the
stimulation of this one very simple feeling, a feeling which depends entirely on the
physical experience of being immersed in the element of water. The physical aspect
is predominant in the course of the symbolical performance: indeed the sensation
caused by being immersed in water ceases as soon as the person emerges again,
confirming the fact that the purely physical sensation is the trigger of the feeling
experienced by the person involved.

   John's water, of course, remains water. On the difference between Christ and
John, Hegel quotes from Luke 3, 16: '[...] in V. 8 sagt Johannes: ich taufte euch im
Wasser; er aber wird in heiligen Geist und in Feuer (Lk 3 16) eintauchen [...]' ('In
verse 8 John says: "I have baptized you with water, but he shall baptize you with the
Holy Ghost" and (as Luke iii.16 adds) "with fire [...]"'.[27] This is a crucial difference:
the object handled by John — which is also in this case, as for the bread, the
medium of the action — does not change its nature, while Christ is able to perform
a paradoxical action, that is immersing or baptizing into spirit and fire, not in water.
Christ performs mystical actions which are able to transform the object from within.
This does not happen when John performs the symbolical action of baptizing.

   In the light of these considerations, the difference between *symbolisch* and *mystisch*
starts to take shape: Christ's action is mystical because it involves a powerful
transformation of the objects on which the action is performed, turning the object
itself into a movement between presence and absence; John's baptism on the other
hand does not involve such radical changes and is based on a simple physical feeling,
which automatically dissolves on emerging out of the water. The water in this sense
is a medium that has an influence on the person who is immersed in it but does not
itself undergo any radical changes. There is no trace in this symbolical performance
of the powerful and unstable connection between object and feeling which was at
the centre of Christ's mystical action.

Problems Left Unsolved: The Broken Ring

This is the basic differentiation which in my opinion it is possible to find in *The
Spirit of Christianity*.[28] As I mentioned before, terminology is not always used
coherently in Hegel's early writings, and in this case too there are problems left

unresolved: not only does Hegel once use the adjective *symbolisch* in referring clearly
to the Last Supper,[29] but he also provides an example which instead of explaining
actually complicates things, namely the example of the broken ring. In order to
clarify the fact that the mystical action performed by Christ does not reveal its real
meaning to an external spectator, Hegel writes that something similar happens with
two friends who break a ring as a sign of their friendship when they have to say
farewell to each other:

> [...] so wie wenn scheidende Freunde einen Ring brachen, und jeder ein Stück
> behielt, der Zuschauer nichts sieht, als das Zerbrechen eines brauchbaren
> Dinges und das Teilen in unbrauchbare, wertlose Stücke; das Mystische der
> Stücke hat er nicht gefaßt. So ist, objektiv betrachtet, das Brot bloßes Brot, der
> Wein bloßer Wein; aber beide sind auch noch mehr.[30]

> [Similarly, when friends part and break a ring and each keeps one piece, a
> spectator sees nothing but the breaking of a useful thing and its division into
> useless and valueless pieces; the mystical aspect of the pieces he has failed to
> grasp. Objectively considered, then, the bread is just bread, the wine just wine;
> yet both are also something more.][31]

What Hegel calls 'das Mystische der Stücke' [the mystical aspect of the pieces] is the
secret meaning of the action: as in the case of the Last Supper, the external spectator
could not grasp the meaning of breaking a ring without knowing that the two parts
will be a sign of the bond of friendship before the friends are reunited. The parallel
with Christ's action however ends here: Christ's mystical action and the creation of
the mystical object are not reflected in the breaking of the ring. The broken ring,
in other words, does not present the same complex, internal movement which we
detected in the mystical objects of the Last Supper. In fact in the text that follows,
Hegel will then concentrate his attention on the mystical character of the Last
Supper, rather than on the broken ring.

Moreover, the breaking of the ring is the typical example used to explain the
conception of the symbol: for instance in *Symbolik und Mythologie* Friedrich Creuzer
recalls that the noun *symbolum* comes from the Greek verb *symballein*, meaning
'putting back together', since it was common to break a coin, or indeed a ring,
keeping the pieces as a sign of friendship and of the hospitality enjoyed.[32]

Does, then, Hegel's parallel between the ring on the one hand and the bread and
wine on the other jeopardize the differentiation between *mystisch* and *symbolisch*
which I have tried to sketch? In my final remarks I will explain why, in my opinion,
it does not, and why it remains important to recognize the crucial differentiation
between *symbolisch* and *mystisch* in *The Spirit of Christianity*.

There is nevertheless a point on which *symbolisch* and *mystisch* seem to converge.
Alongside the distinction between the physical basis of the symbol and the
internal movement of the mystical object, Hegel also makes use of a more general
interpretation of the two terms, according to which they both refer simply to the
gap between the content that they express and the form in which they express it.
In both cases there is something more than what we see, and we need to know the
context in order to decode what that 'more' could be (friendship in the case of the
ring, and Christ's love incorporated in the case of the bread). The border between

mystical and symbolical becomes, from this point of view, very subtle and almost undistinguishable. In other words Hegel seems to employ the terms *symbolisch* and *mystisch* in a broad and in a strict sense at the same time: in the broad sense, something is symbolical, *or* mystical, if there is a hidden meaning which I need to know in order to understand the action performed; while in the strict sense the mystical action presents a precise internal structure, while the symbolical action evokes a sensation by means of a material medium. In my opinion the presence of these two ways of interpreting the meaning of *mystisch* and *symbolisch* is due to the fact that in *The Spirit of Christianity* Hegel is in the process of developing the conceptions of a mystical and of a symbolical action. In the later writings, as I mentioned before, these conceptions, and the difference from one another, emerge in their full complexity. The link with these early speculations is nevertheless still visible.

Indeed I will argue that the differentiation we find in *The Spirit of Christianity* also enables us to understand the genesis of the conceptions of *mystisch* and *symbolisch* in Hegel's later writings, where the two terms are not interchangeable and where Hegel emphasizes and builds on some of the characteristics which we mentioned already in relation to *The Spirit of Christianity*.

Conclusion

What is left of Hegel's understanding of a symbolical action in his later symbol-conception? And what remains of Hegel's description of a mystical action in his later speculations on the nature of mysticism? These questions take us back to underlining the lack of studies of the evolution of Hegel's conception of mysticism: as a consequence, the answers must necessarily consist only in a provisional interpretation, and in a sketch rather than in a complete reconstruction.

As far as the conception of symbolism is concerned, we can rely on a number of studies in reconstructing the link between the symbolical action in *The Spirit of Christianity* and Hegel's later definition of a symbol. If it is true, as Kathleen Dow Magnus has argued, that the conception of symbolism remains stable throughout Hegel's philosophical production, the question about the link between the John the Baptist' symbolical action and the later symbol-conception is legitimate.[33] An investigation of the definition of 'symbolic action' in *The Spirit of Christianity* also offers new material for reflecting on the genesis of Hegel's conception of symbol. In *The Spirit of Christianity*, as well as in the later writings, Hegel indeed insists on one defining characteristic of the symbol, and this is its strong connection to matter, to sensation.[34] In his famous study on Hegel's aesthetics, Paolo D'Angelo wrote for instance that in the symbolical there is always something more than that which can be expressed explicitly: this *remainder* lies precisely in the nature of the symbol, that is in its link to matter and sensation.[35] Matter predominates already in the symbolical action performed by John, where the sensation of feeling the water on the body was the key to the symbol of baptism — and this is why Hegel lingers on the description of the purely physical effect produced by the immersion in the water. From this perspective, Hegel's description of John's baptism in this early text offers a clear and strong connection to his later conception of symbol.

With regard to the role of the mystical action in the Frankfurt text, two aspects deserve to be considered in the light of the evolution of Hegel's conception of mysticism. In commenting on selected passages from *The Spirit of Christianity*, I pointed out in particular the following crucial characteristics of the mystical action: first, the power of bringing together two extremities that can only be forced together, creating an unstable combination; and second, the movement which the mystical action generates. Both are defining characteristics of mysticism in Hegel's later writings too.

In *The Spirit of Christianity* Hegel states that Christ forces into an object a new nature, as his love for the disciples is incorporated in a piece of bread, which becomes his own flesh. This is an action that requires an excessive power, and this is why Hegel calls Jesus an enthusiast, *Schwärmer*.[36] Christ can perform that action because of his enthusiastic, excessive energy. Nevertheless, Christ is not the only figure to whom Hegel attributes a form of mystical acting: in the *Lectures on the History of Philosophy*, Hegel mentions two other important examples, namely the Neoplatonists and Jakob Böhme.[37] They, too, are enthusiasts who talked *mystically*; in both cases their mystical way of speaking was not contrary to philosophy, but quite the opposite: they are rather examples of the way in which speculative philosophy could be expressed mystically — and *mystical* here means that this kind of philosophy is driven by the desire to unite opposites into one.

The defining characteristic of Jakob Böhme's thought — so remarks Hegel in the *Lectures on the History of Philosophy* — is indeed the struggle to unify opposites, which in Böhme's terminology are described as God and the Devil. The content of Böhme's struggle is indeed '[...] die tiefste Idee, die die absolutesten Gegensätze zu vereinigen aufzeigt' [the most profound idea, which points to the unification of the most absolute opposites].[38] In the section on Proclus in the same lectures, the Neoplatonists' mystical striving towards unification is described as follows:

> 'Mystisch' | heißt im eigentlich Sinn 'spekulativ'. Das Mystische oder Spekulative ist, daß diese Unterschiede, die als Totalitäten, als Götter bestimmt sind, als eine Einheit zu erfassen. Bei den Neuplatonikern kommt überhaupt der Ausdruck 'mystisch' oft vor; μύειν heißt dann nichts anderes als 'spekulative Betrachtung'.[39]

> ['Mystical' in the proper sense means 'speculative'. The mystical or speculative consists in the fact that these differences, which are determined as totalities, as divinities, are to be conceived as a unity. Actually in the Neoplatonists we mainly find the term 'mystich'; μύειν means then nothing other than 'speculative consideration'.]

This passage is also echoed in the addition to § 82 of the *Encyclopedia*, in which the conception of mysticism is associated with that of speculation, arguing that mysticism aims at uniting what the mere intellect conceives as opposites:

> [...] das Mystische allerdings [ist] ein Geheimnisvolles, jedoch nur für den Verstand, und zwar einfach um deswillen, weil die abstrakte Identität das Prinzip des Verstandes, das Mystische aber (als gleichbedeutend mit dem Spekulativen) die konkrete Einheit derjenigen Bestimmungen ist, welche dem Verstand nur in ihrer Trennung und Entgegensetzung für wahr gelten.[40]

[The mystical is indeed something secret, and yet only for the intellect, and the reason is this: the abstract identity is the principle of the intellect, but the mystical (as synonymous with the speculative) is the concrete unity of those determinations which for the intellect count for true only in their separation and opposition.]

A mystic in the proper sense of the word is then an enthusiast who is aiming at bringing together the opposites into unity — and this is the defining feature which Hegel attributes to Christ in *The Spirit of Christianity*.

The oscillation between hiding and revealing which we sketched in this text also emerges again in the later writings, where Hegel insists on the fact that mysticism, properly understood, is not esotericism. This is clear already in the passage quoted from the lectures on Proclus, where Hegel states that the word mystical actually refers to 'speculative contemplation'. The addition to § 82 of the *Encyclopedia* also insists on the fact that the term mystical should not be considered as a synonym for mysterious or inapprehensible.

Mysticism is rather exoteric in its attempt to open up the secret, to reveal its content.[41] Hegel builds his understanding of mysticism on a movement of presence and absence, of hiding and revealing, which reminds us of the description of the mystical object in the Frankfurt text, an object that briefly disappears as such in order to become the medium of revelation for Christ's love. In the *Phenomenology* Hegel writes for instance: 'Denn das Mystische ist nicht Verborgenheit eines Geheimnisses oder Unwissenheit, sondern besteht darin, daß das Selbst sich mit dem Wesen Eins weiß, und dieses also geoffenbart ist.' [For the mystical is not concealment of a secret, or ignorance, but consists in the self knowing itself to be one with the divine Being and that this, therefore, is revealed.][42]

The conception of mysticism which emerges in the later writings and at which I can only hint here, is yet to be fully reconstructed. As I hope to have coherently suggested, it is a conception according to which mysticism is not equivalent to esotericism but rather an enthusiastic and yet speculative way of thinking philosophically. Christ's mystical (and not symbolical) action in *The Spirit of Christianity* is in this sense an important starting point for Hegel's further reflections — and this is why it is crucial to recognize this distinction despite the problems which the Frankfurt text leaves partially unsolved.

I am grateful to Claus-Artur Scheier, to Gian Franco Frigo, and to the participants in the workshop 'Hegel und die Freiheit' (Università di Padova, 6–8 October 2010) for their suggestions and comments on the topic at the centre of this essay.

Notes to Chapter 6

1. I shall quote the German text from the following edition: Georg Wilhelm Friedrich Hegel, *Hegels theologische Jugendschriften*, ed. by Herman Nohl (Tübingen: Mohr, 1907). English translations are based on Georg Wilhelm Friedrich Hegel, *Early Theological Writings*, trans. by Thomas Malcolm Knox, with an introduction and Fragments trans. by Richard Kroner (Chicago, IL: University of Chicago Press, 1948). All other translations are my own unless otherwise stated.
2. See in particular the studies on Hegel's philosophy of art by Annemarie Gethmann-Siefert, especially *Einführung in Hegels Ästhetik* (Munich: Fink, 2005). See also Kathleen Dow Magnus,

Hegel and the Symbolic Mediation of Spirit (Albany: State University of New York, 2001); Paolo D'Angelo, *Simbolo e Arte in Hegel* (Rome-Bari: Laterza, 1989).

3. On Hegel's conception of mysticism exist only few publications, most of which tend to understand it in the context of the philosopher's supposed interest in esotericism. See for instance: David Walsh, 'The Esoteric Origins of Modern Ideological Thought: Boehme and Hegel' (unpublished doctoral dissertation, University of Virginia, 1978); Glenn Alexander Magee, *Hegel and the Hermetic Tradition* (Ithaca, NY: Cornell University Press, 2001). In an article entitled 'The Mystical Element in Hegel's *Early Theological Writings*' (*University of California Publications in Philosophy*, 2.4 (1910), 67–102) George Plimpton Adams has argued in favour of a radical change in Hegel's attitude towards mysticism: '[...] Hegel had passed through just that romantic mysticism against which he contends in the preface of the Phenomenology'). In my study *Il primo filosofo tedesco* I argue in favour of a reconstruction of Hegel's understanding of mysticism which does not imply major shifts in his conception and avoids recurring to esotericism as a frame of interpretation — a frame which I consider misleading: Cecilia Muratori, *Il primo filosofo tedesco. Il misticismo di Jakob Böhme nell'interpretazione hegeliana* (Pisa: ETS, 2012). On Hegel's attitude towards mysticism, Frederick C. Copleston rightly argued that 'Hegel was doubtless hostile to the taking of short cuts in philosophy by substituting appeals to institution or to mystical insights in place of the patient effort to understand and to express the truth in a systematic way. [...] But it by no means follows that Hegel did not regard mystical writers as having given expression, even in paradoxical form, to valid insights, which the philosopher should try to conceptualize [...].' (Frederick C. Copleston, 'Hegel and the Rationalization of Mysticism', in *New Studies in Hegel's Philosophy*, ed. by Warren E. Steinkraus (New York: Holt, Rinehart and Wiston, 1971), pp. 187–200 (p. 191)).

4. See further on this topic Cecilia Muratori, *Il primo filosofo tedesco*, part I.2.

5. Commenting on the text *Über das Verhältniß der Naturphilosophie zur Philosophie überhaupt*, published in the *Kritisches Journal der Philosophie*, Rosenkranz refers superficially to a distinction between symbolism and mysticism, associating the first with Christianity and the second with paganism: 'Hegel bestimmte daher das Heidenthum als *Vergötterung der Natur*, während das Christenthum durch die Natur als den unendlichen *Leib Gottes* bis in das Innerste und den Geist Gottes schaue. Dort walte die *Heiterkeit* des unmittelbaren Versöhnt*seins*, hier der *Schmerz* des Versöhnt*werdens*; dort herrschte das *Symbol*, hier die *Mystik*, deren selbst der Protestantismus sich nicht habe entschlagen können.' Karl Rosenkranz, *Hegels Leben* (Berlin: Verlag von Duncker und Humblot, 1844), p. 168. My translation: 'Hegel therefore defined paganism as *idolisation of nature*, whereas Christianity looks through nature, as the infinite *body of God*, into the core and into the spirit of God. In the former prevails the *serenity* of the immediate *being*-reconciled, in the latter, the *pain* of the *becoming*-reconciled; there the *symbol* dominates, here *mysticism*, which not even Protestantism could renounce'. In the present essay I will not consider Hegel's distinction between symbolism and mysticism within this frame, focusing instead on the substantial distinction between a symbolic and a mystical action in Hegel's reflections on the spirit of Christianity only.

6. Jacob Grimm and Wilhelm Grimm, *Deutsches Wörterbuch*, 16 vols (Leipzig: S. Hirzel, 1854–1960), sub voce: 'MYSTISCH, adj. nach dem griech. μυστικος, seit dem vorigen jahrh. völlig eingebürgert, mit der bedeutung des dunkeln und geheimnisvollen, auf grund der vereinigung der seele mit dem göttlichen wesen [...].'

7. Friedrich Creuzer, *Symbolik und Mythologie der alten Völker, besonders der Griechen*, 4 vols (Leipzig and Darmstadt: Karl Wilhelm Leske, 1810), I, 70–80: 'Je mehr es [das Symbol] diesem heiligen Bedürfnis huldigte, desto größer die Neigung zum Unverständlichen, bis es im Äussersten endlich zu einem verkörperten Räthsel ward. [...] In noch höherem Grade gilt dieses von dem eigentlich mystischen Symbol. [...] Man hatte den Schlüssel verloren, den man im Unterricht der Mysterien empfing; wie dann alle Symbolik dieses geheimen Dienstes eine Belherung voraussetzte, die der Eingeweihte nur von den Ordenspriestern und Exegeten erhielt.' See also Tilottama Rajan, 'Toward a Cultural Idealism: Negativity and Freedom in Hegel and Kant', in *Idealism without Absolutes: Philosophy and Romantic Culture*, ed. by Tilottama Rajan and Arkady Plotnitsky (Albany: State University of New York, 2004), pp. 51–71 (p. 63): 'Creuzer distinguishes two kinds of symbol: "plastic" and "mystic", corresponding to the beautiful and

the sublime or the classical and the romantic. Though he wants the aura of symbol for both forms, he verges on deconstructing the traditional concept, by conceding in the "mystic" symbol a mutual inadequacy of form and content, an excess or lack absent from the more conventional "plastic" symbol.' See also Martin Donougho, 'Hegel and Creuzer: or, Did Hegel Believe in Myth?' in *New Perspectives on Hegel's Philosophy of Religion*, ed. by David Kolby (Albany: State University of New York, 1992), pp. 59–80. Donougho alludes to Hegel's conception of a mystic symbol, but without explaining exactly what is meant thereby and especially in which Hegelian texts this conception is to be found (see p. 70: '[...] Hegel agrees [with Creuzer] that the "mystic" symbol constitutes "die eigentliche Symbolik" — Creuzer's phrase — even while he holds that the "plastic" Ideal escapes symbolism altogether').

8. Tilottama Rajan does not seem to consider the term mystic as referring for Hegel to a precise set of phenomena but associates it with symbol: 'For Hegel the symbolic is thus the aporia between these forms, a confusion of mystic with plastic [...]. Hegel, it would seem, denies the symbol as *Darstellung*, but retains its mystic link to ideas' (p. 64).

9. For a full account of Hegel's conception of mysticism in its development see Muratori, *Il primo filosofo tedesco*. In this essay I will only refer to key aspects of this evolution in the conclusion.

10. See *Hegels theologische Jugendschriften*, p. 297: 'Der Abschied, den Jesu von seinen Freunden nahm, war die Feier eines Mahl der Liebe; Liebe ist noch nicht Religion, dieses Mahl also auch keine eigentliche religiöse Handlung [...].' *Early Theological Writings*, p. 248: 'Jesus' leave-taking from his friends took the form of celebrating a love-feast. Love is less than religion, and this meal, too, therefore is not strictly a religious action [...].' I do not agree with the translation of 'Liebe ist nocht nicht Religion' with 'love is less than religion.' I suggest therefore as an alternative translation: 'love is not yet religion.'

11. *Hegels theologische Jugendschriften*, p. 297. *Early Theological Writings*, p. 248.

12. *Hegels theologische Jugendschriften*, p. 297: '[...] und darum schwebt dies Essen zwischen einem Zusammenessen der Freundschaft und einem religiösem Akt, und dieses Schweben macht es schwer, seinen Geist deutlich zu bezeichnen.' *Early Theological Writings*, p. 248: 'Hence this eating hovers between a common table of friendship and a religious act, and this hovering makes difficult the clear interpretation of its spirit.'

13. *Hegels theologische Jugendschriften*, p. 297.

14. Cf. *Early Theological Writings*, pp. 248–49.

15. *Hegels theologische Jugendschriften*, p. 297: 'Jesus brach das Brot: Nehmet hin, dies ist mein Leib, für euch gegeben, tut's zu meinem Gedächtnis; desselbigen gleichen nahm er den Kelch: Trinket alle daraus, es ist mein Blut des neuen Testaments, für euch und für viele zur Vergebung der Sünden vergossen; tut dies zu meinem Gedächtnis!' Cf. *Early Theological Writings*, p. 248: 'Jesus broke bread: "Take, this is my body given for you; do this in remembrance of me". Likewise took he the cup: "Drink ye all of it; this is my blood of the new testament, which is shed for you and for many for the remission of sins; do this in remembrance of me."'

16. *Hegels theologische Jugendschriften*, pp. 297–98.

17. *Early Theological Writings*, p. 249.

18. *Hegels theologische Jugendschriften*, p. 298. *Early Theological Writings*, p. 249.

19. *Hegels theologische Jugendschriften*, p. 298.

20. Cf. *Early Theological Writings*, p. 250.

21. See in this context Hegel's remarks on the difference between the Catholic and the Protestant interpretation of the ritual taking place during Mass. Particularly clear is the following passage from the 1821 *Lectures on the Philosophy of Religion*: 'Hostie hinübergestellt als Ding ist ein Brotteig, *nicht* der Gott. Reformierte *Vorstellung* ohne dies *Mystische — Andenken*, gemein psychologisches Verhältnis; alles Spekulative verschwunden' [The host transposed into a thing is bread-dough, *not* God. Reformed *representation* without this *mystical — remembrance*, mere psychological relation; everything speculative vanished]. Georg Wilhelm Friedrich Hegel, *Vorlesungen über die Philosophie der Religion*, ed. by Walter Jaeschke, in Id., *Vorlesungen. Ausgewählte Nachschriften und Manuskripte* (Hamburg: Meiner, 1983–), v, 91.

22. *Hegels theologische Jugendschriften*, p. 300.

23. Cf. *Early Theological Writings*, p. 251.

24. Cf. the definition of *Transsubstantiation* as formulated by Laarman in *Historisches Wörterbuch*

der Philosophie: 'Der durch seine Schöpfungstat als allmächtig ausgewiesene Gott erfaßt durch die Transsubstantiation die "forma" von Brot und Wein als deren substanztragenden Grund, verwandelt diese sofort und total in den erhöhten Leib des Herrn, aber beläßt die Akzidenzien ohne physische Transformation, so daß für die Sinneserfahrung auch keine Täuschung oder Fiktion vorliegt' (*Historisches Wörterbuch der Philosophie*, ed. by Joachim Ritter, Karlfried Gründer and Gottfried Gabriel, 12 vols (Basel: Schwabe, 1998), vol. x, cols 1349–58). The passage is quoted by Claus-Artur Scheier in his essay 'Zeiten der Metamorphose', in *Dimensionen der Ästhetik. Festschrift für Barbara Ränsch-Trill*, ed. by Manfred Lämmer and Tim Nebelung, Schriften der Deutschen Sporthochschule Köln, 50 (Sankt Augustin: Academia, 2005), pp. 48–61 (p. 57).

25. *Hegels theologische Jugendschriften*, p. 319.
26. Cf. *Early Theological Writings*, p. 275. I have modified the translation at several points: for instance, Knox translates 'in die Mannigfaltigkeit des Bewußtseins' as 'in the consciousness of multiplicity' instead of 'in the multiplicity of consciousness', which is the literal translation.
27. *Hegels theologische Jugendschriften*, p. 319. *Early Theological Writings*, p. 274.
28. It is particularly interesting to compare Hegel's very innovative conception of the terms symbolical and mystical with Schelling's interpretation of the symbolical or mystical character of the Last Supper and of baptism. Indeed Schelling also distinguishes between the mystical and the symbolical with regard to the Last Supper and to the act of baptizing: the differentiation appears nevertheless to be significantly different from Hegel's. See Friedrich Wilhelm Joseph Schelling, *Philosophie der Kunst* (1802) (in Id., *Sämmtliche Werke*, ed. by Karl Friedrich August Schelling (Stuttgart/Augsburg: Cotta, 1859), v, 357–487; reprint: *Ausgewählte Werke* (Darmstadt: Wissenschaftliche Buchgesellschaft, 1979), pp. 1–131). The text is also printed in the following edition, from which I quote: Friedrich Wilhelm Joseph Schelling, *Texte zur Philosophie der Kunst*, ed. by Werner Beierwaltes (Stuttgart: Reclam, 1982), pp. 139–281 (pp. 221–22): 'Es ist ganz dem gemäß, was überhaupt als Prinzip des Christentums anzusehen ist: daß es keine vollendeten Symbole, sondern nur symbolische *Handlungen* hat. Der ganze Geist des Christentums ist der des Handelns. Das Unendlich *ist* nicht mehr im Endlichen, das Endliche kann nur ins Unendliche übergehen; nur in diesem können beide eins werden. Die Einheit des Endlichen und Unendlichen ist also im Christentum Handlung. Die erste symbolische Handlung Christi ist die Taufe, wo der Himmel sich ihm verband, der Geist in sichtbarer Gestalt herabkam, die andere sein Tod, wo er den Geist | dem Vater wieder befahl, zurückgab, und an sich das Endliche vernichtend, Opfer für die Welt wird. Diese symbolische Handlungen werden im Christentum fortgesetzt durch das *Nachtmahl* und die *Taufe*. Das Nachtmahl hat wieder zwei Seiten, von denen es betrachtet werden kann, die ideelle, inwiefern es das Subjekt ist, das sich den Gott schafft, und in das jene geheimnisvolle Einigung des Unendlichen und Endlichen fällt, und die symbolische. Inwiefern die Handlung, wodurch das Endliche hier zugleich das Unendliche wird, als Andacht in das empfangene Subjekt selbst fällt, insofern ist sie nicht symbolisch, sondern *mystisch*; inwiefern sie aber eine äußere Handlung ist, ist sie symbolisch. (Wir werden auf diesen sehr wichtigen Unterschied des Mystischen und Symbolischen in der Folge zurückkommen.)' Friedrich Wilhelm Joseph Schelling, *The Philosophy of Art*, ed. and trans. with an introduction by Douglas W. Stott (Minneapolis: University of Minnesota, 1989), p. 65: 'All this shows us quite clearly what we are to understand as the overriding principle of Christianity: that it has no perfected symbols but rather only symbolic *acts*. The entire spirit of Christianity is that of action. The infinite *is* no longer within the finite; the finite can only pass over into the infinite. Only within the latter can the two become one. The unity of the finite and the infinite is thus an act of Christianity. Christ's first symbolic action is *baptism*, where heaven allies itself with him and the spirit descends in a visible form. The other is his *death*, where he commends the spirit to the Father once again, gives it back, nullifies the finite within his own person and becomes a sacrifice for the world. These symbolic acts are continued in Christianity by means of the *eucharist* and *baptism*. The eucharist itself has two sides from which it can be viewed: the ideal, to the extent that it functions as the subject that creates God for itself and into which falls that mysterious union of the infinite and the finite; and the symbolic. To the extent that the act through which the finite here simultaneously becomes the infinite occurs as devotion or prayer within the receiving subject itself, this act is not symbolic but rather

mystic. To the extent that it is an external act, however, it is symbolic. (We will return later to this extremely important difference between the mystic and the symbolic.)' On mysticism and symbolism according to Schelling see also Henry Crabb Robinson, *Essays on Kant, Schelling, and German Aesthetics*, ed. by James Vigus, MHRA Critical Texts, 18 (London: Modern Humanities Research Association, 2010), pp. 86–89. On Schelling's early conception of 'symbol' see Tonino Griffero, *Senso e immagine. Simbolo e mito nel primo Schelling* (Milan: Guerini, 1994).

29. *Hegels theologische Jugendschriften*, p. 300: '[...] in der symbolischen Handlung soll das Essen und Trinken — und das Gefühl des Einsein in Jesu Geist zusammenfließen; aber das Ding und die Empfindung, der Geist und die Wirklichkeit vermischen sich nicht [...].' *Early Theological Writings*, pp. 251–52: '[...] in the symbolical action the eating and drinking and the sense of being one in Jesus are to run into one another. But thing and feeling, spirit and reality, do not mix.'

30. *Hegels theologische Jugendschriften*, p. 298.

31. *Early Theological Writings*, p. 249.

32. See Creuzer (1810), I, 34: 'Der einfachste Begriff von σύμβολον, unmittelbar aus jener ersten Bedeutung des Verbum entspringend, ist folglich der von Platon gebrauchte: *Eins aus Zweien Zusammengesetztes*, und auf diesem einfachsten Sprachgebrauche beruht auch der älteste Gebrauch der Versicherungszeichen selbst. Ein Täfelchen zu zerbrechen und die getrennten Hälften als Unterpfand und Zeichen eines geschlossenen Gastrechts aufzubewahren, war eine uralte, auch in Griechenland geheiligte Sitte.' In a footnote Creuzer adds: 'In *tessera* liegt der Grundbegriff eines jeden vierseitigen Körpers [...]. Später zerbrach man einen Ring, oder gab dem Gastfreund den Siegelabdruck [...].' On the original meaning of the word symbol see also Umberto Eco, 'Simbolo', in *Enciclopedia Einaudi* (Turin: Einaudi, 1981), XII, 877–915 (p. 877): 'Σύμβολον da συμβάλλω "gettare con", "mettere insieme", "far coincidere": simbolo è infatti originariamente il mezzo di riconoscimento consentito dalle due metà di una moneta o di una medaglia spezzata, e l'analogia dovrebbe mettere in guardia i compilatori di lessici filosofici. Si hanno le due metà di una cosa di cui l'una sta per l'altra (*aliquid stat pro aloquo*, come avviene in tutte le definizioni classiche del segno), e tuttavia le due metà della moneta realizzano la pienezza della loro funzione solo quando si ricongiungono a ricostituire un'unità.' Eco also refers (but only superficially) to Hegel's conception of symbol (p. 894).

33. Magnus, pp. 38–39.

34. See also Hegel's account of the symbolic-mythical nature of metamorphosis in the *Lectures on the Philosophy of Art*, which Claus-Artur Scheier brought to my attention (in Georg Wilhelm Friedrich Hegel, *Werke in 20 Bänden*, XIII, 504 ff.) See for further details: Scheier, 'Zeiten der Metamorphose', p. 54.

35. Paolo D'Angelo, *Simbolo e Arte in Hegel* (Rome-Bari: Laterza, 1989), p. 60: 'Nel simbolico c'è sempre *di più* di quel che può trapassare in significato esplicito, c'è un *resto*, e questo resto risiede proprio nella natura sensibile del simbolo. Dunque, l'inadeguatezza che è caratteristica del simbolico è innanzi tutto uno squilibrio provocato dal predominio della materia sensibile'. On the separation between the external appearance and the secret meaning of a symbol as well as on the tension of reunification that the symbol embodies, Annemarie Gethmann-Siefert writes: 'Hegel bestimmt das Symbol als das äußerliche, für die Anschauung zugängliche Gestalt, die mit der intendierten Bedeutung nur partiell übereinstimmt. Jedes Symbol bleibt deshalb zweideutig, dunkel und die symbolische Kunstform kann insgesamt das Verhältnis der Idee zu ihrer Gestalt lediglich als Suchen, Streben nach Versöhnung beider artikulieren'. (Annemarie Gethmann-Siefert, *Die Funktion der Kunst in der Geschichte. Untersuchungen zu Hegels Ästhetik*, in *Hegel-Studien*, ed. by Friedhelm Nicolin and Otto Pöggeler, suppl. issue 25 (1984), p. 266).

36. *Hegels theologische Jugendschriften*, p. 325: '[...] einige wenige reine Seelen schlossen sich mit dem Triebe, gebildet zu werden, an ihn [Jesus] an; mit großer Gutmütigkeit, mit dem Glauben eines reinen Schwärmers nahm er ihr Verlangen für befriedigtes Gemüt, ihren Trieb für Vollendung, ihre Entsagung einiger bisherigen Verhältnisse, die meist nicht glänzend waren, für Freiheit und geheiltes oder besiegtes Schicksal [...].' Cf. *Early Theological Writings*, p. 282: 'A small group of pure souls attached themselves to him with the urge to be trained by him. With great good nature, with the faith of a pure enthusiast, he interpreted their desire as a satisfied heart, their urge as a completion, their renunciation of some of their previous relationships, which in the majority were not outstanding, as freedom and a healed or conquered fate.' (I substituted the

translation of the German term *Schwärmer* as 'dreamer' with the more precise word 'enthusiast'.) For Hegel's positive account of *Schwärmerei* see especially the *Lectures on the History of Philosophy* (Georg Wilhelm Friedrich Hegel, *Werke in zwanzig Bänden*, ed. by Eva Moldenhauer und Karl Markus Michel (Frankfurt am Main: Suhrkamp, 1969–71), XIX, 440. Kant's work *Von einem neuerdings erhobenen vornehmen Ton in der Philosophie* constitutes the principal dismissal of enthusiasm (*Schwärmerei*) as anti-philosophical, from which Hegel dissociates himself (Immanuel Kant, *Von einem neuerdings erhobenen vornehmen Ton in der Philosophie*, in Id., *Werke*, ed. by Artur Buchenau, Ernst Cassirer, and Benzion Kellermann, 9 vols (Berlin: Bruno Cassirer, 1914), VI: *Schriften von 1790–1796*, pp. 477–96, in particular pp. 486–87). For Hegel's distinction between *Enthusiasmus* and *Schwärmerei* see Klaus Vieweg, *Philosophie des Remis. Der junge Hegel und das 'Gespenst des Skeptizismus'* (Munich: Fink, 1999), p. 85.

37. For a detailed account of Hegel's interpretation of Jakob Böhme's mysticism see Muratori, *Il primo filosofo tedesco*, part III. On Böhme's conception of judgement (*Urteil*) according to Hegel see also Cecilia Muratori, 'Il Figlio caduto e l'origine del Male. Una lettura del § 568 dell'Enciclopedia', in *L'assoluto e il divino. La teologia cristiana di Hegel*, ed. by Tommaso Pierini, Georg Sans, Pierluigi Valenza and Klaus Vieweg (Pisa and Rome: Archivio di Filosofia, 2010), pp. 107–18.

38. Georg Wilhelm Friedrich Hegel, *Vorlesungen über die Geschichte der Philosophie*, in Id., *Ausgewählte Nachschriften und Manuskripte*, IX, 80.

39. Ivi, VIII, 190. On this passage see also Francesca Menegoni, 'Die Frage nach dem Ursprung des Bösen bei Hegel', in *Subjektivität und Anerkennung*, ed. by Barbara Merker, Georg Mohr and Michael Quante (Paderborn: Mentis Verlag, 2004), pp. 228–42, in particular pp. 238–39.

40. Georg Wilhelm Friedrich Hegel, *Enzyklopädie der philosophischen Wissenschaften im Grundrisse*, in Id., *Werke in zwanzig Bänden*, VIII, 178–79.

41. See Georg Wilhelm Friedrich Hegel, *Vorlesungen über die Geschichte der Philosophie*, in Id., *Ausgewählte Nachschriften und Manuskripte*, VI, 261.

42. Georg Wilhelm Friedrich Hegel, *Phänomenologie des Geistes*, in Id., *Werke in zwanzig Bänden*, III, 526. Georg Wilhelm Friedrich Hegel, *Phenomenology of Spirit*, translated by A. V. Miller, with analysis of the text and foreword by J. N. Findlay (Oxford: Clarendon Press, 1977), p. 437.

CHAPTER 7

'All are but parts of one stupendous whole'? Henry Crabb Robinson's Dilemma[I]

James Vigus

Around 1806, probably just after he returned from his five-year period as a student in Germany, Henry Crabb Robinson drafted a translation of one of the central Weimar classicist accounts of symbolism and of aesthetic autonomy: Karl Philipp Moritz's 'Über die bildende Nachahmung des Schönen' [On the Plastic Imitation of the Beautiful] (1788).[2] The translation of this rhetorically complex text is accurate and impressive, and had it been completed and published, Moritz's theory might have played its part in the British Romantic resurgence of interest in Neoplatonism. Robinson's work was not published, however, and another two centuries were to pass before a substantial section of Moritz's essay appeared in English.[3] The present chapter sets out to explain why Robinson considered it important to translate Moritz, and why he was able to do this in so evidently sympathetic a spirit. These questions arise because, as a student in Jena, Robinson had recently absorbed the aesthetic theories of Kant and Schelling, and displayed his grasp of the 'new school' of philosophy in a series of pioneering essays.[4] Given that modern scholarship tends to insist in particular on a clear separation of Kant's account of aesthetic autonomy from that of Moritz, it might appear that Robinson's recourse to 'Über die bildende Nachahmung des Schönen' represented a backward step in his intellectual development. This would accord with the view of critics (writing before the discovery of some of the essays just mentioned) who assumed that Robinson fundamentally misunderstood the 'Kantianism' he attempted to mediate. My argument, on the contrary, is that there were cogent reasons for turning to Moritz's essay in 1805–06. To look through the eyes of Robinson is, indeed, to discover why a 'pre-critical', essentially Neoplatonic approach to symbolism retained its relevance in the period of post-Kantian speculation. Above all, it becomes apparent that in his approach to questions of aesthetics the Jena student Robinson shared a fundamental impulse with Moritz: the religious hope of constructing a theodicy.

I begin this chapter by exploring the account of the symbolic relationship between God and the beauty of creation familiar to Robinson prior to his German studies, using a comparison with a fellow Unitarian in the 1790s: Samuel Taylor Coleridge. This background will illuminate both the systematic and psychological reasons for Robinson's subsequent immersion in Kant's theory respecting the autonomy of beauty. I then sketch the way in which Robinson's absorption of Schelling's new philosophy of art caused him to modify his Kantian perspective on symbolism. Finally, using quotations from the first part of Robinson's manuscript translation, I explore what significance the essay 'Über die bildende Nachahmung des Schönen' may have held for the Englishman.

The Determinism of Symbolic Theodicy and its Kantian Displacement

Robinson's encounter with German thought, which began only a few years before he presented his ideas to Stael, had shaken him to the point where he felt — as he confessed in an article 'On the Philosophy of Kant' (1802) — 'CONFOUNDED'.[5] To see why this was so it is necessary to understand what precisely 'Kantianism' displaced in Robinson's world picture. In the revolutionary decade of the 1790s Robinson had moved toward Unitarianism (or Socinianism). In theological terms, this implied a broad affiliation to the teachings of Joseph Priestley, especially that Christ was a mere man, not divine, and that the Trinity was a late corruption in Christian doctrine. Meanwhile, the philosophical tendency of Unitarianism was, as the name suggests, anti-dualist, and Priestley built on eighteenth-century associationist philosophy to affirm a vision of a purely material *universe* in which the one God was immanently omnipresent. The distinctive tenet of Unitarian thought at this time was, as Robinson notes, *'philosophical necessity'*:[6] the view that events in the universe proceed with mechanistic inevitability according to the law of cause and effect, so that the whole creation, including mankind, is directed by the indwelling providence to an ultimately happy ending. This doctrine was, in Priestley's presentation, deeply optimistic. And the evidence for it might seem to lie all around, open to view: as science and social justice marched forward, the signs of God's benevolence became increasingly clear. Alongside their rational inheritance from Locke and Newton, Unitarian writers also drew on enthusiastic, loosely Platonic and early-Enlightenment visions of man's place in the universal harmony, whether in the poetry of Pope or the philosophy of Shaftesbury. Thus in the words of the leading Unitarian poet, Coleridge, God was 'the Great Invisible (by Symbols seen)':[7] impossible to perceive directly only because of the delightful paradox that all perception of the millions of 'Symbols' in the world was nothing less than apprehension of God himself. 'All that meets the bodily Sense / I deem Symbolical', asserts the poet. Later in the same poem, *Religious Musings*, Coleridge describes God as 'The SUPREME FAIR sole Operant':[8] a formulation that portrays the divinity as a shaping principle at once comprising and creating absolute beauty. Coleridge's vision integrated mankind into this universe, not as an active agent, but as the happily passive percipient of God's power:

> ...'Tis the sublime of man,
> Our noontide Majesty, to know ourselves
> Parts and proportions of one wond'rous whole:
> This fraternizes man, this constitutes
> Our charities and bearings. But 'tis God
> Diffus'd thro' all, that doth make all one whole[.][9]

Contemporary readers would have heard the echo: Coleridge is recalling Alexander Pope's celebration of this supposedly best of all possible worlds in the *Essay on Man*, according to which 'All are but parts of one stupendous whole, / Whose body Nature is, and God the soul'.[10]

The potentially ecstatic Unitarian vision, however, also had a darker aspect. The advance of rational and scientific enquiry on which it depended was, notoriously, diminishing the need to posit a creator-God; and if God is conceived as entirely one with his creation, what distinctive role can he retain?[11] Further, if we refuse reliance on the biblical testimony of miracles, what reason do we still have to speak of God at all? Such questions gathered force as the violence of political events in Europe appeared to cast doubt on the progressive notion of the rational perfectibility of man. In the mid–1790s, then, a sceptical crisis afflicted Unitarianism, a symptom of which was Coleridge's own defection from the cause.[12] Gradually convinced that the Unitarian identification of God with the world was tantamount to pantheism, Coleridge found himself approaching a more extreme position still: atheism. It was at this point that, as he subsequently related, the work of Kant 'took possession of me as with a giant's hand', and Coleridge's thought took a new, transcendentalist turn.[13]

Though Robinson was no poet, his case resembled that of Coleridge. When Robinson travelled to Germany, the one speculative certainty that remained to him was the above-mentioned 'philosophical necessity', the doctrine that the human will in this mechanical world is determined, not free. Whether it was still reasonable to think of a God immanent in the machine he was not sure, but in retrospect he believed himself to have approached the fearful conclusion of atheism: that man's will was indeed determined by a law of cause and effect, and not by a benevolent intelligence. Although he did not know exactly what he sought in Germany, his prolific writing in this period manifests its goal clearly enough. Alongside his attempt to establish his own relationship to society, in the sense of cultivating a profession (the precarious one of literary journalism), Robinson was looking for a new way to conceive man's relationship to the cosmos. His half-conscious hope was to discover a theodicy, a conceptual model to replace the Unitarian vision that had combined the Newtonian mechanical theodicy with the sentimental theodicy of Shaftesbury.[14]

When he struggled through Kant's works, then, what puzzled and eventually delighted him most was the fact that the German philosopher stakes all on the — as Robinson had supposed — discredited doctrine of human free will. It was the fact that Kant asserted this tenet on 'principles so different' from anything Robinson had encountered in English philosophy that led him to 'convert' from his former opinions to a new position called Kantianism.[15] After a year's study, Robinson felt convinced by Kant's account of moral faith: that practical reason demands belief in the propositions that speculative reason cannot prove — those propositions being chiefly 'the freedom of the Will — the Being of God And the Immortality of the Soul'.[16] But this was not yet the 'rational religion' in which Robinson could rest. Not surprisingly, given his former convictions, he shared many contemporaries' unease regarding Kant's dualistic position that whereas our actions are determined by the law of cause and effect in the phenomenal realm, we exercise free will as moral agents in the noumenal realm. Robinson soon began to focus on Kant's attempt to bridge this so-called gap, in the third *Critique*, the work that Robinson described as 'the Key-stone of his general philosophy, [filling] up the critical arch, binding & uniting the distinct systems of theoretical & practical philosophy, unfolded in his former works'.[17]

It may be surmised that Robinson relished the complexity of Kant's account of aesthetic judgment because he was disenchanted with the relatively simple model associated with Unitarianism. For a Unitarian in Priestley's mould, an account of symbolism would amount to reading the moral benevolence of God in the beautiful phenomena of the world. Once God's attributes and even existence are no longer taken for granted, however, the moral significance of beauty becomes problematic. Having questioned the referential utility of beauty, it may be possible to consider that beauty instead provides reassuring evidence about the harmony of the universe precisely because it does *not* bear any intrinsic relation to moral goodness; because (in other words) it may be contemplated as complete in itself without reference to any other principle. This perspective helps to account for Robinson's enthusiasm in relating Kant's articulation of the disinterestedness of aesthetic judgment in the early paragraphs of the *Critique of the Power of Judgment*, in an article he drafted on 'Kant's Analysis of Beauty':

> For where we feel an interest in an object we desire its actual material *existence*, but in a judgement of beauty respect the *idea* of the object alone. This position [... is] pregnant with vast consequences. In the first place it fixes the boundary between the *good*, the *agreeable* & the *beautiful*. The Satisfaction which accompanies those qualities is always connected with Interest. The agreeable is that which gratifies the Sense, & it is always accompanied with a desire to possess the object & it supposes want in him who is gratified. The good is that which pleases, in the mere conception, by means of the Reason. That it is an object of interest is evident from this, that whether it be in itself immediately good, or but mediately (that is, *useful*) it is always an object of the *Will*, & that is identical with Interest in the existence of an object. [...] the agreeable is *enjoyed*, the beautiful *merely pleases*, the good is *esteemed*. The agreeable is felt by the mere *Animal*, the good is approved of by *pure spirit* or *intellect*, the beautiful alone is perceived alike by the sensible & intellectual being. This is the peculiar prerogative & glory of the judgem[en]t of taste, that it occupies, as it were, the whole man, calling into action in like degree his sensibility & his reason. Hence the sort of supremacy assigned by the german metaphysicians to the *beautiful* in reference to the *true* & the *good*.[18]

Among the 'vast consequences' of Kant's premises, then, Robinson sees the fact that judgments of taste involve the 'whole man'. Kant's rigorous distinction between the various mental powers had threatened to exclude any such holism, but Kant's followers, including Schiller and Schelling, had made it central to their aesthetics. The unifying force of judgments of beauty is, as Robinson presents it, the reason for assigning beauty to the highest rung in what is often called the 'rationalist trinity' of the true, the good and the beautiful.[19] And this is an evaluation that Robinson could find not only in Schelling's philosophy of art but also emphatically expressed in the work of Moritz.

Schelling and the Doctrine of Aesthetic Autonomy

Even as he studied Kant, Robinson's omnivorous reading in aesthetics was expanding beyond Kantian bounds. As it happened, his expertise on this topic had a momentous consequence: an illustrious literary couple then visiting Weimar, Madame de Staël and Benjamin Constant, sought instruction in the 'new school' of philosophy in early 1804, and Robinson was commissioned to compose private lectures especially for this purpose. Madame de Staël annotated the lectures and would eventually incorporate some of the material in her popular work *De l'Allemagne*. Robinson's manuscript 'On the German Aesthetick or Philosophy of Taste' thus contains accounts of developments in aesthetics since the publication of Kant's *Critique of Judgment* in 1790, including Schiller's theory of aesthetic education and Friedrich Schlegel's comments on art as play. The same manuscript also distils the essence of the highly detailed notes Robinson compiled from Schelling's lectures on the philosophy of art. Following the discussion of this lecture, Constant entered a prescient coinage in his diary: 'l'art pour l'art'.[20]

Perceiving that Schelling's immoderate claims for aesthetic symbolism conflicted with the apparent modesty of Kant, Robinson found himself attracted to aspects of Schelling's theory. The absorption of Schelling's thought assisted Robinson in questioning Kant's principle of noumenal freedom: in a private letter, reasserting his fundamental Unitarian suspicion of dualism, he even suggests that 'Kant's assertion of liberty rests but upon a suspicious ground, and there is no part of his system so feeble as this'. Robinson continues: 'Schelling is here much more successful And since I have found that *his* Phil[osoph]y is very compatible with necessity I feel myself as it were bribed to his System'.[21] The implication was that Schelling's conception of the universe, compatible in 1802 (as Robinson notes) with Spinozistic pantheism, comprises a one Absolute that subsists in a relationship of *necessity* to its constituent parts.[22] Thus in Robinson's illustration of this world view, he returns to the world of English theodicy that his Kantian conversion had briefly challenged or displaced. In a manuscript exposition of Schelling he quotes the very same lines from Pope to which the Unitarian Coleridge had alluded in the quotation above: 'All are but parts of one stupendous whole / Whose body nature is and God the soul.'[23] Robinson's increasing deference to the exhilarating depth of German metaphysics, meanwhile, is reflected in his caveat that Alexander Pope was hardly aware of the import of his own words.

According to Schelling, as Robinson records in his notes from the latter's lectures, we discover the nature of the one Absolute directly, by intellectual intuition. This intuition manifests itself in art — in the contemplation of a perfectly formed work of art, but above all in the *production* of art: 'In art the secret of the creation becomes objective, and precisely for that reason art is essentially creative or productive. For the absolute informing–into–one that is objective in the production of art is the source of everything, and the production of art is therefore a symbol of divine production.'[24] In this way, art for Schelling retains the (Kantian) principle of autonomy, but exercises greater signifying power. As Robinson rapidly discovered, Schelling offers what might be termed a maximalist account of symbolism, on a continuum with, yet ultimately opposed to, Kant's relatively modest, or minimalist account. But were Schelling's ambitious claims tenable? Robinson attempted for a time to suspend judgment on this question. As he neatly expressed the general antithesis: 'Schelling's Philosophy is the mystical platonic doctrine which it is the fashion in England to laugh at. And [...] Kant's critical system is a sober, innocent, dry, logical system, promising little & exciting to little enthusiasm, which accommodates itself to prevailing popular opinions: While its more lively successor delights in extravagant & bold Assertions'.[25]

As this quotation intimates, Robinson vehemently resisted suggestions — including that of the philosopher himself during an evening conversation — that he had become a discipline of Schelling. He protested, indeed, that 'Schelling considered me as a disciple *which I am not*'.[26] He was not a disciple because, wary of Schelling's 'mystical formularies', he remained attracted to Kantian sobriety. Yet it was at the time when he studied Schelling's philosophy of art that Robinson wrote in his correspondence of experiencing a new and refreshing sense of peace.[27] It was also a stepping-stone to further literary activities, as we will see shortly. I suggest that the psychological satisfaction Schelling's work afforded to Robinson may be summed up in this way: it enabled him to return to the Unitarian frame of theodicy, in which there is no place for free will. This model is, meanwhile, paradoxically guaranteed by an art whose beauty evokes a sense of freedom. Freedom is limited to the aesthetic sphere of the production of beauty, and in doing so it (again, at first sight paradoxically) guarantees a basically determined, necessitated, orderly universe. Since Schelling's account of the productive genius who produces art, and whose creative power is analogous to that of God, develops directly from the Kantian account of genius, it was possible for Robinson — despite his own emphasis on the radical differences between Kant and Schelling — to entertain both types of symbol theory simultaneously.

The great paradigm for Schelling's account of art as self-sufficient, and yet as disclosing the constitution of the universe, is classical mythology. The classical gods seem to signify productive power, but not in any straightforwardly allegorical sense: rather they occupy their own self-sufficient world, which Schelling defines as the world of the fantasy, or imagination. This is the spirit of Schelling's claim: 'Mythology as such and every poetic rendering of it in particular is to be grasped neither schematically nor allegorically, but symbolically.'[28] As Schelling presented it, the realm of ancient mythology was autonomous, connected to nothing beyond itself, and hence self-referential. Though 'plagued' by the difficulty of Schelling's thought, Robinson seems to have found its systematic approach to art a congenial context in which develop an increasing enthusiasm for classical literature and mythology.[29] He took Greek lessons with the Schellingian acolyte and author of a system of aesthetics, Friedrich Ast, and began to study mythology. Crucially, he read the author who had to a significant extent informed Schelling's thought on mythology, Karl Philipp Moritz.

In the above-mentioned lecture 'On the German Aesthetick or Philosophy of Taste', Robinson compressed this intensive course of philosophical reading into a few pithy observations (which caught the imagination of his French interlocutors).

In particular, he summarized Kant's theory of beauty in the third *Critique*, along with the 'new' theories that had simultaneously developed and challenged Kant. Robinson emphasizes the notion that beauty, and beautiful art in particular, must be regarded as autonomous, as strictly independent from any moral or utilitarian goal:

> The beautiful object must have in itself a form that intimates design, i.e. a harmony of parts propriety and fitness, a series of connections & dependencies, which being contemplated excite the Sense of Beauty, but it must not manifest in itself any precise & definite purpose — *it must have no object out of itself.* Every definite purpose limits & chains the aesthetical feeling which must be free.
>
> N.B. This Result, which I have stated very loosely (in Kant it is left very obscure) has also led to many favourite doctrines of the modern Critics. That *pure poetry* and works of pure art must be judged of in this way is obvious [...][30]

First, the 'form that intimates design' without 'any precise & definite purpose' renders Kant's concept of 'Zweckmäßigkeit' [purposiveness] without any particular purpose.[31] However, whereas Kant concentrates more on natural beauty than artistic beauty, and certainly does not specify the latter in his definition of a *pure* judgment of taste, Robinson shows the influence of over a decade of debate surrounding of Kant's theory, by focusing his account decisively on works of art.[32] Robinson is particularly emphatic on the point that Kant's account of beauty is 'obscure', and not to be analysed without considering the doctrines of the 'modern Critics' — who nevertheless exceeded Kantian bounds on speculation to the extent of contemplating the universe itself as a beautiful work of art. An enthusiastic discourse of this nature sends Robinson back, in turn to Platonic sources. Such sources now include a writer who, like Kant, maintains a doctrine of aesthetic autonomy; and, like Schelling, develops this notion in a frame of neoplatonizing mythology.

Robinson Translates Moritz on Beauty

Robinson studied Moritz's essay relatively late: in his manuscript Memorandum Book, he first mentions it on 14 June 1805. However, he is likely to have known of it previously, at least by reputation, since it had aroused controversy in the Weimar circles in which Robinson had moved for the past eighteen months.[33] As an enthusiastic translator of Goethe, Robinson would have been interested by the fact that Moritz had composed the work while staying in Rome with the great poet, who to some extent provided the model for Moritz's conception of productive genius.[34]

The reasons for Robinson's interest in Moritz's 'Über die bildende Nachahmung des Schönen' are reflected in the range of comparisons it has attracted from later commentators. As Sabine Schneider notes, it combines a 'radical new semiotic' with 'fundamentalist Neoplatonism' inspired directly by Plotinus as well as mediately by Leibniz and Shaftesbury.[35] In the view of Wilhelm Dilthey, Moritz's essay contains 'the whole of Schelling in a nutshell'.[36] It has also been read as anticipating the theory of aesthetic autonomy in Kant's *Critique of the Power of Judgment* — a view that Kantian scholars tend to reject indignantly. To look through the eyes of the contemporary translator, however, is to see that it was necessary to try to reconcile Kantian autonomy with the Schellingian model; otherwise the stark choice would remain between Unitarian mechanism on the one hand or spirit–matter dualism on the other, foreclosing the possibility of a satisfactory theodicy. Moritz communicates his metaphysical argument in a rhythmic and evocative prose that confirms Schiller's judgment — half-admiring and half-appalled — that 'seine ganze Existenz ruht auf Schönheitsgefühlen' [his whole being is based on feelings of beauty].[37] In his translation Robinson endeavours to preserve that urgency and vivacity.

The first important step in Moritz's argument is the enforcement of a strict separation between beauty and utility.[38] Moritz posits that beauty is an idea that we strive to imitate, a status that the idea of beauty shares with the idea of nobility. Continuing this *'play of ideas'* ('Ideenspiel'),[39] Moritz establishes the opposition between the useful and the noble/beautiful with a metaphysical argument. An act of physical courage in war is noble if the soldier acts 'merely for the sake of the deed itself', that is to say if his motive is pure. The action would be noble whether or not it turned out to be practically useful — hence the noble/beautiful may be defined as that which needs no purpose beyond itself. If the soldier had merely been obeying orders, however, his deed would not have been noble, but simply good. If on the other hand his motive were selfish (one of personal revenge, say), the deed itself would be neither noble nor good; but it could still be equally useful to his country as in the first two cases. Utility thus comes third in the hierarchy of ideas, after nobility/beauty and good, which latter idea forms a bridge between the other two. Since utility can thus be allied with the bad as well as the good, and the useless attaches naturally to the bad, the hierarchy could be represented diagrammatically as follows:

Noble / Beautiful
Good
Useful
— — — —
Mean
Bad
Worthless

This is more than a hierarchy of ascending and descending ideas, however: it also forms a circle. For the top term, the noble/beautiful, turns out to ally itself with the bottom, the worthless:

> Der Begriff vom Unnützen nehmlich, in so fern es gar keinen Zweck, keine Absicht außer sich hat [...] schließt sich am willigsten und nächsten an den Begriff des Schönen an, in so fern dasselbe auch keines Endzwecks, keiner Absicht, warum es da ist, außer sich bedarf, sondern seinen ganzen Wert, und den Endzweck seines Daseins in sich selber hat.[40]

> [The idea of the worthless [...] in as much as it has no purpose no end beyond itself, readily & easily unites itself with the idea of the beautiful, as that too *needs* no purpose or end beyond itself, but the whole worth & final end of the existence of which, lies in itself.][41]

Further, Moritz defines utility as follows:

> Unter Nutzen denken wir uns nehmlich die Beziehung eines Dinges, als

Teil betrachtet, auf einen Zusammenhang von Dingen, den wir uns als ein Ganzes denken. Diese Beziehung muß nehmlich von der Art sein, daß der Zusammenhang des Ganzen beständig dadurch gewinnt und erhalten wird: je mehrere solcher Beziehungen nun eine Sache auf den Zusammenhang, worin sie sich befindet, hat, um desto nützlicher ist dieselbe.[42]

[Under Utility, we think of a thing as constituting a part, of a certain connection of things which we think as forming a whole. The relation of this part to the whole must be of such a kind, that the connection of the whole is supported & encreased by it. The greater number of references therefore which any thing has to such a connected whole, the more useful such [a] thing is.][43]

Each part must have reference to the whole; the whole itself, however, is by definition self-sufficient. The conceptual logic runs as follows: 'Hieraus sehen wir also, daß eine Sache, um nicht nützlich sein zu dürfen, notwendig ein für sich bestehenden Ganzen unzertrennlich verknüpft ist' [Thus we see that a thing, in order that it may not need utility, must be necessarily a self-subsisting whole];[44] that which does not need utility is the beautiful; therefore the beautiful is a self-subsisting whole. It remains only to be said that for a self-subsisting whole to be called beautiful, it must present itself to our imagination or to our senses — otherwise it would not be beautiful but sublime, since Moritz in accordance with standard definitions treats the sublime as that which baffles the attempt of our imagination to grasp it as a totality.

In fact, continues Moritz, we *cannot* imagine the one true whole, the universe itself — though if we could, it would appear supremely beautiful. Our limited imagination must content itself with smaller wholes, which are not strictly speaking wholes at all (since they themselves form a part of the universe), but merely appear so to us. A smaller whole of this kind is work of fine art, which is beautiful by virtue of reflecting the beauty of the entire universe:

Denn dieser große Zusammenhang der Dinge ist doch eigentlich das einzige, wahre Ganze; jedes einzelne Ganze in ihm, ist, wegen der unauflöslichen Verkettung der Dinge, nur eingebildet — aber auch selbst dies Eingebildete muß sich dennoch, als Ganzes betrachtet, jenem großen Ganzen in unsrer Vorstellung ählnich, und nach eben den ewigen, festen Regeln bilden, nach welchen dieses sich von allen Seiten auf seinen Mittelpunkt stützt, und auf seinem eignen Dasein ruht.

Jedes schöne Ganze aus der Hand des bildenden Künstlers, ist daher im Kleinen ein Abdruck des höchsten Schönen im großen Ganzen der Natur; welche das noch mittelbar durch die bildende Hand des Künstlers nacherschafft, was unmittelbar nicht in ihren großen Plan gehörte.[45]

[This great connexion of things in the universe, is properly speaking the only true & real Whole: All things of nature are so indissolubly bound & connected together that every whole we fancy we find in it, is but the work of our imagination. Yet this fancied whole, must as a whole, conceived in our minds, be formed by the fixed & eternal rules according to which the *Universal whole* is in itself complete, & supposing itself in its centre, rests on its own existence.

Every beautiful Whole therefore which proceeds out of the hand of the plastick artist, is a miniature impression of the supremely beautiful in the great Whole of nature, who as it were by a sort of supplementary creation produces mediately through the forming hand of the artist, what did not immediately belong to her great plan.][46]

Moritz thus argues that a beautiful object, usually a work of art, is a harmoniously proportioned whole and, as such, perfect. This perfection in miniature (or microcosm) functions as a symbol of the whole, perfect universe (or macrocosm), precisely because it does not refer to anything outside itself. The language of the translation returns us to Robinson's above-quoted summary of Kant on beauty: 'The beautiful object must have in itself a form that intimates design, i.e. a harmony of parts propriety and fitness, a sense of connections & dependencies, which being contemplated excite the Sense of Beauty, but it must not manifest in itself any precise & definite purpose — *it must have no object out of itself.*'

As the verbal similarities in these quotations indicate, Robinson perceived a close affinity between Moritz's notion of a self-sufficient, beautiful whole, and Kant's theory of how the perceiving subject apprehends the connectivity of beauty. In general, Kant scholars are unconvinced by such an affinity: they point out that whereas Moritz makes metaphysical claims about the objective qualities of beautiful objects, Kant rejects such speculation as illegitimate, concentrating his investigation purely on the subject's response to such objects.[47] From Robinson's point of view, however, it would have been impossible to seal off all objectivizing claims of aesthetics: as a follower of the speculations of Schiller and Schelling, as well as an admirer of Goethe, he enquired into the nature of creative genius, whose *products* are the works of art that we admire. The driving question, which Kant's carefully placed limit on speculation had not suppressed, remained this: what can works of art can tell us about our place in the universe? The next section of 'On the Plastic Imitation of the Beautiful' addresses this question, as Moritz elaborates the role of the artist as a mirror of nature. This mirroring takes place internally rather than externally, in that nature — which in Moritz's discourse always signifies the 'self-subsisting whole' just discussed — bestows on the artist a measure of her own creative power, and so creates at one remove by operating *through* the artist. Thus the artist is moved by the composite beauty of nature to create according to the very same pattern of beauty that inspired the creation of natural objects:

> Wem also von der Natur selbst, der Sinn für ihre Schöpfungskraft in sein ganzes Wesen, und das Maß des Schönen in Aug' und Seele gedrückt ward, der begnügt sich nicht, sie anzuschauen; er muß ihr nachahmen, ihr nachstreben, in ihrer geheimen Werkstatt sie belauschen, und mit der lodernden Flamm' in Busen bilden und schaffen, so wie sie[.][48]

> [He therefore who has received from Nature a lively & powerful Sense of its her creative power, on whose eye, & in whose breast, the measure of beauty is impressed, he is not contented with contemplating its her operations, he is impelled to imitate & emulate it her, he watches its her secret operations, & warmed by the glowing fire in his bosom like his great model forms & creates.][49]

In a phrase that anticipates Coleridge's famous description of the poetic imagination as that which 'dissolves, diffuses, dissipates, in order to re-create',[50] Robinson renders Moritz's eulogy of the creative genius: 'Indem seine glühende Spähungskraft in das Innre der Wesen dringt, bis auf den Quell der Schönheit selbst, die feinsten Fugen löset; und auf der Oberfläche sie schöner wieder fügend [...]' [His ardent penetration pierces into the internal essences of things, even to the source of beauty itself, he disjoins & as it were disjoints the most delicate members of nature & with greater beauty in works of art reunites & recombines them].[51] The phrase 'reunites & recombines' is especially noteworthy in being an extrapolation rather than a literal translation of the German 'fügend'.

As the images of fire and energetic disjoining have already intimated, Moritz regards the creative process as fundamentally a struggle — a struggle to reveal the idea of beauty beyond recalcitrant physical objects and to re-impress that beauty upon them:

> Die Realität muß unter der Hand des bildenden Künstlers zur Erscheinung werden; indem seine durch den Stoff gehemmte Bildungskraft von innen, und seine bildende Hand von außen, auf der Oberfläche der leblosen Masse zusammentreffen, und auf diese Oberfläche nun alles das hinübertragen, was sonst größtenteils vor unsern Augen sich in die Hülle der *Existenz* verbirgt, die durch sich selbst schon jede Erscheinung aufwiegt.[52]

> [Under the hand of the forming artist, reality itself becomes ideal, & substance, shew; for while the plastick power within, & the forming hand without, are resisted by the matter on which they work they meet on the surface of the lifeless mass, & impress upon that surface what is generally concealed from our own eyes behind the veil of existence, which outweighs in itself all shew.][53]

The reason why the artist must struggle, according to Moritz, lies in the fact that 'the supreme beauty in the harmonious structure of the universe' is (as noted above) too large to be conceived by the imagination: man can only apprehend it 'unmittelbar in der *Tatkraft*' [immediately in his *active power*].[54] 'Tatkraft' is one of the key concepts of this essay, and although Moritz employs it semantically in opposition to 'Einbildungskraft' (usually translated 'imagination'), it is an ancestor of Romantic concepts of the productive imagination.[55]

Moritz pursues at some length the theme of the inadequacy of the senses and imagination to apprehend the supreme beauty in itself: these faculties can only appreciate the *reflection* of beauty as it appears in a work of art. However, since the human being is finite, even his 'Tatkraft' is incommensurate to the infinite connections of nature 'streaming in upon it from all directions' ('allumströmend').[56] Hence the necessity for struggle: when the 'Tatkraft' creates a microcosm — a work of plastic art — it must try to reflect all these infinite connections present in the macrocosm. The artist thus experiences a 'sense of trouble' as an indistinct feeling ('dunklen Ahndung') of a totality takes shape within his 'Tatkraft', without yet taking on a form that satisfies the imagination. To perform this task, the active power must somehow bring all these confusing connections into one 'focus' (the etymology of the German *Brennpunkt* aptly connotes fire): a visible or audible object. Again, Moritz underlines that this object — the work of art — functions as a mirror of the supreme beauty.

Although the artist must struggle to impose his dimly conceived idea upon the material, this difficult process has, according to Moritz, a wonderful compensation:

namely the sense of 'unnenbare Reiz' [ineffable delight] involved in the '*lebendige Begriff*' [*lively* conception] of the plastic imitation of beauty.[57] In the first conception of the work, that is, there is 'a faint presentiment of the work as if already complete'. Such a presentiment is accessible only to the 'active power', not to the reasoning faculty ('Denkkraft').

In addition to distinguishing 'Tatkraft' (active power) from 'Einbildungskraft' (fancy, in this context), Moritz draws a further distinction between 'Tatkraft' and 'Denkkraft'. Robinson at first translates the latter word literally as 'thinking power', and subsequently as 'Understanding', a sensible translation given the similarity between the role played by Moritz's 'Denkkraft' to that of Kant's 'Verstand'. All thought, Moritz had observed at the outset of the essay, consists in distinction; 'Denkkraft', he now consistently avers, deals with the relations of things, with comparisons. The point is that since the essence of beauty is self-subsistence as a pure whole, beauty 'lies beyond the boundaries of the thinking power': it is impossible to compare it to anything else and thus impossible to explain why it is beautiful. 'Denn es mangelt ja der Denkkraft völlig an einem Vergleichungspunte, wornach sie das Schöne beurteilen, und betrachten könnte. Was gibt es noch für einen Vergleichungspunkt für das echte Schöne, als mit dem Inbegriff aller harmonischen Verhältnisse des großen ganzen der Natur, die keine Denkkraft umfassen kann?'[58] [For the Understanding is altogether destitute of a point of comparison by which it may examine & judge of beauty. For with what else could the truly beautiful be compared, than with the result of all the harmonious relations of the great whole of nature, which no power of thought can comprehend?].[59] At this point Moritz's argument reaches a rhetorical climax: 'Das Schöne kann daher nicht erkannt, es muß hervorgebracht — oder *empfunden* werden.'[60] As Robinson freely translates: 'Beauty therefore cannot be understood or known, it must be produced & felt.'[61] This is a further bolster to the position that Moritz's 'play of ideas' was designed to establish in the first section of the essay: that beauty, and hence the beautiful artwork, is perfectly autonomous. Such an approach made Moritz's essay ripe for appropriation in a post-Kantian context in which Neoplatonic metaphysics was re-emerging.

Conclusion

As Thomas P. Saine has convincingly argued, Moritz's argument in 'On the Plastic Imitation of the Beautiful' amounts to an 'aesthetic theodicy'.[62] In *The Genealogy of the Romantic Symbol*, Nicholas Halmi comments on the prevalence of the desire for a theodicy as the stakes rose in the complex of symbol-theories:

> [...] the theorization of the symbol in the Romantic period may be understood as an attempt, however, illogical and methodologically dubious in itself, to foster a sense of the harmony of the human mind with nature, of the unity of seemingly disparate intellectual disciplines, and of the compatibility of individual freedom with a cohesive social structure — all for the sake of reducing anxiety about the place of the individual in bourgeois society (especially in the aftermath of the French Revolution and ensuing European wars) and about the increasing dominance of mechanistic science (which, by opposing mind to nature as

subject to object, undermined the traditional basis on which the world's meaningfulness had been assumed).[63]

The material I have presented in this chapter may to a certain extent be regarded as an illustration of Halmi's thesis. In tracing the development of Robinson's interest in the aesthetic theodicy of Moritz, however, I have tried to emphasize a coherence that reflects a high degree of self-conscious awareness as to both the potential rewards and dissatisfactions of emphatic symbol-theories. I suggest in closing that this is a characteristic that Robinson shared with the author he translated: both writers were sceptically inclined to a sufficient degree to recognize that the appeal of symbolic theodicy was in part a therapeutic one, as a possible reassurance to minds who could no longer directly accept the old certainties of puritan forms of religion (pietism, for Moritz; Presbyterianism and then Unitarianism, for Robinson). As Jutta Heinz's contribution to this volume (Chapter 3) demonstrates, Moritz's awareness of the therapeutic motivation for this line of theorization constitutes a complicating factor in his fictional writing, in which, as it turns out, 'pure' symbols or an ideally symbolic mode are not to be found. Robinson, too, explicitly recognized his own religious anxieties. As he explored Moritz's thought in 1806, after the principal period of his study of the aesthetics of Kant and Schelling, he continued to approach the Enlightenment manifesto 'All are but parts of one stupendous whole' as a troubling question rather than an achieved world view. Robinson was long to remain 'what the Quakers call a seeker' in matters of religion and philosophy.[64]

Notes to Chapter 7

1. I thank David Wykes, the Director of Dr Williams's Library, London, for his kind permission on behalf of the Trustees to quote from manuscript material in the Henry Crabb Robinson collection. I would like to make special mention of the assistance provided by the late Jonathan Morgan, archivist of Dr Williams's Library, in finding the manuscript discussed in this chapter and tracking down further information about it. My thanks also to Graham Davidson for his comments on an early draft.

2. As Norbert Christian Wolf remarks in a review essay, this is the 'Programmschrift deutscher Autonomieästhetik': 'Karl Philipp Moritzens endgültige Erhebung zum Klassiker. Über Alessandro Costazzas große Arbeit zu Moritz und der Ästhetik des 18. Jahrhunderts' <http://www.iaslonline.de/index.php?vorgang_id=2506> [accessed 9 February 2012].

3. See Stefan Bird-Pollan's translation in *Classic and Romantic German Aesthetics*, ed. by J. M. Bernstein (Cambridge: Cambridge University Press, 2003), pp. 131–44. Both Robinson and Bird-Pollan translate approximately two-thirds of Moritz's work, omitting the concluding, dark section on the danger of beauty and the disastrousness of dilettantism.

4. See Henry Crabb Robinson, *Essays on Kant, Schelling, and German Aesthetics*, ed. by James Vigus, Critical Texts, 18 (London: MHRA, 2010).

5. Ibid., p. 28.

6. Ibid.

7. *Religious Musings* (1794), line 19, in *Coleridge's Poetry and Prose*, ed. by Nicholas Halmi, Paul Magnuson and Raimonda Modiano (New York and London: Norton, 2004), p. 22.

8. Ibid., line 62, p. 23.

9. Ibid., lines 135–40, p. 25.

10. *An Essay on Man in Four Epistles to H. St John Lord Bolingbroke* (1733–1734), lines 267–68, in Alexander Pope, *The Major Works*, ed. by Pat Rogers (Oxford and New York: Oxford University Press, 1993), p. 279.

11. Compare Jonathan Loesberg, *A Return to Aesthetics: Autonomy, Indifference, and Postmodernism* (Stanford, CA: Stanford University Press, 2005), p. 14.

12. On Coleridge's struggle to attain a confident register in pronouncements on symbolism, see Ben Brice, *Coleridge and Scepticism* (Oxford: Oxford University Press, 2007).

13. See James Vigus, 'The Philosophy of Samuel Taylor Coleridge', in *The Oxford Handbook of British Philosophy in the Nineteenth Century*, ed. by William Mander (Oxford: Oxford University Press, 2013).

14. For these terms I draw principally on Thomas P. Saine, *Die Ästhetische Theodizee. Karl Philipp Moritz und die Philosophie des achtzehnten Jahrhunderts* (Munich: Fink, 1971), p. 67.

15. *Essays on Kant, Schelling, and German Aesthetics*, p. 28; compare p. 1 f.

16. Ibid., p. 123.

17. Ibid., p. 50.

18. Ibid., p. 51.

19. On this background, compare Frederick Beiser's defence of eighteenth-century rationalist aesthetics, *Diotima's Children: German Aesthetic Rationalism from Leibniz to Lessing* (Oxford and New York: Oxford University Press, 2010).

20. See Robinson, *Essays on Kant, Schelling, and German Aesthetics*, pp. 18–25.

21. Ibid., p. 57.

22. Ibid., p. 18. Compare the beginning of Schelling's introduction to his *Philosophie der Kunst*, in F. W. J. Schelling, *Texte zur Philosophie der Kunst*, ed. by Werner Beierwaltes (Stuttgart: Reclam, 1982), p. 139: 'Der ist noch weit zurück, dem die Kunst nicht als ein geschlossenes, organisches und ebenso in allen seinen Teilen notwendiges Ganzes erschienen ist, als es die Natur ist' [He to whom art does not appear as a closed, organic and in all its parts equally necessary whole, just like nature, is still very backward].

23. Robinson, *Essays on Kant, Schelling, and German Aesthetics*, p. 127.

24. Ibid., p. 77. For Robinson's remarks on Schelling's notion of intellectual intuition, see 'Introduction', above.

25. Ibid., p. 58.

26. Letter to Thomas Robinson, 23 December 1802, quoted in *Essays on Kant, Schelling, and German Aesthetics*, p. 18.

27. 'Yet I believe & feel in myself the happy effects of this study: I feel myself so entirely at ease; All the questions of religion & in particular concerning revelation appear to me so little & so low': *Essays on Kant, Schelling, and German Aesthetics*, p. 58.

28. Ibid., p. 81.

29. Robinson wrote to his brother Thomas on 1–2 June 1803: '[... I] *plagued* myself literally with the new Philosophy of Schelling'. Quoted in *Essays on Kant, Schelling, and German Aesthetics*, p. 16.

30. Henry Crabb Robinson, 'On the German Aesthetick or Philosophy of Taste', in *Essays on Kant, Schelling, and German Aesthetics*, pp. 129–38 (p. 130); cf. his elaboration of this point in an earlier essay (p. 53).

31. Immanuel Kant, *Critique of the Power of Judgment*, trans. by Paul Guyer and Eric Matthews (Cambridge: Cambridge University Press, 2000), §10, p. 105.

32. Kant: 'A judgment of taste on which charm and emotion have no influence [...], which thus has for its determining ground merely the purposiveness of the form, is a pure judgment of taste' (ibid., §13, p. 108). A. W. Schlegel, one of the 'modern Critics' to whom Robinson here refers, thought that Kant had unduly limited the scope of beauty; and Friedrich Schiller, another of the 'modern Critics', adapted Kant's argument to a detailed consideration of artistic beauty in his 1793 'Kallias or Concerning Beauty: Letters to Gottfried Körner': translated in *Classic and Romantic Aesthetics*, ed. by J. M. Bernstein, pp. 145–84.

33. One of Robinson's closest friends, Karl Ludwig von Knebel, had even composed a retort to Moritz's essay: see Mark Boulby, *Karl Philipp Moritz: At the Fringe of Genius* (Toronto, Buffalo and London: University of Toronto Press, 1979), pp. 189–90.

34. Many commentators have denied Moritz any originality, claiming that he simply recorded Goethe's ideas; but for important differences between them see Norbert Christian Wolf, *Streitbare Ästhetik. Goethes kunst- und literarische Schriften, 1771–1789* (Tübingen: Max Niemeyer,

2001), pp. 486, 493–99; and Alessandro Costazza, *Schönheit und Nützlichkeit. Karl Philipp Moritz und die Ästhetik des 18ten Jahrhunderts* (Bern: Peter Lang, 1996), pp. 16–26.

35. See Sabine M. Schneider, *Die schwierige Spraches des Schönen. Moritz' und Schillers Semiotik der Sinnlichkeit* (Würzburg: Königshausen & Neumann, 1998), p. 178.

36. 'Diese wundevolle Stelle im Keime der ganze Schelling', quoted in Günter Niklewski, *Versuch über Symbol und Allegorie (Winkelmann — Moritz — Schelling)* (Erlangen: Palm & Enke, 1979), p. 63.

37. Schiller to Körner, 2 February 1789, quoted in Schneider, *Die schwierige Sprache des Schönen*, p. 7.

38. Thus Moritz breaks from the rationalist aesthetic theories associated with Wolff: see Costazza, *Schönheit und Nützlichkeit*, esp. pp. 66–69. Quotations of Moritz's German are from Karl Philipp Moritz, *Werke in zwei Bänden*, ed. by Heide Hollmer and Albert Meier (Frankfurt am Main: Deutscher Klassiker Verlag, 1997), II, 958–91.

39. Moritz, 'Über die bildende Nachahmung des Schönen', p. 965; Robinson, 'Moritz on Imitation' (MS in the Crabb Robinson collection, Dr Williams's Library, Bundle 6.XII.42), p. 8.

40. Moritz, 'Über die bildende Nachahmung des Schönen', pp. 964–65.

41. Henry Crabb Robinson, 'Moritz on Imitation', p. 7.

42. Moritz, 'Über die bildende Nachahmung des Schönen', p. 966.

43. Robinson, 'Moritz on Imitation', pp. 8–9.

44. Moritz, 'Über die bildende Nachahmung des Schönen', p. 967; Robinson, 'Moritz on Imitation', p. 9.

45. Moritz, 'Über die bildende Nachahmung des Schönen', p. 969.

46. Robinson, 'Moritz on Imitation', p. 11.

47. 'Einen wichtigen Unterschied wird man darin erblicken dürfen, daß Kants *Zweckmäßigkeit ohne Zweck* ein Phänomen der Empfindung, nämlich das *freie Spiel* der Gemütskraft meint, also im Rahmen der Wirkungsästhetik bleibt, während die *innere Zweckmäßigkeit*, von der Moritz spricht, eine des Kunstwerks ist, die gerade in ihrer Objektivität, ohne Bezugnahme auf das aufnehmende Subjekt, wenngleich nur durch dieses festgestellt werden kann.' Peter Szondi, *Poetik und Geschichtsphilosophie I*, ed. by Senta Metz and Hans-Hagen Hildebrandt (Frankfurt am Main: Suhrkamp, 1974, 1980), p. 97. Cf. also Costazza, pp. 141–43, and Paul Guyer, 'The Perfections of Art: Mendelssohn, Moritz, and Kant', chapter 4 of *Kant and the Experience of Freedom* (Cambridge: Cambridge University Press, 1996), pp. 131–60.

48. Moritz, 'Über die bildende Nachahmung des Schönen', p. 969.

49. Robinson, 'Moritz on Imitation', p. 11.

50. Samuel Taylor Coleridge, *The Collected Works of Samuel Taylor Coleridge*, gen. ed. Kathleen Coburn (Princeton, NJ: Princeton University Press, 1971–2002), VII: *Biographia Literaria or Sketches of My Literary Life and Opinions*, ed. by James Engell and W. Jackson Bate, 2 vols (1993), I, 304.

51. Moritz, 'Über die bildende Nachahmung des Schönen', p. 969; Robinson, 'Moritz on Imitation', p. 11.

52. Moritz, 'Über die bildende Nachahmung des Schönen', p. 970.

53. Robinson, 'Moritz on Imitation', p. 12.

54. Moritz, 'Über die bildende Nachahmung des Schönen', p. 970; Robinson, 'Moritz on Imitation', p. 12.

55. The hierarchical distinction between *Einbildungskraft* and *Tatkraft* in Moritz parallels Coleridge's later distinction between fancy and imagination, whereby fancy mechanically recombines sense-impressions in an order different from that received by the memory, whereas imagination actively fuses component sense-perceptions into a new whole. (See Coleridge, *Biographia Literaria*, I, 304–05). Robinson, indeed, had read enough of the German Romantics to have gained a sense of this distinction for himself, and he begins accordingly to translate *Einbildungskraft* as 'fancy'.

56. Cf. Moritz, 'Über die bildende Nachahmung des Schönen', p. 972; Robinson, 'Moritz on Imitation', p. 14.

57. Moritz, 'Über die bildende Nachahmung des Schönen', p. 973; Robinson, 'Moritz on Imitation', pp. 15, 14.

58. Moritz, 'Über die bildende Nachahmung des Schönen', p. 974.

59. Robinson, 'Moritz on Imitation', p. 15.

60. Moritz, 'Über die bildende Nachahmung des Schönen', p. 974.

61. Robinson, 'Moritz on Imitation', p. 16.

62. Saine, *Die Ästhetische Theodizee*; cf. Seraina Plotke, 'Der ästhetische Trost. Karl Philipp Moritz' ästhetische Schriften im Spiegel der Sinnsuche', *Monatshefte*, 95.3 (2003), 421–41 (p. 427): 'Das Schöne stellt nach Moritz eine Ganzheit, eine Ordnung dar, die auf einen der Annahme nach vollkommenen und harmonischen Kosmos rekurriert. Das Kunstwerk wird zum Indikator einer *Sinn-vollen* Welt. Es signalisiert die Dauerhaftigkeit und Zeitlosigkeit des Universums. Der tatsächliche Zweck des Schönen also "In-sich-selbst-Vollendeten" liegt also darin, dem Menschen Halt und Geborgenheit zu geben.' [The beautiful, according to Moritz, presents a totality, an order, which appeals to a supposedly perfect and harmonious cosmos. The artwork becomes an indicator of a meaning-full world. It signals the permanence and timelessness of the universe. The actual goal of the beautiful and so 'the complete in itself' thus lies in providing man with support and security.] Both Plotke and Saine (p. 126) maintain that Moritz's arguments on aesthetics remained essentially consistent throughout his theoretical works.

63. Nicholas Halmi, *The Genealogy of the Romantic Symbol* (Oxford: Oxford University Press, 2007), p. 24.

64. Robinson to Wilhelm Benecke, 26 January 1834, in *Diary, Reminiscences, and Correspondence of Henry Crabb Robinson, Barrister-at-Law, F.S.A.*, ed. by Thomas Sadler, 3 vols (London: Macmillan, 1869), III, 38. For an account of Robinson's religious development, see Timothy Whelan, 'The Religion of Crabb Robinson', *Transactions of the Unitarian Historical Society*, 24.2 (April 2008), 112–34.

CHAPTER 8

The Spark of Intuitive Reason: Coleridge's 'On the Prometheus of Aeschylus'[1]

James Vigus

This chapter is an invitation to read Samuel Taylor Coleridge's neglected essay 'On the Prometheus of Aeschylus'.[2] Prometheus, the Titan who brought fire to mankind and suffered the wrath of the upstart tyrant, Zeus, for bestowing this supernatural gift on a wretched race, was an attractive figure for many Romantic writers. Some, including Shelley, identified with Prometheus as a gesture of resistance to authority, whether in its religious or political manifestations. Coleridge, on the other hand, who presented 'On the Prometheus' as a lecture to the Royal Society of Literature in 1825,[3] had no such anti-authoritarian purpose. He identified with the Greek Titan in a different, increasingly rueful way. Nearly thirty years previously he had exclaimed in a letter: 'I have [...] made up my mind that I am a mere *apparition* — a naked Spirit!'[4] Now, as Coleridge found himself oppressed by corporeal afflictions and addictions, what remained was a wistful longing: 'O! might Life *cease*, and selfless *Mind* / Whose Being is *Act*, alone remain behind!'[5] In this mood, he would ironically emphasize the spirit's imprisonment in the recalcitrant matter of the body: 'For in this bleak World of Mutabilities, & where what is not changed, is chilled, and in this winter-time of my own Being,' he confessed, 'I resemble a Bottle of Brandy in Spitzbergen — a Dram of alcoholic Fire in the center of a Cake of Ice.'[6] It was natural for Coleridge, thus troubled by the relationship between mind and body,[7] to meditate on Prometheus, the divine spirit punished by being chained to a rock. This chapter examines the extreme extent to which Coleridge thought his way into a version of the Promethean role.

'On the Prometheus' provides a haunting distillation of the philosophical and religious concerns that exercised Coleridge in his later years. As such, the subject matter is as complex as the style is knotty: much of the essay consists of philosophical postulates, at times in the form of notes rather than continuous prose, and interspersed with Greek and Latin tags that visibly obstruct the flow of reading. Coleridge courted this esoteric mode of expression partly on grounds of social conservatism: as befits a disquisition on Greek religion, he speaks to those who have ears to hear, to (potential) initiates. For he had come to believe that to openly and publically present arguments that could appear to problematize the foundations of religious belief was — in an ironically Promethean fashion — to 'arm fools with fire'.[8] Its wilful textual obscurity is no doubt the main reason why 'On the Prometheus' has suffered even greater neglect than most of Coleridge's post-1817 works. Yet despite the difficulties it presents to the interpreter, it is — so I will argue — valuable for its insights into the very nature of interpretation itself. Through an introductory exposition of 'On the Prometheus', this chapter makes the claim that it is a uniquely complete instance of Coleridge's 'practical criticism'. The latter term was coined by Coleridge but distorted in the twentieth century to denote an anti-theoretical mode of reading, as free as possible from contextual presumptions. In the process, it has often been forgotten that what Coleridge had originally attempted was 'the application of [philosophical] principles to purposes of practical criticism'.[9] In Coleridge's own work, indeed, practice flows inseparably from a — boldly presumption-filled — theory. Following a brief contextual introduction, 'On the Prometheus' accordingly proceeds with methodical strictness in two parts: first, Coleridge outlines a metaphysical system, which he labels (for convenience) 'Greek'; and second, he maps this system onto Aeschylus's play, showing which concepts each character in turn symbolizes.[10]

For according to Coleridge's fundamental intuition, *Prometheus Bound* is a 'philosopheme', or a work of mythology that bodies forth a philosophical idea.[11] (He foregoes discussion of the poetic dimension of Aeschylus's play, in contrast to his treatment a few years previously of another 'philosophic poet' and tragedian, Shakespeare.) In this context Coleridge defines an 'idea' as 'the presence of the Whole under the paramouncy of some one of its eternal and infinite Modes.'[12] The idea in question regards the genesis of the human mind, or, to use the Greek term, *nous*. This Greek word is congenial to Coleridge's purpose since it connotes, without being limited to, 'Reason'.[13] This genesis of *nous* is best conceived, in Coleridge's view, as a struggle. For Reason, the completing factor and highest aspect of the mind, is unable tranquilly to fulfil its function of producing principles: embodied, it finds itself subject to the painful intrusions of other forces. In this sense, Coleridge sums up his whole view of the play with the pithy phrase *nous agonistes*.[14] As I will elaborate below, Coleridge interprets the fire that Prometheus brings and for which he suffers as a symbol of that which is distinctive about humanity, namely *nous*, which includes the powers of both Reason and conscience.

Coleridge also applies another favourite term to describe *Prometheus Bound*, when he calls it 'a *philosopheme* and a *tautegorikon*'.[15] The latter coinage signals that Coleridge brings to his reading the controversial symbol-theory of F. W. J. Schelling,[16] which in part developed through dialogue with another contemporary German mythographer, Friedrich Creuzer. I will argue that the concept of taute-gory appropriately reflects the bold method of interpretation with which Coleridge approaches Aeschylus's work. The term 'tautegory' underlines the distinctive quality of symbolic as opposed to allegorical presentation and modes of thought. According to this conception, an *allegory*, consisting of a set of images designed to convey a meaning quite different from those images, is characterized by contingency, or arbitrariness: the images chosen are in principle replaceable by others which could convey an identical meaning. A *tautegorical symbol*, by contrast, conveys a meaning which is co-extensive with itself. It is characterized by necessity: the network of thoughts it provides is supposedly impossible to convey in any other way. Such a theory clearly rests on a universalizing view of human nature, for it assumes that a core meaning remains constant (albeit with possibilities of development and progression) over the centuries. In this particular case, Coleridge will interpret Promethean fire as truly integral to the human mind, with regard to its powers both of reasoning and moral self-legislation.

Even from this brief introduction it is clear that the mode of practical criticism Coleridge applies to *Prometheus Bound* — the abstract system first, followed by the discovery of traces of that same system in the text — is deeply appropriative. In other words, Coleridge imports his own philosophical concerns into his reading, investigating historical questions not with any attempt at objective neutrality, but with an explicit 'Moral Interest'.[17] How he justifies this method — and to what extent it still deserves sympathetic attention from modern readers — is the topic of the first of the five sections in which this chapter now proceeds. Here I will outline the link that Coleridge posits between Aeschylus's conception and the Greek mystery religions, especially the Eleusinian and Samothracian Mysteries, as he goes about a speculative (re)construction of the quintessentially 'Greek' system of metaphysics. In the second part, I offer a brief account of the metaphysical section of Coleridge's essay, explicating the sense in which he sees (Greek) philosophizing as the search for first principles. Third, I consider the contrast Coleridge draws between the Greek myth's status as 'symbol' and the 'allegory' of the story of Adam and Eve in Genesis. This lays the foundation for the fourth section, in which I analyse the symbolism Coleridge identifies in *Prometheus Bound*, character by character. Finally, I consider the ways in which the symbolism of fire resonates with the process of interpretation. While defending the work's coherence as practical criticism, then, I aim to show the centrality of Coleridge's moral intuitionism to his whole approach.

Overleaping the Hermeneutic Gap: Coleridge on the Greek Mysteries

Coleridge intended his exposition of the philosophical meaning of *Prometheus Bound* to form part of a larger project (never completed) that would unveil the connections between Greek drama and the Mystery religions. He announces as his guiding 'hypothesis' the following: 'that it was the office of the tragic poet, under a disguise of the sacerdotal religion, mixed with the legendary or popular belief, to reveal as much of the mysteries interpreted by philosophy, as would counteract the demoralizing effects of the state religion, without compromising the tranquility of the state itself'.[18] The immediate occasion for this remarkable suggestion is the ancient story, recently reported anew by Creuzer, that Aeschylus was prosecuted for illegally divulging elements of the Eleusinian Mysteries.[19] Coleridge's hypothesis is further based on the intuition that, whereas Athenian state religion promulgated an unrefined polytheism, which from a Christian no less than a Platonic perspective must be regarded as immoral, the Mysteries preserved the key elements of the patriarchal monotheistic law. Coleridge thus proposes a hermetic narrative according to which fundamental doctrines of Genesis were transmitted (via the 'corrupt channel' of the seafaring Phoenicians) and reappear later in fragmentary form in Greek texts.[20]

The next section of this chapter will enter into more detail regarding these doctrines, at the centre of which was the teaching of monotheism, the one God. At this point, even though the experiences of the initiates of the Mysteries are not explicitly thematized in 'On the Prometheus', two questions arise. Why was Coleridge committed to this speculative interpretation of the spiritual background and content of the Greek mysteries? And to what extent can the modern reader still bring sympathetic attention to Coleridge's thought experiment?[21]

What is at stake in Coleridge's project is the continuity of religious principles. For reasons to be considered presently, he considers (triune) monotheism to be the vehicle of the universally binding moral law, whereas any alternative scheme, whether pantheism or polytheism, conduces immorality. The unspoken anxiety behind his work is this: if so crucial a doctrine as the One God had evolved, rather than having being revealed at the very dawn of human life, it would forfeit that status of absolute truth that Christianity required of it. This may be regarded as a modern version of the 'virtuous pagan' dilemma that especially engaged medieval Christian thinkers: were morally admirable ancient pagans necessarily damned owing to their ignorance of Christ and their worship of multiple divinities? The happiest solution would be to posit, in the tradition of the 'Ancient Theology', an unbroken line of revelatory insight that went underground but was never lost until the time when Christ brought religious principles into a universally comprehensible, exoteric form. The project of producing such a history was further stimulated by the cultural pressure of its rival. As Coleridge complains at the beginning of 'On the Prometheus', certain French authors (in the wake of Hume's *Natural History of Religion*) had claimed that monotheistic religion gradually emerged from the relatively unsophisticated polytheism of Egypt. Such explanations were freshly topical following Jean-François Champollion's announcement of the discovery of hieroglyphics in 1822.[22] To counter this narrative, Coleridge tacitly avails himself of Creuzer's theory that monotheism actually preceded the (in Coleridge's view) 'corrupt' phase of Egyptian sensuous polytheism.[23] Since he finds no proof to the contrary in the Bible, Coleridge can then propose what he considers the most morally acceptable early genealogy of religious faith: 'viz. that the sacerdotal religion of Egypt had, during the interval from Abimelech to Moses, degenerated from the patriarchal or arkite monotheism into a pantheism, cosmotheism, or worship of the world as God.'[24]

A recipient of the pure tradition of original monotheism, Aeschylus was one of the 'mythic poets' who, writes Coleridge, 'adapted the secret doctrines of the mysteries as the (not always safely disguised) antidote to the debasing influence of the religion of the state.'[25] A reader could well object that the above-mentioned story of Aeschylus divulging elements of the Mysteries is insufficient ground for making *secret* doctrines central to a reading of the dramatist's work. Any such judgment, however, involves wider questions of hermeneutics. Modern scholars are in no better position than Coleridge and his contemporaries to deduce the concealed doctrines of the Mysteries: even though archaeology has revealed much about material aspects of the rituals at Eleusis and Samothrace, the deeper meanings known only to the initiates remain impenetrable. Why were these *mystes* said to experience a profound sense of calm in the face of death; what were the significations of the sacred objects the hierophants showed them; and what form did their encounter with a procession of gods take? The names of the six gods or 'Cabiri' worshipped at Samothrace are known to have constituted a vital part of the secrets of the Mysteries, but information about them has barely advanced since the Romantic period.[26] Then as now, the available evidence about the Mysteries' symbolism is fragmentary and often untrustworthy.[27]

This means that the Mysteries confront us in an extreme form with the hermeneutic gap that notoriously divides (modern) interpreters from (ancient) texts or experiences. It is possible to take various different attitudes to that gap. Friedrich Schleiermacher, often regarded as the founder of the modern discipline of hermeneutics, considered the interpreter to be in a position of so-called 'radical dependence', reliant on faith where knowledge was lacking.[28] The historicism of more recent times, on the other hand, prefers to reconstruct the relevant context as neutrally as possible, abstaining from further speculation for fear of betraying an ideologically motivated standpoint.

Coleridge follows another way, rooted in the speculative mythography in which he had steeped himself in the 1790s and now fortified by his reading of Schelling and Creuzer.[29] Coleridge optimistically proposes to sweep away the hermeneutic gap that divides us from the Mysteries:

> The difficulty of comprehending any scheme of opinion is proportionate to its greater or lesser unlikeness to the principles and modes of reasoning in which our own minds have been formed. [...] This difficulty the author anticipates as an obstacle to the ready comprehension of the first principles of the eldest philosophy, and the esoteric doctrines of the Mysteries; but to the necessity of overcoming this the only obstacle, the thoughtful inquirer must resign himself, as the condition under which alone he may expect to solve a series of problems the most interesting of all that the records of ancient history propose or suggest.[30]

The willingness to bridge the acknowledged gap is, in Coleridge's view, nothing less than a pre-condition for grasping 'the esoteric doctrines of the Mysteries'. It is a condition that scholars ever since the Romantic period have rejected as a headlong plunge into ideology. Nevertheless, Coleridge will propose a 'key' that will open a view on the whole conceptual complex.[31] The notion that such a key is possible follows from the assumption — admittedly unpalatable to more conventional methodologies — that we, as modern readers, can intuit these ancient 'principles'. As will appear shortly, Promethean fire in the sense of a spark of illumination thus becomes a symbol not just for *nous* considered abstractly, but also for the interpretative process itself. It is precisely this self-reflexive suggestion that can still prove fruitful for modern readers. By way of preparatory initiation, however, Coleridge first requires that we follow him in an excursion into 'the holy jungle of transcendental metaphysics'. Even if this section of his essay must inevitably (in Coleridge's own words) 'seem strange and obscure at first reading — perhaps fantastic', it sustains a strong level of systematic coherence.[32]

The Holy Jungle of Transcendental Metaphysics

Pursuing the impulse of the mythological criticism of his age to trace all myths back to some one, single source, Coleridge declares that Greek philosophy consisted of an investigation 'ta peri arkon', 'concerning the first principles'. The nature of this investigation was introspective, for philosophy in the strictest sense began when '[g]reat minds' reflected on the very distinctiveness of mind itself, in which consists the '*diversity* between Man and beast'. To this definition of original philosophy Coleridge adds: 'as far as man proposes to discover the same in and by the pure reason alone'.

The term 'pure reason', appearing at this crucial moment, signals a Kantian subtext that is rarely absent from Coleridge's prose. Kant's *Critique of Pure Reason* had in fact shown that reason, considered as the faculty that strives a priori after principles, cannot discover answers to the great questions of metaphysics, but becomes trapped in antinomies. Kant, however, had then turned to a different aspect of reason — 'practical reason', or conscience — to provide the desired certainty. Kantian 'moral faith' appealed to a transcendental mode of argument: if the moral law is as binding as our conscience informs us that it is, then certain necessary conditions must be in place, including the existence of God (to guarantee appropriate rewards and punishments). Coleridge was one of those post-Kantians who followed and extended this line of argument, casting aside Kant's caution and looking to the conscience as the single foundational principle that would at once unite the diverse endeavours of the three *Critiques* and provide a ground for metaphysical knowledge. Coleridge, however, rejected what he perceived as Kant's excessively rigid separation between the aspects of reason. In treating *Prometheus Bound* as a 'philosopheme', Coleridge proposes to discover in it a symbolically expressed outline of the faculties of the human mind, distinguishing the various powers, but avoiding absolute divisions. When Coleridge describes the genesis of mind or *nous* (how helpfully flexible was the Greek word!), he thus programmatically alternates between the Kantian terms: 'pure reason', 'practical reason', or sometimes both together.[33] This terminological flexibility reflects Coleridge's own scheme of transcendental psychology. He retains the three mental categories of sense, Understanding (Verstand) and Reason (Vernunft), as well as the Kantian notion of a conflict between the latter two: 'even the human understanding in its height of place seeks vainly to appropriate the IDEAS of the pure reason, which it can only represent by IDOLA.'[34] At the same time, however, he regards the role of Reason (when not usurped) as that of 'irradiating' and improving the Understanding. In Greece, when 'Great minds turned inward on the fact of the *diversity* between Man and beast', investigating the structure and function of that hierarchy, it was discovered that 'the mere understanding, considered as the power of adapting means to immediate purposes, differs indeed from the intelligence displayed by animals, and not in degree only; but yet does not differ by any excellence which it derives from itself, or by any inherent diversity, but solely in consequence of a combination with far higher powers of a diverse kind in one and the same subject.'[35]

Further, in constructing a philosophical system, Coleridge pursues the Kantian method of transcendental argument to an extreme:[36] he enquires what conditions must be presupposed in order for conscience, or the consciousness of a binding moral law, to be operative. Thus the introspective discovery of a fundamental principle implies a metaphysical enquiry beyond Kantian bounds into the nature of the creation — or rather of the 'producent power — the *productivity*' (p. 1266). In this way the Greek philosophical endeavour, in Coleridge's eyes, regains its currency in the modern age. The project of the *Opus Maximum*, composed roughly contemporaneously with Coleridge's work on 'On the Prometheus', is to establish a logical (i.e. non-temporal) sequence to account for the emergence of diverse forms from the Godhead — above all to account for the emergence of evil, which is itself a necessary condition of the moral law.[37]

In thinking of evil as constituted by a will that diverges from the divine will, Coleridge insists on the actuality of a multiplicity of powers, thus firmly rejecting pantheism. A complete conflation of God (or the creative force) with the creation would mean that there could be no will other than original creative force, no possibility that a finite will could choose positive evil. The sense of the binding force of the moral law instead provides Coleridge, as just noted, with the basis for belief in God — specifically in a God who remains transcendent of as well as immanent within his creation. In 'On the Prometheus' Coleridge expresses this antithesis in a simple equation in which 'W' stands for 'world' and 'G' for 'God'. Both theist and pantheist maintain that the world without God is inconceivable, i.e.:

$$W - G = 0$$

But the pantheist adds the converse:

$$G - W = 0$$

for which the theist substitutes

$$G - W = G \ [38]$$

Coleridge refers to basic pantheism, or the teaching that God is perfectly immanent in the world (i.e. $G - W = 0$), as 'the Phoenician scheme'. The polar opposite of pantheism is theism, which asserts God's transcendence: in Coleridge's terminology it is 'the Hebrew scheme'. This latter, he repeatedly avers, is the 'true' scheme, since it is taught by biblical authority. Yet the so-called 'Greek scheme' he constructs in 'On the Prometheus' significantly turns out to constitute a medium between those two extremes.

Greek Symbol versus Hebrew Allegory: A *via media* Cosmology

In order to contextualize the myth of *Prometheus Bound*, Coleridge compares it with the story of Adam and Eve in Genesis. Both provide a mythological account of the problem (just outlined) of the origin of the will-to-evil, but they do so with enormous differences in style: 'The most venerable, and perhaps the most ancient, of Grecian mythi, is a philosopheme, the very same in subject-matter with the earliest record of the Hebrews, but most characteristically different in tone and conception'.[39] Coleridge's deepest study of Genesis would be made in the safe privacy of his notebooks in the coming years,[40] but at this time he has already formed one strong conjecture: that the story of the 'forbidden fruit and serpent' originated as a relatively simple narrative, probably in the form of Egyptian hieroglyphic inscriptions.[41] It is, he claims, an 'allegory' — a term Coleridge associates with 'picture-language' and with a relatively undeveloped level of understanding.[42] Not, of course, that this myth can be anything other than 'profound truth — a truth that is indeed the grand and indispensable condition of all moral responsibility'; yet its presentation involves 'an accommodation to the then childhood of the human race'.[43] In this way, Coleridge implies that the apple and serpent are replaceable rather than essential or constitutive images. Coleridge's investigation suggestively parallels Hegel's remark that it is ridiculous to insist on the importance of consuming an apple. For Coleridge, as for Hegel, the Hebrew narrative takes a naïve form – a simple picture of eating the forbidden fruit.[44]

The Greeks, who according to Coleridge's hermetic scheme had preserved the essence of the same (ultimately Egyptian-derived) wisdom in the Mystery doctrines, were no longer children, but 'approaching manhood'. This means that they can express the same intuition regarding the moral basis of humanity in a more complex form. Indeed, Coleridge considers that the use of symbol, as opposed to allegory, was a relatively late cultural development, introduced by the Greeks.[45] Here, the implication is that the myth of Prometheus bringing the gift of fire conveys unique connotations that could not be expressed in any other way. Coleridge sums up the contrast as follows: 'The Prometheus is a *philosopheme* and *tautegorikon*: the tree of knowledge of good and evil, an allegory (ieropaideuma), though the noblest and most pregnant of its kind.' This comparison to some extent reflects a shift in Coleridge's own sensibility over the years. He had always admired the sublimity of the Hebrew scriptures, but whereas he had once contrasted this robust imagery with the 'poor Stuff' of Greek myth, he now even ventures to detect an aspect of superiority in Aeschylus over Moses.[46]

In Coleridge's view, the presentational contrast significantly reflects differences in the respective 'Hebrew' and 'Greek' accounts of creation. Coleridge describes the difference in foundational cosmogony in the following way. Genesis describes an abrupt *creatio ex nihilo*: 'The Hebrew wisdom imperatively asserts an unbeginning creative One who neither became the world; nor is the world eternally; nor made the world out of himself by emanation or evolution; but who willed it, and it was!'[47] By contrast, the 'Greek' scheme describes a procession of divinities, such as the initiates in the Mysteries presumably saw represented. Coleridge's reconstruction of this scheme accrues even further complexity because he is tacitly disagreeing with the text on which he relied for his general approach, Schelling's 'Über die Gottheiten von Samothrake'.[48] Schelling posited a chain of gods, revealed by the hierophants in the Mystery rites, in which the humblest deity came first, the greatest last. Since a *dependency* of the greatest on the lowest would amount, in Coleridge's view, to pantheism, he is anxious to reinterpret the lowest deities in exclusively 'psychological' terms.[49]

All material things, then, according to Coleridge's representation of the 'Greek scheme', have to be contemplated as emerging from 'the Indistinguishable', or the primal chaos. Coleridge describes chaos as 'the essentially unintelligible, yet necessarily presumed basis or sub-position of all positions.'[50] In contrast to Schelling, Coleridge does not include it in the Mystery pantheon, nor does he assert it as an empirically demonstrable reality. He accords it rather the status of a necessary assumption, 'an indispensable idea for the human mind'. Coleridge adds that 'As an idea, it must be interpreted as a striving of the mind to distinguish *being* from *existence*, or *potential* being, the ground of being containing the possibility of existence, from being *actualised*.'[51] This emphasis on potential is important to Coleridge. He guards against a vision of the primal chaos as an 'omnium gatherum' swarm of phenomena,[52] for this would amount once again to a pantheism that fails to explain diversification from the One and would consequently imply denial of the reality of evil. In order to explain the genesis of *nous* Coleridge needs a description of how the potentiality of this chaos became actuality, how the 'ground' gave rise to specific forms. At this point he finds a richer mythological frame in 'the language of the Mysteries' than in the brief description of the 'darkness' in Genesis — though he once again syncretically insists upon a link between the two: '[I]t was the Esurience, the pothos, or desiderium, the unfueled fire, the Ceres, the ever-seeking maternal goddess, the origin and interpretation of whose name is found in the Hebrew root signifying hunger, and thence capacity.'[53] Of these various terms and images, it is that of fire that Coleridge will pick up again when he turns specifically to Prometheus. It is significant for Coleridge's method that fire here takes its place among a number of other figures: a tautegorical symbol should precisely resonate with such various possibilities that all intimate the same mystery of longing. Emphasizing this mystery, Coleridge's does not allow us to forget that this metaphysical stage is still to be thought of as pre-human: he thus resists taking up the sexual dimension prominent in most of the myths as they have been transmitted to us.[54]

Thus far, chaos has merely the status of an absolute 'identity', a potential ground of all being.[55] To explain how the potential became actuality, or in simpler terms, why there is something rather than nothing, Coleridge's hypothetical Greek thinkers must make one more assumption: that of a mysterious 'XYZ' prior even to the chaos, which is 'supersensuous and divine'.[56] This 'antecedent ground of corporeal matter' is neither transcendent, nor operative as a cause, but rather best described as the 'still continuing *substance*' of the physical world. To recur to the terms of the philosophy contemporary with Coleridge, he is reviving the controversial Kantian concept of the *Ding an sich* [thing in itself], or 'noumenon', in a modified form. He does so by positing a kind of spiritual energy behind all things. This energy has an intimate connection with the *nous* whose generation in human beings 'On the Prometheus' is designed to explain.

Nous agonistes

The tension within the primal identity, or, to use Coleridge's more specific expression, the 'polarization into thesis and antithesis', arose from the mysterious 'desiderium' just mentioned. In more clearly mythological terms, the explosive beginning of differentiation within the One may be represented as a 'schism in the *to theion*'[57] — a war of the gods. Coleridge now introduces two new terms to describe this primal polarity: the 'thesis' (or supersensuous, divine ground) and 'antithesis' (initially chaotic material) equate respectively to 'nomos' (law) and 'idea'. As we will see shortly, 'nomos' is symbolized in Coleridge's interpretation by Zeus, while Prometheus himself stands for 'idea'. Rather than see the relationship between these gods as purely one of authority versus insurrection, Coleridge emphasizes the extent to which they intertwine. Nomos is the antecedent unity just discussed, in this context manifested as the 'principle' effectively ensuring that a particular phenomenon — especially a plant, animal or man, in that order of complexity — develops in one particular way rather than another. Nomos 'strives to become idea'. Importantly, it engages in constant polar interplay with idea: whereas Nomos connotes necessity, idea connotes freedom. Idea is the overflowing productive energy; but the activity of producing results in a product, which, being relatively static, must again submit to Nomos. At this point, however, Coleridge's Kantian inspiration once again comes to the fore: in channelling itself into the pinnacle of creation, the human being, Idea becomes not just Nomos but a 'nomos autonomos', 'autonomous law' — the ultimate combination of necessity and freedom in the form of self-legislation. At this advanced stage the 'product' formed from this process is no longer merely body, but the 'self-consciousness' that we know by immediate intuition to be integral to human being. Thus Coleridge concludes that 'Idea' is both Will (the desire, as it were, to flow out and form products) and Reason (the highest level of law, a shaping principle): these terms coincide in the Greek word 'Nous'. Encompassing the cogitative and moral faculties, Nous thus equates, depending on one's emphasis, to 'the rational will, [or] the practical reason'.[58]

Coleridge has now returned to his philosophical starting-point. We know intuitively — as the basic fact of consciousness — that we have a responsible will (or in Kantian terms a capacity of self-legislation), because our conscience persistently informs us that we fail to fulfil the moral law. The resulting sense of remorse, Coleridge tells us, is symbolized in the vulture that gnaws Prometheus.[59] The cosmology I have just summarized is a construction designed to answer a question like this: what preconditions must be thought in order to guarantee the moral law's coherence? Coleridge has posited a cosmic fall, symbolically represented by warring gods, which can in turn explain how the human will has the potential to stray, i.e. to will evil — indeed that the finite will has, by definition, always already strayed. It has not been necessary, in Coleridge's view, to look exclusively to the Bible for such an account: for in Greek mythology 'the fact of a moral corruption connatural with the human race was again recognized. In the assertion of ORIGINAL SIN the Greek Mythology rose and set.'[60]

When Coleridge now comes to explain that Zeus stands for 'nomos', his symbolic method enables him to trace a fourfold significance. Zeus represents, firstly, nomos 'as opposed to Idea or Nous'; second, law in the sense of ruling; third, nomos damnetes, i.e. coercing law,[61] and — most importantly — the curiously named 'nomos politikos', further defined as 'law in the Pauline sense'. This latter addition seems to suggest that the 'nomos' incorporated by Zeus is a law felt by the individual as being imposed from outside. To the extent that we feel that our transgressions will be punished by an external authority, we are under the sway of Zeus. In this way,

Zeus (or Jove: Coleridge now begins to use the Latinate form of the god's name) is as important a character as Prometheus in Coleridge's account of the faculties that constitute humanity: for human being is unthinkable without a moral law which from a certain perspective appears to be threateningly imposed from without.

The significances of Prometheus form an approximately dialectical opposition to those of Zeus. Firstly, Prometheus represents 'Idea pronomos', idea prior to law:[62] for in the 'Greek' cosmological scheme law could not take effect until idea had begun to strive against it. Secondly, Prometheus is 'Idea philonomos', in the capacity of Zeus's 'friend and counsellor'. Thirdly, he is 'logos philanthropos',[63] the 'divine humanity', who stole a spark 'from the living *spirit* of law' and gave it to mankind. This gift, 'by which we are to understand reason, theoretic and practical',[64] is to be regarded as an addition bestowed on 'an elect, a favoured animal', beyond what was necessary for the constitution of a living creature. Animals have understanding, whereby under-standing literally implies a sub-stance of their being, but the universalizing, self-legislating reason is in the Greco-Coleridgean mythology a bonus attribute, unique to humanity. Earlier in the essay Coleridge had noted as one of the significances of the story of Prometheus giving stolen fire to man: 'The generation of the Nous, or pure reason in man. 1st, Superadded or infused, a supra, to mark that it was no mere evolution of the animal basis — that it could not have grown out of the other faculties of man, his life, sense, understanding, as the flower grows out of the stem, having pre-existed *potentially* in the seed.'[65] It is striking that Coleridge allows the possibility that a principle of 'evolution' could explain any feature of animal life, yet cannot explain Reason itself, which we must think of as beginning and sustaining the whole process.

Fourth, Prometheus is 'both the gift and the giver'. This double function makes the figure of Prometheus a perfect example of a 'tautegory', though Coleridge does not repeat the term here. In the myth, Prometheus is 'the gift, whence the soul received REASON; and reason is her being, says our Milton.'[66] Whereas law has power, idea has 'Prophecy, Foresight': here Coleridge exploits the root meaning of the Greek word 'prometheus', as forethought. The secret that Zeus tries to wrest from Prometheus is that of 'the transitoriness inherent in all antithesis; for the *Identity* or the *Absolute* is alone eternal'. (Zeus is unable to do so, of course: in the play, Prometheus proclaims with heroic stubbornness that 'There is no torture, no ingenuity, by which / Zeus can persuade me to reveal my secret, till / The injury of these bonds is loosed from me.')[67] At this point the terminology Coleridge employs is Schellingian, and the mode of insight to which Coleridge is appealing is akin to Schelling's 'intellectual intuition'. Yet the terms 'identity' and 'absolute' are enlisted in the broadly anti-Schellingian project of indicating the *rational* basis of the universe. Coleridge is suggesting that Reason, the power that is inexplicable by the process of evolution, gives us insight into the absolute identity by virtue of continuing to participate in it. A correlative point is that, as noted earlier, Coleridge underlines Prometheus's chronological seniority to Zeus: for Nous is 'anterior to the schism'.[68] Thus Prometheus is kindred, yet lonely; and fastened to a rock, to signify the non-productivity of nous once its product is fixed: 'The Nous is bound to a rock, the immovable firmness of which is indissolubly connected with its barrenness, its non-productivity. Were it *productive* it would be Nomos; but it is Nous, because it is *not* Nomos.'[69] Most importantly, the fact that a vulture lacerates Prometheus signifies the pangs of remorse 'incident to and only possible in consequence of the Nous, as the rational, self-conscious, and therefore responsible will'.[70]

The Hermes in Hermeneutics

That Nous be personified as a god, and in particular a fire-bringing god, is a point central not only to Coleridge's 'Greek' cosmology, but also to his method of interpretation. It is at the same time the point at which those two elements coincide. He emphasizes that the heavenly provenance of the 'gift' marks its difference in kind from all the faculties that human beings share with animals.[71] The idea of a 'spark' symbolizes, in Coleridge's reading, an agency that transforms what it acts upon (in this case the ordinary, animal faculties of the human being) without undergoing a change in its own nature: for fire continues to burn even as it 'converts' whatever it comes into contact with. The notion of Reason as a divine 'spark' also appeals to Coleridge because it suggests sudden, instantaneous illumination, of the kind that occurs in the biblical myth when the Word makes nature out of chaos with the declaration 'let there be light'. In Coleridge's account, Reason provides us with flashes of intuitive insight, energizing the lower power of the Understanding, which by itself can do no more than process and classify the data supplied by sense experience. In other texts, Coleridge describes Reason as being its 'own evidence'.[72]

This conception once again reflects a complex engagement with the German texts that broach similar topics. Whereas Schelling looks to Greek mythology for evidence that the divine principle provides incremental revelation, gradually unfolding itself in a process of cosmic evolution, Coleridge regards the primary content of this revelation as occurring instantaneously.[73] Further, Coleridge takes up and characteristically modifies the ideas of Creuzer. In Creuzer's view, the disturbing and awakening properties characteristic of the symbol in ancient mythology are associated with brevity ('Kürze'). A symbol, writes Creuzer, 'ist wie ein plötzlich erscheinender Geist, oder wie ein Blitzstrahl, der auf Einmal die dunkele Nacht erleuchtet' [is like a spirit suddenly appearing, or like a flash of lightening that in a moment illuminates the dark night].[74] In another formulation: 'Es ist ein Moment, der unser ganzes Wesen in Anspruch nimmt, ein Blick in eine schranklose Ferne, aus der unser Geist bereichert zurückkehrt' [It is a moment that occupies our whole being, a glimpse into a boundless distance, from which our spirit returns enriched]. In this way, the interpreter-initiate envisaged by Creuzer resembles the poet of Shelley's 'Alastor', who 'gazed, till meaning on his vacant mind / Flashed like strong inspiration, and he saw / The thrilling secrets of the birth of time.'[75] For such Romantic writers the image of pitch darkness lit up in a sudden flash assisted in assimilating the Mystery initiates' experience of illumination to the task of interpretation in the modern age.

Creuzer's evocation of the sublime in the form of endless night and boundless distance, occasionally illuminated by a lightning flash, would have stimulated

Coleridge's reflections but would not have satisfied him. Despite his various differences with Schelling's position, Creuzer still clings (in Coleridge's view) to a version of pantheism that fails to assert the primacy of Reason and its difference in kind from the subordinate powers.[76] In drawing out the connotations of Promethean fire, then, Coleridge emphasizes not only the irrevocable, instantaneous quality of its operation, but also its permanent and ever-deepening effects. Like the story of Adam and Eve, the story of Prometheus tells of the defining moment in the genesis of the human mind, and in both cases this moment colours all that follows. But the fire of Prometheus is a tautegorical symbol, one especially rich in implication: fire connotes danger (in the form of the newly descending moral law, whose breach brings punishment in the form of hell-fire);[77] yet it is also the condition of the possibility of practical skills such as tool-making, supposedly impossible to animals and only possible to humans because our Reason illuminates our Understanding.

This is the kind of conclusion toward which Coleridge's practical criticism is working in 'On the Prometheus'. Insight into the 'key' that will unlock the whole 'cypher' of Aeschylus's mythology may occur in a flash of intuition, but its effects will linger, colouring all our thoughts thereafter. An equally vital notion is that Reason is continually engaged in a struggle, by virtue of its condition as (so to speak) a misfit in the world. This aspect emerges forcefully in a passage of self-reflexive commentary close to the end of the essay. Coleridge observes that Prometheus as Nous is both 'solitary' and 'kindred': *solitary* to the extent that Nous was (as a potential) the antecedent ground under-lying the primal chaos and so pre-dates all other powers, but *kindred* because he is now part of a pantheon, an array of divinities that emerged from the absolute identity. So it is that in Aeschylus's play 'The kindred deities come to him, some to soothe, to condole; others to give weak, yet friendly counsels of submission; others to tempt, or insult.'[78]

Coleridge focuses on the role of Hermes in the latter respect. Hermes is primarily 'the symbol of INTEREST'. As the 'GO-BETWEEN' who carries messages from Zeus and torments Prometheus with prudent advice, Hermes represents moral heteronomy: in Coleridge's words, 'interests or motives intervening between the reason and its immediate self-determinations'.[79] As the personification of mediacy, that is, Hermes militates against intuition, whose operation is immediate. Hermes opposes 'nomos autonomos', or self-legislation in the sense of the pure will to follow the dictate of conscience for its own sake. Even more than this: 'The HERMES impersonates the eloquence of cupidity, the cajolement of power regnant; and, in a larger sense, custom, the irrational in language [...] the fluent [...] the rhetorical in opposition to logoi, ta noeta.'[80] For in the play, Hermes counsels the 'self control and prudence' that Prometheus has hitherto spectacularly lacked. He tells the chorus that Prometheus is clearly mad. Although he seems to admit that his rhetoric is ineffectual, he then gathers himself for a final verbal assault, describing the tortures that Zeus will inevitably inflict if Prometheus remains stubborn.

It is significant that Coleridge identifies this worldly figure with both 'custom' and 'the rhetorical'. His suggestion is that in our fallen, embodied state, we cannot maintain Promethean purity. In particular, words do not only function to communicate truth, but also obstruct the enquiring mind. In applying a radical hermeneutic method to Aeschylus's play, Coleridge struggles with Hermes — with the problem, that is, of mediating the fundamental 'idea' of this philosopheme. His use of awkward Greek and Latin terms and conspicuously non-fluent style throughout the essay seem designed to take a stand against 'custom', understood as the easy familiarity of everyday notions. In more philosophical terms, when Nous turns inward to discover its own situation and powers (the original 'Greek' project), it cannot succeed without the mediation of language; but the inevitable dependence of language upon positive images makes it difficult for Nous to reconnect to the purely potential, or 'negative' ground. Whilst the tautegorical symbol of Aeschylus's Prometheus provides (for Coleridge) the richest expression of the genesis of Nous, symbolism is itself a function of Hermes. The hermeneutic imagination can be enlightened by tautegorical symbols, but it needs them because it finds itself in a state of mystification: Greek symbolism manifests, as Coleridge's discussion implies, a rich yet not entirely healthy cultural development from the allegory of Genesis.

Conclusion

'On the Prometheus of Aeschylus' is an example of Coleridgean 'practical criticism' in the original sense of that term. Far from being anti-theoretical, it imports a pre-conceived theory into a reading of a text. It does so to a radical extent, since the philosophical prologue is nothing less than a speculation on 'first things', on the necessary conditions of human Reason, both theoretical and moral. In this way, the essay compresses much of Coleridge's systematic moral philosophy into a small compass. To elaborate his conception, Coleridge then finds the most fitting language in ancient mythology.

Such a procedure is provocative, and invites various objections, including that Coleridge has made no real contribution to classical scholarship. Further, Coleridge's firm denial that Reason could have emerged from a process of 'evolution' appears to raise a fundamental question about his philosophical endeavour. Did the impending Darwinian theory render Coleridge's thought obsolete at its very root? My chapter has implied the beginning of an answer: Coleridge's postulation of a Nous necessarily underlying any conceivable process of evolution at least cannot be dismissed by means of evolutionary discourse itself. George Eliot's prescient remark about Darwin implicitly puts the case for Coleridge: 'to me the Development theory and all other explanations of processes by which things came to be, produce a feeble impression compared with the mystery that lies under the processes.'[81] Coleridge is concerned precisely with this higher-order investigation of 'the mystery that lies under the processes': in this sense 'On the Prometheus' tenaciously resumes Coleridge's longstanding effort to 'solve the process of Life & Consciousness'.[82] The true achievement of 'On the Prometheus', thereby, is that it holds a mirror up to the enquiring mind. On first reading, the essay appears to bear little relation to Aeschylus, yet it draws the reader into an introspective approach to the myth. Once grasped in an act of intuition that may occur after much reflection on the narrative, the philosopheme of the Coleridgean Aeschylus is likely to flash upon the inward eye again and again.

Notes to Chapter 8

1. The research for this chapter began several years ago, as work for a graduate reading group organized by Douglas Hedley in Cambridge — a group that included Jeffrey Einboden and Cecilia Muratori, both contributors to the present volume. It would not have been possible without discussions with these scholars. Related work was fruitfully discussed at Klaus Vieweg's Colloquium for German Idealism at Friedrich-Schiller-University, Jena, in 2008. Graham Davidson kindly provided feedback on a draft.

2. All references are to 'On the Prometheus of Aeschylus', in Samuel Taylor Coleridge, *The Collected Works of Samuel Taylor Coleridge*, gen. ed. Kathleen Coburn, Bollingen Series 75, 16 vols in 34 (Princeton, NJ: Princeton University Press, 1971–2002), XI: *Shorter Works and Fragments*, ed. by H. J. Jackson and J. R. de J. Jackson, 2 vols (1995), II, 1251–1301. I am indebted to the editors' fine introduction and notes; I will not repeat the information they provide about the genesis of the work around 1821 and its relation to the draft notes included in this edition. Especially given the relative inaccessibility of the critical edition, however, I also cite here the original publication (now available online): S. T. Coleridge, 'On the Prometheus of Æschylus; an Essay, preparatory to a series of Disquisitions respecting the Egyptian in connection with the Sacerdotal Theology, and in contrast with the Mysteries of ancient Greece', *Transactions of the Royal Society of Literature of the United Kingdom* (London: John Murray, 1834), II, 384–404.

3. Since the question of the attribution of *Prometheus Bound* to Aeschylus had at this time not yet been raised, I do not consider it in this chapter.

4. Coleridge to John Thelwall, 31 December 1796: *The Collected Letters of Samuel Taylor Coleridge*, ed. by Earl Leslie Griggs, 6 vols (Oxford: Oxford University Press, 1956–71), I, 295.

5. Album Verses: 'Dewdrops are the Gems of Morning', *The Poetical Works of Samuel Taylor Coleridge* (vol. XVI of *The Collected Works of Samuel Taylor Coleridge*, as in note 2), ed. by J. C. C. Mays, 3 vols in 6 (2001), I.2, 1015 (poem 593), dated 1832–33.

6. S. T. Coleridge to Mrs Charles Aders, 3 January 1826, in *Letters*, VI, 532. For a full list of Coleridge's references to Prometheus, see the editor's note in *Aids to Reflection* [1825] (vol. IX of *The Collected Works of Samuel Taylor Coleridge*), ed. by John Beer (1993), p. 561.

7. For the most recent and substantial treatment of this topic see Susanne E. Webster, *Body and Soul in Coleridge's Notebooks, 1827–1834* (Basingstoke: Palgrave Macmillan, 2010), but Webster deals almost exclusively with material written after 'On the Prometheus'.

8. Plato, says Coleridge, had 'a sense of high responsibility not to do mischief and arm fools with fire under the pretence of conveying truth': *Lectures 1818–1819 on the History of Philosophy* (vol. VIII of *The Collected Works of Samuel Taylor Coleridge*), ed. by J. R. de J. Jackson, 2 vols (2000), I, 185. For more on the Platonic context of Coleridge's distinction between the esoteric and exoteric see James Vigus, *Platonic Coleridge* (Oxford: Legenda, 2009), esp. pp. 93–96 and pp. 104–06. Nigel Leask, *The Politics of Imagination in Coleridge's Critical Thought* (Basingstoke: Macmillan, 1988), pp. 147–209, interprets Coleridge's detection in ancient Greek drama and philosophy of the practice of simultaneously concealing and selectively revealing speculative tenets — the distinction, that is, between esoteric and exoteric presentations — as an expression of Coleridge's 'authoritarian cultural politics', informing his own vision of how the contemporary learned class, the 'clerisy', ought to operate in a time of deep political and cultural anxiety. Leask's work remains one of the few accounts to recognize the centrality of 'On the Prometheus' to the vision of providential history Coleridge developed from around 1817.

9. Samuel Taylor Coleridge, *Biographia Literaria: or Biographical Sketches of My Literary Life and Opinions* [1817] (vol. VII of *The Collected Works of Samuel Taylor Coleridge*), ed. by James Engell and Walter Jackson Bate, 2 vols (1983), II, 19.

10. Thus 'On the Prometheus of Aeschylus' falls approximately into the following sections: first, contextual introduction (pp. 1258–63); second, philosophical system (pp. 1264–78); third, mapping the system on to *Prometheus Bound* (pp. 1278–86).

11. 'On the Prometheus of Aeschylus', p. 1267; cf. p. 1271, and p. 1273: 'this most profound and pregnant philosopheme'. The definition, I suggest, seems appropriate to the context, though the term 'philosopheme' generally referred to a philosophical statement, system or axiom: cf.

Samuel Taylor Coleridge, *Marginalia* (vol. XII of *The Collected Works of Samuel Taylor Coleridge*), ed. by George Whalley and H. J. Jackson, 6 vols (1980–2001), II, 389n. Coleridge probably gained some impetus for his use of this term from Creuzer, who uses it in his 1810 preface (p. x) and proceeds to distinguish various types of myth, including the theological and the natural, the highest being the 'Philosopheme', which incorporates genuine thought and ancient wisdom (p. 105). Coleridge referred to both the first and the substantially revised second edition of Creuzer's *magnum opus*. Quotations in this chapter are from Friedrich Creuzer, *Symbolik und Mythologie der alten Völker, besonders der Griechen*, 4 vols (Leipzig and Darmstadt: Karl Wilhelm Leske, 1810–12).

12. *The Notebooks of Samuel Taylor Coleridge*, ed. by Kathleen Coburn, Merton Christensen and Anthony John Harding, 5 vols in 10 (New York, London, and Princeton, NJ: Routledge and Kegan Paul, 1957–2002), IV, 4839 (dated 1821–22 by the editors).

13. See 'On the Prometheus of Aeschylus', p. 1267. I have referred to H. G. Liddell and R. Scott, *Greek–English Lexicon* [1843] (Oxford: Oxford University Press, 1996). For the sake of clarity (rather than implying any specific interpretation) I capitalize some of the terms Coleridge uses in a special sense, such as Reason.

14. 'Prometheus, or Nous Agonistes' was the title Coleridge suggested that his son Hartley should use for an original work (quoted in *Aids to Reflection*, p. 563). Compare a similar recommendation of the title 'Nous Agonistes: An Orphic Mystery': *Shorter Works and Fragments*, II, 1298.

15. 'On the Prometheus of Aeschylus', p. 1268; cf. p. 1288. Here and in the following I have transliterated Greek words used by Coleridge for ease of reading. On tautegory, see also Jeffrey Einboden's contribution to this volume, p. 165.

16. For more on this reception and the controversy surrounding Coleridge's symbol-theory, see the introduction to this volume. As Jackson and Jackson note, the question of the relation of 'On the Prometheus of Aeschylus' to Coleridge's German sources (above all Böhme, Creuzer and Schelling) 'cannot be considered closed' (p. 1255, n. 1) — though plagiarism was not involved. Especially important is F. W. J. Schelling, *Ueber die Gottheiten von Samothrake. Vorgelesen in der öffentlichen Sitzung der Baier'schen Akademie der Wissenschaften am Namenstage des Königs den 12. Oct. 1815. Beylage zu den Weltaltern* (Stuttgart and Tübingen: J. G. Cotta, 1815; facsimile reprint Amsterdam: Rodopi, 1968). In the following, I also cite this text in the following abridged translation: Robert F. Brown, *Schelling's Treatise on 'The Deities of Samothrace'* [1974] (Missoula, MT: Scholar's Press, 1977). The connection between the essays of Schelling and Coleridge was first noted in William K. Pfeiler, 'Coleridge and Schelling's Treatise on the Samothracian Deities', *Modern Language Notes*, 52.3 (March 1937), 162–65.

17. *Marginalia*, II, 183.

18. 'On the Prometheus of Aeschylus', p. 1264.

19. Aeschylus is Coleridge's only example at this point, but several years later he also mentions 'Sophocles the purest Emanation from the Mysteries, the only Antidote to the corruptive influence of the popular or established Religion': *Notebooks*, V, 6646 (11 September 1830).

20. Such syncretizing narratives may be unfashionable, but they have by no means disappeared, a distinguished instance being Thomas McEvilley, *The Shape of Ancient Thought: Comparative Studies of Greek and Indian Philosophies* (New York: Allworth Press, 2002). McEvilley, however, employs a less nuanced concept of 'pantheism' than Coleridge (see below): for instance, he describes Aeschylus's Zeus as 'both immanent and transcendent' (p. 27), and then as 'pantheistic' (p. 61).

21. In developing a 'sympathetic' reading of Coleridge's speculations I have drawn inspiration from Tim Milnes, *The Truth about Romanticism* (Cambridge: Cambridge University Press, 2010). I thus take a different approach from that of Anthony John Harding in *The Reception of Myth in British Romanticism* (Columbia: University of Missouri Press, 1995), for whom 'Coleridge's reinterpretations of myth serve an ideology that requires historicist analysis' (p. 13).

22. For Coleridge's peremptory dismissal of the significance of Champollion's deciphering work, see *Notebooks*, IV, 5219. For an introduction to the cultural context, see Stefanie Fricke, '"Pleasant riddles of futurity": Egyptian Hieroglyphs in the Romantic Age', in *Romantic Explorations: Selected Papers from the Koblenz Conference of the German Society for English Romanticism*, ed. by Michael Meyer (Trier: Wissenschaftlicher Verlag Trier, 2011), pp. 173–84.

23. On the original monotheism that 'must have existed previously to the great apostasy of the

pantheists', see Samuel Taylor Coleridge, *Opus Maximum* (vol. xv of *The Collected Works of Samuel Taylor Coleridge*, as in note 2), ed. by Thomas McFarland with the assistance of Nicholas Halmi (2002), p. 263.

24. 'On the Prometheus of Aeschylus', p. 1261. 'Abimelech' here is not, *pace* the editorial note, 'a slip for Abraham'. In Abraham's time, Abimelech was the Philistine King of Gerar (Genesis 26. 1): just as Abraham had dealings with Abimelech, so Moses with Pharaoh. I have referred to *The Bible: The Authorized King James Version*, ed. by Robert Carroll and Stephen Prickett (Oxford: Oxford University Press, 1997).

25. 'On the Prometheus of Aeschylus', p. 1277. Aeschylus is Coleridge's only example at this point, but several years later he also remarks that 'Sophocles [was] the purest Emanation from the Mysteries, the only Antidote to the corruptive influence of the popular or established Religion': *Notebooks*, v, 6646, 11 September 1830. Coleridge tacitly takes issue with Schelling, who writes that such explanations based on systematic priestly deception merely reflect the corrupt spirit of modern times and are alien to the ancients: 'Undenkbar wäre schon an sich ein solcher Widerspruch zwischen dem öffentlichen Götterdienst und der Geheimlehre' [Such a contradiction between the public cult of the gods and the secret doctrine plainly would be unthinkable]. *Ueber die Gottheiten von Samothrake*, p. 28; *Deities of Samothrace*, pp. 24–25; and cf. *Ueber die Gottheiten von Samothrake*, p. 86, note 87; *Deities of Samothrace*, p. 37.

26. As Susan Guettel Cole notes, 'little new light has been shed on their identity by the excavations': *The Samothracian Mysteries and the Samothracian Gods: Initiates, 'Theoroi', and Worshippers* (unpublished doctoral dissertation, University of Minnesota, 1975), p. 6.

27. Much of the evidence comes from the Church Fathers, who in general had polemical motives for disparaging pagan rites. Coleridge, however, explained the situation in this way: 'The corruption and debasement of the Eleusinian, and, in a somewhat less degrees, of the Cabiric mysteries, must have followed with rapid steps on the loss of liberty in Greece, and probably commenced with its abuse, and with the consequent licentiousness in principles and practice that ended in the destruction of its forms and safeguards. Making due allowance for the misconceptions and exaggerations incident to all accounts received at second-hand, I see no reason to doubt the general accuracy of the statements given by the fathers of the first four centuries, respecting the mysteries as they existed in their times. Varro had already endeavoured to check the degeneracy of the more independent and cosmopolite Graeco-Phoenician mysteries of Samothrace, and to decipher for its priests the original principles of their theology, or rather cosmogony.' *Shorter Works and Fragments*, II, 1017.

28. See Friedrich Schleiermacher, *Hermeneutics and Criticism and Other Writings*, ed. and trans. by Andrew Bowie (Cambridge: Cambridge University Press, 1998), p. xvii.

29. The continuities and contrasts between Coleridge's research into biblical and mythological history in the 1790s and the 1820s deserve further investigation; in a sense he was constantly engaged in the 'new kind of pleasure' memorably described by Edward B. Hungerford in *Shores of Darkness* (Cleveland, OH: Meridian, 1963 [1941]), p. 18: 'The thing was to take the most daring liberties with the received notion of well-known myths and yet not really depart from the authority of ancient texts.' I borrow the term 'speculative mythographer' from Hungerford.

30. 'Summary of an Essay on The Fundamental Position of the Mysteries in Relation to Greek Tragedy', in *Notes and Lectures Upon Shakespeare and some of the Old Poets and Dramatists with Other Literary Remains of S. T. Coleridge*, ed. by Mrs H. N. Coleridge, 2 vols (1849), II, 218–22, p. 221. This admirably clear text is written in the third person ('Mr Coleridge supposes...') and may perhaps have been composed by Sara Coleridge, Coleridge's daughter and the editor of these volumes.

31. 'key to the whole cypher', *Shorter Works and Fragments*, II, 1291. The notion of a key reminds the modern reader of George Eliot's Mr Casaubon in *Middlemarch* (1871–72), who pursues a 'key to all mythologies'. Coleridge's most recent authority for such a search was Creuzer: see e.g. *Symbolik und Mythologie*, 1810 edition, p. xii, and, respecting later interpretations of oracles, p. 80 (§34): 'Man hatte den Schlüssel verloren, den man im Unterricht der Mysterien empfing' [the key was lost that was received in the lessons of the mysteries].

32. 'On the Prometheus of Aeschylus', pp. 1277, 1272.

33. Thus Coleridge writes of 'Nous, or pure reason' ('On the Prometheus of Aeschylus', p. 1268) and of 'This gift (by which we are to understand reason, theoretic and practical)' (p. 1281). Compare

Coleridge's quotation from Plato's *Phaedrus* (pp. 1276–77), cited here in translation: 'do you think it possible to understand the nature of soul satisfactorily without taking it as a whole?'

34. 'On the Prometheus of Aeschylus', p. 1285.

35. 'On the Prometheus of Aeschylus', pp. 1266–67.

36. In this characterization of Coleridge's method I draw on Tim Milnes's fine chapter 'Coleridge's Logic', in *Handbook of the History of Logic*, ed. by John Woods and Dov M. Gabbay (Amsterdam: Elsevier, 2008), IV: *British Logic in the Nineteenth Century*, pp. 33–74.

37. For a fuller account, see James Vigus, 'The Philosophy of Samuel Taylor Coleridge', in *The Oxford Handbook of British Philosophy in the Nineteenth Century*, ed. by William Mander (Oxford: Oxford University Press, forthcoming 2013).

38. 'On the Prometheus of Aeschylus', p. 1263.

39. 'On the Prometheus of Aeschylus, p. 1267; cf. p. 1287.

40. On Coleridge's notes on Genesis, largely made in 1829, see Jeffrey W. Barbeau, *Coleridge, The Bible, and Religion* (New York: Palgrave Macmillan, 2007), pp. 49–55.

41. 'On the Prometheus of Aeschylus', p. 1287.

42. Cf. the introduction to this volume, above p. 9.

43. 'On the Prometheus', p. 1267.

44. G. W. F. Hegel, *Vorlesungen. Ausgewählte Nachschriften und Manuskripte* (Hamburg: Meiner, 1983–), III–V: *Vorlesungen über die Philosophie der Religion*, ed. by Walter Jaeschke, V, 40.

45. *Notebooks*, IV, 4839.

46. The dismissal of Greek 'poor stuff' appears in a letter to William Sotheby, 10 Sept 1802: *Letters*, II, 865. John Beer has written helpfully on the interplay between Hebrew and Hellenic motifs in Coleridge's thought, most recently in *Coleridge's Play of Mind* (Oxford: Oxford University Press, 2010), p. 88. Coleridge took pride in 'the independence of my System on any preconceptions of mine derived from Moses': *Notebooks*, IV, 4562, dated June 1819.

47. 'On the Prometheus of Aeschylus', p. 1271.

48. Coleridge's avoidance of the term 'emanation' in his positive description of the 'Greek scheme' probably reflects the fact that Schelling criticized Creuzer for imposing the later, Neoplatonic theory of emanation on ancient thought (*Deities of Samothrace*, pp. 34–35; n. 74). It was indeed to be this very tendency that would bring Creuzer's work into widespread disrepute. Coleridge shared Schelling's cautious interest with respect to Neoplatonism, preferring where possible to pursue Neoplatonic hints *ad fontes* to the work of Plato himself.

49. In marginalia to George Stanley Faber, *A Dissertation on the Mysteries of the Cabiri [...]*, 2 vols (Oxford: Oxford University Press, 1803), Coleridge explains his view further: 'The ancient Mystae were so far Pantheists, that they made the lowest first, the highest posterior [...]. If we however take the whole in the order of manifestation not of Power & Being, the system is then susceptible of a safe and orthodox interpretation — The 3 first Cabiri are psychological Deities, Gods of Chaos — then comes the caller forth, the Word, Hermes, Mercury — then appear the supreme Triad, in which the Hermes appears again as Apollo, or Minerva — & lastly, the mysterious 8th, in which is again to appear, as the infant Bacchus, the Son of a most high of a mortal Mother.' *Marginalia*, II, 576. These convolutions are explained by the fact that 'The Samo-thracian Mysteries contained the Patriarchal Faith & Expectations disfigured by their forced combination with Pantheism or the Worship of Nature.' Ibid., II, 582–83; cf. *Notebooks*, IV, 4839.

50. 'On the Prometheus of Aeschylus', p. 1269.

51. 'On the Prometheus of Aeschylus', p. 1269.

52. Coleridge underlines this in *Lectures 1818–1819 on the History of Philosophy*, I, 27. Here Jackson's note compares Coleridge's marginalia on Jakob Böhme (*Marginalia*, I, 604), a vital connection previously made by Richard Haven, 'Coleridge and the Greek Mysteries', *Modern Language Notes*, 70.6 (June 1955), 405–07. A detailed study of Coleridge's marginalia to Böhme is outside the scope of this chapter, but would assist in understanding the fire-symbolism I discuss here. There are significant parallels between the figure of Prometheus in Coleridge and the figure of Lucifer in Böhme; for new research on the latter, see Cecilia Muratori, 'Il figlio caduto e l'origine del male. Una lettura del §568 dell' Enciclopedia', in *L'assoluto e il divino. La teologia cristiana di Hegel*, ed. by Tommaso Pierini et al. (Pisa and Rome: Fabrizio Serra Editore, 2011),

pp. 107–18.

53. 'On the Prometheus of Aeschylus', pp. 1269–70. The moral dimension of this thought of Coleridge's becomes clear in a subsequent notebook passage in which he again uses the term 'esurience'. He believes that the result of this 'desiderium' is, translated into the terms of another mythology, the fall of Lucifer: 'The Desiderium of Proserpine charmed up the dark King into the sunny flower-field of Enna: that he <sunk down again to the Region of Hollowness and endless Burnings> & carried her down with him — the fiery Esurience, was the Fall.' *Notebooks*, v, 5794, dated March 1828.

54. Compare Kevin Clinton, 'Stages of Initiation in the Eleusinian and Samothracian Mysteries', in *Greek Mysteries: The Archaeology and Ritual of Ancient Greek Secret Cults*, ed. by Michael B. Cosmopoulos (London and New York: Routledge, 2005), pp. 50–78 (p. 68).

55. 'On the Prometheus of Aeschylus', p. 1273.

56. 'On the Prometheus of Aeschylus', p. 1271.

57. 'On the Prometheus of Aeschylus', p. 1273.

58. 'On the Prometheus of Aeschylus', p. 1277.

59. 'On the Prometheus of Aeschylus', p. 1285.

60. *Aids to Reflection*, p. 284, in the context of the myth of Cupid and Psyche: the fact that Coleridge can discern this pattern in multiple myths strengthens in his view the probability of his thesis. This remark appears at the decisive moment in *Aids to Reflection* in which Coleridge challenges readers to discover by simple introspection whether we have a responsible will.

61. Not, *pace* the editors' translation (p. 1279, n. 4), 'law subjugating law'.

62. Not, *pace* the editors' translation (p. 1280, n. 4), 'idea *of things* prior to law' (emphasis mine).

63. Coleridge persistently linked the term *nous* to *logos*, as used at the beginning of the Gospel of John: see the editor's note in *Aids to Reflection*, pp. 551–52.

64. 'On the Prometheus of Aeschylus', p. 1281.

65. 'On the Prometheus of Aeschylus', p. 1268.

66. Coleridge liked to quote thus from John Milton, *Paradise Lost* (V 486–87 var.) at crucial moments: compare *Biographia Literaria*, I, 295 (chapter 13).

67. 'On the Prometheus of Aeschylus', p. 1282. Aeschylus, *Prometheus Bound; The Suppliants; Seven Against Thebes; The Persians*, trans. by Philip Vellacott (London: Penguin, 1961), p. 50.

68. 'On the Prometheus of Aeschylus', p. 1282.

69. 'On the Prometheus of Aeschylus', p. 1282.

70. 'On the Prometheus of Aeschylus', p. 1285.

71. 'On the Prometheus of Aeschylus', p. 1268.

72. See e.g. *Biographia Literaria*, I, 243.

73. Cf. Douglas Hedley, *Living Forms of the Imagination* (London: T&T Clark, 2008), p. 122.

74. Creuzer, *Symbolik und Mythologie*, I, 69 (§31).

75. P. B. Shelley, *Alastor*, lines 126–28. *Shelley's Poetry and Prose*, ed. by Donald H. Reiman and Neil Freistat [1977] (New York and London: Norton, 2002), p. 77.

76. Coleridge asserts that Creuzer, notwithstanding his theory of 'Urmonotheismus', retains 'an undue estimation of pantheism', treating it as a 'congener' with rather than as a degeneration from monotheism. It is in this sense that Creuzer is too close an adherent of the 'Schellingian scheme': *Notebooks*, IV, 4839 (f121). For further critique of Creuzer, see *Lectures 1818–1819 on the History of Philosophy*, I, 87.

77. The connection with hell-fire appears vividly in *Notebooks*, IV, 5077.

78. 'On the Prometheus of Aeschylus', p. 1283.

79. 'On the Prometheus of Aeschylus', p. 1283.

80. 'On the Prometheus of Aeschylus', p. 1283.

81. George Eliot to Barbara Bodichon, 5 December 1859, quoted in Beer, *Coleridge's Play of Mind*, p. 240.

82. Coleridge to Thomas Poole, 16 March 1801, in *Letters*, II, 706.

CHAPTER 9

Emerson's Exegesis:
Transcending Symbols

Jeffrey Einboden

Introduction

> Born unto God in CHRIST — in Christ, my ALL!
> What, that Earth boasts, were not lost cheaply, rather
> Than forfeit that blest Name, by which we call
> The HOLY ONE, the Almighty God, OUR FATHER?
> FATHER! in Christ we live: and Christ in Thee.
> Eternal Thou, and everlasting we!
>
> The Heir of Heaven, henceforth I dread not Death.
> In Christ I live, in Christ I draw the Breath
> Of the true life. Let Sea, and Earth, and Sky
> Wage war against me: on my front I shew
> Their mighty Master's Seal.[1]

Emerson's famed meeting with Coleridge at Highgate on 5 August 1833 was punctuated by the latter's recitation of these lines. Celebrating his 'Baptismal Birth-day', Coleridge's sonnet rehearses the beginnings of his life even as he approaches its end, anticipating his death in 1834 while recalling his birth and christening in 1772. For Emerson, hearing these verses in 1833 would mark neither a beginning nor an end, but a pivotal intersection in his early life. Straddling two discrete phases of his career, Emerson arrives at Highgate nearly a year after his resignation from the Unitarian ministry, and just a few months before assuming his new role as public lecturer in Boston. The theology of Coleridge's verses, no less than the lifespan they imply, may also have seemed alien to his American guest. Staunch defender of Trinitarianism, Coleridge naturally assumes Christ's divinity in his verses — a doctrine rejected by Unitarian Emerson. Perhaps most ironic is the sacramental occasion for this anniversary poem. Commemorating his baptism, Coleridge was surely unaware that another Christian sacrament — the Lord's Supper — had very recently provoked his young listener to quit his New England church and vocation, sceptical as to the efficacy of traditional religious rites.[2]

Amid such discrepancies, a commonality between British host and American visitor is faintly evident in these lines, hinting at the decisive role which Coleridge will play in Emerson's development through the early 1830s. Invoking first the verbal 'Name' of God, Coleridge turns by his tenth line to the objective sign of

God's grace. Defying 'Sea, and Earth, and Sky', the poet boasts that 'on my front I shew | Their mighty Master's Seal', envisioning his salvation in aesthetic terms, with his baptism exhibited as a mark, both visible and significant. This 'shewing' of God's 'Seal' — rendering spiritual reality as interpretable image — intersects powerfully with Emerson's own evolution during this formative period. It will be the American's shifting attitude towards 'signs' and 'symbols' that serves as critical index to his early development, gauging his transition from Unitarian minister, in 1832, to founder of Transcendentalism by 1836. Underlying this key transformation is an idea of the symbol mediated and shaped by Coleridge himself, with Emerson's 1833 visit to Highgate — and his hearing these emblematic verses — epitomizing broader tendencies in his unfolding thought.

'One Symbolical Act of Christ' (1832)

Ten months before hearing Coleridge deliver his 'Baptismal Birth-day', Emerson had delivered his 'Lord's Supper' sermon — a valediction to his congregation at Boston's Second Church, and his apology for rejecting the rite of communion. Resigning only three years after his installation in 1829, Emerson's farewell sermon contends that 'Jesus did not intend to establish an institution for perpetual observance when he ate the passover', and moreover, that 'it is not expedient to celebrate it as we do'.[3] Clearly informed by contemporary trends in exegesis, Emerson recruits higher critical methods to challenge scriptural proofs, noting inconsistencies between synoptic accounts of 'the supper', and emphasizing the conditioned perspective of biblical authors. Expanding its hermeneutic frame, his sermon gradually shifts from interrogating the reliability of gospel narratives to exploring the cultural circumstances of their composition. The rite's imperative formula — 'This is my body which is broken for you. Take, Eat. This is my blood which is shed for you. Drink it' — is deemed by Emerson to be 'not extraordinary' if understood within its proper rhetorical context:

> [Jesus] always taught by parables and symbols. It was the national way of teaching and was largely used by him. Remember the readiness which he always showed to spiritualize every occurrence. He stooped and wrote on the sand. He admonished his disciples respecting the leaven of the Pharisees. He instructed the woman of Samaria respecting living water. He permitted himself to be anointed, declaring that it was for interment. He washed the feet of his disciples. These are admitted to be symbolical actions and expressions.[4]

Denying the uniqueness of Jesus's *paschal* imperative, Emerson aligns the Lord's Supper with a range of sibling 'actions and expressions'. Unifying this diverse group is their 'symbolical' character — a 'way of teaching' which too seems unexceptional, being a 'national', rather than a personal, means of instruction. At stake in this classification is, of course, the definition of 'symbol' itself, with Emerson's polemic against the Supper now dependent upon the significance, and authority, of 'symbolical actions'. Accordingly, the sermon continues to sketch the implications of categorizing the Supper under this new label:

> I cannot help remarking that it is very singular we should have preserved this

> rite [the Lord's Supper] and insisted upon perpetuating one symbolical act of
> Christ whilst we have totally neglected others, particularly one other which
> had at least an equal claim to our observance. Jesus washed the feet of his
> disciples and told them that 'As he had washed their feet, they ought to wash
> one another's feet [...].[5]

Corollary to equating 'every occurrence' which Jesus 'spiritualized', Emerson
recognizes the inconsistency of celebrating some rites and not others: why observe
one 'symbolical act' (the Lord's Supper), while neglecting another (foot-washing)?
This logic would suggest, of course, that *both* be observed — or neither. However,
as Emerson notes, the washing of feet 'has been very properly dropped' by New
England churches, and proceeds to ask:

> Why? 1. Because it was a local custom, and unsuitable in western countries, and
> 2. because it was typical, and all understand that humility is the thing signified.
> But the passover was local too, and does not concern us; and its bread and wine
> were typical, and do not help us to understand the love which they signified.[6]

The force of defining the Lord's Supper as a 'symbolical act' now becomes clear.
By means of analogy, Emerson finds this rite to be merely 'local' and 'typical' —
both culturally and semantically distinct from 'us'. As a figurative 'custom', the
Passover is neither universal nor necessary, but rather regional and accidental, with
no relationship enduring for 'western countries' between symbol ('bread and wine')
and symbolized ('love'). This interpretive breach is reinforced, and further widened,
as Emerson nears the conclusion of his sermon:

> To pass by other objections, I come to this: that the *use of the elements*, however
> suitable to the people and the modes of thought in the East, where it originated,
> is foreign and unsuited to affect us. [...] We are not accustomed to express our
> thoughts or emotions by symbolical actions. Most men find the bread and
> wine no aid to devotion and to some persons it is an impediment. To eat bread
> is one thing; to love the precepts of Christ and resolve to obey them is quite
> another.[7]

The conventional definition of 'symbol' as an agent of synthesis is here inverted.
Rather than a 'throwing together' (σύν-βολή; *sun-bolē*), Emerson's 'symbolical'
becomes an adjective of antithesis, an 'impediment' to genuine communion.[8]
Set in opposition is a range of dichotomous pairs, with East–West, Ancient–
Modern, Action–Meaning, Form–Content all fixed in contradiction. Embodying
'foreignness' rather than bridging it, the *paschal* symbol discriminates between
'peoples' and 'modes', dividing 'us' from 'them', even while it fails to reconcile 'eating
(bread)' and 'loving (precepts)'. In finding Emerson conclude his 1832 sermon —
and his ministerial career — with this ironic reversal of the 'symbol', we also find,
however, a deeper irony inscribed into the American's early development. While
it is his definition here of 'symbolical acts' as empty 'signs' which marks Emerson's
resignation from the church, transitioning him from preacher to philosopher, the
philosophy he will now pioneer will be premised upon a definition of the symbol
directly opposed to the one here critiqued. Although it is his rejection of 'symbols'
which helps Emerson close his years as Unitarian clergy, it will be their veneration
which will open the way for Transcendentalism.

'One Mighty Alphabet' (1833–35)

Ten weeks after departing England in the summer of 1833 — having met not only Coleridge, but also Wordsworth and Carlyle — Emerson would launch his new career, giving his initial public lecture in Boston on 5 November. Speaking at the city's Masonic Lodge, Emerson's first address makes an intriguing complement and contrast to his 'Lord's Supper', delivered just over a year earlier. Introducing a series of four lectures entitled 'The Uses of Natural History', Emerson's opening talk was devoted simply to 'Science' — a remarkable topic, not only in its ambitious breadth, but also in its radical departure from his work as Unitarian minister. Although trading biblical studies for natural inquiry, however, there remain profound continuities between Emerson's first speech as lecturer and his final sermon as minister. Echoing his 1832 'Lord's Supper', the American's 1833 'Science' will be an exegetical performance, tackling hermeneutic issues, and — more specifically — the problems of interpreting signs and symbols.[9]

Emerson's intervening visit to Highgate, and his personal encounter with Coleridge, had signalled the culmination of a literary encounter between the two reaching back to 1829. This year's publication of *Aids to Reflection* in an American edition provided Emerson with Coleridgean definitions which pervade his first lectures, prompting him to emphasize, for example, the crucial 'distinction' between 'Reason & Understanding'.[10] Coleridge's influence is also suggested in Emerson's selection of 'Natural History' for the subject of his 1833 lectures, betraying the philosophic aspirations formed by the American during his transatlantic travels the preceding August. More targeted, yet less conspicuous, is Coleridge's impact upon 'Science' itself, with Emerson's very first lecture on 5 November indelibly marked by his recent engagement with his British predecessor. Nearing the end of this lengthy opening address, Emerson builds to the following description:

> The strongest distinction of which we have an idea is that between thought and matter. The very existence of thought and speech supposes and is a new nature totally distinct from the material world; yet we find it impossible to speak of it and its laws in any other language than that borrowed from our experience in the material world. We not only speak in continual metaphors of the morn, the noon and the evening of life, of dark and bright thoughts, of sweet and bitter moments, of the healthy mind and the fading memory; but all our most literal and direct modes of speech — as right and wrong, form and substance, honest and dishonest etc., are, when hunted up to their original signification, found to be metaphors also. And this, because the whole of Nature is a metaphor or image of the human Mind. The laws of moral nature answer to those of matter as face to face in a glass. 'The visible world,' it has been well said, 'and the relations of its parts is the dial plate of the invisible one.' In the language of the poet,
>
>> For all that meets the bodily sense I deem
>> Symbolical, one mighty alphabet
>> For infant minds.[11]

This passage from 'Science' begins where the 'Lord's Supper' had concluded, drawing a sharp ontological contrast. Rather than Form–Meaning or East–West, the 'strongest distinction' here is between 'thought' and 'matter', with these two realms understood as 'totally distinct'. However, while Emerson had ended his 1832 sermon with such contradiction — finding 'symbolical acts' helpless to overcome division — his 1833 lecture inverts this approach, discovering 'metaphor' to be the effective bridge between physical and metaphysical. Opening with the 'idea' of division, this passage soon reverses, finding 'modes of speech' to be directly 'borrowed' from the 'material world' — a figurative link which extends and expands as Emerson continues, with 'Nature' itself revealed as 'metaphor' for 'the human Mind'. This chain of correspondence is supported by the citation of closing lines from a certain 'poet', verses which also mark a surprising reversal. Authored by none other than Coleridge himself, this selection from his 'The Destiny of Nations: A Vision' finds the Briton's poetry intersecting another pivotal moment in Emerson's early career.[12] However, rather than Emerson visiting London, this citation imports Coleridge to Boston, domesticating his verses anonymously within the American's address. Echoing the 'Baptismal Birth-day' heard in August, these lines in November celebrate the intuition of 'infant minds', transforming the sensible world into 'one mighty alphabet' ripe for translation. No longer alien in culture and theology, Coleridge's poetic voice is now Emerson's own, recruited to support his newly acquired theory of the 'symbolical' universe. Conceiving 'the whole of Nature' to be a sequence of metaphors, this passage represents a critical shift in Emerson's exegesis; rather than critiquing scriptural symbols as conditioned by history and nation, here the American celebrates the world itself as a material bible — a 'great book' inviting figurative interpretation.

Marrying the poetic and the natural, the aesthetic and the physical, 'Science' anticipates the trend of Emerson's thought during his transition from ministerial resignation (1832) to the publication of *Nature* (1836) — his first major work, and the recognized launch of Transcendentalism. Despite being Emerson's initial public address, the 1833 'Science' unveils a symbol theory which continues to resonate within the final lectures he will deliver before the opening of the critical year 1836. The fading days of 1835 would find Emerson lecturing on 'Shakspear', still meditating upon the sequence of metaphor which links language with nature, and nature with mind:

> The power of the Poet depends on the fact that the material world is a symbol or expression of the human mind and part for part. Every natural fact is a symbol of some spiritual fact. Light and darkness are our familiar expression for knowledge and ignorance and heat for love. Who looks upon a river in a meditative hour and is not reminded of the flux of all things?[13]

As with 'Science', the figurative relation between 'material world' and 'human mind' is here associated with the poetic. However, rather than simply quoting a 'poet' to exemplify his emergent ideas, Emerson now insists that 'the Poet' is wholly *dependent* upon this exact correspondence between matter and mind. The force of aesthetic language — 'the power of the Poet' — is only made possible by an anterior correlation of the 'natural' and the 'spiritual', with these two arenas of 'fact' directly aligned. Far from his 1832 definition of 'symbolical acts' as contingent and accidental, the 'symbol' is now refigured by 1835 as a universal relationship which is both necessary and strict — a phenomenal 'expression' of the noumenal, which synthesizes these antitheses 'part for part'. Delivered only a few weeks before Emerson would begin to author his pioneering *Nature*, this passage from 'Shakspear' offers an embryonic formula of the new American philosophy, foreseeing the birth of Transcendentalism in revising the parameters of the symbol.

'The Circumference of the Invisible World' (1836)

Although the appearance of *Nature* in September 1836 marks a new phase in Emerson's career, the publication of his 'little book' would involve as much revision as creation, refashioning and re-using ideas previously included within his lectures as delivered between 1833 and 1835. The passage cited above from 'Science', for instance, is adapted for use within the book's fourth chapter, while the quote from 'Shakspear' just referenced is partially repeated in Chapter 3. *Nature* is unique, however, in attempting to construct a coherent structure, representing Emerson's initial efforts to unify the divergent strains of his thought. The book's seven body chapters are each dedicated to a single topic, but are also ordered in sequence, building an ontic ladder from low to high, beginning with the physical ('Nature'; Chapter 1) and rising to the metaphysical ('Spirit'; Chapter 7).[14] In such a scheme, it is perhaps not surprising to find that the chapter which appears directly in the middle of the book — Chapter 4 — is devoted to 'Language', particularly as 'modes of speech' had assumed such a pivotal role within Emerson's early lectures. It is also unsurprising, however, to find that at the core of this central chapter on 'Language' is the idea of the 'symbol' itself, with this trope thus forming the very heart of *Nature*, serving as the book's medial point, bridging its beginning and end, its lowest and highest.

From the first sentences of 'Language', it is clear that defining the symbol will once again determine the trajectory of Emerson's argument within his early writings. Situated after his discussions of 'Commodity' (Chapter 2) and 'Beauty' (Chapter 3), Emerson's fourth chapter addresses his 'third' topic of concern, opening with this oft-quoted introduction:

> Language is a third use which Nature subserves to man. Nature is the vehicle
> of thought, and in a simple, double, and threefold degree:
> 1. Words are signs of natural facts.
> 2. Particular natural facts are symbols of particular spiritual facts.
> 3. Nature is the symbol of spirit.[15]

Immediately striking in this initial passage is not its substance, but its style, with Emerson opening his chapter with a series of postulates, rather than crafted prose. Adopting a categorical and prescriptive tone, these propositions seem tailored more for logical mathematics, than exploring the nuanced origins of human language. Such clarity of form is all the more striking due to the density of this passage's content, its numerical simplicity contrasting sharply with the complex ideas Emerson outlines here. Being familiar with selections from his early lectures, we do have some advantage in tackling this introduction to 'Language'; Emerson's second postulate, for example, was previously encountered in 'Shakspear', which had proposed that 'Every natural fact is a symbol of some spiritual fact.' The difference here, however, is that such an assertion is now accommodated to a larger design, comprising just a single element within a dynamic complex. Mapping the system suggested by Emerson's introduction, we find his formulae lend themselves to a diagram such as in Fig. 1:

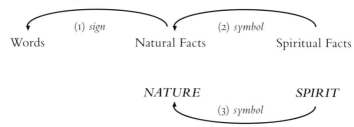

Recalling his 1833 'Science', Emerson here constructs a figurative chain linking 'Words', 'Nature' and 'Spirit', with the physical world intervening between the verbal and the noumenal. Inspiring the former and concretely expressing the latter, 'Nature' is positioned as a 'vehicle', a conduit which leads from the spiritual to the linguistic. However, while Emerson had previously described these three levels simply as 'metaphors' of each other, 'Language' introduces a crucial distinction, specifying the kind of figurative relationships which govern this sequence. Although 'words' are *signs* of 'natural facts', these 'natural facts' are themselves *symbols*, not merely *signifying* the spiritual world but serving as its embodiment. Reinforcing this unique correspondence between 'Nature' and 'Spirit' is its twofold expression within Emerson's scheme. Postulate 2 finds repetition and expansion in Postulate 3, with these two formulae positioned as mirrors for each other, articulating the same relationship at different levels. Postulate 2 asserts a correspondence between individual parts, aligning 'particular facts', both natural and spiritual; according to examples Emerson will later provide in 'Language': 'A lamb is innocence; a snake is subtle spite'.[16] These specific correspondences in Postulate 2 are then contained and summarized in Postulate 3, which asserts a global correspondence, aligning the totalities of 'Nature' and 'Spirit'. Shared between these two levels (particular and general), is the identical relationship of 'symbol' — a relationship which equates Postulates 2 and 3, even while distinguishing them both from Postulate 1, which concerns the origin of mere verbal 'signs'.

The distinction here suggested at the opening of 'Language' — identifying the physical world as 'symbol' of the spiritual — is consistent with the remainder of Emerson's *Nature*, as well as his broader indebtedness to the Romantic tradition first mediated by Coleridge's works. In *Nature*'s culminating Chapter 7, for example, Emerson will echo Continental predecessors by suggesting that 'the world' — akin to man's own 'body' — stands as an 'incarnation of God', positioning the physical not as arbitrary *representation* of the divine, but its manifestation.[17] Later, in his celebrated 1844 essay 'The Poet', Emerson will strengthen this teaching further, asserting that '[t]he Universe is the externization of the soul' — a formula which distinguishes material and spiritual only in terms of exoteric and esoteric, with the 'Universe' standing as phenomenal exterior for the interior 'soul'.[18] Approaching a depiction of the symbol as 'tautegorical' — as *self*-referential, referring to the *same* as itself (ταὐτο-) — Emerson's depiction of Nature as symbol seems to imply not mere signification, but rather participation, with the physical serving as the worldly form of the spiritual, embodying it 'part for part'.[19]

Returning to *Nature*'s pivotal Chapter 4, we find Emerson's final sentences offering an instructive complement to his formulaic introduction, parsing the implications of his symbolic equation of Nature and Spirit; nearing the end of his chapter, Emerson writes:

> There seems to be a necessity in spirit to manifest itself in material forms; and day and night, river and storm, beast and bird, acid and alkali, preëxist in necessary Ideas in the mind of God, and are what they are by virtue of preceding affections, in the world of spirit. A Fact is the end or last issue of spirit. The visible creation is the terminus or the circumference of the invisible world. 'Material objects,' said a French philosopher, 'are necessarily kinds of *scoriæ* of the substantial thoughts of the Creator, which must always preserve an exact relation to their first origin; in other words, visible nature must have a spiritual and moral side.'[20]

Opening his conclusion to 'Language', Emerson reiterates and exemplifies his core postulates, providing a list of dichotomous pairs which 'manifest' the 'mind of God'. Polarities of 'particular facts' — day/night, river/storm, beast/bird, acid/alkali — all share the same origin, each being a 'material form' of a divine 'Idea'. Now gesturing to a Neoplatonic model, Emerson here describes symbolic correspondence not in terms of interior–exterior, but rather in terms of ascent–descent, with the 'visible creation' located at the bottom of a hierarchy, cascading down from 'the world of the spirit'.[21] The physical is accordingly recognized as the 'last', the 'end', the 'terminus' — the liminal 'circumference' of the metaphysical. Perhaps most conspicuous in these sentences, however, is simply Emerson's emphasis and insistence, repeatedly labelling the Nature–Spirit relationship as a 'necessity', as 'necessary', as 'necessarily' active. Seeking to bolster further his central tenet, Emerson ends the above with a supporting quotation — one whose source is perhaps more significant than its content. Attributed to a 'French philosopher', this proposal that 'material objects' are '*scoriæ*' of divine 'thoughts' is in fact original to *Le Vrai Messie* — a 1829 work by Guillaume Oegger (*c.* 1790–1853), a prominent Catholic priest and, later, disciple of Swedenborg. Recruiting a text dedicated to the 'True Messiah' as means of support, Emerson performs another ironic reversal, both recalling and inverting his 'Lord's Supper' delivered just four years earlier. No longer critiquing 'symbolic acts' to refute Christian practice, Emerson now invokes Christian thought to validate his theory of the symbol, finding his newly acquired belief in Nature's 'circumference' of Spirit anticipated by the theories of this Catholic 'philosopher'.[22]

Such recollection and reversal of his 1832 sermon culminates as Emerson continues his conclusion to Chapter 4, bringing *Nature*'s 'Language' to a close with the following remarks:

> This doctrine is abstruse, and though the images of 'garment,' 'scoriæ,' 'mirror,'

&c., may stimulate the fancy, we must summon the aid of subtler and more vital expositors to make it plain. 'Every scripture is to be interpreted by the same spirit which gave it forth,' — is the fundamental law of criticism. A life in harmony with nature, the love of truth and of virtue, will purge the eyes to understand her text. By degrees we may come to know the primitive sense of the permanent objects of nature, so that the world shall be to us an open book, and every form significant of its hidden life and final cause.

A new interest surprises us, whilst, under the view now suggested, we contemplate the fearful extent and multitude of objects; since 'every object rightly seen, unlocks a new faculty of the soul.' That which was unconscious truth, becomes, when interpreted and defined in an object, a part of the domain of knowledge, — a new weapon in the magazine of power.[23]

Although Chapter 4 had begun with simple and strict postulates, this same chapter ends by endorsing 'subtler and more vital' approaches to interpretation, urging us to 'purge the eyes' so we may better apprehend Nature's 'primitive sense'. Contrasting its opening formulae of signs and symbols, 'Language' closes by meditating upon the nuanced and complex task of reading these tropes. As with his farewell address to the ministry, Emerson again features the problem of hermeneutics at the climax of his writings — and, more specifically — the problem of interpreting 'scripture'. However, as anticipated by early lectures such as 'Science', the sacred text which here becomes subject to exegesis is not a verbal bible, but the physical world; rather than gospel 'parables' and 'teachings', the interpretive target is 'defined in an object', no longer a discursive sign, but a material symbol. Having found the 'modes of thought in the East' to be 'unsuitable' in his 1832 sermon, Emerson by 1836 discovers the American landscape itself to be 'significant' in 'every form', marvelling at the 'fearful extent and multitude' of interpretable symbols in this familiar setting. Attempting to escape the contingencies of culture, Emerson takes refuge now in 'the permanent objects of nature', privileging 'local' over 'foreign', 'necessary' over 'accidental'. This shift in interpretive focus is accompanied by a shift in interpretive practice. While the 'Lord's Supper' had adopted a higher critical approach, weighing textual proofs and contextual evidence, 'Language' now understands the 'law of criticism' to be intuitive union between author and reader, recommending 'every scripture [...] be interpreted by the same spirit which gave it forth'. Advocating dynamic intimacy rather than analytic distance, Emerson defines the project of criticism here in existential terms: it is leading a 'life in harmony with nature' that ultimately reaches Nature's own 'hidden life and final cause'.

This change of exegetical focus and exegetical practice ultimately leads to a change in exegetical prospects as well. Unlike the epistemic limits inherent to the 'Lord's Supper' — with biblical significance and integrity always left uncertain — *Nature* promises a limitless potential in reading the symbols of the physical world. Rather than a closed canon of scripture, Emerson predicts that Nature 'shall be to us an open book', becoming a 'text' which 'by degrees' will be made 'plain'. Reversing historical direction, Emerson no longer seeks to recover past revelation, but rather to augur the future, celebrating all things 'new' as he concludes the chapter, repeating this word three times in his final paragraph alone. Accentuating this fresh potential, Emerson again recruits an anonymous quotation, affirming that 'every object rightly seen, unlocks a new faculty of the soul' — an axiom which has traditionally been ascribed to none other than Coleridge himself, identified as a paraphrase from his *Aids to Reflection*. And while Emerson's quotation seems rather to have been borrowed from Goethe — who proclaimed in 1823 that 'Jeder neue Gegenstand, wohl beschaut, schließt ein neues Organ in uns auf' — critics' readiness to acknowledge Coleridge as the voice prompting these final lines of Chapter 4 is nevertheless fitting.[24] As an intervening presence in Emerson's career, inducing his transition from minister to philosopher, Coleridge is naturally understood also to haunt the climax of 'Language', witnessing Transcendentalism's coming of age, even as he had helped baptize and foster this tradition in the years of its infancy.[25]

Epilogue

> All that you say is just as true without the tedious use of that symbol as with it. Let us have a little algebra, instead of this trite rhetoric, — universal signs, instead of these village symbols, — and we shall both be gainers. The history of hierarchies seems to show, that all religious error consisted in making the symbol too stark and solid, and, at last, nothing but an excess of the organ of language.
>
> 'The Poet' (1844)[26]

Considering the boundless promise claimed for the symbol in 1836, it is perhaps surprising to find Emerson lamenting the 'excesses' of this very same trope just eight years later. Shifting focus from natural to poetic symbols in 1844, Emerson seems also to have shifted his faith in their potential, here invoking pejorative terms such as 'tedious' and 'trite' to describe their use. While the symbol had stood as a paragon of necessity and stability in *Nature*, we find its 'stark and solid' character symptomatic of 'error' in 'The Poet'. Particularly striking is the reversed privileging of 'symbol' and 'sign' in the above, with the former characterized as 'universal' and the latter relegated to the 'village', understood as merely provincial — a curious inversion of Romantic convention. And despite being published a dozen years after his 'Lord's Supper', we may even be tempted to hear in this quotation a distant echo of Emerson's own resignation sermon, and more particularly, his rejection of 'symbolical acts'. Concerned with aesthetics rather than sacraments, 'The Poet' nevertheless veers here towards a critique of the 'religious', lamenting its history of fixed symbols — a polemic which had formed the very core of Emerson's 'Lord's Supper' more than a decade earlier.

This ironic turn — with 'The Poet' appearing to retreat from *Nature*'s ideal symbol — seems all the more surprising when we realize that this quotation from 1844 is not an anomaly, but rather signals a growing trend within Emerson's later writings. Although *Nature* would come to define the first years of his career, Emerson would soon produce works of equal strength, authoring two series of *Essays* in 1840 and 1844, the second of which features 'The Poet' as quoted above. These succeeding efforts serve to repeat and extend the central tenets of *Nature*; however, they also subtly revise Emerson's earliest works — revisions again evidenced most clearly in his shifting approach to the symbol. The principal text which follows 'The Poet', Emerson's *Representative Men*, offers an intriguing blend of such continuity and contrast. Published in 1850, this biographic collection celebrates many of the figures already revealed as having influenced Emerson in 1836 — Plato, Shakespeare, Goethe, Swedenborg. It is the chapter dedicated to the latter, however, which most distinctly recalls, as well as adjusts, ideas from Emerson's youth. Treating Swedenborg as an exemplary 'mystic', *Representative Men* celebrates this modern 'Church Father' as a 'colossal soul'; yet, nearing the midpoint of his chapter, Emerson also elects to highlight a crucial point of contention with his predecessor, critiquing Swedenborg by noting that:

> He fastens each natural object to a theologic notion; — a horse signifies carnal understanding; a tree, perception; the moon, faith; a cat means this; an ostrich that; an artichoke this other; — and poorly tethers every symbol to a several ecclesiastic sense. The slippery Proteus is not so easily caught. In nature, each individual symbol plays innumerable parts, as each particle of matter circulates in turn through every system. The central identity enables any one symbol to express successively all the qualities and shades of real being. In the transmission of the heavenly waters, every hose fits every hydrant. Nature avenges herself speedily on the hard pedantry that would chain her waves. She is no literalist. Every thing must be taken genially, and we must be at the top of our condition to understand any thing rightly.[27]

Consistent with his earliest lectures, Emerson continues to understand the 'natural' as a 'symbol' of the 'theologic', echoing his previous belief that there is a 'necessity in spirit to manifest itself in material forms'. However, while 'Language' had opened by positing that 'particular natural facts are symbols of particular spiritual facts', such easy equivalence is now challenged, with Emerson deriding any attempt to correlate 'each natural object' with a single 'theologic notion'. In 1836, Emerson had exemplified the second postulate of his Chapter 4 by asserting that 'a lamb is innocence; a snake is subtle spite'; by 1850, Emerson ridicules Swedenborg's own tendency to claim that 'a cat means this; an ostrich that; an artichoke this other'. Although the identity of physical and metaphysical 'facts' laid the foundation for *Nature*, it now becomes the very grounds of critique, rejected as 'trite rhetoric' in 'The Poet', and disdained as 'hard pedantry' in *Representative Men*.[28]

Perhaps more instructive than simply recognizing this reversal is discerning its motivation: what accounts for yet another turn in Emerson's approach to the symbol? In this regard, it is the diction used to challenge Swedenborg which becomes most telling. According to Emerson, the problem with his symbol is that it *tethers* 'object' to 'notion', it *fastens* them, serving to bind Nature and Spirit together in a *chain*. Recruiting language of captivity and confinement, Emerson frames his protest against Swedenborg in terms of interpretive liberty, resisting his symbol's lack of exegetical freedom. Defined as a static object — with exclusive and permanent meaning — Swedenborg's symbol is stripped of its hermeneutic potential; endowed with particular significance, the symbol ironically loses its significant promise. Discovering this to underlie Emerson's latest critique, we are returned, however, to the very beginnings of his career, finding a broad consistency in his treatment of the symbol which embraces its many variations and digressions. Whether criticized or celebrated, the symbol seems always invoked to expand interpretive parameters, dilating the latitude and scope of our 'domain of knowledge'. In 1832, 'symbolical acts' were seen as 'impediments' to spiritual growth, rejected as 'dead forms' of a foreign institution.[29] In 1836, the 'symbol' had become a key to 'unlocking' endless potential, a stable bridge leading from 'natural facts' to 'spiritual facts'. By 1844 and 1850, this very stability would be questioned, refuted for yielding a symbol which is too 'stark and solid'. Initially rejecting a religious orthodoxy through criticizing symbols ('Lord's Supper'), Emerson is led to establish a philosophic orthodoxy that celebrates symbols (*Nature*) — an orthodoxy which itself demands revision, requiring amendment as his career unfolds ('The Poet', *Representative Men*).

These irregular contours of Emerson's symbol culminate in a final model, one sketched in outlines both flexible and fluid. Adopting mythic allusion to exposit his new ideal, Emerson personifies the symbol now as *protean* — as the physical face of that 'slippery Proteus' who is 'not so easily caught'. Evading definition, the symbol here embodies a liquid divine, transformed into a rolling 'wave' of the 'heavenly waters'.[30] Mirroring the 'circulation' of 'each particle' through 'every system', we discover that any 'one symbol' may manifest 'all the qualities and shades of real being', an agility which makes the task of interpretation both perpetual and dynamic. That Emerson should arrive at such a flexible concept of the symbol in his mature writings is, moreover, entirely fitting — not only as this fluid model helps comprehend the variety of symbols espoused through his career, but also as it expresses well Emerson's own fluidity as a thinker. Although 'Proteus' is invoked to characterize the semantic flexibility of symbols, this label may equally be applied to Emerson himself, serving as an apt self-portrait for an author who has also proved 'not so easily caught'. Willing to redefine his terms as well as alter his terminology (symbol/sign; natural symbol/poetic symbol), Emerson himself has become remarkably 'slippery', eluding his scholarly pursuers through gradual transformation from 1832 to 1850. Mimicking his own description of Nature, Emerson too is 'no literalist', ready to 'speedily avenge himself' on any attempt to narrowly construe, or definitively apprehend, a single theory of his symbol. Following this parallel to its conclusion, however, we may also find it possible to discern a 'central identity' amid his variations, a 'real being' glimmering through the diverse 'qualities and shades' of Emerson's symbol. It seems no coincidence that the above quotation from *Representative Men* culminates by once again questioning our own capacity to 'rightly understand', shifting emphasis from interpreted object ('Nature') to interpreting subject ('we') — a transition which recalls Emerson's consistent effort to expand hermeneutic prospects, preserving the wonder and potential of our 'infant minds'. And while his readers are admonished to approach Nature's symbol with a 'genial' temperament, it is perhaps Emerson's own works which most urgently demand such an approach, requiring us to 'be at the top of our condition' as his career increasingly confronts us with the 'flux of all things'.

Notes to Chapter 9

1. For these first ten and a half lines of Coleridge's sonnet ('My Baptismal Birth-day' [c. 1832]) see *The Collected Works of Samuel Taylor Coleridge*, gen. ed. Kathleen Coburn, 16 vols in 34, Bollingen Series (Princeton, NJ: Princeton University Press, 1971–2002), XVI: *Poetical Works*, ed. by J. C. C. Mays, 3 vols in 6 (2001), I.2, 1136.

2. This 1833 meeting is memorialized in Emerson's *English Traits* (1856) which notes that Coleridge 'burst into a declamation on the folly and ignorance of Unitarianism' before reciting his 'baptismal anniversary' poem. See *The Collected Works of Ralph Waldo Emerson*, ed. by Alfred R. Ferguson and others, 8 vols (Cambridge, MA: The Belknap Press of Harvard University Press, 1971–2010), v (1994), 5–6.

3. *The Complete Sermons of Ralph Waldo Emerson*, ed. by Albert J. von Frank and others, 4 vols (Columbia: University of Missouri Press, 1989–91), IV (1991), 186.

4. *Complete Sermons*, IV, 188.

5. Ibid.

6. *Complete Sermons*, IV, 189.

7. *Complete Sermons*, IV, 192.

8. I appeal here to the etymology of 'symbol'; however, see Nicholas Halmi, *The Genealogy of the Romantic Symbol* (Oxford: Oxford University Press, 2007), pp. 103–08 for the varied history of its use in both 'Christian and non-Christian' contexts. While the symbol has been recognized as essential to Transcendentalism from its first major study (see, e.g., Octavius Frothingham's *Transcendentalism in New England: A History* (New York: G. P. Putnam's Sons, 1876)), insufficient attention has been paid to the evolution of Emerson's symbol theory from his Unitarian ministry to his mature writings.

9. For Emerson's transition between his time abroad and first lecture series, see Robert D. Richardson, *Emerson: The Mind on Fire* (Berkeley: University of California Press, 1995), pp. 143–55.

10. Coleridge's decisive impact on Emerson's development has long been a topic of concern for his critics. As early as 1834, Emerson himself associated the 'distinction' between 'Reason & Understanding' with 'Coleridge & the Germans' (and 'Milton'); see *The Letters of Ralph Waldo Emerson*, ed. by Ralph L. Rusk, 6 vols (New York: Columbia University Press, 1939), I, 412. For the importance of James Marsh's 1829 *Aids to Reflection* to Coleridge's reception in America, see Philip Gura, *The Wisdom of Words: Language, Theology and Literature in the New England Renaissance* (Middletown, CT: Wesleyan University Press, 1981), pp. 44–50.

11. *The Early Lectures of Ralph Waldo Emerson*, ed. by Robert E. Spiller and others, 3 vols (Cambridge, MA: The Belknap Press of Harvard University Press, 1959–72), I (1959), 24. Recalling his recent transatlantic travels, and his encounter with Coleridge, Emerson's choice of 'Science' for his inaugural lecture in 1833 may also echo contemporary British concern with 'the progress of modern science'; just two months before Emerson's Highgate visit, Coleridge had himself participated in the third meeting of the 'British Association for the Advancement of Science' (June, 1833), at which the coinage 'scientist' was passionately debated. See Richard Holmes, *The Age of Wonder: How the Romantic Generation Discovered the Beauty and Terror of Science* (New York: Pantheon Books, 2008), pp. 446–50, 458.

12. For these lines from Coleridge's 'The Destiny of Nations', see Poetical Works, I.I, 282.

13. *Early Lectures*, I, 289.

14. Labelled by Emerson his 'little book' (*Letters*, II, 26), *Nature* comprises an 'Introduction', seven body chapters ('Nature'; 'Commodity'; 'Beauty'; 'Language'; 'Discipline'; 'Idealism'; 'Spirit'), and a final eighth chapter ('Prospects'), which serves as the work's epilogue. For *Nature's* extensive reliance on material previously delivered in Emerson's early lectures, see *Emerson's Nature: Origin, Growth, Meaning*, ed. by Merton M. Sealts, Jr. and Alfred R. Ferguson (New York: Dodd, Mead & Company, Inc., 1969), pp. 46–65.

15. *Collected Works of Ralph Waldo Emerson*, I (1971), 17.

16. *Collected Works of Ralph Waldo Emerson*, I, 18.

17. *Collected Works of Ralph Waldo Emerson*, I, 38. Gustaaf Van Cromphout convincingly links Emerson's pantheistic leanings to his reading of Goethe in particular; see *Emerson's Modernity and the Example of Goethe* (Columbia: University of Missouri Press, 1990), pp. 27–40.

18. *Collected Works of Ralph Waldo Emerson*, III (1983), 9.

19. Although Coleridge's coinage '*tautegorical*' — 'expressing the *same* subject but with a *difference*' — does not occur in *Nature*, this definition of the symbol was available to Emerson through his reading of *Aids to Reflection*; for Coleridge's 'neologism', see Halmi, p. 17, and the present volume, pp. 140–41.

20. *Collected Works of Ralph Waldo Emerson*, I, 22–23.
21. Not only 'Language', but much of *Nature*, is infused with Neoplatonic language. Most conspicuously, the book's 1836 epigram is ascribed to Plotinus (*Collected Works of Ralph Waldo Emerson*, I, I); see also note 25 below.
22. This quotation from Oegger's *Le Vrai Messie* was first copied by Emerson from a manuscript translation in July 1835; see *Emerson's Nature*, p. 59.
23. *Collected Works of Ralph Waldo Emerson*, I, 23.
24. In *Emerson's Modernity* (1990), Van Cromphout presents solid proof for the Goethean origin of Emerson's quotation, as well as recognizing the tendency of 'modern editors' to 'trace this statement to Coleridge' (p. 32). Recent critics have, however, continued to identify *Aids to Reflection* as Emerson's source; see, for example, James Engell, 'Coleridge (and His Mariner) on the Soul: "As an exile in a far distant land"', in *The Fountain Light: Studies in Romanticism and Religion*, ed. by J. Robert Barth (Bronx, NY: Fordham University Press, 2002), pp. 128–51 (pp. 137–38).
25. 'Language' does echo Coleridge, for example, in noting that the 'relation between the mind and matter' either 'appears to men, or it does not appear' — an assertion which recalls a quotation from Plotinus regarding 'intuitive knowledge' featured in *Biographia Literaria* ('it either appears to us or it does not appear'); see *Collected Works of Ralph Waldo Emerson*, I, 22; *Collected Works of Samuel Taylor Coleridge*, VII, 1 (1983), 241; and *Emerson's Nature*, p. 57.
26. *Collected Works of Ralph Waldo Emerson*, III, 20.
27. *Collected Works of Ralph Waldo Emerson*, IV (1987), 68.
28. For previous recognition of the 1832 echoes in Emerson's 1850 critique, and his increasing emphasis upon 'metamorphosis' in his later writings, see Julie Ellison, *Emerson's Romantic Style* (Princeton, NJ: Princeton University Press, 1984), pp. 204–07.
29. For Emerson's association of his ministerial duties with 'dead forms', see Van Cromphout, p. 24.
30. Emerson's 'protean' allusion seems again to have been anticipated by Coleridge, who also cites 'that Proteus Essence' in describing 'the sense of analogy or likeness' engendered by 'a Symbol'; see *The Notebooks of Samuel Taylor Coleridge*, ed. by Kathleen Coburn, Merton Christensen and Anthony Harding, 5 vols in 10 (London: Routledge, 1957–2002), II (1961), 2274.

CHAPTER 10

Pointing at Hidden Things:
Intuition and Creativity

Temilo van Zantwijk

Modern analytic philosophy usually uses the word 'intuition' synonymously with 'emotion'. This usage rests on the assumption that talk about intuition as a cognitive capacity amounts to illuminatism, which is the reliance on externally inaccessible fundamental insights. Our thesis against this widely shared assumption is that the concept of intuition in the sense of awareness of principles and constructive operations depending on basic insights, as it is used for instance by Spinoza, is to be understood as a presupposition of basic mereological claims. Intuition is our faculty to grasp wholes of a certain sort. Examples like 'organisms', 'continua', 'persons' or 'totalities' come both from everyday and from scientific language. In this essay we thus explore the concept of intuition in the sense of a cognitive capacity as it is used in classical philosophy. First we provide an analytic approach to the concept of intuition. Secondly we will explore the relations between intuition and imagination, which is the faculty to represent individuals, which are not definitely determinable by concepts and propositions. Drawing on reflections from F. W. J. Schelling's transcendental idealism we provide criteria for external objectivity of intuition by way of imaginative representation of organic wholes in some works of art. Finally we stress the importance of a theory of intuition for an adequate understanding of creativity which is the power to construct the unity of things and theories seemingly opposite to one another.

Overcoming Illuminatism: Holistic Definite Descriptions

To the assumption that man possesses the faculty to grasp certain basic concepts and truths by intuition has been objected, prominently by Arthur Schopenhauer, that this very idea amounts to illuminatism, which is a dangerous form of irrationalism.[1] If we accept a rationalist worldview in the sense of Descartes, we must support the claim that we know certain basic innate ideas and principles immediately by intuition. Again, if we assume with transcendentalists like Fichte or Schelling that the mind provides a formation of our experience by way of self-construction, we must assume some sort of immediate self-consciousness as the construction principle. Both rationalists and idealists therefore in a somewhat different way claim that besides imagination, which is the faculty to perceive of individuals appearing in space and time, and propositional knowledge, which is the capacity to conceive of things with the help of general concepts and to form, express and infer judgments, man possesses intuitive awareness of fundamental truths and self-consciousness. Both rationalism and idealism are thus open to the objection of being versions of illuminatism.

A general version of the objection consists of at least five somewhat different charges. First it seems to be inexplicable how an identity of subjectivity and objectivity is to be conceived of. In every perception a subject seems to refer to an object he is perceiving of. Now if we assume a reflective self-perception this lets the perceiving self turn into an object which is experienced by the self more or less distinctly. The self that is perceived of is not identical with the self perceiving of it.

Secondly, there are problems involved in the idea of immediateness. Intuition is supposed to provide an evidence beyond any sceptical doubt; furthermore, this evidence is gained immediately. But to be gained immediately, according to Hegel's well-known objection against self-consciousness as a principle of philosophy, means the same as to be conceptually inconceivable.[2] Therefore intuition seems to be undefinable. As a result it seems to be impossible to determine the scope of intuition and to find an object to which it refers.

Thirdly, intuition depends on internalism. Suppose someone ascertains that he meets the requirement of immediate self-consciousness, how can someone else check that he fulfils it? Some mysterious self-evidence which cannot even be put to a test seems not to be very worthwhile.

Fourthly, the concept of absolute assent makes sense only with respect to logical tautologies, where the contrary of any true proposition implies a logical contradiction. But why should we say that we do not feel any doubts concerning our intuitions? If anything, we can only claim that we are emotionally involved in our intuitions: we want our intuitions to be true. The assumption that nobody can withdraw his assent from truths he recognizes intuitively thus puts the difference between intuition and emotion into question.

Finally, if we set aside all these doubts for a moment and assume that we still have intuitions and are aware of them, how could we express our intuitions by meaningful signs? Intuition still would mean nothing to us, because nobody would be able to communicate his insight to others and an insight you have alone is not an insight at all.

As a result, the concept of intuition seems to be of very little value in the context of justification of reasonable beliefs. Most philosophers therefore consider it best to take intuitions to be unjustified beliefs stemming from emotions.[3] For our emotions are imposed immediately upon us. Moreover intuitions in the sense of emotions still have some relevance in ethics. For instance compassion is a feeling that can motivate people to bestow benefits on others.

A successful defence of intuition is not to be expected from an attempt to refute such reasonable objections. In fact philosophers like Spinoza, Fichte or Schelling and later defenders of intuition like Husserl and Bergson were completely aware of many difficulties related to a theory of intuition. The only reasonable defence of intuition in the face of these familiar objections in accordance with modern analytic philosophy must be that notwithstanding these problems everyday as well as scientific language presupposes intuitive rationality. This proves to be the case indeed. In order to show this we have to define the concept of holistic definite descriptions.

Following standard semantics for referring terms we may say that to make use of definite descriptions like 'the last assistant of Gottfried Gabriel' in sentences like: 'The last assistant of Gottfried Gabriel spent the rest of his life in solitude', presupposes firstly the existence of the object of reference, in this case a person who is the last assistant of Gottfried Gabriel, and secondly uniqueness, which means as much as that the extension of the referring expression consists of just one object. Needless to say that by the words 'to presuppose' we do not mean that fulfilment of these requirements can be logically inferred from these expressions but that they just belong to the pragmatics of such descriptive signs: normally they are used in contexts in which these requirements are fulfilled. This is standard philosophy of language. Now let us focus on the difference between the first definite description which is 'the last assistant of Gottfried Gabriel' and another definite description contained in this example: 'the rest of his life'. Now we say that there is a fundamental difference between these two expressions concerning the uniqueness condition, which they may both fulfil. The first kind of uniqueness we may call numerical uniqueness, because the referring expression here invites us to pick out one single object from the set of assistants of Gottfried Gabriel, namely exactly the last one. If we examine the second descriptive term 'the rest of his life' we can easily show that it puts us on the trace of a different form of uniqueness. We are not asked to pick out the rest of his life from a set of different lives. An expression like this behaves like expressions such as 'reality': they are referring to one single object, but there is nothing apart from this object that allows us to distinguish it from others and pick it out of a set. At the same time it is clear that the rest of my life does not basically consist of a sequence of events. It is an individual which does not allow of being composed from parts, but only of differentiation into parts. We may say therefore that the objects referred to by these examples are different kinds of mereological objects. In the first case the individual is one of the elements contained in a set, in the second case it is a whole which can be differentiated only by the construction of internal distinctions like 'the rest of his time in Jena', 'the Tübingen intermezzo', 'the Chemnitz period' etc. We may call wholes which can be composed out of elements apart from the order of the contained elements, like sets, 'extensional wholes'. When talking about ordered sets requiring formation rules, we speak of 'intensional wholes'. In the interesting case of wholes that we do not identify by composition at all, but only by way of internal differentiation, like 'the rest of someone's life', we will speak of 'organic wholes'. From this we may conclude that we concede the existence of organic wholes whenever we make use of everyday language. Moreover we usually presuppose that we know a good deal about organic wholes, since we are differentiating them into parts.

Now the question arises, from what source might our information about organic wholes stem? Empirical perception gives us information about individuals in as far as they are distinct from one another. This however is only numerical uniqueness.

Another source of information is our common practice to determine objects with the help of general concepts. This helps us to assign properties to objects. But 'the Tübingen intermezzo' is not a property of the last assistant of Gottfried Gabriel like being a biped, or going bald. Organic wholes are not determined by way of subsumption under general terms. We have to be familiar with them already before we can differentiate them into parts. Therefore we claim that everyday language presupposes a faculty of the mind to grasp organic wholes. Now in all cases in which our perception of parts depends on the ability to perceive of the whole we say that we know the whole by intuition.

From this we can conclude that the mere fact that you cannot deny the existence of an organic mereological object as soon as you grasp it does not really differ from the existence presupposition we generally make with respect to the objects referred to by definite descriptions. From this point of view there is nothing nebulous about organic wholes: we usually immediately accept their existence as a result of their presupposed uniqueness. That we cannot deny that existence in some cases is simply a pragmatic presupposition resulting from our use of referring terms. This result does not at all imply that you have to assert with total assent anything you perceive of with respect to organic wholes. The organic is open to unlimited differentiation and of course it is possible that we are conceiving of a character that is familiar to us and nevertheless misunderstand it simply because we distinguish features in it which are in reality foreign to this person. In other words: perceiving of an organic whole is not total perception or omniscience.

Spinoza: Intuition, Imagination and Emotion

For various reasons Spinoza deserves some attention in the context of elucidations about the concept of intuition. First there is the scarcely hidden central role Spinoza played since the *Letters* of Friedrich Heinrich Jacobi to Lessing on the subject in the controversies about the possibility of systematic philosophy in the wake of the renewed German philosophy by Fichte, Schelling and Hegel. Spinoza's concept of intuition was a source of inspiration not only for idealist philosophy in which Kant's rejection of intellectual intuition as an uncritical way of conceiving of things-in-themselves was overrun. The idealists on the contrary were in need of a faculty of the mind powerful enough to let human intelligence grasp the absolute principle of all thinking and perceiving, which was alternately named the transcendental I (Fichte), the Absolute (Schelling) or the absolute Spirit (Hegel). Although they almost never take a firm stand towards Spinoza (in fact Schelling's attitude changes from a seemingly ironic expression of admiration in his early years to an overt but not very satisfying criticism in the *Investigations into the Essence of Human Liberty (1809)*), the importance of Spinoza as a starting point of philosophical reflection in the classical German era is beyond doubt. Secondly Goethe's theory of intuition-guided thinking ('anschauendes Denken') in his *Morphology* explicitly draws on Spinoza's concept of a *scientia intuitiva*, thereby placing Spinoza at the very centre of a transition process from classificatory natural history towards constructive natural science. Goethe's studies in botany and mineralogy, especially, use a constructive method of ordering phenomena in series and searching for connecting links.

In this section we draw on the sharp distinction between intuition and imagination which is established in *Propositio* 40 of Book II of the *Ethics*.[4] This distinction provides a conceptual framework, which allows Spinoza to separate intuition as a cognitive faculty from both passions of the mind (Spinoza rejects the idea of a substantially independent soul and thus of passions of the soul) and images represented in the mind by the faculty of imagination. Intuition is unimaginative, passionless understanding. It is not completely devoid of affection, however, since in Spinoza's view not all affections are passions. The striving to persist effectuates a series of affections by which the intellect gives assent to its own perseverance. The intellectual love to the one and only substance called *Deus sive Natura* is the utmost of these affections of the mind in favour of its own being. The crucial question is of course if we can under these conditions know anything about this seemingly mysterious faculty of the mind at all. Spinoza recurs to an example he also gives in the *Tractatus de Intellectus Emendatione*. The central argument says that basic concepts of mathematics presuppose a faculty to grasp the logically simple. Given the three numbers *a*, *b* and *c* the task is to find a number *x* which stands in the same proportion to the third number *c* as the second to the first: $a{:}b = c{:}x$. This exercise sometimes is done by way of recollection of the correct solution. In this case a student just remembers the signs as images and makes use of the faculty of imagination, which is the way man conceives of singular objects. If the student is able to find the solution by application of a rule, in this case: 'Multiply *a*:*b* by *x*, then multiply *c* by *b*:*a*', he makes use of the faculty of understanding. This is the faculty to prescind general concepts from many cases. For our purposes we can desist from exploring Spinoza's conviction that abstract concepts, insofar as they are well-defined and reducible to simple concepts, represent the essences of things adequately. Enough to say that our conclusion that, for example, the proportionality of 5 and 25 is identical with the proportionality of 15 and 75 is an inference founded upon a rule which presupposes an understanding of proportionality. The concept of proportionality we use in determining the rule itself is simple and cannot be defined by higher rules. Thus Spinoza concludes that there must be cases in which we immediately grasp the content of this concept, for instance when we apprehend the identity of 1:2 and 3:6.

At the bottom of Spinoza's reflection we find a transcendental argument which he does not state explicitly: the act of expressing a rule, which enables us to find the proportional number to a third number given the proportion between two other numbers presupposes an immediate adequate understanding of the concept of proportionality we are making explicit in the statement of this rule. In other words: we could not establish this rule without having an intuitive understanding of proportionality. It is to be noticed that Spinoza's argument does not say that it is necessary to have the intuition in order to make an appropriate use of the rule. You can apply the rule correctly without understanding its principle. But you cannot establish the rule without an adequate understanding of the constructing principle, which is intuitive.

Intuition thus is the faculty of understanding the logically simple, since simple concepts are undefinable and still are used adequately. Secondly, intuition is the faculty to construct rules from the logically simple, which also implies that intuition is the awareness of the mind of its own operations in as far as these are conveyed adequately.[5] Finally, intuition is the faculty of conceiving of (organic) wholes, in the sense that the ability to establish a mathematical rule enables us to construct any special application of it without exception, whereas it is impossible to state the rule from a set of examples alone. In Spinoza's view, we always need to this end a construction of the examples from the principle. A rule is not just an abstraction from a set of examples but a device to differentiate a principle into cases determined by it. Thus the intuition of the principle implicitly includes the totality of its applications.

Imagination, on the contrary, is the faculty of apprehending individual bodies and thus is complex.[6] The complexion of features of the individual thing cannot be exhaustively determined by concepts and thus is represented in an image taken to be the thing in imagination. For instance the teleological determination of nature as a divine creation is nothing but a confusion of imaginative representations with things in themselves, 'quae omnia [...] imaginationes affectiones pro rebus accepisse'.[7] The principal subject of imagination is the state of the body as it is affected by other bodies. Imagination thus depends on the effects bestowed on the sense organs by other bodies or events. But the images do not depict the figures of the bodies they represent.[8] Imagination is thus a faculty of constructing things out of our perception of the effects they cause upon our bodies. A reality beyond imaginative representation is not available to us. Therefore the images we are taking to be things in some 'outer' world do not stand in relations of similarity to things they depict. On the contrary, to speak with Fichte, images are 'all there is' in the world of empirical perception.[9] Adequacy is achievable only to the extent that rational construction from self-evident principles by adequate universals is possible. As a result of this imagination is supposed to cause the mind to give assent to false judgments. In the *Tractatus de Intellectus Emendatione* Spinoza attaches indeed very little value to our imaginations, which 'possint esse causa multorum, magnorumque errorum'.[10] It must be admitted however that Spinoza maintains that imagination itself is not erroneous, he only claims that one-sided imaginations lacking ideas excluding the existence of the thing imagined lead to false judgments.[11]

Imagination is thus of vital importance.[12] It informs the mind about the state of the body which is a perception from a point of view of temporal extension. It is thus responsible for the changing states of the mind, which would otherwise be nothing else than the mode of eternal self-approval of the substance. Change is caused by passions effectuated by images. Again we refrain from exploring the whole system of passions and active self-affections of the mind Spinoza provides in the third book of the *Ethics* and just give an example. Envy is a passion caused by a deeper affection of a beloved person for a person other than the lover.[13] Usually the image of the beloved person loving someone else nourishes the mind with hatred against the formerly beloved person and jealousy against the rival. Passions influence one another within chains of causation, in which they become stronger or weaker, depending on the images supporting them. If someone sees the image of the beloved body, such that 'excrementis alterius jungere cogitur',[14] he will feel disgust and misinterpret the adequate cause of his frustration, which is an obstruction of his will to persevere ('conatus perseverandi').

As a result it becomes clear that imagination in Spinoza is on the one hand of vital importance, in that it is the only source of information in the mind about states of the body. On the other hand the imagination definitely never provides an adequate understanding of the body. On the contrary it leads the understanding astray in that it suggests the substantial existence of things which are in fact only modifications of reality seen from a point of view of limited duration. The images it produces affect the mind with passions preventing it from understanding the adequate causes which would appease its state of agitation. Adequate understanding in Spinoza's view therefore always depends on a radical change of perspective: given that what we perceive of by intuition can never be represented to us by images or vice-versa, the imagination is always and necessarily a deficient mode of understanding.

Kant: Productive and Reproductive Imagination

One of the systematic starting points of the classical German era in philosophy and literature, — say the period reaching from Goethe's *Werther* (1774), the Jacobi–Lessing discussion on Spinoza and Kant's first *Critique* until Hegel's *Encyclopedia* and the deaths of Goethe (1749–1832) and Hegel (1770–1831) — is the question of the scope and cognitive value of imagination. This becomes immediately clear when we consider for a moment the basic features of Kant's 'Transcendental Aesthetic' in his *Critique of Pure Reason*. Kant argues that space and time are necessary for the possibility of experience. Furthermore, space and time are not just empirical attributes; they cannot be found by way of an abstraction procedure starting from things given in our perception. Space is not just the common feature of many extended things, which besides properties like colour, smell etc. have also the property of spatial and temporal extension. Space and time are not just empirical concepts. At the same time Kant argues that it is impossible for space and time to be counted as empirical objects. To be an empirical object means to be counted as an object in an outer world and this means to be a thing or an event which can be found in space and time. To count as empirical means to appear to us, which is to be temporally and spatially extended. Furthermore, all appearing objects are coordinated with one another. Therefore it does not make sense to assume more than one space or time. Several spaces can be counted as different only relatively to a common space, in which they are different. 'Space' and 'time' therefore are referring terms with an extension of exactly one object. At the same time Kant states that 'space' and 'time' are logically simple expressions, which cannot be defined by general properties included in their content: it is impossible to give a definition drawing on a higher genus and expressing the specific difference here. 'Space' and 'time' are thus proper names, referring to ideal individuals not given in empirical perception. From this it follows that space and time are independent from one another, an assumption which contradicts relativity theory and caused the neo-Kantian schools a lot of problems in the twentieth century. Finally, Kant draws a distinction between concepts and intuitions ('Anschauungen') such that any perception we have is either discursive or intuitive. As a result space and time are: (i) pure forms underlying empirical perception; (ii) ideal individual objects, not given to us in empirical perception; (iii) the operation of the mind apprehending these ideal forms and objects. Kant combines these features in the notion of 'pure intuition' ('reine Anschauung').

Before we highlight the consequences to be drawn from this theory with respect to the concept of imagination it will be useful to dwell upon the transcendental argument Kant puts forward in support of his view. Generally speaking, Kant accepts Hume's empiricist criterion for legitimate usage of referring terms. This means that concepts must apply to possible objects of empirical perception. Thus at first sight Kant's use of the terms 'space' and 'time' is not justified. By way of a transcendental argument pure imagination can be justified however. In the 'Transcendental Aesthetic' Kant speaks of a 'transcendental review' ('Erörterung'); in the 'Transcendental Logic', the same operation is called 'transcendental deduction', both expressions being reminiscent of judicial terminology. The core of the argument is the assumption that there are synthetic a priori judgments. Hume had equated all synthetic judgments with statements of empirical, only a posteriori valid matters of facts, whereas only analytic judgments are a priori valid (since the opposite of an analytic judgment expressing a logically valid 'relation of ideas' implies a contradiction). However, Kant, as is commonly acknowledged, maintains that there is a class of a priori valid synthetic judgments. These include the law of causality (the same causes are always connected with the same effects) and also the basic judgments of mathematics.[15] The idea of the proof is to show that mathematical axioms follow immediately from the assumption that space and time are ideal individual objects we perceive of in pure imagination. In this sense Kant states that the sentence 'Space is three dimensional' is an a priori valid synthetic judgment, immediately following from our pure imagination. If this judgment were false, the notion that any two points in a plane are connected by exactly one direct line would not be a self-evident truth, which is the same as saying that it would not be an axiom. On the assumption that there is only one geometry, namely the Euclidean, which provides the laws of the one and only space which also is the space of everyday experience, Kant is convinced that axioms of geometry must be true statements, not in the sense of logical validity but in the sense of adequacy to an object, which is established by way of geometrical construction in pure imagination.

Kant's 'Transcendental Aesthetic' has far-reaching consequences for the concept of imagination. If we accept the concept of pure imagination and argue that it is necessary for the possibility of experience, then we must assume that the power of imagination is at least in part constructive. It cannot receive all of its images from sense perception; on the contrary sense perception is making use of spatial and temporal schemes produced by the imagination.[16] No wonder that a vast discussion on productive imagination ('produktive Einbildungskraft') began in close connection with the reception of Kant's Critiques in the 1790s. One of the most far-reaching amplifications of imagination takes place in Schelling's transcendental idealism, thereby turning upside down Spinoza's conviction that intuition and imagination are totally separated faculties of the mind.

Schelling: Imagination as Aesthetic Intuition

In the final part of his *System of Transcendental Idealism* (1800) Schelling addresses imagination in the context of philosophy of art, where it is connected with genius and creativity. As we read in his *Philosophy of Art* a few years later: 'Das treffliche deutsche Wort Einbildungskraft bedeutet eigentlich die Kraft der *Ineinsbildung*, auf welcher in der That alle Schöpfung beruht. Sie ist die Kraft, wodurch ein Ideales zugleich auch ein Reales, die Seele Leib ist, die Kraft der Individuation, welche die eigentlich schöpferische ist' [The splendid German word 'imagination' actually means the power of *mutual informing into unity* upon which all creation really is based. It is the power whereby something ideal is simultaneously something real, the soul simultaneously the body, the power of individuation that is the real creative power].[17] Imagination is not, as in Spinoza, perception of individual objects in space–time, but consciousness of the difference and unity of the individual and the whole. By 'polarity' in the context of Schelling's natural philosophy is meant the unity of seemingly opposed thoughts. Intellectual intuition is the point of separation of spatio-temporal things and the representations of them in discursive thinking, which in itself never becomes an object represented to the mind. It is also the subjective self-awareness of the mind as a reality constructing power. Now pure self-consciousness cannot be an object of imagination. We do not have an image of the self at our disposition. This is the crucial assumption which leads Schelling to the thesis that art is to be conceived of as a tool or organ of philosophical speculations: 'Das Kunstwerk nur reflectirt mir, was sonst durch nichts reflectirt wird, jenes absolut Identische, was selbst im Ich schon sich getrennt hat; was also der Philosoph schon im ersten Act des Bewusstseyns sich trennen läßt, wird, sonst für jede Anschauung unzugänglich, durch das Wunder der Kunst aus ihren Producten zurückgestrahlt' [The work of art merely reflects to me what is otherwise not reflected by anything, namely that absolutely identicality which has already divided itself even in the self. Hence, that which the philosopher allows to be divided in the first act of the consciousness, otherwise inaccessible to any intuition, comes, through the miracle of art, to be radiated back from the product thereof].[18]

Art thus provides the self-conscious mind an ultimate self-perception, which is the construction principle of experience in transcendental idealism, as a genius. Now genius is the realized form of the subject within the sphere of its own experience. It is a mode of being, however, in which the subject does not master its own operations and thus in some sense loses control over its own experience: 'Wird also jenes Absolute reflectirt aus dem Product, so wird es der Intelligenz erscheinen als etwas, das über ihr ist, und was selbst entgegen der Freyheit zu dem, was mit Bewußtseyn und Absicht begonnen war, das Absichtslose hinzubringt' [Hence, if this absolute is reflected from out of the product, it will appear to the intelligence as something lying above the latter, and which, in contrast to freedom, brings an element of the unintended to that which was begun with consciousness and intention].[19] The concept of genius thus lays a final constraint on the idealist project of 'self-construction' which makes explicit the fundamental architecture of 'Wissen', for Schelling an all-embracing term for everything an intelligent being is conscious of. Creativity consists of the unification of the seemingly opposed and can be understood at this level of abstraction.[20] But it proves to be impossible to construct creativity from the principle of self-consciousness within the system of the mind's self-reflected truths. Creativity, which is the ontological principle that brings the self and its reflected world into existence, is manifested within self-consciousness as a matter of fact but at the same time resists construction from self-consciousness.

Pointing at Hidden Things: Intuition and Creativity

In Caspar David Friedrich's painting *Chalk Cliff at Rügen* three figures are represented. One of them, an artist, is looking into the distance; the other male figure is a natural scientist closely examining some plants immediately in front of him on the ground. The third figure is a woman pointing into the depth of the space beyond the rocks hidden to the eyes of the spectator. She is pointing at hidden things and that is what this painting is about.[21] Let's examine the painting more closely, making use of the painters reflections on his own work. Some German Romantic painters such as Philipp Otto Runge explicitly draw on Schelling. It is unknown to us if Friedrich knew Schelling personally or was familiar with his work, but Friedrich's reflections on the cognitive value of art are exactly in line with Schelling's ideas. Starting from this claim that there is a systematic conformity between Schelling and Friedrich we will assume that Friedrich's work is intended to be creative in the sense of producing an insight in the spectator by way of aesthetic intuition.

Against the background of our definition of creativity we will say that works of art are creative if they give us an insight into an underlying unity between things seemingly irreconcilably opposed to one another. In the case of this painting this is the dialectical relation between revealing and hiding. In letting the female figure point at hidden things the painting reveals the relevance of the hidden to man. It does not intend to make us think of a specific hidden thing. Our experience is perception of limited things as the case of the natural scientist exemplifies metaphorically.[22] But limited experience depends on or presupposes an understanding of the unlimited. In the same way our experience is perception of things and events in time. But to conceive of things from a perspective of duration presupposes an understanding of eternity. In the same way spatial limitation draws our attention to infinity. Accordingly Friedrich writes, referring to ideas of Ludwig Tieck, that his works are metaphorical 'pointing gestures' without specific reference, for example a representation of the ruins of an old Gothic church, expressing the need for 'clarity and truth' in a period of history, in which the former 'majesty of the temple' has vanished.[23] If we want know what his paintings mean, we can thus according to Friedrich only make conjectures starting from the discovery of similarities between things seemingly opposed to one another. But such conjectures may trigger what we term an aesthetic intuition, which is creative, in this case an exemplification of historical time, by which we know how it is to experience points of no return. Again we have to emphasize that aesthetic intuition does not provide propositional beliefs, which can be true or false.[24] What we gain by it is an insight into the condition of living in a specific (modern) period of history.

Finally we shall address the question of the external criteria of intuition. We conclude that intellectual intuition is made externally accessible by aesthetic intuition, claiming that aesthetic intuition is the faculty to perceive of symbolic exemplifications. This claim clearly refers to Schelling. Neither in Baumgarten nor Kant's third *Critique*, neither in Cassirer nor in Goodman is it to be found in this strong version. But Schelling's proposal makes considerable sense, as soon as we are prepared to accept just a few more assumptions. The concept of metaphorical exemplification is founded on the relations of denotation, representation and transfer. If we say, for instance, that the fog represented in some painting expresses sadness, than we may say that the predicate 'grey' denotes the grey colour on the canvas. Thus, following Goodman, we may say that the grey colour on the canvas exemplifies the predicate 'grey' literally. But there is also a transfer taking place as soon as we say that sadness is represented as an overcast day in grey colours. Sadness usually does not denote grey objects. We just interpret some grey objects as if they were denoted by sadness. This is the core of metaphorical exemplification.

Now Goodman states generally that denotation is a necessary condition of exemplification. This means to say that an object can only exemplify predicates denoting this object. In order for a term to be denotative it is not necessary that it actually denotes: it is completely sufficient if it can denote anything. Goodman has never explicitly stated this condition also for metaphorical exemplification, leaving it to readers to decide whether transfer from one predicate to another may omit denotation. We can consider several cases here. The very idea of metaphorical exemplification suggests that we have to accept that a predicate metaphorically exemplified must not denotate the object exemplifying it. Now we can nevertheless insist on denotativity and demand that there must at least be objects denoted by the predicate to be transferred. We might argue for instance that 'sadness' denotes a specific psychological state of affairs. We assume that Goodman would support this view himself. We can also go one step further and claim that the transferred predicate need not necessarily be denotative at all. If we accept this then we can also claim that predicates like 'free', 'good', 'infinite', 'meaningful' etc. can be exemplified metaphorically. Furthermore, quasi-referring expressions like 'the absolute', 'the self', 'the cause' and dispositions like 'infinity', 'causality' or 'intelligence' could be exemplified metaphorically. A drama like Schiller's *Don Carlos* could be said to exemplify metaphorically a father–son conflict, for instance.

Now we can draw two consequences from this result, one with respect to intuition and another with respect to creativity. Holistic definite descriptions are quasi-referring expressions. If we refer to 'the last assistant of Gottfried Gabriel' we refer to one specific existing person, but we usually do not mean someone's body appearing in space-time. We mean the whole biophysical self-conscious organization, whose identity is not extended in space and time. Organisms (organizational processes) as well as self-conscious minds are to be identified by their functionality, not by localization at space-time coordinates. If we accept this, then it is also clear that our source of information about such wholes is the intuitive faculty of our mind by which we have an understanding of how it is to be a self-conscious organism, and so on. Now how can we communicate our intuitive knowing-how to others? The answer is: by metaphorical exemplification. Since we cannot give an extensional definition of 'metaphorical exemplification' we may exemplify even this expression metaphorically in saying that we communicate intuition by way of pointing to hidden things. Pointing is a gesture specific to human beings, who communicate cooperatively and share information in situations of joint attention. This opens a door to creativity theory. Our faculty to represent in our imagination hidden things, that is to say those objects not to be found in space or time, is our capacity of aesthetic intuition. This means that human beings have the ability to call into being things not yet existent, because they have the ability to focus and join their attention on these hidden things.

Notes to Chapter 10

1. Arthur Schopenhauer, 'Über Philosophie und ihre Methode', in *Parerga und Paralipomena. Kleine philosophische Schriften II* (Leipzig, 1979), pp. 9–28 (pp. 16 f.).
2. G. W. F. Hegel, *Die Phänomenologie des Geistes*, vol. 9 of *Werke* (Hamburg: Meiner, 1980), p. 134: 'Die Vernunft beruft sich auf das *Selbst*bewußtsein eines jeden Bewußtseins: *Ich bin Ich*, mein Gegenstand und Wesen ist Ich; und keines wird ihr diese Wahrheit ableugnen. Aber inwiefern sie sich auf diese Berufung gründet, sanktioniert sie die Wahrheit der anderen Gewißheit, nämlich der: *es ist Anderes für mich*; Anderes als *Ich* ist mir Gegenstand und Wesen, oder indem *Ich* mir Gegenstand und Wesen bin, bin ich es nur, indem ich mich von dem Anderen überhaupt zurückziehe und als eine Wirklichkeit *neben* es trete'. [Reason appeals to the *self*-consciousness of each consciousness: *I am I*, my object and my essence is the *I*, and no one will deny this truth to reason. However, since reason grounds its appeal on this truth, it sanctions the truth of that other certainty, namely, that there is an *other* for me, that is, to me, an other than the *I* exists and is to me the object and essence, that is, in that *I* am object and essence to myself, I am so merely in that I completely withdraw myself from that other, and I come on the scene *alongside* it as an actuality.] Translation by Terry Pinkard: <http://web.mac.com/titpaul/Site/Phenomenology_of_Spirit_page_files/2012 Phenomenology English GERMAN.pdf> [accessed 1 April 2012].
3. Eliyahu M. Goldratt, *The Choice* (Great Barrington, MA: North River Press, 2008), p. 156.
4. Spinoza, *Tractatus de Intellectus Emendatione, Ethica*, ed. by Konrad Blumenstock (Darmstadt: Wissenschaftliche Buchgesellschaft, 2008).
5. This claim may seem questionable to the reader, since it might undermine the distinction between discursive reasoning and intuition. It is important, however, to see that a division of the mind into different, distinct faculties does not make much sense. There is just one operating mind; what we call 'reasoning' and 'imagining' is from a Spinozist point of view a reduction of the mind's total capacities. Thus intuition includes in some sense reason and imagination. Adequacy is provided for discursive reasoning in as far as it is reduced to basic intuition. Compare also *Ethica*. V, *Propositio* 29, which clearly points in this direction.
6. *Tractatus de Intellectus Emendatione*, nr. 82: 'Dico etiam corporem: nam a solis corporibus afficitur imaginatio'.
7. *Ethica* I, appendix, 156.
8. *Ethica* II, 17, schol.: 'Corporis humani affectiones, quarum ideae Corpora externa, velut nobis praesentia representat rerum imagines vocabimus; tametsi rerum figuras non referunt'.
9. Following Jacobi's criticism, Birgit Sandkaulen supposes Fichte to maintain a 'nihilism of the imaginative', in which both reality and the picture get lost or become at least precarious. Birgit Sandkaulen, '"Bilder sind". Zur Ontologie des Bildes im Diskurs um 1800', in *Denken mit dem Bild*, ed. by Johannes Grave and Arno Schubbach (Munich: Fink, 2010), pp. 131–51 (pp. 133, 149). Compare Spinoza, *Ethica* II, Prop. 23: 'Mens se ipsam non cognoscit, nisi quatenus Corporis affectionum ideas percipit'.

10. *Tractatus de Intellectus Emendatione*, nr. 88.

11. *Ethica* II, 17, schol.

12. Piet Steenbakkers, 'Spinoza on the Imagination', in *The Scope of the Imagination: 'imaginatio' between Medieval and Modern Times*, ed. by L. Nauta und D. Petzold (Leuven: Peeters, 2004), pp. 175–93.

13. *Ethica* III, 35, prop. and schol.

14. Cf. ibid., III, 35, schol.

15. Kant's assumption that mathematical sentences are synthetic has been subject to heavy attacks. It contradicts logicism which is the claim that mathematics is founded upon logic in connection with the view that logical forms are contentful. But it also contradicts formalism which is the notion that axiomatic systems do not refer to objects, but only lay down rules for the use of basic (relational) concepts. As Pirmin Stekeler-Weithofer, *Formen der Anschauung. Eine Philosophie der Mathematik* (Berlin: De Gruyter, 2008) points out, however, Kant's basic idea that mathematics are dealing with ideal objects, irreducible to mere talk about logical forms, still makes sense, because they are indeed neither empirical judgments nor analytic consequences from nominal definitions (p. 78).

16. In their fine paper 'Limitation als Erkenntnisfunktion der Einbildungskraft' Gerhard Schwarz and Matthias Wunsch note a structural analogy between imagination ('Einbildungskraft') and pure reason in Kant. Starting from mereological reflections which we find everywhere in Kant's work they show that the cognitive function of 'Einbildungskraft' is a disposition to draw borders which is necessary for the sensual perception of the form ('Gestalt') of objects given to us in space-time. Imagination thus does not just represent objects in 'images', it forms these images. Like reason, imagination provides a perception of wholes independent from the perception of its parts. Cf. Gerhard Schwarz and Matthias Wunsch, 'Limitation als Erkenntnisfunktion der Einbildungskraft. Eine Strukturverwandtschaft zwischen reiner Vernunfterkenntnis und reiner sinnlicher Erkenntnis bei Kant', in *Archiv für Begriffsgeschichte*, 52 (2010), 93–112.

17. Friedrich Wilhelm Joseph Schelling, *Philosophie der Kunst*, in *Sämtliche Werke*, ed. Karl Friedrich August Schelling, I, 5, 386.

18. Friedrich Wilhelm Joseph Schelling, *Historisch-kritische Ausgabe. Reihe I: Werke*, IX: *System des transzendentalen Idealismus* (1800), ed. by Harald Korten and Paul Ziche, 2 vols (Stuttgart: Frommann-Holzboog, 2005), I, 325–26.

19. Op. cit., p. 315.

20. Interesting surveys are Heinrich Schmidinger, 'Das Auszeichnende des Menschen als seine Kreativität. Eine geistesgeschichtliche Einstimmung', in *Der Mensch — ein kreatives Wesen? Kunst — Technik — Innovation*, ed. by Heinrich Schmidinger and Clemens Sedmak (Darmstadt: Wissenschaftliche Buchgesellschaft, 2008), pp. 7–24; and Ekkehard Knörer, *Entfernte Ähnlichkeiten. Zur Geschichte von Witz und Ingenium* (Munich: Fink, 2007).

21. Cf. Reinhard Wegner, 'Der geteilte Blick. Empirisches und imaginäres Sehen bei Caspar David Friedrich und August Wilhelm Schlegel', *Kunst — die andere Natur*, ed. by Reinhard Wegner (Göttingen: Vandenhoeck und Ruprecht, 2004), pp. 13–34 (p. 15).

22. I use the term 'metaphorical exemplification' here in the sense of Nelson Goodman, *Languages of Art: An Approach to a Theory of Symbols* (Indianapolis, IN: Hackett, 2008). Exemplification is some kind of semantic turnaround: an object exemplifies a predicate when it is referring to this predicate and the predicate is denoting the object. Exemplification is metaphorical if the object is referring to predicates that do not usually denote it. A dark-coloured painting may be said to exemplify the predicate 'sadness' for instance.

23. Caspar David Friedrich, 'Brief an Unbekannt' (1833–34), in idem, *Die Briefe*, ed. by Hermann Zschoche (Hamburg: ConferencePoint, 2005), Nr. 125, pp. 214 f. Cf. J. L. Koerner, *Caspar David Friedrich. Landschaft und Subjekt* (Munich: Fink, 1998).

24. Gottfried Gabriel discusses the distinction between propositional beliefs and non-propositional cognition within the framework of a complementary epistemology, aiming at a rehabilitation of non-propositionality, especially claiming a cognitive value to literature and assigning philosophy a place in between truth-functional scientific and metaphorical literary use of language. Cf. Gottfried Gabriel, *Logik und Rhetorik der Erkenntnis* (Paderborn: Schöningh, 1997).

CHAPTER 11

Aesthetic Cognition and Aesthetic Judgment

Gottfried Gabriel

Like Adorno, I view the 'Bestimmtheit des Unbestimmten' [determinacy of the indeterminate] to be a fundamental characteristic of the work of art,[1] more precisely, the key to understanding the cognitive value of art. I hope to explain this cognitive value in the following essay. To this end, insights from continental aesthetics will be reconstructed with the aid of concepts from Nelson Goodman's analytic aesthetics.

The connection between the conceptual indeterminacy of the work of art and aesthetic cognition was already established by A. G. Baumgarten. Fundamentally important in this regard is his view of *perceptio praegnans* as a representation that is significant, meaningful, literally 'pregnant with meaning'. Epistemologically, the pregnancy of a representation is directly connected to its 'confusion'.[2] Baumgarten is here largely using the terminology of Leibniz, who established 'confusion' as being in epistemic contradistinction to 'distinctness', both concepts in turn subcategories of the general concept 'clarity'.[3]

In Leibniz's view, confused concepts and confused cognition are less perfect than distinct concepts and cognition. He considers especially sense perception to be confused, as its objects cannot be analysed in terms of distinct marks. Baumgarten reformulated the hierarchical relationship between the distinctness of concepts and the confusion of sensibility as a complementary relationship between two equally valid modes of cognition. According to Baumgarten, confused sensory cognition has its own kind of perfection. This perfection is not determined by the degree of *intensive* clarity (that is, logical distinctness), but by the degree of *extensive* clarity (that is, sensitive richness).[4]

By replacing the poetics of rules with the aesthetics of genius, Kant obscured a central contribution of Baumgarten's aesthetics, namely the role that Baumgarten's concept of 'perceptio praegnans' played in the formation of Kant's concept of the aesthetic idea. For Kant, a genius is characterized by his 'ability to represent aesthetic ideas'.[5] He characterizes the aesthetic idea as 'diejenige Vorstellung der Einbildungskraft, die viel zu denken veranlaßt, ohne daß ihr doch irgend ein bestimmter Gedanke, d.i. Begriff, adäquat sein kann' [the representation of imagination that gives rise to much thinking, but which cannot be appropriately designated by a determinate thought, i.e., concept].[6] It should be emphasized here that Kant only means that the aesthetic idea cannot be explicated exhaustively by a *determinate* concept. But he does not say that thinking in concepts is inappropriate for an understanding of the aesthetic idea.

The shared property of aesthetic ideas and pregnant perceptions is their power to give rise to connotations ('Nebenvorstellungen').[7] Poetic fiction, for example, uses them as a way of re-presenting ('Vergegenwärtigung'), i.e. making-present objects and the world by conveying, instead of propositional cognition *about* objects, non-propositional acquaintance *with* objects. (We might compare Bertrand Russell's distinction between 'knowledge by description' and 'knowledge by acquaintance'.) Poetic fiction can thus be positively distinguished from mere ordinary fiction by precisely this mode of re-presentation, arising semantically from the richness of meaning of its language.

It has long been the general goal of scientific explications to transform confused concepts into distinct ones. Confusion is thus — in the negative sense — equated with mere vagueness or ambiguity. In addition to this, however, a positive interpretation is valid in the aesthetic domain, an interpretation that sees a concentrated connotative surplus of meaning at work in *pregnant* confusedness. This confusion is not to be criticized for its logical deficiency, but to be welcomed for its aesthetic richness. It forms the epistemic basis for aesthetic indeterminacy. Now the concept of indeterminacy is itself a semantically indeterminate, that is to say, vague and ambiguous concept. It is important to differentiate the above-mentioned view (of an indeterminate *surplus* of meaning) from indeterminacy as a *lack* of determinacy ('Unterbestimmtheit'). This lack of determinacy is aesthetically relevant, too. It comes into play when something particular re-presents or visualizes something general, without specifying precisely what general is meant. The particular is the meaningful singular entity and thus the very quintessence of the determinate indeterminate. Goodman's concept of exemplification is well suited to explicate this idea analytically.[8]

Indeterminacy is not arbitrariness. A symbol (or object) can exemplify much, but not everything. So there are limits to exemplification. The symbolism it effectuates is a reference to a *selection* of characteristics which the symbol (the object) possesses. Goodman's standard example for making this clear is a tailor's swatches of cloth: as samples, they exemplify the colour, weave, texture, and pattern of the cloth in question, but not its size nor its value.

This conception acquires aesthetic relevance because of the fact that, in addition to such *literal* exemplification, a *metaphorical* exemplification enters in. With metaphorical exemplification, which Goodman calls 'expression', possession is metaphorical. A picture painted in dull greys expressing sadness possesses the property of sadness in a metaphorical sense.[9] The following holds for both kinds of exemplification: a symbol or object does not exemplify all the characteristics that it possesses, it only exemplifies the characteristics to which it, in addition, refers. It is primarily the metaphorical exemplification that can be associated with the traditional concept of the symbol.

The fact that a symbol does not exemplify all the characteristics that it possesses does not make the situation any easier; quite to the contrary, it becomes more complex. What a symbol refers to is a matter of interpretation, which in turn requires 'practice' in order to determine the relevant, that is to say the exemplified characteristics.[10] Here we can bridge the gap with the hermeneutic tradition. The practice is based on a schooling of judgment which, as Kant justly emphasized, cannot be reduced to rules. Exemplification is a matter of transition from the particular (the symbol) to the general (the exemplified characteristics). It is hence not so much the determining faculty of judgment ('bestimmende Urteilskraft') that comes into play, but rather the reflective judgment ('reflektierende Urteilskraft'). This increases the factor of indeterminacy.

The cognition to which reflective judgment gives rise is thus not only inexhaustible, it remains fundamentally open to a completely different interpretation or view of things as well. At this point, we must call in the continental concept of intentionality to complement the analytic concept of exemplification. This is at any rate the case as long as we are dealing not with "natural" objects, but with artifacts (in the broadest sense of the term) and their characteristics. The concept of intention is necessary here in order to make exemplification, in the sense of a reference to *relevant* characteristics, comprehensible. Relevance is a matter of interpretation, and reliable interpretations are impossible without taking intentions into account. Artifacts exemplify characteristics they do not possess incidentally, but with which they were intentionally provided — whether these characteristics are literal or metaphorical.

Aesthetic cognition is based — and its connection with sense perception consists precisely in this — on re-presentation. Aesthetic re-presentations, whether they occur through depiction, as in painting, or linguistic condensation, as in literature, can be *taken up in* statements, but never *replaced* by them. This is not a matter of non-conceptual immediacy, but simply of the obvious fact that the interpretation of a visual or literary work of art cannot replace viewing or reading the work of art itself.

Taking for granted the difference between the aesthetic object and a discourse about this object, speaking about a determinate indeterminacy is not actually paradoxical, but rather a fitting characterization of the particular, here in the sense of something that is special ('das Besondere'). The particular in this sense is determinate insofar as it is a singular entity, but indeterminate with respect to its meaningfulness. By making use of a poignant distinction derived from Adorno, this paradox can be resolved in the following manner: the literary work of art re-presents the world in the mode of *showing*: 'so ist es' [so it is].[11] When this determinate 'so' is more closely determined in its 'so-ness' by interpretation, i.e. predicatively described in the mode of *saying* 'it is so and so', the individual determinacy of the work passes into conceptual indeterminacy of interpretation. This is already the case when not only the interpretation, but also the interpreted work of art is formulated in language. With visual works, the situation is even more difficult, since with the change of medium a different symbolic system comes into play. To speak about visual objects is additionally indeterminate due to the fact that object and interpretation obey different forms of logic: viewing with the senses in space and time obeys the logic of part and whole, whereas discursive concepts, on the other hand, obey the logic of superordination and subordination. From this categorial difference arise as a result several difficulties with respect to the mediatory discourse about art.[12]

I am defending the possibility of aesthetic cognition in the spirit of a *moderate* cognitivism based on the view that art is *also* capable of conveying cognition, and thus possesses a cognitive power to shed light on the world. In this connection it is essential that we should not confine the concept of cognition to propositional cognition, that is, to the truth of statements. We must instead recognize the validity of non-propositional cognition. If this step were not made, the cognitive value of art would appear questionable. This cognitivism is moderate to the extent that the emotive function of art is not contested.

Now aesthetic cognitivism is not limited to defending the cognitive value of art. It is often also thought to entail the view that aesthetic *judgments* have a cognitive basis, so that judgments of a work of art as an aesthetic success or failure can be justified by argument. Although the one view does not strictly imply the other, a connection between both forms of aesthetic cognitivism does exist to the extent that we could hardly grant a work of art the function of conveying cognition if it is held to be a failure. However, the possibility of aesthetic cognition can very well be defended without discussing the problem of the grounds for aesthetic value judgments, and Goodman's position is a good example of this. And conversely, works of art can be aesthetically judged without touching on the question of whether or not they convey cognition. This is the case, for example, in the traditional discussion of aesthetic judgment as a judgment of taste.

In contrast to Kant's view, it is possible to 'dispute' about aesthetic questions as long as a definitive *proof* is not sought, but rather a plausible *argument*. To summarize my point: our aesthetic judgment fundamentally depends on our aesthetic description, on how we see something. Ways of seeing — seeing something as something — can be formulated as kinds of exemplification. What something exemplifies is not fixed once and for all, but is indeterminate within certain limits. This indeterminacy also carries over to our judgment, which depends on which exemplification forms the basis of our perception, what we see. For this reason, our judgment — like our perception — can switch. To the extent that we are able to make things to be seen in a certain way, we can accordingly prepare our arguments for our aesthetic judgment from the corresponding descriptions, and in this way we can even make our aesthetic judgment plausible.

Translated by Aaron Epstein and Christian Kästner

Notes to Chapter 11

1. Theodor W. Adorno, *Gesammelte Schriften in zwanzig Bänden*, ed. by Rolf Tiedemann (Frankfurt am Main: Suhrkamp, 1996), VII: *Ästhetische Theorie*, p. 188: 'Der Zweck des Kunstwerks ist die Bestimmtheit des Unbestimmten' [The purpose of the work of art is the determinacy of the indeterminate].
2. Alexander Gottlieb Baumgarten, *Metaphysica/Metaphysik* [1779]. Historisch-kritische Ausgabe, trans. and ed. by Günter Gawlick and Lothar Kreimendahl (Stuttgart-Bad Cannstatt: Frommann-Holzboog, 2011), p. 274 f. (§ 517). Cf. Baumgarten, *Meditationes philosophicae de nonnullis*

ad poema pertinentibus (Halle, 1735), § LV; in the Latin–English edition, *Reflections on Poetry*, ed. by Karl Aschenbrenner and William B. Holther (Berkeley and Los Angeles: University of California, 1954), p. 56; Gottfried Gabriel, 'Baumgartens Begriff der "perceptio praegnans" und seine systematische Bedeutung', in *Alexander Gottlieb Baumgarten. Sinnliche Erkenntnis in der Philosophie*, ed. by Alexander Aichele and Dagmar Mirbach (Hamburg: Meiner, 2008) (= vol. 20 of *Aufklärung. Interdisziplinäres Jahrbuch zur Erforschung des 18. Jahrhunderts und seiner Wirkungsgeschichte*), pp. 61–71.

3. Gottfried Wilhelm Leibniz, *Philosophische Schriften*, ed. by Carl Immanuel Gerhardt (Berlin, 1880, repr. Hildesheim: Georg Olms, 1965), IV: *Meditationes de Cognitione, Veritate et Ideis* (1684), pp. 422–26.

4. Baumgarten, *Reflections on Poetry*, pp. 42 f. (§§ xv–xvii).

5. Kant, Immanuel, *Kants gesammelte Schriften*, herausgegeben von der Königlich Preußischen Akademie der Wissenschaften (Berlin: Walter de Gruyter & Co., 1900–; repr. 1968), V: *Kritik der Urteilskraft*, § 49, pp. 313 f.

6. Ibid., p. 314.

7. With respect to the distinction of 'perceptio primaria' and 'perceptio secundaria', cf. Baumgarten, *Metaphysik*, trans. from Latin into German by Georg Friedrich Meier (Halle, 1776), p. 169 (§ 392).

8. Nelson Goodman, *Languages of Art: An Approach to a Theory of Symbols* (Indianapolis, IN: Bobbs-Merrill, 1976), chapter 2.

9. Ibid., pp. 50, 85 f.

10. Goodman, *Ways of Worldmaking* (Indianapolis, IN: Hackett, 1992), p. 185.

11. Cf. Theodor W. Adorno, 'Erpreßte Versöhnung. Zu Georg Lukács. Wider den mißverstandenen Realismus', in *Gesammelte Schriften*, ed. by Rolf Tiedemann (Frankfurt am Main: Suhrkamp, 1996), XI: *Noten zur Literatur*, 251–80 (p. 270).

12. Cf. Gottfried Gabriel, 'Warum es so schwerfällt, etwas über Kunst zu sagen', in *Kunst und Philosophie. Kunstvermittlung in den Medien*, ed. by Julian Nida-Rümelin and Jakob Steinbrenner (Ostfildern: Hatje Cantz, 2011), pp. 61–84.

AFTERWORD

Nicholas Halmi

Goethe once defined the symbol as that which 'by fully representing itself refers to everything else'. By representing German thought about the symbol in the 'Goethezeit' — not exhaustively, to be sure, but in full recognition of its variety and complexity — the present collection refers to the influence and implications of that body of thought beyond the linguistic, cultural, and chronological boundaries of its grounding, and particularly in nineteenth- and twentieth-century Anglo-American thought, from Henry Crabb Robinson, Coleridge, and Emerson, to Nelson Goodman. This initiative is valuable, it seems to me, less because of a resurgent interest in philosophical aesthetics, even if there are signs of such a resurgence, than because the development of modern critical theory out of German Romantic philosophy has been increasingly occluded in the last two decades — notwithstanding the distinguished efforts of philosophers such as Manfred Frank and Andrew Bowie and literary critics such as Ernst Behler and Tilottama Rajan — by the assimilation of anglophone Romantic studies to nineteenth-century studies, ostensibly a broader field but in practice almost exclusively restricted to British literature and culture, with a particular emphasis on socio–political issues in Victorian Britain.[1] Of course, to speak of the development of critical theory is to imply transformation as well as continuity (and one of the burdens of my own research in this area has in fact been to distinguish a particular Romantic concept of the symbol from its appropriations by later theorists); but neither can be identified outside a shared context. The contributions to the present volume abundantly supply such a context.

A shared context is one thing, however, and a shared concept another. Thus the reader of the collection is confronted with the question of family resemblances: that is, do the assembled essays, ranging in authors discussed roughly from Leibniz in the seventeenth century to Goodman in the twentieth, have a unified subject, or rather a series of more or less distinct concerns nominally connected under the designations *symbol* and *intuition*? Or to rephrase the question: is the collection a contribution to *Begriffsgeschichte*, conceptual history, or to *Wortgeschichte*, historical semantics? The question arises both because of the volume's subject matter and because of its general methodological orientation. With regard to the former, Stephan Meier-Oeser's erudite essay observes that analysing specific concepts under the names of *symbol* and *intuition* is unavoidably complicated by the 'variety of conceptual implications that accrued to them from the long history of their use in philosophical language'. So the adoption of these terms (and their equivalents) by Kant and his successors could never be semantically 'innocent'.

Secondly, a tension between the claims of unity and multiplicity is discernible already in the editors' Introduction, which postulates a 'newly charged' post-Kantian concept of the self-referential symbol while questioning the legitimacy of speaking of 'the Romantic symbol'. To an extent, this tension reflects a methodological difficulty inherent in the discipline of *Begriffsgeschichte*, with its characteristic focus on individual concepts and keywords: a difficulty in distinguishing pragmatically between the historicity of discourse and that of philosophical understanding. It may have been presumptuous on my part to privilege a particular concept (which I identified primarily in Goethe, Schelling, and Coleridge) as distinctively Romantic, but the restrictive designation was intended precisely to avoid effacing the radical differences among concepts, such as G. H. Schubert's and Friedrich Creuzer's (the latter interestingly discussed here by Cecilia Muratori), which might otherwise be classed together on chronological, linguistic, or cultural grounds.[2] In the event, Helmut Hühn's differentiation of Goethe's concept from Schelling's implies that my definition, however exclusionary, may still have been too capacious.

Such tension dissolves, however, if the question of the collection's unity is viewed not from the perspective of the content of the concepts gathered here under the name of the symbol, but from the perspective of their conceptuality. Whereas interpretations of symbols must posit or presuppose a particular concept of the symbol, the present essays address themselves to the logically prior process of establishing the conditions and means of symbolization. Thus their subject is *discursive constructions* of the symbol. Although symbols of any kind must be 'instituted' in Hans-Georg Gadamer's sense — that is, recognized as symbols — in order to function semiotically, the enabling act of institution does not have to be performed discursively when the relevant semiotic conventions are already understood. If, for example, we are familiar with Renaissance Christian iconography, we shall not require a discursive identification of the subject of a painting in which a woman draped in blue is confronted by a winged man holding a lily. That the '*Goethezeit*' witnessed a proliferation of accounts of the symbol in and across various theoretical contexts — epistemology (Leibniz, Wolff), aesthetics (Moritz, Schelling, Friedrich Schlegel, Crabb Robinson, Goodman), aesthetics and moral philosophy (Kant), natural philosophy (Goethe), theology (the young Hegel), history of religion (Creuzer), cosmology and theology (Coleridge, Emerson) — suggests not only that 'the means of representation afforded by discursive types of cognition alone' were widely considered to be insufficient (as the editors state in the Introduction), but equally that the conceivable alternative or supplementary means of intuitive cognition were themselves insufficiently accessible to intuition. Hence the need for new theoretical institutions of symbolism, developed in more or less explicit contradistinction to the symbol-concepts of Enlightenment semiotics.

For all their differences, then, the emergent concepts analysed in this collection may be understood — as the editors' Introduction also emphasizes — as responses to an epistemological crisis precipitated by the perceived limitations of existing taxonomies of representation. In that respect, these concepts are characteristic manifestations of European Romanticism generally, a field whose heterogeneous and contradictory contents have common origins in a distinctive set of historical and cultural provocations, that is, as 'possible answers' to a situation in which 'nothing can be taken for granted any more and in which a reaching out for new (or old) securities is the order of the day'.[3] The paradox, and perhaps the tragedy, of the symbolisms of Romanticism is that they needed to be conceptualized discursively if they were to be comprehended intuitively.

Notes to the Afterword

1. See Tilottama Rajan, '"The Prose of the World": Romanticism, the Nineteenth Century, and the Reorganization of Knowledge', *Modern Language Quarterly*, 67 (2006), 479–504, and 'Romanticism and the Unfinished Project of Deconstruction', *European Romantic Review*, 23 (2012), 293–303.
2. Cf. *The Genealogy of the Romantic Symbol* (Oxford: Oxford University Press, 2007), pp. 1–2, 17–19.
3. Christoph Bode, 'Europe', in Nicholas Roe (ed.), *Romanticism: An Oxford Guide* (Oxford: Oxford University Press, 2005), pp. 127–36 (p. 135); and see also his 'Romantik—Europäische Antwort auf die Herausforderung der Moderne? Versuch einer Rekonzeptualisierung', in Anja Ernst and Paul Geyer (eds.), *Die Romantik: Ein Gründungsmythos der europäischen Moderne* (Göttingen: Bonn University Press, 2010), pp. 85–96.

BIBLIOGRAPHY

Primary Sources

AESCHYLUS, *Prometheus Bound; The Suppliants; Seven Against Thebes; The Persians*, trans. by Philip Vellacott (London: Penguin, 1961)

ALANUS AB INSULIS, *Textes inédits*, ed. by Marie-Thérése d'Alverny (Paris: J. Vrin, 1965)

ALBERT THE GREAT, *Super Dionysium de caelesti hierarchia*, Opera omnia 36/1, ed. by Paul Simon and Wilhelm Kübel (Münster: Aschendorff, 1993)

ARISTOTLE, *Aristotle's Metaphysics; Metaphysica; a revised text with introduction and commentary*, ed. by William D. Ross (Oxford: Clarendon Press, 1924)

——*Metaphysik*, ed. by Ursula Wolf (Reinbek bei Hamburg: Rowohlt-Taschenbuch-Verlag, 2002)

BAUMEISTER, FRIEDRICH CHRISTIAN, *Elementa philosophiae recentioris* (Leipzig: Gleditsch, 1747)

——*Institutiones metaphysicae* (Wittenberg and Zerbst: Zimmermann, 1774; first published 1738)

——*Institutiones metaphysicae* (Wittenberg et al.: Ahlfeldt, 1765)

BAUMGARTEN, ALEXANDER GOTTLIEB, *Metaphysica/Metaphysik* [1739, 1757]. Historisch-kritische Ausgabe, trans. and ed. by Günter Gawlick and Lothar Kreimendahl (Stuttgart-Bad Cannstatt: Frommann-Holzboog, 2011)

——*Metaphysik*, trans. from Latin into German by Georg Friedrich Meier (Halle, 1776)

——*Reflections on Poetry*, ed. by Karl Aschenbrenner and William B. Holther (Berkeley and Los Angeles: University of California, 1954)

BERNSTEIN, J. M. (ed.), *Classic and Romantic German Aesthetics* (Cambridge: Cambridge University Press, 2003)

The Bible: The Authorized King James Version, ed. by Robert Carroll and Stephen Prickett (Oxford: Oxford University Press, 1997)

BILFINGER, GEORG BERNHARD, *Dilucidationes philosophicae* (Tübingen: Cotta, 1725)

——*Praecepta logica* (Jena: Marggraf, 1742)

BOEHM, ANDREAS, *Metaphysica* (Giessen: Krieger, 1767)

CARLYLE, THOMAS, *Sartor Resartus: The Life and Opinions of Herr Teufelsdröckh* (London: Chapman and Hall, 1869)

CICERO, MARCUS TULLIUS, *De oratore*, trans. and ed. by Harald Merklin (Stuttgart: Reclam, 2006)

COLERIDGE, SAMUEL TAYLOR, *Coleridge's Poetry and Prose*, ed. by Nicholas Halmi, Paul Magnuson and Raimonda Modiano (New York and London: Norton, 2004)

——'On the Prometheus of Æschylus; an Essay, preparatory to a series of Disquisitions respecting the Egyptian in connection with the Sacerdotal Theology, and in contrast with the Mysteries of ancient Greece', *Transactions of the Royal Society of Literature of the United Kingdom* (London: John Murray, 1834), II, 384–404

——*The Collected Letters of Samuel Taylor Coleridge*, ed. by Earl Leslie Griggs, 6 vols (Oxford: Oxford University Press, 1956–71)

——*The Collected Works of Samuel Taylor Coleridge*, gen. ed. Kathleen Coburn, 16 vols in 34, Bollingen Series (Princeton, NJ: Princeton University Press, 1971–2002), especially:

vol. I: *Lectures 1795: On Politics and Religion*, ed. by Lewis Patton and Peter Mann (1971)

vol. VI: *Lay Sermons*, ed. by R. J. White (1972)

vol. VII: *Biographia Literaria or Sketches of My Literary Life and Opinions*, ed. by James Engell and W. Jackson Bate, 2 vols (1983)

vol. VIII: *Lectures 1818–1819 on the History of Philosophy*, ed. by J. R. de J. Jackson, 2 vols (2000)

vol. IX: *Aids to Reflection*, ed. by John Beer (1993)

vol. XI: *Shorter Works and Fragments*, ed. by H. J. Jackson and J. R. de J. Jackson, 2 vols (1995), containing 'On the Prometheus of Aeschylus', II, 1251–1301

vol. XII: *Marginalia*, ed. by George Whalley and H. J. Jackson, 6 vols (1980–2001)

vol. XV: *Opus Maximum*, ed. by Thomas McFarland with the assistance of Nicholas Halmi (2002)

vol. XVI: *Poetical Works*, ed. by J. C. C. Mays, 3 vols in 6 (2001)

—— *The Notebooks of Samuel Taylor Coleridge*, ed. by Kathleen Coburn, Merton Christensen and Anthony John Harding, 5 vols in 10 (New York, London, and Princeton, NJ: Routledge and Kegan Paul, 1957–2002)

—— 'Summary of an Essay on The Fundamental Position of the Mysteries in Relation to Greek Tragedy', *Notes and Lectures Upon Shakespeare and some of the Old Poets and Dramatists with Other Literary Remains of S. T. Coleridge*, ed. by Mrs H. N. Coleridge, 2 vols (1849), II, 218–22

CREUZER, FRIEDRICH, *Symbolik und Mythologie der alten Völker, besonders der Griechen*, 2 vols (Leipzig and Darmstadt: Leske, 1810–12); 2nd edn, 4 vols (Leipzig and Darmstadt: Leske, 1819)

CRUSIUS, CHRISTIAN AUGUST, *Weg zur Gewißheit und Zuverläßigkeit der menschlichen Erkenntnis* (Leipzig: Gleditsch, 1747)

EMERSON, RALPH WALDO, *The Collected Works of Ralph Waldo Emerson*, ed. by Alfred R. Ferguson and others, 8 vols (Cambridge, MA: The Belknap Press of Harvard University Press, 1971–2010)

—— *The Complete Sermons of Ralph Waldo Emerson*, ed. by Albert J. von Frank and others, 4 vols (Columbia: University of Missouri Press, 1989–91)

—— *The Early Lectures of Ralph Waldo Emerson*, ed. by Robert E. Spiller and others, 3 vols (Cambridge, MA: The Belknap Press of Harvard University Press, 1959–72)

—— *The Letters of Ralph Waldo Emerson*, ed. by Ralph L. Rusk, 6 vols (New York: Columbia University Press, 1939)

FABER, GEORGE STANLEY, *A Dissertation on the Mysteries of the Cabiri [...]*, 2 vols (Oxford: Oxford University Press, 1803)

FICHTE, Johann Gottlieb, *Gesamtausgabe der Bayerischen Akademie der Wissenschaften*, ed. by Reinhard Lauth et al. (Stuttgart-Bad Cannstadt: Friedrich Frommann Verlag, 1977–) [=GA], especially

FICHTE, *Vorlesungen über Logik und Metaphysik* [1797], in GA, vol. IV, 1

FRIEDRICH, CASPAR DAVID, *Die Briefe*, ed. by Hermann Zschoche (Hamburg: ConferencePoint, 2005)

GARVE, CHRISTIAN, 'Betrachtungen einiger Verschiedenheiten in den Werken der ältesten und neuern Schriftsteller, insbesondere der Dichter', in *Neue Bibliothek der schönen Wissenschaften und der freyen Künste*, vol. X (Leipzig: Dyck, 1770), pp. 1–37

GOETHE, JOHANN WOLFGANG VON, *Goethes Werke*, ed. by commission of the Grand Duchess Sophie von Sachsen. Sections I–IV, 133 vols in 143 (Weimar, 1887–1919; photomechanical reprint Munich, 1987 [=WA, i.e. Weimarer-Ausgabe], especially:

'[Mein Verhältniß zu Schiller]', in WA I, 42.2, p. 146

'Betrachtung über Morphologie überhaupt', in WA II, 6, pp. 292–99

'Der Versuch als Vermittler von Object und Subject', in WA II, 11, pp. 21–37

Aus meinem Leben. Dichtung und Wahrheit, Erster Theil, in WA I, 26

'Die Metamorphose der Pflanzen', in WA I, 1, pp. 290–92

'Erfahrung und Wissenschaft', in WA II, 11. pp. 38–41

'Über die Gegenstände der bildenden Kunst', in WA I, 47, pp. 91–95

—— *The Collected Works*, executive ed. Victor Lange, 12 volumes (Princeton, NJ: Princeton University Press, 1984–95)

—— *Scientific Studies*, ed. and trans. by Douglas Miller (New York: Suhrkamp, 1988)

GOETHE, JOHANN WOLFGANG VON, and FRIEDRICH SCHILLER, *Correspondence between Goethe and Schiller, 1794–1805*, trans. by Liselotte Dieckmann (New York: Peter Lang, 1994)

GOLLING, JOHANN WILHELM, *Theses philosophicae de cognitione symbolica et intuitiva* (Altdorf: Meyer, 1725)

GOTTSCHED, JOHANN CHRISTOPH, *Erste Gründe der gesamten Weltweisheit*, erster Theil (Leipzig: Bernhard Christoph Breitkopfen, 1733)

GRIMM, JACOB, and WILHELM GRIMM, *Deutsches Wörterbuch*, 16 vols (Leipzig: S. Hirzel, 1854–1960)

HARDENBERG, FRIEDRICH VON [Novalis], *Die Schriften Friedrich von Hardenbergs*, ed. by Paul Kluckhohn and Richard Samuel (Stuttgart: Kohlhammer, 1960–), especially:

Das Allgemeine Brouillon (1798/99), in *Schriften*, vol. III

—— *Werke*, ed. by Gerhard Schulz, second edition (Munich: Beck, 1981)

HEGEL, GEORG WILHELM FRIEDRICH, *Vorlesungen. Ausgewählte Nachschriften und Manuskripte*, (Hamburg: Meiner, 1983–), especially:

Vols III–V: *Vorlesungen über die Philosophie der Religion* (ed. by Walter Jaeschke)

Vols VI–IX: *Vorlesungen über die Geschichte der Philosophie* (ed. by Pierre Garniron and Walter Jaeschke)

—— *Hegels theologische Jugendschriften*, ed. by Herman Nohl (Tübingen: Mohr, 1907)

—— *Werke in zwanzig Bänden*, ed. by Eva Moldenhauer and Karl Markus Michel (Frankfurt am Main: Suhrkamp, 1969–71), i.e. Theorie-Werkausgabe, especially:

Vol. III: *Phänomenologie des Geistes*

Vols VIII–X: *Enzyklopädie der philosophischen Wissenschaften im Grundrisse*

Vols XIII–XV: *Vorlesungen über die Ästhetik*

Vols XVIII–XX: *Vorlesungen über die Geschichte der Philosophie*

—— *Vorlesungen über die Philosophie der Kunst*, ed. by Annemarie Gethmann-Siefert (Hamburg: Meiner, 2003)

—— *Die Phänomenologie des Geistes*, vol. IX of *Werke* (Hamburg: Meiner, 1980)

Translations of Hegel:

—— *Early Theological Writings*, trans. by Thomas Malcolm Knox, with an introduction and Fragments trans. by Richard Kroner (Chicago, IL: University of Chicago Press, 1948)

—— *Phenomenology of Spirit*, trans. by A. V. Miller, with analysis of the text and foreword by J. N. Findlay (Oxford: Clarendon Press, 1977)

—— *Phenomenology of Spirit*, trans. by Terry Pinkard (2008), online: <http://web.mac.com/titpaul/Site/Phenomenology_of_Spirit_page_files/2012 Phenomenology English GERMAN.pdf > [accessed 24 January 2012]

HERDER, JOHANN GOTTFRIED, *Werke in zehn Bänden*, ed. by Martin Bollacher et al. (Frankfurt am Main: Deutscher Klassiker-Verlag, 1985–2000), especially:

Kalligone, vol. VIII, ed. by Hans Dietrich Irmscher (Frankfurt am Main: Deutscher Klassiker-Verlag, 1998)

HÖLDERLIN, FRIEDRICH, *Theoretische Schriften*, ed. by Johann Kreuzer (Hamburg: Meiner, 1998)

HOLLMANN, SAMUEL CHRISTIAN, *Philosophiae rationalis quae Logica vulgo dicitur editio auctior et emendatior* (Göttingen: Vandenhoeck, 1767 [first edition 1746])

KANT, IMMANUEL, *Gesammelte Schriften*, ed. by Königlich Preußische Akademie der Wissenschaften (Berlin: Walter de Gruyter & Co., 1900–) [=Akademie-Ausgabe], especially:
    'Preisschrift über die Fortschritte der Metaphysik' (1791), in Akademie-Ausgabe, vol.
      XX
    'Untersuchung über die Deutlichkeit der Grundsätze der natürlichen Theologie und
      der Moral' (1764), in Akademie-Ausgabe, vol. II
    'Von einem neuerdings erhobenen vornehmen Ton in der Philosophie' (1796), in
      Akademie-Ausgabe, vol. VIII
    'Welches sind die wirklichen Fortschritte, die die Metaphysik seit Leibnizens und
      Wolfs Zeiten in Deutschland gemacht hat?', in Akademie-Ausgabe, vol. XX
    Anthropologie in pragmatischer Absicht, in Akademie-Ausgabe, vol. VII
    Entwürfe zu dem Colleg über Anthropologie aus den 70er Jahren, in Akademie-Ausgabe,
      vol. XXV
    Kritik der praktischen Vernunft, in Akademie-Ausgabe, vol. V
    Kritik der reinen Vernunft, in Akademie-Ausgabe, vol. III
    Kritik der Urteilskraft, in Akademie-Ausgabe, vol. V
    Vorlesungen über Metaphysik, in Akademie-Ausgabe, vol. XXVIII
——*Kritik der Urteilskraft*, ed. by Manfred Frank and Véronique Zanetti (Frankfurt am
Main: Suhrkamp, 2001)
——*Werke*, ed. by Artur Buchenau, Ernst Cassirer and Benzion Kellermann, 9 vols
(Berlin: Bruno Cassirer, 1914)
Translations of Kant:
——*Anthropology, History and Education*, ed. and trans. by Robert B. Louden and Günter
Zöller (Cambridge: Cambridge University Press, 2007)
——*Critique of Judgement*, trans. by James Creed Meredith; revised, edited, and introduced
by Nicholas Walker (Oxford: Oxford University Press, 2007)
——*Critique of Judgment*, trans. by J. H. Bernard (Amherst, NY: Prometheus Books,
2000)
——*Critique of Judgment*, trans. by Werner S. Pluhar (Indianapolis, IN: Hackett Publishing
Company, 1987)
——*Critique of the Power of Judgment*, ed. and trans. by Paul Guyer and Eric Matthews
(Cambridge: Cambridge University Press, 2000)
——*Critique of Pure Reason*, ed. and trans. by Paul Guyer and Allen W. Wood (Cambridge:
Cambridge University Press, 1998)
——*Lectures on Logic*, trans. by Michael Young (Cambridge: Cambridge University Press,
1992)
——*Lectures on Metaphysics*, trans. by Karl Ameriks and Steve Naragon (Cambridge:
Cambridge University Press, 1997)
——*Prolegomena to Any Future Metaphysics*, ed. and trans. by James W. Ellington, 2nd edn
(Indianapolis, IN: Hackett Publishing Company, 2001)
——*Theoretical Philosophy after 1781*, ed. by Henry Allison and Peter Heath (Cambridge:
Cambridge University Press, 2002)
——*Theoretical Philosophy, 1755–1770*, trans. by David Walford and Ralf Meerbote
(Cambridge: Cambridge University Press, 1992)
LAMBERT, JOHANN HEINRICH, *Neues Organon oder Gedanken über die Erforschung des Wahren
und dessen Unterscheidung von Irrthum und Schein*, vol. II: *Semiotik* (Leipzig: Wendler,
1764)
LEIBNIZ, Gottfried Wilhelm, *Opera omnia*, ed. by Louis Dutens, 6 vols (Geneva: Fratres de
Tournes, 1768)
——*Sämtliche Schriften und Briefe*, ed. by Carl Immanuel Gerhardt (Berlin: Akademie
Verlag, 1923 ff. [= A]), especially:

De arte combinatoria, in A vi, 1

'De modis combinandi characteres', in A vi, 4

'Dialogus', in A vi, 4

'Quid sit idea', in A vi, 4

'Vocabula', in A vi, 4

Meditationes de cognitione, veritate et ideis, in A, vi, 4

Nouveaux Essais sur L'entendement humain, in A vi, 6

LESSING, GOTTHOLD EPHRAIM, *Erziehung des Menschengeschlechts und andere Schriften* (Stuttgart: Reclam, 1994)

LOCKE, JOHN, *Essay concerning Human Understanding*, ed. by P. H. Nidditch (Oxford: Clarendon Press, 1975)

MEIER, GEORG FRIEDRICH, *Anfangsgründe aller schönen Wissenschaften*, 3 vols (Halle: Carl Hermann Hemmerde, 1748–50; repr. 1755)

MEYER, JOHANN HEINRICH, 'Über die Gegenstände der bildenden Kunst', in Johann Wolfgang von Goethe, *Sämtliche Werke nach Epochen seines Schaffens*, ed. by Karl Richter et al., 20 vols in 33 (Munich: Hanser, 1985–98), vol. 6.2, pp. 27–68

MICRAELIUS, JOHANNES, *Lexicon Philosophicum Terminorum Philosophis Usitatorum* (Jena: Freyschmid, 1653)

MORITZ, KARL PHILIPP, *Götterlehre oder mythologische Dichtungen der Alten* (Berlin: Unger, 1791)

——*Schriften zur Ästhetik und Poetik*, ed. by Hans Joachim Schrimpf (Tübingen: Niemeyer, 1962)

——*Werke in drei Bänden*, ed. by Horst Günther, 3 vols (Frankfurt am Main: Insel Verlag, 1981)

——*Werke in zwei Bänden*, ed. by Heide Hollmer and Albert Meier, 2 vols (Frankfurt am Main: Deutscher Klassiker Verlag, 1997–99), vol. I: *Dichtungen und Schriften zur Erfahrungsseelenkunde*; vol. II: *Popularphilosophie. Reisen. Ästhetische Theorie*, especially:

'Über die Allegorie' (1789), II, 1008–11

'Über die bildende Nachahmung des Schönen' (1788), II, 958–91

previous trans. by Stefan Bird-Pollan, in *Classic and Romantic German Aesthetics*, ed. by J. M. Bernstein (Cambridge: Cambridge University Press, 2003), pp. 131–44

'Versuch einer Vereinigung aller schönen Künste und Wissenschaften unter dem Begriff des in sich selbst Vollendeten' (1785), II, 943–49

Andreas Hartknop. Eine Allegorie (1786), vol. I

POPE, ALEXANDER, *The Major Works*, ed. by Pat Rogers (Oxford and New York: Oxford University Press, 1993)

PORPHYRY, 'Vita Pythagorae', in *Opuscula selecta*, ed. by August Nauck (Leipzig: Teubner, 1886)

PROCLUS, *Procli Diadochi In Platonis Cratylum commentaria*, ed. by Giorgio Pascuali (Leipzig: Teubner, 1908; repr. Stuttgart: Teubner, 1994)

QUINTILIAN, MARCUS FABIUS, *The Orator's Education*, ed. and trans. by Donald A. Russell (Cambridge, MA: Harvard University Press, 2001)

ROBINSON, HENRY CRABB, *Diary, Reminiscences, and Correspondence of Henry Crabb Robinson, Barrister-at-Law, F.S.A.*, ed. by Thomas Sadler, 3 vols (London: Macmillan, 1869)

——*Essays on Kant, Schelling, and German Aesthetics*, ed. by James Vigus, Critical Texts, 18 (London: MHRA, 2010)

——MEMORANDUM BOOK FOR 1804–1805, MS IN THE CRABB ROBINSON, DR WILLIAMS's Library, (London), Bundle I.VI.1

——'Moritz on Imitation', MS in the Crabb Robinson collection, Dr Williams's Library (London), Bundle 6.XII.42

ROSENKRANZ, KARL, *Hegels Leben* (Berlin: Verlag von Duncker und Humblot, 1844)

SCHELLING, FRIEDRICH WILHELM JOSEPH, 'Fernere Darstellungen aus dem System der Philosophie', in *Ausgewählte Werke*, ed. by Manfred Frank (Frankfurt am Main: Suhrkamp, 1985), II, 77–169

SCHELLING, FRIEDRICH WILHELM JOSEPH, *Sämmtliche Werke*, ed. by Karl Friedrich August Schelling (Stuttgart, Augsburg: Cotta, 1856–61) [=SW], especially:

    Philosophie der Kunst (1802–03), in SW, vol. I/ 5

    Philosophie der Mythologie, in SW, vol. II/ 1–2

    System des transscendentalen Idealismus (1800), in SW, vol. I, 3

—— *System des transzendentalen Idealismus*, ed. by Horst D. Brandt and Peter Müller (Hamburg: Meiner, 2000)

—— *System des transzendentalen Idealismus* (1800), *Werke*, IX, ed. by Harald Korten and Paul Ziche, 2 vols (Stuttgart: Frommann-Holzboog, 2005)

—— *Texte zur Philosophie der Kunst*, ed. by Werner Beierwaltes (Stuttgart: Reclam, 1982)

—— *Ueber die Gottheiten von Samothrake. Vorgelesen in der öffentlichen Sitzung der Baier'schen Akademie der Wissenschaften am Namenstage des Königs den 12. Oct. 1815. Beylage zu den Weltaltern* (Stuttgart and Tübingen: J. G. Cotta, 1815; facsimile reprint Amsterdam: Rodopi, 1968)

Translations of Schelling:

    —— *Schelling's Treatise on 'The Deities of Samothrace'*, trans. by Robert F. Brown (Missoula, MT: Scholar's Press, 1977 [1974])

    —— *The Philosophy of Art*, ed. and trans. by Douglas W. Stott (Minneapolis: University of Minnesota, 1989)

SCHILLER, FRIEDRICH, *Werke. Begründet von Julius Petersen, fortgeführt von Lieselotte Blumenthal und Benno von Wiese*, ed. by Norbert Oellers et al. (Weimar: Hermann Böhlaus Nachfolger, 1943–) (=NA, i.e. Nationalausgabe), especially:

    'Was heisst und zu welchem Ende studiert man Universalgeschichte?'(1789), in NA, vol. XVII, pp. 359–76

Ueber naive und sentimentalische Dichtung (1795–96), in NA, vol. XX

—— *On the Naive and Sentimental in Literature*, trans. by Helen Watanabe-O'Kelly (Manchester: Carcanet, 1981)

SCHLEGEL, FRIEDRICH, *Kritische Friedrich-Schlegel-Ausgabe*, ed. by Ernst Behler (Paderborn, Darmstadt, Zürich: Schöningh, 1958–)

SCHLEIERMACHER, FRIEDRICH, *Hermeneutics and Criticism and Other Writings*, ed. and trans. by Andrew Bowie (Cambridge: Cambridge University Press, 1998)

SCHOPENHAUER, ARTHUR, 'Über Philosophie und ihre Methode', in *Parerga und Paralipomena. Kleine philosophische Schriften II* (Leipzig, 1979), pp. 9–28

SHELLEY, P. B., *Shelley's Poetry and Prose*, ed. by Donald H. Reiman and Neil Freistat (New York and London: Norton, 2002 [1977])

SPINOZA, BENEDICT, *Tractatus de Intellectus Emendatione, Ethica*, ed. by Konrad Blumenstock (Darmstadt: Wissenschaftliche Buchgesellschaft, 2008)

STAËL [-Holstein, Anne Louise Germaine de], *De l'Allemagne,* Nouv. éd. publ. d'après les ms. et les éd. orig. avec. des variantes, une introd., des notices et des notes par la Ctesse Jean de Pange avec le comours de Simone Belayé (Paris: Hachette, 1958–60)

TENNEMANN, W. G., *Geschichte der Philosophie*, 11 vols (Leipzig: Barth, 1798–1819)

THOREAU, HENRY DAVID, *Walden: or Life in the Woods* (Boston, MA: Ticknor and Fields, 1854)

VILLAUME, PETER, *Practische Logik für junge Leute, die nicht studieren wollen* (Berlin, 1787; 3rd edn Leipzig: Rein, 1819)

WOLFF, CHRISTIAN, *Gesammelte Werke*, ed. by Jean École et al. (Hildesheim: Georg Olms, 1965 ff. [= Works]), especially

    Psychologia empirica, in Works, sect. 2, vol. V

Vernünftige Gedancken von Gott, der Welt, und der Seele des Menschen (Deutsche Metaphysik), in Works, sect. I, vol. II

Vernünftige Gedanken von den Kräften des menschlichen Verstandes und ihrem richtigen Gebrauche in Erkenntnis der Wahrheit (1712), in Works, sect. I, vol. I

WORDSWORTH, WILLIAM, *The Poetical Works*, ed. by Thomas Hutchinson (Oxford: Oxford University Press, 1996)

Secondary Sources

ADAMS, GEORGE PLIMPTON, 'The Mystical Element in Hegel's *Early Theological Writings*', *University of California Publications in Philosophy*, 2.4 (1910), 67–102

ADAMS, HAZARD, *Philosophy of the Literary Symbolic* (Tallahassee: Florida University Press, 1983)

ADICKES, ERICH, *Kant und die Als-Ob-Philosophie* (Stuttgart-Bad Cannstatt: Frommann, 1927)

ADORNO, THEODOR W., *Gesammelte Schriften in zwanzig Bänden*, ed. by Rolf Tiedemann (Frankfurt am Main: Suhrkamp, 1996), especially:
    Vol. VII: *Ästhetische Theorie*
    Vol. XI: *Noten zur Literatur*

ALT, PETER-ANDRÉ, *Begriffsbilder. Studien zur literarischen Form der Allegorie* (Tübingen: Niemeyer, 1995)

BARASH, JEFFREY ANDREW, 'Was ist ein Symbol? Bemerkungen über Paul Ricœurs kritische Stellungnahme zum Symbolbegriff bei Ernst Cassirer', *Internationales Jahrbuch für Hermeneutik*, 6 (2007), 259–74

BARBEAU, JEFFREY W., *Coleridge, The Bible, and Religion* (New York: Palgrave Macmillan, 2007)

BATLEY, E. M., 'Masonic Thought in the Work of Karl Philipp Moritz: Sheen or Substance?', *London Germanic Studies*, 6 (1998), 121–46

BEER, JOHN, *Coleridge's Play of Mind* (Oxford: Oxford University Press, 2010)

BEHLER, ERNST, 'Schellings Ästhetik in der Überlieferung von Henry Crabb Robinson', *Philosophisches Jahrbuch der Görres-Gesellschaft*, 83 (1976), 133–83

——— *Frühromantik* (Berlin and New York: de Gruyter, 1992)

BEISER, FREDERICK, *Diotima's Children: German Aesthetic Rationalism from Leibniz to Lessing* (Oxford and New York: Oxford University Press, 2010)

——— *The Fate of Reason: German Philosophy from Kant to Fichte* (Cambridge, MA, and London: Harvard University Press, 1987)

BENJAMIN, WALTER, 'Der Begriff der Kunstkritik in der deutschen Romantik', in *Gesammelte Schriften*, ed. by Rolf Tiedemann and Hermann Schweppenhäuser (Frankfurt am Main: Suhrkamp, 1991), vol. I.1, pp. 9–123

——— *The Origin of German Tragic Drama*, trans. by John Osborne (London: NLB, 1977)

BERNDT, FRAUKE, and HEINZ J. DRÜGH (eds.), *Symbol. Grundtexte zur Ästhetik, Poetik und Kulturwissenschaft* (Frankfurt am Main: Suhrkamp, 2009)

BERTSCH, MARKUS, et al. (eds.), *Kosmos Runge. Der Morgen der Romantik*, im Auftr. der Hamburger Kunsthalle und der Kunsthalle der Hypo-Kulturstiftung, München (Munich: Hirmer, 2010)

BIELEFELDT, HEINER, *Symbolic Representation in Kant's Practical Philosophy* (Cambridge: Cambridge University Press, 2003)

BLECHSCHMIDT, STEFAN, *Goethes lebendiges Archiv. Mensch — Morphologie — Geschichte* (Heidelberg: Winter, 2010)

BODE, CHRISTOPH, *The Novel: An Introduction*, trans. by James Vigus (Oxford: Wiley-Blackwell, 2011)

BOULBY, MARK, *Karl Philipp Moritz: At the Fringe of Genius* (Toronto, Buffalo and London: University of Toronto Press, 1979)

BOWIE, ANDREW, 'Romantic Aesthetics and the Ends of Contemporary Philosophy', in *Das Neue Licht der Frühromantik. Innovation und Aktualität frühromantischer Philosophie*, ed. by Bärbel Frischmann and Elizabeth Millán-Zaibert (Paderborn: Schöningh, 2009), pp. 213–24

BRECHT, CHRISTOPH, 'Die Macht der Worte. Zur Problematik des Allegorischen in Karl Philipp Moritz' Hartknopf-Romanen', *Deutsche Vierteljahrsschrift für Literaturwissenschaft und Geistesgeschichte*, 64 (1990), 624–51

BREIDBACH, OLAF, *Goethes Metamorphosenlehre* (Munich: Fink, 2006)

—— *Goethes Naturverständnis* (Paderborn: Schöningh, 2011)

BRICE, BEN, *Coleridge and Scepticism* (Oxford: Oxford University Press, 2007)

CASSIRER, ERNST, *Gesammelte Werke* [Hamburger Ausgabe], ed. by Birgit Recki (Hamburg: Felix Meiner, 1998–) [=GW], especially

    Vols XI–XIII: *Philosophie der symbolischen Formen I–III*, ed. by Birgit Recki (2001–02)

    Vol. XXIII: *An Essay on Man: An Introduction to a Philosophy of Human Culture* ed. by Birgit Recki (2006)

CAYGILL, HOWARD, *A Kant Dictionary* (Oxford: Blackwell, 1995)

CLASS, MONIKA, *Coleridge and Kantian Ideas in England, 1796–1817* (London: Continuum, 2012)

CLINTON, KEVIN, 'Stages of Initiation in the Eleusinian and Samothracian Mysteries', in *Greek Mysteries: The Archaeology and Ritual of Ancient Greek Secret Cults*, ed. by Michael B. Cosmopoulos (London and New York: Routledge, 2005)

COLE, SUSAN GUETTEL, *The Samothracian Mysteries and the Samothracian Gods: Initiates, 'Theoroi', and Worshippers* (unpublished doctoral dissertation, University of Minnesota, 1975)

COPLESTON, FREDERICK C., 'Hegel and the Rationalization of Mysticism', in *New Studies in Hegel's Philosophy*, ed. by Warren E. Steinkraus (New York: Holt, Rinehart and Wiston, 1971), pp. 187–200

COSTAZZA, ALESSANDRO, *Schönheit und Nützlichkeit. Karl Philipp Moritz und die Ästhetik des 18ten Jahrhunderts* (Bern: Peter Lang, 1996)

D'ANGELO, PAOLO, *Simbolo e Arte in Hegel* (Rome-Bari: Laterza, 1989)

DE MAN, PAUL, 'Allegorie und Symbol in der Frühromantik', in *Typologia litterarum*, ed. by Stefan Sonderegger et al. (Zürich: Atlantis, 1969), pp. 403–27

—— 'The Rhetoric of Temporality', in *Blindness and Insight: Essays in the Rhetoric of Contemporary Criticism* (London: Methuen, 1983), pp. 187–228

DONOUGHO, MARTIN, 'Hegel and Creuzer: or, Did Hegel Believe in Myth?' in *New Perspectives on Hegel's Philosophy of Religion*, ed. by David Kolby, (Albany: State University of New York, 1992), pp. 59–80

ECO, UMBERTO, 'Simbolo', in *Enciclopedia Einaudi* (Turin: Einaudi, 1981), vol. XII, pp. 877–915

—— 'Vom offenen Kunstwerk zum Pendel Foucaults', *Lettre International*, 5 (1989), 38–42

ELLISON, JULIE, *Emerson's Romantic Style* (Princeton, NJ: Princeton University Press, 1984)

ENGEHAUSEN, FRANK, ARMIN SCHLECHTER and JÜRGEN PAUL SCHWINDT (eds), *Friedrich Creuzer 1771–1858. Philologie und Mythologie im Zeitalter der Romantik* (Heidelberg: Verlag Regionalkultur, 2008)

ENGELL, JAMES, 'Coleridge (and His Mariner) on the Soul: "As an exile in a far distant land"', in *The Fountain Light: Studies in Romanticism and Religion*, ed. by J. Robert Barth (Bronx, NY: Fordham University Press, 2002), pp. 128–51

FAVARETTI CAMPOSAMPIERO, MATTEO, *Conoscenza simbolica. Pensiero e linguaggio in Christian Wolff e nella prima età moderna* (Hildesheim and New York: Olms, 2009)

FISCHER, BERNHARD, 'Kunstautonomie und Ende der Ikonographie. Zur historischen Problematik von "Allegorie" und "Symbol" im Winckelmanns, Moritz' und Goethes Kunsttheorie', *Deutsche Vierteljahrsschrift für Literaturwissenschaft und Geistesgeschichte*, 64 (1990), 247–77

FRANK, MANFRED, FRANK, MANFRED, *Das Problem 'Zeit' in der deutschen Romantik* (Paderborn and Munich: Schöningh, 1990)

——*Einführung in die frühromantische Ästhetik* (Frankfurt am Main: Suhrkamp, 1989)

——'Unendliche Annäherung'. *Die Anfänge der philosophischen Frühromantik* (Frankfurt am Main: Suhrkamp, 1997)

——'Wechselgrundsatz. Friedrich Schlegels philosophischer Ausgangspunkt', *Zeitschrift für philosophische Forschung*, 50 (1996), 26–50

FRICKE, STEFANIE, ' "Pleasant riddles of futurity": Egyptian Hieroglyphs in the Romantic Age', in *Romantic Explorations: Selected Papers from the Koblenz Conference of the German Society for English Romanticism*, ed. by Michael Meyer (Trier: Wissenschaftlicher Verlag Trier, 2011), pp. 173–84

FRIED, DANIEL, 'The Politics of the Coleridgean Symbol', *Studies in English Literature*, 46.4 (Autumn 2006), 763–79

FROTHINGHAM, OCTAVIUS, *Transcendentalism in New England: A History* (New York: G. P. Putnam's Sons, 1876)

GABRIEL, GOTTFRIED, 'Baumgartens Begriff der "perceptio praegnans" und seine systematische Bedeutung', *Aufklärung. Interdisziplinäres Jahrbuch zur Erforschung des 18. Jahrhunderts und seiner Wirkungsgeschichte*, 20 (2008), Themenschwerpunkt: Alexander Gottlieb Baumgarten, ed. by Alexander Aichele and Dagmar Mirbach, pp. 61–71

——'Bestimmte Unbestimmtheit — in der ästhetischen Erkenntnis und im ästhetischen Urteil', in *Das unendliche Kunstwerk. Von der Bestimmtheit des Unbestimmten in der ästhetischen Erfahrung*, ed. by Gerhard Gamm and Eva Schürmann (Hamburg: Philo, 2007), pp. 141–56

——'Kontinentales Erbe und analytische Methode. Nelson Goodman und die Tradition', *Erkenntnis*, 52 (2000), 185–98

——*Logik und Rhetorik der Erkenntnis* (Paderborn: Schöningh, 1997)

——'Warum es so schwerfällt, etwas über Kunst zu sagen', in *Kunst und Philosophie. Kunstvermittlung in den Medien*, ed. by Julian Nida-Rümelin and Jakob Steinbrenner (Ostfildern: Hatje Cantz, 2011), pp. 61–84

GABRIEL, GOTTFRIED, HELMUT HÜHN and TEMILO VAN ZANTWIJK, 'Heuristik im Spannungsfeld von Wissenschaft und Poesie', in *Ereignis Weimar-Jena. Kultur um 1800*, ed. by Olaf Breidbach (Munich: Fink, forthcoming 2013)

GADAMER, HANS-GEORG, *Wahrheit und Methode. Grundzüge einer philosophischen Hermeneutik* (Tübingen: Mohr, 1986)

GEISENHANSLÜKE, ACHIM, *Der Buchstabe des Geistes. Postfigurationen der Allegorie von Bunyan zu Nietzsche* (Munich: Fink, 2003)

GETHMANN-SIEFERT, ANNEMARIE, *Die Funktion der Kunst in der Geschichte. Untersuchungen zu Hegels Ästhetik*, *Hegel-Studien*, supplementary issue 25 (1984) , ed. by Friedhelm Nicolin and Otto Pöggeler

——*Einführung in Hegels Ästhetik* (Munich: Fink, 2005)

GOLDRATT, ELIYAHU M., *The Choice* (Great Barrington, MA: North River Press, 2008)

GOODMAN, NELSON, *Languages of Art: An Approach to a Theory of Symbols* (Indianapolis, IN: Hackett, 2008)

——*Ways of Worldmaking* (Indianapolis, IN: Hackett, 1992)

GÖTZE, MARTIN, *Ironie und absolute Darstellung* (Paderborn and Munich: Schöningh, 1999)

GRIFFERO, TONINO, *Senso e immagine. Simbolo e mito nel primo Schelling* (Milan: Guerini, 1994)

GURA, PHILIP, *The Wisdom of Words: Language, Theology and Literature in the New England Renaissance* (Middletown, CT: Wesleyan University Press, 1981)

GUYER, PAUL, *Kant* (London: Routledge, 2006)

——*Kant and the Experience of Freedom* (Cambridge: Cambridge University Press, 1996)

HALMI, NICHOLAS, 'Coleridge, Allegory and Symbol', in *The Oxford Handbook of Samuel Taylor Coleridge* (Oxford: Oxford University Press, 2008), pp. 345–58

——'Coleridge's Most Unfortunate Borrowing from A. W. Schlegel', in *British and European Romanticisms: Selected Papers from the Munich Conference of the German Society for English Romanticism*, ed. by Christoph Bode and Sebastian Domsch (Trier: Wissenschaftlicher Verlag Trier, 2007), pp. 131–42

——*The Genealogy of the Romantic Symbol* (Oxford: Oxford University Press, 2007)

HAMILTON, PAUL, *Coleridge and German Philosophy: The Poet in the Land of Logic* (London: Continuum, 2007)

HARDING, ANTHONY JOHN, *The Reception of Myth in British Romanticism* (Columbia: University of Missouri Press, 1995)

HARTER, JOEL, *Coleridge's Philosophy of Faith* (Tübingen: Mohr Siebeck, 2011)

HAVEN, RICHARD, 'Coleridge and the Greek Mysteries', *Modern Language Notes*, 70.6 (June 1955), 405–07

HEDLEY, DOUGLAS, *Living Forms of Imagination* (London: T&T Clark, 2008)

HEIDEMANN, DIETMAR H., 'Kann Erkenntnis kreativ sein? Die produktive Einbildungskraft in der Ästhetik und Erkenntnistheorie Kants', in *Kreativität* (XX. Deutscher Kongress für Philosophie, 26.–30. September 2005, Sektionsbeiträge vol. 1), ed. by Günter Abel, (Berlin: Universitätsverlag der TU Berlin, 2005), pp. 565–76

HENRICH, DIETER, *Between Kant and Hegel: Lectures on German Idealism*, ed. by David S. Pacini (Cambridge, MA, and London: Harvard University Press, 2003)

HIGGONET, MARGARET R., 'Madame de Staël and Schelling', *Comparative Literature*, 38 (1986), 159–80

HOFFMANN, PAUL, 'Goethes "wahre Symbolik" und die "Wälder der Symbole"', in *Von der Natur zur Kunst und zurück. Neue Beiträge zur Goethe-Forschung*, ed. by Moritz Baßler, Christoph Brecht and Dirk Niefanger (Tübingen: Max Niemeyer Verlag, 1997), pp. 199–218

HOLMES, RICHARD, *The Age of Wonder: How the Romantic Generation Discovered the Beauty and Terror of Science* (New York: Pantheon Books, 2008)

HÜHN, HELMUT, '"Epídosis eis hauto". Zur morphologischen Geschichtsbetrachtung bei Johann Gustav Droysen', in *Morphologie und Moderne. Goethes 'anschauliches Denken' in den Geistes- und Kulturwissenschaften seit 1800*, ed. by Jonas Maatsch and Thorsten Valk (Berlin and New York: de Gruyter, 2012)

HUNGERFORD, EDWARD B., *Shores of Darkness* (Cleveland, OH: Meridian, 1963 [1941])

HUNNEKUHL, PHILIPP, 'Reconstructing the Voice of the Mediator: Henry Crabb Robinson's Literary Criticism', in *Informal Romanticism*, ed. by James Vigus (Trier: Wissenschaftlicher Verlag Trier, 2012), pp. 61–76

HUTTER, AXEL, 'Hegels Philosophie des Geistes', *Hegel-Studien*, 42 (2007), 81–97

JAMME, CHRISTOPH, '"Göttersymbole". Friedrich Creuzer als Mythologe und seine philosophische Wirkung', Heidelberger Jahrbücher, 51 (2008), 487–98

KEANE, PATRICK J., *Emerson, Romanticism, and Intuitive Reason: The Transatlantic 'Light of All Our Day'* (Columbia: University of Missouri Press, 2005)

KEARNEY, RICHARD, and DAVID M. RASMUSSEN (eds.), *Continental Aesthetics: Romanticism to Postmodernism: An Anthology* (Hoboken, NJ: Wiley-Blackwell, 2001)

KNELLER, JANE, *Kant and the Power of Imagination* (Cambridge: Cambridge University Press, 2007)

KNÖRER, EKKEHARD, *Entfernte Ähnlichkeiten. Zur Geschichte von Witz und Ingenium* (Munich: Fink, 2007)

KOBUSCH, THEO, 'Intuition', in *Historisches Wörterbuch der Philosophie*, ed. by J. Ritter, K. Gründer, and G. Gabriel (Basel: Schwabe, 1976), vol. IV, col. 524

KOERNER, J. L., *Caspar David Friedrich. Landschaft und Subjekt* (Munich: Fink, 1998)

KUBIK, ANDREAS, *Die Symboltheorie bei Novalis. Eine ideengeschichtliche Studie in ästhetischer und theologischer Absicht* (Tübingen: Mohr Siebeck, 2006)

KUHN, DOROTHEA, 'Goethes Morphologie. Geschichte — Prinzipien — Folgen', in *Typus und Metamorphose. Goethe-Studien*, ed. by Renate Grumach (Marbach am Neckar: Deutsche Schillergesellschaft, 1988), pp. 188–202

LEASK, NIGEL, *The Politics of Imagination in Coleridge's Critical Thought* (Basingstoke: Macmillan, 1988)

LIDDELL, H. G., and R. SCOTT, *Greek–English Lexicon* (Oxford: Oxford University Press, 1996 [1843])

LOESBERG, JONATHAN, *A Return to Aesthetics: Autonomy, Indifference, and Postmodernism* (Stanford, CA: Stanford University Press, 2005)

MAATSCH, JONAS, *'Naturgeschichte der Philosopheme'. Frühromantische Wissensordnungen im Kontext* (Heidelberg: Winter, 2008)

MAGEE, GLENN ALEXANDER, *Hegel and the Hermetic Tradition* (Ithaca, NY: Cornell University Press, 2001)

MAGNUS, KATHLEEN DOW, *Hegel and the Symbolic Mediation of Spirit* (Albany: State University of New York, 2001)

MARQUARDT, HERTHA, *Henry Crabb Robinson und seine deutschen Freunde*, 2 vols (Göttingen: Vandenhoeck & Ruprecht, 1964–67)

McEVILLEY, THOMAS, *The Shape of Ancient Thought: Comparative Studies of Greek and Indian Philosophies* (New York: Allworth Press, 2002)

McFARLAND, THOMAS, 'Involute and Symbol in the Romantic Tradition', in *Coleridge, Keats and the Romantic Imagination: Romanticism and Adam's Dream*, ed. by J. Robert Barth and John L. Mahoney (Columbia and London: University of Missouri Press, 1990), pp. 29–57

McKUSICK, JAMES C., 'Symbol', in *The Cambridge Companion to Coleridge*, ed. by Lucy Newlyn (Cambridge: Cambridge University Press, 2002), pp. 217–30

MEIER-OESER, STEPHAN, 'Sprache und Bilder im Geist. Skizzen zu einem philosophischen Langzeitprojekt', *Philosophisches Jahrbuch der Görres-Gesellschaft*, 111 (2004), 312–42

—— 'Symbol I', in *Historisches Wörterbuch der Philosophie*, ed. by Joachim Ritter, Karlfried Gründer, Gottfried Gabriel (Basel: Schwabe, 1998), vol. x, cols 710–23

—— 'Wort, inneres / Rede, innere', in *Historisches Wörterbuch der Philosophie*, ed. by J. Ritter, K. Gründer, G. Gabriel (Basel: Schwabe, 2004), vol. XII, cols 1037–50

MENEGONI, FRANCESCA, 'Die Frage nach dem Ursprung des Bösen bei Hegel', in *Subjektivität und Anerkennung*, ed. by Barbara Merker, Georg Mohr and Michael Quante (Paderborn: Mentis Verlag, 2004)

MILNES, TIM, 'Coleridge's Logic', in *Handbook of the History of Logic*, ed. by John Woods and Dov M. Gabbay (Amsterdam: Elsevier, 2008), IV: *British Logic in the Nineteenth Century*, pp. 33–74

—— *The Truth about Romanticism* (Cambridge: Cambridge University Press, 2010)

MORGNER, ULRIKE, *'Das Wort aber ist Fleisch geworden'. Allegorie und Allegoriekritik im 18. Jahrhundert am Beispiel von Karl Philipp Moritz' 'Andreas Hartknopf. Eine Allegorie'* (Würzburg: Königshausen & Neumann, 2002)

MOSER, CHRISTIAN, 'Sichtbare Schrift, lesbare Gestalten. Symbol und Allegorie bei Goethe, Coleridge und Wordsworth', in *Allegorie. Konfigurationen von Text, Bild und Lektüre*, ed. by Eva Horn and Manfred Weinberg (Opladen and Wiesbaden: Westdeutscher Verlag, 1998), pp. 118–32

MURATORI, CECILIA, 'Il Figlio caduto e l'origine del Male. Una lettura del § 568 dell'Enciclopedia', in *L'assoluto e il divino. La teologia cristiana di Hegel*, ed. by Tommaso Pierini, Georg Sans, Pierluigi Valenza and Klaus Vieweg (Pisa and Rome: Archivio di Filosofia, 2010), pp. 107–18

——*Il primo filosofo tedesco. Il misticismo di Jakob Böhme nell'interpretazione hegeliana* (Pisa: ETS, 2012)

MÜRI, WALTER, 'ΣΥΜΒΟΛΟΝ. Wort- und sachgeschichtliche Studie', in id., *Griechische Studien. Ausgewählte wort- und sachgeschichtliche Forschung zur Antike*, ed. by Eduard Vischer (Basel: Reinhardt, 1976), pp. 1–44

NIKLEWSKI, GÜNTER, *Versuch über Symbol und Allegorie (Winckelmann — Moritz — Schelling)* (Erlangen: Palm & Enke, 1979)

PALMIER, JEAN-MICHEL, *Walter Benjamin* (Frankfurt am Main: Suhrkamp, 2009)

PÉPIN, JEAN, *Mythe et allégorie* (Paris: Aubier, 1958)

PERCONTI, PIETRO, *Kantian Linguistics: Theories of Mental Representation and the Linguistic Transformation of Kantism* (Münster: Nodus Publikationen, 1999)

PICHT, GEORG, *Aristoteles' De anima* (Stuttgart: Klett-Cotta, 1987)

PFEILER, WILLIAM K., 'Coleridge and Schelling's Treatise on the Samothracian Deities', *Modern Language Notes*, 52.3 (March 1937), 162–65

PLOTKE, SERAINA, 'Der ästhetische Trost. Karl Philipp Moritz' ästhetische Schriften im Spiegel der Sinnsuche', *Monatshefte*, 95.3 (2003), 421–41

PÖRKSEN, UWE, 'Goethes Kritik naturwissenschaftlicher Metaphorik und der Roman *Die Wahlverwandtschaften*', *Jahrbuch der Schiller-Gesellschaft*, 25 (1981), 285–315

RAJAN, TILOTTAMA, 'Toward a Cultural Idealism: Negativity and Freedom in Hegel and Kant', in *Idealism without Absolutes: Philosophy and Romantic Culture*, ed. by Tilottama Rajan and Arkady Plotnitsky (Albany: State University of New York, 2004), pp. 51–71

REID, NICHOLAS, 'Why we need the Opus Maximum to understand the Coleridgean Symbol', *The Coleridge Bulletin*, n.s. 38 (Winter 2011), 93–99

——*Coleridge, Form and Symbol: Or, the Ascertaining Vision* (Farnham: Ashgate, 2006)

RICHARDSON, ROBERT D., *Emerson: The Mind on Fire* (Berkeley: University of California Press, 1995)

RICŒUR, PAUL, *Die Interpretation. Ein Versuch über Freud* (Frankfurt am Main: Suhrkamp, 1974)

——*Symbolism of Evil*, trans. from French by Emerson Buchanan (Boston, MA: Beacon Press, 1967)

RITTER, JOACHIM, KARLFRIED GRÜNDER and GOTTFRIED GABRIEL (eds.), *Historisches Wörterbuch der Philosophie*, 13 vols (Basel: Schwabe, 1971–2007)

ROSS, ALISON, *The Aesthetic Paths of Philosophy: Presentation in Kant, Heidegger, Lacoue-Labarthe, and Nancy* (Stanford, CA: Stanford University Press, 2007)

SAFRANSKI, RÜDIGER, *Goethe und Schiller. Geschichte einer Freundschaft* (Munich: Hanser, 2009)

SAINE, THOMAS P., *Die Ästhetische Theodizee. Karl Philipp Moritz und die Philosophie des achtzehnten Jahrhunderts* (Munich: Fink, 1971)

SANDKAULEN, BIRGIT, ' "Bilder sind". Zur Ontologie des Bildes im Diskurs um 1800', in *Denken mit dem Bild*, ed. by Johannes Grave and Arno Schubbach (Munich: Fink, 2010), pp. 131–51

SCHEIER, CLAUS-ARTUR, 'Zeiten der Metamorphose', in *Dimensionen der Ästhetik. Festschrift für Barbara Ränsch-Trill*, ed. by Manfred Lämmer and Tim Nebelung, Schriften der Deutschen Sporthochschule Köln, 50 (Sankt Augustin: Academia, 2005), pp. 48–61

SCHLAFFER, HEINZ, *Faust Zweiter Teil. Die Allegorie des 19. Jahrhunderts* (Stuttgart: Metzler, 1989)

SCHMIDINGER, HEINRICH, 'Das Auszeichnende des Menschen als seine Kreativität. Eine geistesgeschichtliche Einstimmung', in *Der Mensch — ein kreatives Wesen? Kunst —*

Technik — Innovation, ed. by Heinrich Schmidinger and Clemens Sedmak (Darmstadt: Wissenschaftliche Buchgesellschaft, 2008), pp. 7–24

SCHNEIDER, SABINE M., *Die schwierige Sprache des Schönen. Moritz' und Schillers Semiotik der Sinnlichkeit* (Würzburg: Königshausen & Neumann, 1998)

SCHOLL, CHRISTIAN, *Romantische Malerei als neue Sinnbildkunst. Studien zur Bedeutungsgebung bei Philipp Otto Runge, Caspar David Friedrich und den Nazarenern* (Munich and Berlin: Deutscher Kunstverlag, 2007)

SCHOLZ, OLIVER R., 'Symbol, 19. und 20. Jahrhundert', in *Historisches Wörterbuch der Philosophie*, ed. by J. Ritter, K. Gründer, G. Gabriel (Basel: Schwabe, 1998), vol. x, cols 723–38

SCHULTE, JOACHIM, 'Chor und Gesetz. Zur "morphologischen Methode" bei Goethe und Wittgenstein', in Joachim Schulte, *Chor und Gesetz. Wittgenstein im Kontext* (Frankfurt am Main: Suhrkamp, 1990), pp. 11–42

SCHWARZ, GERHARD, and MATTHIAS WUNSCH, 'Limitation als Erkenntnisfunktion der Einbildungskraft. Eine Strukturverwandtschaft zwischen reiner Vernunfterkenntnis und reiner sinnlicher Erkenntnis bei Kant', *Archiv für Begriffsgeschichte*, 52 (2010), 93–112

SEALTS, MERTON M., JR, and ALFRED R. FERGUSON (eds.), *Emerson's Nature: Origin, Growth, Meaning* (New York: Dodd, Mead & Company, Inc., 1969)

SØRENSEN, BENGT ALGOT, *Symbol und Symbolismus in den ästhetischen Theorien des 18. Jahrhunderts und der deutschen Romantik* (Copenhagen: Munksgaard, 1963)

STEENBAKKERS, PIET, 'Spinoza on the Imagination', in *The Scope of the Imagination: 'imaginatio' between Medieval and Modern Times*, ed. by L. Nauta und D. Petzold (Leuven: Peeters, 2004), pp. 175–93

STEKELER-WEITHOFER, PIRMIN, *Formen der Anschauung. Eine Philosophie der Mathematik* (Berlin: De Gruyter, 2008)

SWIATECKA, MARIE JADWIGA, *The Idea of the Symbol: Some Nineteenth-Century Comparisons with Coleridge* (Cambridge: Cambridge University Press, 1980)

SWIFT, SIMON, *Romanticism, Literature and Philosophy: Expressive Rationality in Rousseau, Kant, Wollstonecraft and Contemporary Theory* (London: Continuum, 2006)

SZONDI, PETER, *Poetik und Geschichtsphilosophie I*, ed. by Senta Metz and Hans-Hagen Hildebrandt (Frankfurt am Main: Suhrkamp, 1974, 1980)

THUMS, BARBARA, *Aufmerksamkeit. Wahrnehmung und Selbstbegründung von Brockes bis Nietzsche* (Munich: Fink, 2008)

——'Das feine Gewebe der Organisation. Zum Verhältnis von Biologie und Ästhetik in Karl Philipp Moritz' Kunstautonomie und Ornamenttheorie', *Zeitschrift für Ästhetik und Allgemeine Kunstwissenschaft*, 49.2 (2004), 237–60

TITZMANN, MICHAEL, *Strukturwandel der philosophischen Ästhetik 1800–1880. Der Symbolbegriff als Paradigma* (Munich: Fink, 1978)

TODOROV, TZVETAN, *Symboltheorien* (Tübingen: Niemeyer, 1995)

——*Theories of the Symbol*, trans. by Catherine Porter (Ithaca, NY: Cornell University Press, 1982)

URBICH, JAN, *Darstellung bei Walter Benjamin. Die 'Erkenntniskritische Vorrede' im Kontext ästhetischer Darstellungstheorien der Moderne* (Berlin: De Gruyter, 2011)

——'"Die Kunst geht auf den letzten Messias". Friedrich Schlegels Ideen-Fragmente und das Verhältnis von Revolution und Religion', in *Romantik und Revolution. Zum politischen Reformpotential einer unpolitischen Bewegung*, ed. by Klaus Ries (Heidelberg: Winter, 2012), pp. 171–95

——'Epoche und Stil. Überlegungen zu zwei Deutungsmustern der Jenaer Frühromantik', in *Jena. Ein nationaler Erinnerungsort?*, ed. by Jürgen John and Justus H. Ulbricht (Köln and Weimar: Böhlau, 2008), pp. 123–38

——'"Mysterium der Ordnung". Anmerkungen zum Verhältnis von Absolutem und

Sprache bei Friedrich Schlegel und Walter Benjamin', *Sprache und Literatur*, 1 (2009), 93–111

VAN CROMPHOUT, GUSTAAF, *Emerson's Modernity and the Example of Goethe* (Columbia: University of Missouri Press, 1990)

VIEWEG, KLAUS, *Philosophie des Remis. Der junge Hegel und das 'Gespenst des Skeptizismus'* (Munich: Fink, 1999)

VIGUS, JAMES, *Platonic Coleridge* (Oxford: Legenda, 2009)

—— 'The Philosophy of Samuel Taylor Coleridge', in *The Oxford Handbook of British Philosophy in the Nineteenth Century*, ed. by William Mander (Oxford: Oxford University Press, 2013)

—— 'Zwischen Kantianismus und Schellingianismus. Henry Crabb Robinsons Privatvorlesungen über Philosophie für Mme de Staël 1804 in Weimar', in *Germaine de Staël und ihr erstes deutsches Publikum. Literaturpolitik und Kulturtransfer um 1800*, ed. by Gerhard R. Kaiser and Olaf Müller (Heidelberg: Winter, 2008), pp. 355–92

VLASOPOLOS, ANCA, *The Symbolic Method of Coleridge, Baudelaire and Yeats* (Detroit, MI: Wayne State University Press, 1983)

VOGES, MICHAEL, *Aufklärung und Geheimnis. Untersuchungen zur Vermittlung von Literatur- und Sozialgeschichte am Beispiel der Aneignung des Geheimbundmaterials im Roman des späten 18. Jahrhunderts* (Tübingen: Niemeyer, 1987)

WALSH, DAVID, 'The Esoteric Origins of Modern Ideological Thought: Boehme and Hegel' (unpublished doctoral dissertation, University of Virginia, 1978)

WEBSTER, SUSANNE E., *Body and Soul in Coleridge's Notebooks, 1827–1834* (Basingstoke: Palgrave Macmillan, 2010)

WEGNER, REINHARD, 'Der geteilte Blick. Empirisches und imaginäres Sehen bei Caspar David Friedrich und August Wilhelm Schlegel', *Kunst — die andere Natur*, ed. by Reinhard Wegner (Göttingen: Vandenhoeck und Ruprecht, 2004), pp. 13–34

WELLBERY, DAVID, 'Rhetorik und Literatur. Anmerkungen zur poetologischen Begriffsbildung bei Friedrich Schlegel', in *Die Aktualität der Frühromantik*, ed. by Ernst Behler and Jochen Hörisch (Paderborn and Munich: Schöningh, 1987), pp. 161–74

—— 'The Transformation of Rhetoric', in *The Cambridge History of Literary Criticism*, vol. V: *Romanticisms*, ed. Marshall Brown (Cambridge: Cambridge University Press, 2000), pp. 185–202

WELLEK, RENÉ, 'Symbol and Symbolism in Literature', in *Dictionary of the History of Ideas*, ed. by Philip Paul Wiener, 5 vols (New York: Scribner, 1973–74), IV, 337–45

WHELAN, TIMOTHY, 'The Religion of Crabb Robinson', *Transactions of the Unitarian Historical Society*, 24.2 (April 2008), 112–34

WOLF, NORBERT CHRISTIAN, 'Karl Philipp Moritzens endgültige Erhebung zum Klassiker. Über Alessandro Costazzas große Arbeit zu Moritz und der Ästhetik des 18. Jahrhunderts' <http://www.iaslonline.de/index.php?vorgang_id=2506> [accessed 9 February 2012]

—— *Streitbare Ästhetik. Goethes kunst- und literarische Schriften 1771–1789* (Tübingen: Max Niemeyer, 2001)

WOLFF-METTERNICH, BRIGITTA-SOPHIE VON, *Die Überwindung des mathematischen Erkenntnisideals. Kants Grenzbestimmung von Mathematik und Philosophie* (Berlin and New York: de Gruyter, 1995)

ZANTWIJK, TEMILO VAN, 'Ästhetische Anschauung. Die Erkenntnisfunktion der Kunst bei Schelling', in *Der Körper der Kunst*, ed. by Johannes Grave and Reinhard Wegner (Göttingen: Wallstein, 2007), pp. 132–61

—— 'Das Ereignis Weimar-Jena als Symbol einer geistigen Welt', in *Anna Amalia, Carl August und das Ereignis Weimar*, ed. by Hellmut Th. Seemann (Göttingen: Wallstein, 2007), pp. 118–31

INDEX